Comhairle Contae Thiobraid Árann
Tipperary County Council
Library Service

www.tipperarycoco.ie (0504) 21555

Items should be returned on or before the last date shown below.
Items can be renewed by phoning your local library: give the date
due back and the number on the barcode label below. Fines will
be charged for overdue items at the rate 60.25per item per week.

DATE DUE	DATE DUE	DATE DUE
TEMPLEMORE (0504) 32555		
06/15		
23. JUL 15.		
2 4 NOV 2015		
08 FEB 16.		
2 4 OCT 2019		

TOM SEMPLE

AND

THE THURLES BLUES

LIAM Ó DONNCHÚ

First published in 2015

Tom Semple and The Thurles Blues

© Liam Ó Donnchú 2015

ISBN 978-0-9560755-3-6

Design and layout: Tom Beirne

Typeset in 10pt Stone Serif

Printed in Ireland by:
Walsh Colour Print, Castleisland, County Kerry

This book is dedicated to
Tom Semple and to all the hurlers of his era.

Upon his native sward the hurler stands
To play the ancient pastime of the Gael
And all the heroes famed of Inisfáil
Are typified in him . . .
– JAMES DOLLARD

Ní bheidh a leithéidí arís ann

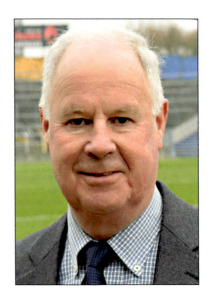

Liam Ó Donnchú is a native of Hollyford, County Tipperary. Having spent over four decades as a primary teacher, Liam, now retired, is a founder and director of Lár na Páirce, the museum of Gaelic Games in Thurles and P.R.O. of Semple Stadium. He is a former player, secretary and chairman of Thurles Sarsfields GAA Club and at present its vice-president. He is author of such publications as *Pouldine School – Inné agus Inniu*, co-author of *Tipperary's GAA Ballads*, *Horse and Jockey – a Pictorial Record* and numerous articles on Gaelic games. Liam was, for many years, secretary of Tipperary GAA Yearbook committee.

Liam is married to Catherine and they have four adult children: Eoghan, Muireann, Neasa and Kilian.

Contents

A Superb Addition to the G.A.A. Library

IS CÚIS MHÓR áthais an deis seo a bheith agam fáilte a chur roimh an leabhar iontach seo atá dirithe ar cheann den daoine agus sloinnte is cailiúla i gCumann Lúthchleas Gael.

It gives me great pleasure to pen these words in acknowledgement of a publication that is a superb addition to the G.A.A. library, focussing as it does on a name that is synonymous with the G.A.A. and most notably with supporters of the wonderful game of hurling.

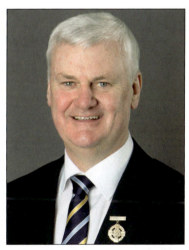

Semple Stadium may be the official title for the G.A.A.'s second largest stadium but to members of a certain generation the reference of 'Tom Semple's Field' would not have been uncommon.

Such informal titling may have belonged to a different era but the venue's reputation as an esteemed one for our games grew from people's familiarity with it and fondness for it.

Thurles is not only the birthplace of Cumann Lúthchleas Gael, it is a place that has always occupied a special place in the mindset of our members.

Some of the greatest Munster hurling finals have taken place at the famed venue and in more recent times it has been a regular host of League finals and All-Ireland quarter-finals.

That is, of course, before mention of the 1984 All-Ireland hurling final, which was moved to Semple Stadium as part of the G.A.A.'s centenary celebrations.

With all of this in mind it is some tribute to have such an exalted venue named after you and that is a measure of the contribution that Tom Semple made to the fabric of the G.A.A. in the roles of player, captain, trainer, referee and administrator.

That this fine work by Liam Ó Donnchú connects Tom Semple with the 'Thurles Blues' hints at the club as the cornerstone of this great story and by extension how it came to take on a national relevance. That can only be a good thing.

It was not so long ago that the G.A.A. library was sparingly stocked.

I am glad to say that this is no longer the case and superb publications such as this preserve important aspects of our history and enlighten younger generations about the rich tapestry of storied existence.

I commend everyone involved in its publication and wish you Liam every success with it.

Rath Dé ar an obair,

AOGÁN Ó FEARGHÁIL
Uachtarán Chumann Lúthchleas Gael

Tom Semple
– An Immortal
G.A.A. Name

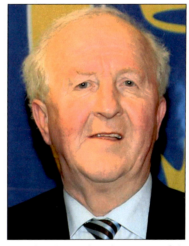

THAR CHEANN Comhairle na Mumhan, ba mhaith liom traoslú le Liam Ó Donnchú ar son na hoibre atá déanta aige chun an foilseachán tábhachtach seo a chur ós ár gcóir. Is iontach an cuimhneachán é agus táim cinnte go mbainfidh a lán daoine an-taitneamh as an leabhar suimiúil seo.

Tom Semple's name is immortalised forever among G.A.A. people, and hurling followers in particular, in the stadium that bears his name in Thurles. His contribution to the G.A.A. was extraordinary and it is fitting that Liam Ó Donnchú has written this biography of Tom Semple which also aptly records the history of the Thurles 'Blues' teams with which he played. Tom Semple fulfilled roles as a player, trainer, administrator and referee and did so at the highest level and to the highest standards. He was also a great leader both on and off the pitch and will be forever remembered as captain of the famed Thurles 'Blues' and for leading Tipperary to All-Ireland titles in 1906 and 1908. His skills as an administrator benefitted the G.A.A. at club, county, provincial and national level and Comhairle na Mumhan was privileged to have him serve as a Tipperary representative for a decade.

Today Comhairle na Mumhan is proud to stage many championship games including the famed Munster senior hurling final in Tom Semple's field, a place that is a magnificent and fitting tribute to a man who played such a key role in the growth of the G.A.A. and acquiring and developing the grounds that became Semple Stadium.

I congratulate Liam Ó Donnchú on his research and dedication in bringing this important book to fruition. I'm sure it was a labour of love for a man who himself has become synonymous with Semple Stadium as public address announcer for many years.

On behalf of Comhairle na Mumhan, I want to welcome the publication of 'Tom Semple and the Thurles Blues'. I know it will bring knowledge and pleasure to all who read it and will be an important addition to the treasure trove of G.A.A. historical and biographical publications.

ROIBEÁRD AN tSEACA
Cathaoirleach
Comhairle na Mumhan

Semple was synonymous with Hurling

S INCE THE foundation of the G.A.A. in Thurles in 1884, Tipperary has provided the association with many outstanding players and administrators, but few, if any, can match the status that Tom Semple has gained in G.A.A. lore. This well-deserved status was hard won by Tom Semple and his gallant 'Blues' who carved for themselves and Tipperary a legendary and special niche in the annals of our county. Ever since those far off days, the name of Semple is associated with courageous leadership, disciplined endeavour and high achievement. Tom was a native of my own parish, Upperchurch/Drombane, a fact that has always been a source of pride for all parishioners.

As a hurler, Semple was a top class player, winning numerous county titles, four Munster and three All-Ireland medals. Playing days over, Tom became an accomplished administrator at all levels of the G.A.A. Semple Stadium, named in his honour, is synonymous with hurling people and the G.A.A.

I compliment Liam Ó Donnchú on the excellent achievement of producing a book of this calibre, detailed and accurate. I trust that it will receive well-deserved support.

Mícheál de Búrca.

MÍCHEÁL DE BÚRCA
Cathaoirleach, Bord Thiobraid Árann

A Welcome Record of Semple's Achievements

TOM SEMPLE'S name is known far and wide within G.A.A. circles for his association with Thurles G.A.A. grounds but for many he remains a historical figure that little is known about.

I welcome this publication which will put on record Tom's achievements as both a hurler and a captain of Tipperary and Thurles Sarsfields and also as a referee and chairman of Mid Tipperary G.A.A. board.

I compliment Liam Ó Donnchú for his work in making this publication possible and I know it will be of great interest to all Gaels within Tipperary and further afield.

Seosamh Ó Cinnéide.

SEOSAMH Ó CINNÉIDE
Cathaoirleach
Bord Thiobraid Árann Meánach

The Blues wrote an indelible page in G.A.A. history

THE STORY of hurling as it evolved through the end of the nineteenth century and into the twentieth is adorned by legendary clubs and giants of the game brought to life in the graphic reportage of the time.

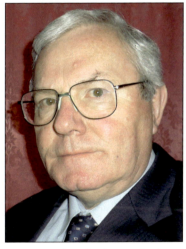

Blackrock, Dungourney, Toomevara, Tullaroan, Mooncoin and Tubberadora are just a few of the great clubs that were to the fore in those early years and in that illustrious company the famed Thurles Blues wrote their indelible page in the history of the game. So too did the men who led those teams; Kelleher, Meagher, Walton, Walsh, Maher and the great Tom Semple of whom Carbery said: "Few men playing the game in Ireland today have achieved the fame that the Thurles captain, Tom Semple has known".

Not alone was Tom Semple a great All-Ireland captain, he was also an organiser of note and his name is listed on the original committee that began the development of Thurles Sportsfield. The sportsfield was later named "Semple Stadium" in honour of the great Thurles 'Blues' man; it is the premier hurling stadium in Ireland and as long as the ancient game is played on that hallowed turf the name Tom Semple will never be forgotten.

In publishing the history Liam Ó Donnchú has made a major contribution not alone to the story of the G.A.A. in Thurles and Tipperary, but also to understanding how the game of hurling evolved nationally in the early years of the G.A.A..

Nobody could have been better equipped to undertake this task than Liam Ó Donnchú. Already a noted G.A.A. publicist and local historian, Liam has devoted his life to the service of Thurles Sarsfields and Semple Stadium and remains active in the service of both. He has been PRO of Semple Stadium for many years and is the "voice" of the stadium on big match days.

Go n-éirí go geal leis an stair seo agus go mbainfidh lucht a léite mór-thaitneamh agus sult as.

CONCHÚIR Ó hÓGÁIN
Cathaoirleach
Semple Stadium

An Overdue Recognition
for Semple

GROWING UP in Killinan, I heard my late father speak many times about Tom Semple. Even to a young lad like me, the respect in which Tom Semple was held, and the weight his opinion carried among my father's generation, was very evident. To him, and to the Sarsfields and Tipperary players of my father's time, Tom Semple was a special man.

Down the years, Tom Semple has always held a special place in the hearts of Thurles Sarsfields people. His deeds as a player, administrator, and as a leader in our club, are the stuff of legend.

His memory is honoured by the dedication to his name of the Thurles stadium he did so much to promote as a venue for big games, an initiative, which we are proud to say, came from Thurles Sarsfields Club.

He is also remembered in the staging for the past four years of our annual hurling festival which features the Semple Cup as the top award for clubs participating. Now our club vice-president, Liam Ó Donnchú, has added a further hugely important dimension to honouring the Tom Semple legend with the publication of his life story. This extensively and painstakingly researched publication, written by a Sarsfields man so very conversant with the role of Tom Semple in the history of the Gaelic Athletic Association at local and national level, will serve as a lasting tribute to the great man. How fortunate that a man of Liam's background was available and willing to undertake the project.

No longer will hurling enthusiasts and scholars have to rely on anecdotal evidence as to the status and influence of Tom Semple in the formation and development of the association in his home town of Thurles and indeed nationally. Liam's work ensures that Tom Semple's name and his deeds have been accorded an overdue recognition that will serve well the coming generations.

As chairman of Thurles Sarsfields Club I am particularly proud and pleased to be associated with this publication. Our club is also pleased that for the family of Tom Semple, there is a fitting and lasting testimonial to his life, one that does due justice to his memory.

On behalf of Thurles Sarsfields Club and its members, I congratulate Liam on his dedication to, and enthusiasm for, the production of such a valuable work.

Generations of G.A.A. people to come will appreciate his scholarship. I wholeheartedly recommend it to readers.

MÍCHEÁL Ó MEACHAIR
Cathaoirleach
Thurles Sarsfields Club

Foreword

TWO YEARS ago I was a guest on Graduation Day at L.I.T, formerly Tipperary Institute. There was colour and pageantry aplenty with proud parents and family as a son or daughter came forward in cap and gown to receive their precious parchment. What took me by surprise, however, was the number of new nationals who came to the stage.

I had expected that the graduates of Rearcross would be the rarest recipients but, as the names were called, there were Poles, Filipino, Brazilians, Africans from Nigeria and Zimbabwe as well as French Canadians and Mexicans. Then, as we marvelled at people from "faraway places with strange sounding names" the words "Thomas Semple" brought the assembly to attention! You could almost read the lips, *"was he Tom Semple's grandson or great grandson or other close relative?"* There are not many of the name in our part of the country!

The name Tom Semple was once a household name everywhere hurling was played. It still resonates in Tipperary and, of course, Semple Stadium, being named in his memory. Since I came to this county in 1986 I have often asked G.A.A. people why the biography of Tom Semple has never been written. I was told that there was very little known about Tom Semple. Then, in April 1993, we commemorated the 50th anniversary of his death, in St Mary's cemetery in Thurles, and I had the privilege of meeting many of his family and it became clear that they had some material for a book and only awaited an author with the skill and the enthusiasm to capture the essence of this *"giant in the days of giants"* and *"champion among champions"* as Canon Philip Fogarty described him in his obituary in 1943.

It was both fortunate and fitting that the ideal biographer took on the task of compiling and writing the story of Tom Semple's life and times. Liam Ó Donnchú is an historian who is steeped in G.A.A. culture. He is also the *"Voice of Semple Stadium"*. In his gentle tones in Irish and English he keeps the patrons informed of the team selections on a need to know basis! You would never guess from his courteous manner, never issuing orders or warnings, that he has been a teacher for most of his life! And an extremely gifted one, I might add.

Liam situates his subject in post-Famine Ireland. Born in 1879 at Glebe Cross, Moyaliffe, Drombane, the memory of the "Great Hunger" was fresh and painful to the memory. The Land League was engaged in a bitter campaign against large scale evictions of poor smallholders with boycotts and outbreaks of rural violence the order of the day. The Cathedral of the Assumption, Thurles, was blessed and officially opened by Archbishop Thomas W. Croke in June 1879. The funeral of the poet patriot, Charles J. Kickham, took place in August 1882. The social history of Tipperary at the time is most interesting to the modern reader.

When he was a boy of eight, three of Tom's neighbours were on the Tipperary hurling selection which won Tipperary's very first All-Ireland in 1887. He grew up in awe of these local heros and longed to emulate their feats.

The name "Semple" Liam tells us, is a corruption of "St. Paul". The Semple family came originally from the southern border lands of Scotland and they came as employees of the Armstrongs of Farney Castle. Tom's father, Martin, worked as a butler and coachman at Farney Castle. Tom, in his turn, became a railway guard with Great Southern Railways, later C.I.E.

Tom developed into an athletic young man, over six feet tall and a natural hurler. Added to his exceptional ability on the hurling field was, possibly an even greater quality, namely an innate genius for leadership. He was a born leader and others responded to his example and his short, terse speeches more like today's soundbites. Most of his recorded speeches would fit comfortably in text messages.

When you read accounts of his achievements on the field of play, he is invariably named first as Tom Semple, Captain. Called after St. Paul yes but he was always given the primacy of Peter among his disciples being the first named in every team. Having assisted other selections to All-Ireland glory, Tom crowned his success with victories for "the Blues" (Thurles Sarsfields) in two famous years, 1906 and 1908.

We have only one record of a dressing room speech. For one thing dressing rooms were few and far between in those days. But, at half-time in a crucial game against Cork in Tipperary town, The Munster final 1909, with his team four points down, he addressed his fellow players as follows:

"Now, lads, listen! Cork can't play without the ball so don't let 'em have it. Do ye hear?". "We do", they all replied".

Tom Semple's team won by four points in a hectic second half.

Noted for his long puck, he scored a point on one occasion and the ball ended up embedded in a thatched house away up the hill. A ladder had to be commandeered before the game could continue! Later, he used to urge the players to *"aim for the thatch"*. One notices in passing that Tom Semple directed all his attention to the ball.

I heard a humorous account from the late Bishop Michael Russell of a later Tipperary manager who instructed his charges before a game as follows, *"Hurl your hearts out for the first ten minutes and never mind the ball"*! What a pity that the Long Puck competition did not exist in his day! He would probably confound Hawkeye of recent times.

Almost as important as the All-Ireland championship games in those days were the contests for the very unusual trophy, the Croke-Fennelly Cup. This drew large crowds to Fethard. Tom Semple, captain, was presented with the trophy by Archbishop Thomas Fennelly after their victory in 1909 against Limerick Young Irelands and it went on display in Anthony Carew's shop window in Thurles.

In 1913 the "Blues" were given a walk-over by the Limerick Caherline side who were unable to field half their team on the day so the cup became the permanent property of Thurles Sarsfields now named *"the best hurling team in Ireland"*. When it was damaged in a house fire in 1930, Tom Semple, now club chairman, was instrumental in having it restored to its original condition.

This chapter was of special interest to me since the trophy of solid silver was in the Archbishop's House in Thurles when I arrived there, sent for safe keeping by the Thurles Sarsfield Club in 1948. When Lár na Páirce was opened in 1994, I sent it there to the Museum of Gaelic Games with the blessing of Thurles Sarsfields Club.

When the Blues lost the 1909 All-Ireland final against a Kilkenny selection, the hurling world was shocked and saddened at Tom Semple's retirement at the age of 30. Canon Philip Fogarty reported as follows: *"One has to regret that the heyday of this gallant band of hurlers had run its course so unexpectedly, but the master brain of the team – the gifted immortal Semple – definitely retired. Had he remained history would likely continue"*.

Tom Semple continued to serve the G.A.A. as an administrator at club, county and Munster Council level. He acted as trainer and coach and passed on his skills and his sportsmanship to succeeding generations of hurlers of Sarsfields and of Tipperary. Among his protégés was Michael O'Dwyer who was destined to become Superior General of the Columban Fathers and a great missionary.

Tom was one of the principal movers in the purchase of the Showgrounds as a sportsfield in 1910. Canon M.K. Ryan and a working committee of twelve paid £900 for the field and they collected the money by issuing shares to the people of Thurles. They set about developing the Sportsfield and in due course it became a worthy setting for the epic contests between Tipperary and Cork, Tipperary and Limerick, which made the Munster final in Thurles an institution in the world of sport. To Tom Semple must go much of the credit for this success. Thurles people loved to go to the sports field, even when there was no game on; they liked just to walk around and admire the pitch. It is still without question the finest hurling pitch in the world.

Tom was also the chief steward at the games. Older people recalled himself and comrade-in-arms, Jack Mockler, walking round the side-lines and keeping youngsters off the pitch in the days of the side-line seats. He was still a formidable man, with a hat sideways on his head and an ash plant in his hand. He never had to use it, however. He had natural authority of the kind teachers would envy today.

When one thinks of the army of stewards it takes to keep the young lads from crowding in over the wire on to the pitch nowadays and they do not succeed on occasion, one appreciates the respect in which he was held. He loved young people but he loved them even better when they conducted themselves. And that went for young lads on the Thurles to Dublin trains. He was a strict disciplinarian, but then so were most fathers in those days.

The saga of the Croke Memorial and the battle between the Tipperary County Board and the Central Council is an intriguing one. A national competition in hurling and football, set up to raise funds for a memorial to Dr. Croke, was so successful financially that Central Council decided to purchase the field on Jones's Road and name it the "Croke Memorial Park". This bright idea did not impress the locals in Tipperary.

Tom Semple declared that they would accept nothing but the full amount collected from the competitions organised for a monument in Tipperary. *"The idea of buying a field to perpetuate the memory of the illustrious Dr. Croke is ridiculous"* he said. *"We would be unworthy of the name of Tipperary men if we did not fight the Central Council."* The Charities Act 2009 would vindicate Tom Semple's position! After much heated exchanges, Thurles got its Croke Memorial and the Central Council bought the field from Frank Dineen and named it, *"The Croke Memorial Park"*, shortened to Croke Park and vulgarised to *"Croker"* by many who should know better. Happily, the funds stretched to cover both projects so everyone was a winner.

Tom Semple was to play a further role when he stood "shoulder to shoulder" with Dr. John M. Harty as he laid the foundation stone for the Croke Memorial in Liberty Square on St Patrick's Day, 1920. The Black and Tans were lined up across the street and with some of them on the rooftops with guns pointed at the Archbishop. The event was viewed as an act of defiance to the authorities. Little did they know that Tom Semple carried regular dispatches on the train for Michael Collins. Tom Semple was on the committee for the official unveiling of the Croke Memorial and on Whit Sunday, 4 June 1922, Dr. John M. Harty declared; *"I can promise you that the Gaels in Thurles and Tipperary will guard this monument as it would its own life"*.

I sometimes wonder how things would have turned out if the Tipperary County Board had prevailed in the dispute over Croke Park versus the memorial. It is possible that Croke Park would now be in Thurles! Tom Semple would have been deprived of his stadium!

The late Fr. James Feehan always told me that it was he proposed that the Thurles Sports Field be named in memory of Tom Semple. A good story, and as a classmate of Fr. Feehan would say, *"what is more it is true!"* Liam Ó Donnchú documents the fact that Fr. James Feehan proposed the name Semple Stadium on behalf of Thurles Sarsfields Club.

Those who said that too little was known about the life of Tom Semple to warrant a full-size book, will be pleasantly surprised at the extent and depth of Liam Ó Donnchú's research. He has unearthed hitherto unsuspected treasures. Tom Semple's family, who contributed their own memories so willingly and generously will be very pleased with the outcome. I am very pleased for them.

As I said earlier, Tom Semple was once a household name wherever hurling was played or discussed. Liam Ó Donnchú now brings his memory and his achievements alive for new generations of Gaels. And he refreshes the memories of the older generations on the life and times of Tom Semple, champion hurler and natural leader of men. He belongs to that body of men whom Thomas Jefferson described as *"the natural aristocracy of talent and virtue"*.

Liam Ó Donnchú, "the voice of Semple Stadium" up to now, has made a very important contribution to the G.A.A. history and to the social history of the times when Tom Semple was boy and man. And, by the way, lest I forget, Thomas Semple, the graduate, is a son of T.J.'s and a great-grandson of the great Tom himself!

Mar focal scoir, cuireann sé árd-taithneamh dom an brollach seo a chur le sár-obair Liam Úi Dhonnchú. Más maith is mithid!

+ Dermot Clifford

MOST REV. DERMOT CLIFFORD, DD,
Archbishop Emeritus of Cashel & Emly.

Acknowledgements

THE IDEA of writing this book was first suggested to me by Tom Semple's youngest son, Martin. It was August 2011 and we were celebrating the golden jubilee of Fr Jim Semple's ordination. At first I dismissed the idea, citing the passage of time and the lack of sources etc. However, the seed was sown and surfaced again in September 2013, when I agreed to undertake the task of writing a biography of *Tom Semple and The Thurles Blues*. I am very glad that I changed my mind, as working on this book has been a most interesting journey:- meeting so many people, drinking numerous cups of tea, spending endless hours in the Local Studies in Thurles and other libraries, evenings walking graveyards looking for invaluable information on tombstones etc., and in the process expanding my knowledge and appreciation of that golden era of hurling in Thurles and Tipperary and of the men that made it.

Everywhere I went I was welcomed and helped. The mention of Tom Semple and the Thurles Blues opened many doors and descendants were proud and thrilled that their ancestor, whom they thought was long forgotten, was remembered in this fast-moving high tech era.

Before I came to live in Thurles, in the early 1960s, I was aware of the name, Tom Semple, an awareness that was enhanced when I joined Thurles Sarsfields. The name of Semple seemed to have a certain mystique and awe about it and was always referred to with an uncommon reverence, seldom equalled. The re-naming of Thurles Sportsfield as Semple Stadium in 1971 gave deserved recognition to Tom Semple, yet the story of his achievements, while known by a previous generation, remained undocumented. I hope that this book fills that void and that a new generation will be enthused by the ideals and achievements of Tom Semple and the Thurles Blues and will be challenged to emulate them

'to raise their name again to fame with Gaels around Thurles town'.

The task of thanking people is daunting, there are so many who helped me compile this book that listing them is impossible, but a deserved thanks to all. However, there are a few that deserve special mention:- Joe Tobin, Turtulla for his years of support, valued opinion and forensic scrutiny of the draft texts, Seamus J. King, Cashel and Michael Dundon, Thurles, for reading and correcting the drafts. Thanks to Paddy Doherty, Árd na Croise, for use of his valuable tape-recordings. Thanks to those who helped with photographs, John O'Loughlin, and particularly Seamus Loughnane who allowed me access to his amazing collection, regrettably, I have been unable to trace the original owners for a number of the images used. Thanks to Eugene Shortt and Denis (Dinny) Dwyer, Drombane for their informative guided tour of Moyaliffe and all the places associated with Tom Semple's childhood. Thanks to the officers and members of Thurles Sarsfields Club for their encouragement and loyalty.

The Tipperary Studies Department of Tipperary County Library, Thurles, was invaluable to my research and librarians Mary Guinan Darmody and John O'Gorman were most courteous and helpful. Much of the information was gleaned from their files of the *Tipperary Star*. The help given by the late Gerry Slevin of *The Guardian,* Nenagh, deserves grateful mention. I also received valuable assistance from the National Library of Ireland and the Limerick Glucksman Library.

I am deeply grateful to Tom Beirne for his layout and design of the book and to Walsh Colour Print, Castleisland, County Kerry.

Thanks to all the Semple family for their support for this project:- T.J. in Thurles, Anne in Dublin and Martin in Denver, Colorado. Martin encouraged me from the start and without his initial idea and ongoing support, this book would not have come to fruition.

Thurles has its own heroes, none more than its hurlers.

'Mo bheannacht leat a scribhinn'.

LIAM Ó DONNCHÚ
Lá Bealtaine 2015

CHAPTER 1

The Drombane Years
1879-1888

THOMAS, Joseph Semple was born at Glebe Cross, Moyaliffe, Drombane, on Holy Saturday, 12 April 1879 and was baptised on the same day at the local St Mary's Church. He was the third child born to Martin and Anne Semple, who had married in the Big Chapel,[1] Thurles, on 19 November 1868. Martin was a native of Drombane, while his wife, Anne Long, was from Stradavoher in Thurles. As was the custom of the time, Thomas (Tom) was named after his maternal grandfather, Thomas Long. At his baptism, his sponsors were John Scanlon and Mary Semple. Tom had an older brother and two older sisters, Hanora born 25 November 1869, James born 22 February 1872 and Catherine born 11 July 1875. He also had a younger brother, born on 16 September 1885, christened Michael John but usually referred to as John.

The exact location of the Semple family home in Drombane is somewhat uncertain, the most popular opinion being Glebe House[2] or a building adjacent to it. Glebe House had been the home of the Church of Ireland rectors for decades. It had a large basement, its own well in the yard, barracks attached and mill

Glebe House, Moyaliffe, Drombane.

---

[1] Note – The Big Chapel predated the Cathedral of the Assumption, Thurles.
[2] Eugene Shortt, 'The Shooting of Rector Going 1829' in *Upperchurch/Drombane Historical Journal 2013*, p. 14. Note: Mention has also been made of Keeffe's Cross and Coolbawn as possible locations.

stream passing by. The building is now demolished.

The Semples had given decades of service to the Armstrong family, who were the principal employers in the locality. They were a Scottish family from the border country, many of whom headed for Ireland in the turbulent years of the seventeenth century to fight for the Royalist cause. Among them was Captain William Armstrong (c.1630-1695), whose father, Sir Thomas Armstrong, had been a supporter of Charles I throughout the Civil War. When Charles II was restored to power, he favoured Captain William Armstrong with a lease of Farneybridge, in 1660. He established himself at Farney Castle and his younger son, Thomas Armstrong established the Moyaliffe branch about the year 1695, settling in a small stone house built close to the ruins of Moyaliffe Castle. Tom Semple's grandfather, James, worked as a servant at Farney Castle, while Tom's father, Martin, is recalled locally as being a coachman and butler at Farney Castle and later at Moyaliffe.[3]

Farney Castle, Holycross.

Moyaliffe Castle, c.1870s, showing the south wing and garden, with Captain Edward Armstrong and his wife Frances née Steele seated on a bench.
(Image reproduced courtesy of the Armstrong Papers at the University of Limerick Glucksman Library)

It is clear, from the following account of a celebration at Moyaliffe, that Martin Semple was held in high esteem by the Armstrongs and could be trusted with a position of responsibility. In October 1878, Captain Edward Armstrong celebrated the annual 'Harvest Home' at Moyaliffe Castle. Invitations had been sent to his tenants, labourers, tradesmen and their families and the celebrations began at

---

[3] Interview with William Corbett, Roskeen, Drombane (27 July 2000). John and Breda Stakelum are the present owners of Moyaliffe House.

about 4.00 p.m. for the assembled gathering of all ages, numbering about one hundred and fifty-five. They assembled in the vicinity of the farmyard, in an area specially built for such festivities, where a dance-floor had been laid and the area decorated with evergreens, corn sheaves and appropriate slogans, some in the Irish language. Fiddle music filled the autumnal air and the tables were 'full and plenty' and well-decked with a selection of meats including roast beef and a selection of hot smoking puddings. Captain Armstrong arrived with his wife and her companion, Miss Bagwell, about 8.00 p.m. amid welcoming cheers. The flowing bowl followed with plenty for all and the captain drank to the health of his tenants, labourers and his invited friends from Farney Castle and Templemore. At 10.30 p.m. the captain and his entourage retired. Tea, punch and porter were liberally distributed during the remainder of the night, under the supervision of Mr. Semple (Tom's father), Mr. Hogan, Mr. Harrington and Mr. Aduett, all appointed by Captain Armstrong to act in his absence. Celebrations continued until 7.00 a.m., when all wished each other good-bye in friendship.[4]

The surname Semple is uncommon in the southern counties of Ireland and is most likely of French origin, being derived from Sampol, a corruption of Saint Paul. It's a surname of great antiquity and was possibly introduced into England by followers of William the Conqueror after the Norman conquest of 1066. From the middle ages, the surname Semple was popular in the southern borderland of Scotland in the counties Renfrewshire and the two adjoining counties of Ayr and Lanark. In the 1901 and 1911 censuses the Semple surname is predominantly recorded in the Ulster counties,[5] thus re-enforcing a Scottish link. Coincidentally, southern Scotland is also the ancestral homeland of the Armstrong family to whom the Semple family gave service at Farney Castle and Moyaliffe. It was common for families such as the Armstrongs to bring workers with them to work their estates and this may explain the Semple presence in Tipperary. The surname Semple appears on a tombstone in Ballycahill cemetery, indicating Semple habitation in the area in the late eighteenth century. The townland named is Farneybridge, which is in close proximity to Farney Castle. Perhaps the Semple family had come to Moyaliffe sometime after 1851, when Richard Griffith carried out his valuation, as it is not listed therein, nor in the earlier Tithe Applotment Book of 1821.[6]

Tom's mother, Anne, born in 1853, was a midwife[7]. As such she played a very important role in the life of the community with the delivery of new-born

---

[4] *Clonmel Cronicle*, 30 Oct. 1878, p. 2.
[5] Note – National Archives of Ireland (henceforth NAI). The Semple surname is recorded on 716 occasions in 1901 and 745 occasions in 1911.
[6] *Irish Times*, 20 May 1991.
[7] NAI, Census of Ireland 1901.

babies and associated matters. This was an onerous and responsible position, where Anne would have come into contact with great social diversity as she dealt with all levels of society. She would have been well aware of the hardships suffered by many, due to poor housing, lack of sanitation, destitution, poverty and challenging economic circumstances. As a midwife she had the ear of the female folk, who traditionally confided in midwives, due to their status as knowledgeable trusted counsellors. Her position would also have been a source of income for her that gave her an independence not enjoyed by many of her peers.

During Tom's childhood, the memories of the Great Famine of the 1840s, a mere generation away, were still fresh in the minds of the people. This was a time when famine and fever had ravaged the population and emigration scattered many a family to the four corners of the globe. In Tom's native townland of Glebe, Drombane, the population fell from thirty-one in 1841 to thirteen by 1881.[8] In 1841 the parish of Upperchurch/Drombane had a total population of 6,346, a decade later this figure had declined to 4,603 and by 1901 was 2,822. The local town of Thurles was not faring well either. In 1897, Thurles town commissioner J.L. Johnston was very vocal concerning the housing situation in the town. In a sworn statement given to the Local Government Board, which was assessing the need for erecting houses for workers, he stated, "out of a total population of approximately 5,000, more than 500 families were living in very poor conditions – mainly one roomed hovels, often accommodating twelve to fourteen people with no sanitation, backyards or backdoors".[9]

About the year 1870, the average wage of an agricultural labourer was 8p per day. By the mid 1890s this had, on average, increased to around 14p per day. Some labourers' families had to survive on as little as 5p a day – half fed, half clad and pinched looking.[10] Thurles, in the mid 1870s experienced outbreaks of typhoid fever. The patients were treated in the local fever hospital. Such outbreaks struck fear into the local community and are indicative of the poor sanitary conditions prevailing in the town and hinterland at that time.[11]

The Semple family were devout Roman Catholics, who found strength, comfort and solace in their faith. The family rosary and lengthy trimmings would be recited daily, support for the clergy was unquestioned, religious attendance at Sunday Mass and the required observance of fasting and

---

[8] *Pobal Ailbhe, Cashel and Emly*, Census of Population 1941-1971 (Thurles, 1975), p. 16.
[9] *Nationalist*, 3 Mar. 1897, p. 3.
[10] D.G. Marnane, 'The Struggle for the Land in South Tipperary' in *Nationalist Centenary Supplement* (1990), p. 26.
[11] *Irish Times*, 24 Sept. 1874, p. 2.

abstinence were dutifully performed. Their home at Glebe would no doubt contain a picture of the 'Sacred Heart' or of a favourite saint or statue with the rosary beads hanging in a convenient position. These might have been purchased at a stall in Drombane during a mission.

In his youth, Tom, no doubt, was aware of the active role played by the local priest, Fr. Robert Prout, during the Land League campaign of the late 1870s and 1880s. These were the years when the 'Land War' was at its height as the league struggled to gain fair rents, fixity of tenure and free sale for the impoverished tenants. Evictions were common and boycotting as a protest tactic was invented. Such involvement by the clergy was not unusual at the time, as no less than 77% of the total priesthood played some public part in politics from 1850 to 1891.[12] Fr. Prout, a native of Ballingarry, served as curate in Upperchurch and Drombane from 1878 until his untimely death on 12 November 1885, following a fall from his horse as he answered a late night sick-call.[13]

A major event, in the life of the locality was the consecration of the Cathedral of the Assumption, Thurles, on Sunday, 22 June 1879, by Archbishop Thomas Croke. This was the year of Tom Semple's birth. The building was begun in 1865 by Archbishop Patrick Leahy and completed in 1872. It could not be consecrated until 1879, as only then was it free of debt. Considering the poverty and the economic problems of the time, the erection of the cathedral

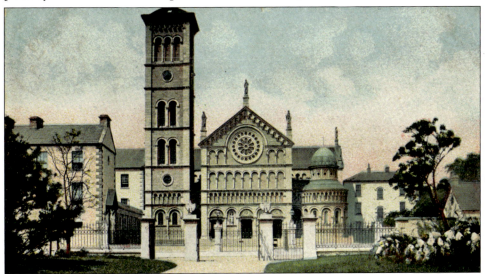

Cathedral of the Assumption, Thurles. Note the absence of the clock. In 1895, to mark his Episcopal Silver Jubilee, Dr Croke presented the cathedral clock to the people of Thurles.
(Image courtesy of the National Library of Ireland)

---

[12] James O'Shea, *Priest, Politics and Society in Post Famine Ireland* (Dublin, 1983), p. 232.
[13] Christy O'Dwyer, *Archdiocese of Cashel and Emly – Pobal Ailbhe* (Strasbourg, 2008), p. 355.

demonstrated the unflinching faith and generosity of the people of Thurles and the Archdiocese of Cashel and Emly. It further demonstrates the strong communal and confessional identity of the people, a factor also noted regarding the local response to the Land League. Mass attendance in Thurles was an amazing 90%, while cathedral receipts (Sunday and Holyday collections) for 1882 stood at £379-12s-2d.[14]

Growing up in a home where the Roman Catholic faith was prominent in the daily lives of the family, Tom would have heard of James Ryan, Ruan, Upperchurch, who entered Mount Melleray Abbey, County Waterford in August 1888, taking the religious name Bruno. In 1914, Fr Bruno and a small group of monks from Mount Melleray were sent to New Melleray Abbey, Iowa, U.S.A. and successfully rejuvenated the mission there. Dom Bruno later became Prior, then Superior and Abbot in 1935.

Charles J. Kickham
1828-1882

One of the most discussed events in the locality, in 1882, was undoubtedly the funeral of the poet, novelist[15] and patriot – Charles Joseph Kickham on Sunday, 27 August. Kickham, the Fenian activist, had died, at the age of fifty-four, in Blackrock, Dublin on 22 August and his remains, en route to Mullinahone, were brought to Thurles by train from Kingsbridge (Hueston) station.

A belated request was made to have the coffin admitted overnight to the cathedral in Thurles. The practice of automatically receiving the remains of the Catholic dead in church had not yet been fully established in Ireland. Therefore, a refusal did not amount to denial of an accepted right as later commentators have assumed, being accustomed to seeing every Catholic rest overnight in a church before burial. In effect, a privilege with obvious political over-tones was being sought for Kickham.[16] Archbishop Thomas Croke was on an extended visit to England at the time, so the decision rested with the administrator Father James Cantwell. He firmly refused, arguing that he could not give permission in the absence of the archbishop.

What would have happened if Archbishop Croke had been in Thurles at the time of the funeral? It is true that Croke had great regard for Kickham, having

---

[14] James O'Shea, *Priest, Politics and Society in Post Famine Ireland* (Dublin, 1983), p. 15.
[15] Note – Kickham was author of the historical novel *Knocknagow* (The Homes of Tipperary) and of many popular local ballads such as *Slievenamon* and *She Lived Beside the Anner*.
[16] R.V. Comerford, *Charles J. Kickham: A Biography* (Dublin, 1979), p. 174.

contributed £10 towards the Kickham Fund in 1878 adding that 'I take him to be of all men, that I have ever met, about the gentlest, the most amiable, the most truthful and the most sorely and searchingly tried'.[17] However, in a letter of condolence to the Kickham family following the funeral, Croke does not explicitly state that he would have allowed Kickham's remains to rest in the cathedral, although he states 'I should have paid them all due honour'.[18]

Kickham's remains rested in the oratory at the residence of Margaret Kirwan on Main Street (now Skehan's Bar, Liberty Square) and the following day the final stage of the funeral proceeded to Mullinahone. Vast crowds were present when the funeral left at 11.30 a.m. and a standard bearer with the flag inscribed, "Tipperary Mourns her Truest Patriot", headed the lengthy procession. Many of his loyal supporters, who had tramped the long roads of Tipperary to vote for him, were here again to bid a final farewell. A long line of cars and two hundred horsemen followed two thousand men, marching six deep. P.G. O'Brien (Dublin) was chief marshal from Thurles to Mullinahone and was assisted by a Thurles committee, which included P. Kirwan, D. Kirwan, T.P. Eviston, Tim Dwyer, and T. Moloney.[19] The name Tim Dwyer will be seen again later at the G.A.A. foundation meeting in 1884.

In Tom Semple's youth there was time for storytelling particularly during the long winter evenings and it was through these that many local folk-tales and native lore was handed on to the rising generation. Tales and ballads of the rapparee Edmond Ryan, Éamonn a' Chnoic or Ned o' the Hill (1670-1724), from the neighbouring townland of Athshanboy would have thrilled the young Tom Semple. However, Tom had more recent heroes to fire his imagination. The foundation of the Gaelic Athletic Association in his local town of Thurles and its ideals were embraced wholeheartedly in Drombane.[20] Some of Tom's neighbours were on the first winning All-Ireland hurling team, when he was but a child of eight years of age. John Leamy, Roskeen, Michael Carroll, Rosmult and Ned Lambe, Drombane, played on the Thurles selection which captured Tipperary's first All-Ireland senior hurling title in 1887, the final of which was played at Birr, County Offaly, on 1 April 1888. These sporting exploits and those of Fergus Moriarty and the Riordans of Rosmult influenced Tom Semple. Such events fostered a pride in the local place and challenged the younger generation to emulate their heroes.

When Tom was four years of age he was registered on the roll of Roskeen

---

[17] Mark Tierney, *Croke of Cashel* (Dublin, 1976), p. 94.
[18] James Maher, *The Valley Near Slievenamon* (Mullinahone.1942), p. 56.
[19] J.M. Kennedy, *A Chronology of Thurles* (Rev. ed.), (Thurles, 1978), p. 46.
[20] Note – In the first quarter century of the G.A.A., seven natives of Drombane won between them eleven All-Ireland hurling and two All-Ireland football medals.

National School. At the time this was a two-teacher school, having been opened on 1 May 1860. The pupil-teacher ratio was high with each teacher having at least four classes to teach. There was much concentration on rote learning and of acquiring the skills of reading, writing and arithmetic, better remembered as the

Roskeen Naional School.

'Three Rs'. The school fostered a strong Roman Catholic ethos, with regular prayer and daily instruction in religious knowledge. Here also Tom was prepared for the church sacraments of Penance and First Communion and where visits from the local clergy were regular. The annual visit from the Catholic diocesan inspector, when each pupil was examined in religious knowledge, was a milestone in the school-year.

But for Tom change was afoot as the family moved residence from Drombane to Thurles.

A desolate rainy day on Main Street, now Liberty Square, Thurles, at the end of the 19th century.

CHAPTER 2

Thurles at the End of the Nineteenth Century

T HE SEMPLE family moved residence from Drombane to the town of Thurles about the year 1888. The main reason for the move was so that Tom's mother, Anne, could be the maternity nurse for the Thurles area. For her, this move was like going home as she was a native of the town, having grown up in Stradavoher. Another Stradavoher native, Margaret (Maggie) Tobin, recalling Anne Semple, would declare that she delivered most of the babies born in Thurles in her time.[1]

Tom Semple was now nine years of age and he was registered as a pupil at Thurles C.B.S. on 2 July 1888. On the school's registration record, his father's occupation is given as 'coachman'. Tom continued to attend the school until 1 July 1894.[2]

Thurles CBS (The Monastery) on Pudding Lane (Jail Street), now O'Donovan Rossa Street. (Image courtesy of the National Library of Ireland)

The Semple family home was at No. 20, The Mall and in 1901 Tom lived there with his mother, Anne, his older sister Catherine and his younger brother, John. Anne is still busy as a practicing mid-wife and both Tom and John are gainfully employed. John was employed as a shop-clerk in the town.[3]

---

[1] Interview with Martin Semple, Tom Semple's son (20 Dec. 2013).
[2] Thurles C.B.S. Archive.
[3] NAI, Census of Ireland, 1901.

Tom secured a position with the railway company Great Southern and Western Railways (G.S.W.R), and started work on 9 June 1899[4]. The rail company was later known as C.I.E. (Córas Iompair Éireann) and at present Irish Rail. Tom's position was described as a railway porter.[5] The porter was a familiar sight at railway stations across the country. He would usually be seen carrying bags

Thurles Railway Station

or wheeling barrows between trains and the station buildings. The duties of the porters included carrying and loading luggage and parcels, assisting passengers with prams and wheelchairs, watering the floral tubs and baskets and putting up new timetables and posters. No day was the same as the next for a porter, and before long Tom Semple became well known to the station's regular users. The Dublin/Cork railway line that passes through Thurles is Ireland's 'premier rail line' and the station was opened on 13 March 1848. The weekly wage of a railway porter in 1909 was one pound and two shillings, rising by a shilling each year in subsequent years.[6]

Through the years, Tom became a well-known figure in all the stations on the line. Through his work he also got to know people of all walks of life, from all parts of the country. Travelling to G.A.A. matches in Thurles by train was popular for teams and supporters during Tom's era. It was also a time when many vital G.A.A. meetings were held in Thurles. Working at the railway station gave Tom a great opportunity for meeting and networking with people. The station was also the hub for the daily news and stories from up and down the line were dissected and discussed. Tom was always up-to-date with current local and national news. Affectionately known as 'Big Tom', he cut quite a figure at

---

[4] Interview with Oliver Doyle, Irish Railway Record Society Sec. (9 Apr. 2014).
[5] NAI, Census of Ireland, 1901.
[6] Interview with Oliver Doyle, Irish Railway Record Society Sec. (9 Apr. 2014).

the station, described as a man of fine physique, standing over six feet three inches in height, erect, uniformed, and moustached.

In 1889, the year following Tom Semple's arrival in Thurles, George Henry Bassett's directory entitled *'The Book of County Tipperary'* was published. It is a treasure-chest of knowledge of the Tipperary of that time and gives a unique insight into community life towards the end of the nineteenth century. Bassett described Thurles thus:-

'Thurles, in the parish of same name, barony of Eliogarty, is on the Great Southern and Western Railway, 86½ miles, English, south-west of Dublin, and 20½ miles, north-east of Limerick Junction. At a short distance to the south-west the G.S. & W. line is joined by the Southern Railway, which terminates at Clonmel, 25½ miles south. The town is situated in the valley of the Suir, occupying a considerable area at both sides of the river. A connection is formed by a stone bridge. The Catholic Cathedral, Protestant parish church, convents and college are at the eastern side. There are also several business houses here, but the greater number is on the western side, following the lines of the Main Street to its junction with New Street and the West Gate, leading to the railway station.

Thurles has suffered from the causes that have affected the prosperity of nearly all the southern towns, but it still maintains a foremost place among the best of the size. It is surrounded by a first rate agricultural country, with plenty of limestone. The land is adapted for pasture and tillage. Oats, barley, potatoes and turnips are the principal crops. Nearly all the extensive farmers divide attention between the raising of young stock, dairying, sheep fattening, and tillage, with the result that they are able to contribute largely to the supplies which maintain the reputation of the markets and fairs.

Charles II granted a patent to Lady Elizabeth Mathew and heirs for two markets in every week, Tuesday and Saturday, and for three fairs every year, each to be held for two days. The successors of Lady Mathew have permitted the markets to be held toll free, and only collect at one fair, Easter Monday, when it happens to be the first Monday of the month, the great day for pigs. The fairs are now held on the first Tuesday of every month for horses, cattle and sheep: pigs on the previous day. They are held in the street and are all good. The markets (Saturday) are also held in the streets with the exception of that for butter. It is held in a yard in New Street, under the supervision of a committee. Sellers are charged 4d per cask. This covers the cost of coopering and delivery at the railway station for buyers, who have nothing to pay. The owner of the yard receives 1d per cask. Corn finds a market every day in the season. The market house in the Main Street, was destroyed by fire in 1869, and continues in ruins, all but one end, occupied for business purposes by Mr. Patrick Ryan. A movement was on foot in 1889 to acquire Mr. Ryan's interest with a view to the erection of a Town Hall'.[7]

The modern parish of Thurles represents the union of the old civil parishes of Thurles, Shyane and Athnid, in full together with most of Rahealty and a small portion of Two-Mile-Borris civil parishes. Bassett's account, admirable as it is, fails to comment on the drastic decrease in the population when, in a period of fifty years, the numbers fell by 50% in the parish and by 40% in the town.

POPULATION OF THURLES[8]

Year	Parish	Town
1841	12,684	7,523
1851	11,792	5,908
1861	7,554	4,866
1871	6,846	5,008
1881	6,497	4,850
1891	5,981	4,511
1901	5,837	4,411

Indeed, between the years 1841 and 1911, the population of County Tipperary fell by 65% – the highest figure in Munster and considerably higher than the national figure of 46%.

LOCAL GOVERNMENT

The day-to-day running of the town was in the hands of the town commissioners. Twelve of these were elected for a period of three years. From 1885 onwards they were also responsible for the maintenance of the streets, which had previously been undertaken by the Grand Jury. In 1886 rates of one shilling in the pound were struck on buildings and three pence on land for town purposes. For repairs of roads, bridges etc., the rates levied were two shillings in the pound on building and nine pence on land. Water supply was from street pumps and a well near the eastern bank of the Suir.[9] Paraffin lamps provided street lighting until 1866, when the Gas Company began providing

---

[7] G.H. Bassett, *The Book of County Tipperary* (Dublin, 1889), p. 369 (henceforth Bassett).
[8] *Pobal Ailbhe, Census of Population Cashel and Emly 1841-1971* (Thurles, 1975), pp 22-5.
[9] Bassett, p. 373.

the service.[10] By 1880, the town commissioners had street lamps lighting nightly until 2.00 a.m., except before fair-days when they were not extinguished until daylight.[11] Chairman of the

Fair day in Thurles.
(Image courtesy of the National Library of Ireland)

town commissioners in 1888, elected 20 June, was Hugh Ryan, Westgate, who was also the first chairman of Thurles G.A.A. Club. Solicitor to the town commissioners was Joseph O'Ryan, Cathedral Street,[12] who was present at the G.A.A. foundation meeting in 1884. Since 1898, the local authority was known as Thurles Urban District Council.

LOCAL PRESS AND COMMUNICATION

There was no telegraph office in the town until 1870, when permission was granted on 15 June, to the post office authorities to erect poles to convey a telegraph wire from the railway station to the post office. Before that time, messages were dealt with from the railway office. The rate was one shilling for twenty words. The Magnetic Company supplied this service. For delivery, a messenger was paid three pence per message. The post office was for many years in the premises now known as the "The County" on Liberty Square.

Local newspapers in circulation in the 1880s include T.P. Gill's *'Tipperary'* which first appeared on 15 October 1881. Gill, who resided at Liscahill, had the publication printed in Charlie Culhane's[13] store at Jail Street (Pudding Lane). *'The Tipperary Leader'*, which survived but three years, succeeded this paper on 22 September 1882. The pages of this weekly newspaper reflect an increase in

---

[10] J.M. Kennedy, *Historic and Important Dates in the Civic tLife of Thurles* (Thurles, 1940), p. 5.
[11] *Nenagh Guardian*, 17 Sept. 2005, p. 16.
[12] J.M. Kennedy, *Historic and Important Dates in the Civic Life of Thurles* (Thurles, 1940), p. 5.
[13] Charlie Culhane was present at the foundation of the G.A.A. on 1 Nov. 1884. The property on Jail St (now O'Donovan Rossa St.) was later owned by the Gleeson family.

business enterprise with the numerous advertisements evidencing the growing significance of local commercial activity. The printing of posters, pamphlets, etc. was carried on by Edward Shanahan of Main Street (now Ryan's Jewellers). The most successful Thurles newspaper has been the *'Tipperary Star'*, which was first published in September 1909. Their premises on Friar Street were once the coach office of a Mr. Curry, who was in the employment of Carlo (Charles) Bianconi (1785-1875), the transport pioneer.[14]

THE TEACHING ORDERS

In the 1880s the Ursuline Sisters had a community of over fifty at their convent on Cathedral Street. Their duties included the teaching of ladies, both boarding and day and also the teaching of about sixty poor children.[15] Superioress was Melbourne born Sister de Pazzi O'Connell. The Ursulines had been in Thurles since 1787, when a local, Sister Clare Ursula (Anastasia) Tobin (b.1759), founded the school. The curriculum of that time is of interest: Young ladies are taught reading, writing, arithmetic, geography, embroidery, needlework and painting on silk.[16]

The Presentation Sisters have been in the town since July 1817, when Sister Mary Francis Cormack of Stradavoher founded the school at Stradavoher, in a building given to the community by her father, John. They later transferred residence to Chapel Lane and moved again in 1824 to their present location on Cathedral Street. By the 1880s the community had increased to thirty-five. The work of the sisters included the teaching of a national school of six-hundred children, both male and female. They also had an orphanage and an industrial school certified for forty-five girls. About three-hundred of the children were fed and clothed by the sisters. Thirteen acres of land belonging to the convent served, among other purposes, for the training of dairymaids.[17] Indeed the Presentation Sisters have a unique connection with Thurles. The order was founded in 1777 by Nano Nagle (1718-1784), whose mother was Anne Mathew of Annfield, Thurles – the daughter of George Mathew the Elder.[18]

The Christian Brothers School has been in Thurles since 1816, when local man William Cahill (1771-1843) and Callan native Thomas Cahill (1781-1858) founded the school on Pudding Lane (Jail Street), now O'Donovan Rossa Street. In the 1880s Rev. Br Thomas J. Nugent was Superior and approximately

---

[14] Daniel Maher, Thurles Local History Notes (unpublished) p. 100. Note: For more on Bianconi's connection with Thurles see: Sister Mercedes Lillis, *The Story of the Ursulines in Thurles, Two Hundred Years Agrowing 1787-1987* (Thurles, 1987), pp 25-6.

[15] Bassett, p. 375.

[16] *Leinster Journal*, 1 Oct. 1788.

[17] Bassett, pp 373-5.

[18] Souvenir Booklet – *Blessing and Opening of the Church of St. Joseph and St. Brigid* (Thurles, 1971), p. 27.

four-hundred boys attended. It was at this time that a secondary department was added to the original national school.[19] Pressure from the Society for the Preservation of the Irish Language had resulted in Irish being taught from 1878. A questionnaire, regarding the status of the Irish language in schools, sent to headmasters in 1882, prompted this response from Br. J. Murphy, Thurles, C.B.S. "About fifty of the pupils' parents speak Irish and I am anxious to start a class as soon as a competent teacher can be found".[20] Archbishop Thomas Croke was on very friendly terms with the Christian Brothers. Not only did he subscribe fifty pounds annually to them but also his pony and trap was always at their command, a privilege they frequently used.

SEMINARIES

St Patrick's College, which opened 1 September 1837, had about one hundred students studying for the priesthood in 1889, of whom twenty were boarded outside. The Pallottines also known as the Society of Catholic Apostolate came to Thurles in 1909. The first Pallottine student to be ordained in Thurles was John Boyle of Cassestown, Thurles, who was ordained in June 1915. Franciscan Friars were present in the town since the late seventeenth century and their friary, on Friar Street, continued until its closure in 1892.

St Patrick's College, Thurles. (Image courtesy of the National Library of Ireland)

STANNIX HOME

A great subject for discussion, in Thurles, during 1889 was the attractive building project nearing completion at the top of Pike Street (now Kickham Street). The building was constructed of red brick, with half-timbered gables

---

[19] Christy O'Dwyer, *Pobal Ailbhe – Archdiocese Cashel and Emly* (Strasbourg, 2008), p. 316.
[20] Barry Coldrey, *Faith and Fatherland* (Dublin, 1988), p. 161.

Stannix Home, Pike Street, now Kickham Street, Thurles.

and verandas and was built at a cost of £2,500 by J. Kiernan, Talbot St., Dublin.[21] It was called the Stannix Home (Widows' Home), after its benefactor Miss Emma Slaughter Stannix, who had left a charitable foundation to build a complex to house widows aged over sixty. She had stipulated that her own tenants, in Moycarkey, were to get first preference and that there was to be no distinction as to religion. Four times a year each resident was to receive five shillings. Miss Stannix was a character of immense generosity and amazing foresight with many local links, particularly with the parish of Moycarkey/Borris.

HOUSING

Thurles Urban Council in March 1899 had applied for the sanction of a loan of £5,000 for the purpose of erecting working class dwellings. Patrick J. Ormonde, surveyor to the urban council said that it was proposed to erect seventy-four houses in all. For these he believed there was an absolute necessity to secure proper accommodation for the labouring class. He considered there were about two hundred of the existing houses absolutely unfit for human habitation. They were chiefly thatched houses, with small windows, badly constructed walls and a great number had but one room. Dr Martin Callanan, medical officer of the district, gave evidence regarding the unsanitary conditions of the houses referred to. These have no sanitary accommodation whatever, at present.[22] This lack of sanitation in Thurles, no doubt, contributed to the recent outbreak of typhoid in the town, an event which spurred local politicians to demand improvements.[23] The medical officer reported to the urban council in September, 'that fifteen cases of typhoid fever had occurred in Stradavoher Street and one in Quarry Street. Eleven patients have been removed to hospital and five were under treatment. A sample of water from the pump in

---

[21] *Irish Builder*, 1 June 1890.
[22] *Nationalist*, 8 Mar. 1899.
[23] *Nenagh Guardian*, 3 Jan. 1900.

Thurles streetscape, Main Street, now Liberty Square, 1898.

Stradavoher was sent for analysis'. The report went on to say that a large number of houses and attached piggeries in Pudding Lane and elsewhere had been unfit for human habitation and closed as a result.[24]

THE STRUGGLE FOR THE LAND

Michael Davitt's Land League, founded in 1879, quickly attained a strong foothold in Tipperary. John Trant of Dovea House, near Thurles, had good reason to remember the early years of the 1880s. The Land League insisted in November 1880 on a reduction of 25% in the rent. This Trant refused but a reduction of 20% was agreed the following spring. Turf cutting was also affected. It was customary for the Trants to let the bog for the season's cutting. But no rate could be agreed in March 1881, which, according to John Trant, was again 'the influence of the Land League'. No turf was cut that year and the want of fuel was severely felt by the farmers and labourers on the nearby Neville Estate.[25]

John Trant was also boycotted in November 1881. Only two of his thirty-five Catholic labourers reported for work. A valuable crop of potatoes in danger of

---

[24] *Nationalist*, 20 Sept. 1899.
[25] National Library of Ireland. P.C. 24 Trant Papers.

over exposure was saved, by organising all the Protestant children and ladies to complete the task. He also had to resort to using Emergency men to save his harvest. As Catholic traders in Thurles refused to supply goods, the Trants responded by building a shop at Killahara and bringing supplies from Dublin to supply their own Protestant families and any other boycotted people.[26] The Trants were constantly under police protection during these years. In February 1882 the police were replaced by soldiers of the 20th Hussars.

Boycotting and public ostracization of land grabbers and their associates was common in the town of Thurles at this time. Indeed the town had a well-deserved reputation for boycotting. Eight locals, charged with boycotting, appeared at the Thurles assizes on 18 December 1881.[27] In 1885 Ryan's Hotel, in the town, was almost ruined by local shopkeepers refusing to buy from any commercial travellers who stayed there.[28] In 1889 shopkeepers here were victimised for supporting a bailiff in the local elections. Tradesmen refused to repair their windows, the children of the local Christian Brothers school refused to associate with their children. The porter van-men were warned to avoid them and the people of Stradavoher boycotted a milk supplier, who gave them milk.[29]

Thurles Ladies' Land League committee was very active during these years. The following were present at their meeting in February 1882:- Mrs. Moloney – President, Misses Murray, Power, McNamara, McGrath, Culhane[30], Stokes, Stapleton, and Hayes.[31]

The sale of farms of evicted tenants, which was advertised to take place at the Courthouse in Thurles on 17 May 1880, provided an opportunity for the local branches of the Land League to show their strength and confront the landlords. It proved to be a massive show of organisational ability and of solidarity with the evicted tenants. Land League branches marched in military formation headed by their own bands, while flags bearing national sentiments were carried aloft. The local excitement was at fever pitch as the streets were thronged in anticipation. A high level of security was obvious as extra constabulary and military were drafted in from Templemore and Tipperary barracks. A Hussar unit from Cahir was also on standby. At the auction, the tenancy of the farms went for sums well below the overdue rent to members of the Landlords Property Defence Association. By the turn of the twentieth century, successive Land Acts had diluted the power base of the landed gentry.

---

[26] Ion Trant, *Just Across the Water* (Thurles, 1996), p. 82.
[27] *Nenagh Guardian*, 11 Feb. 2006, p. 33.
[28] Ibid, 14 Oct. 1885.
[29] *Nationalist*, 13 Mar. 1889.
[30] Miss Culhane's brother, Charlie, was present at the foundation of the G.A.A. on 1 Nov. 1884.
[31] *Tipperary*, 18 Feb. 1882.

THURLES WORKHOUSE

Thurles workhouse, also referred to as 'poorhouse', opened its doors on 9 November 1842, at Gortataggart.[32] Built by the Poor Law Union to accommodate seven hundred inmates, it attempted to tackle the growing local problem of poverty, homelessness and destitution. It provided basic food, clothing and shelter for the utterly destitute and its operation was overseen by an elected board of guardians. Inmates were subject to harsh laws in the workhouse and there was a strict separation of age groups and sexes. Once inside adults were forbidden to leave and children could only do so under the supervision of a teacher. During the Famine years and into the early 1850s, such was the demand for assistance, that the workhouse was seriously overcrowded. This overpopulation of the workhouse, and the already poor health of many new inmates, meant that disease was rife. Between the years of 1847 and 1851 it is recorded that 3,149 inmates succumbed to disease and malnutrition, with over half of these being children under the age of fifteen.[33] From November 1877, the Sisters of Mercy took responsibility for the workhouse.

In charge of Thurles workhouse in 1889 were: John G. Coppinger (clerk), Patrick Russell (master), Mrs. Mary Russell (matron) and Dr John Russell (medical officer).[34]

YOUNG MEN'S CLUB

In October 1883, a preliminary meeting was held in the presbytery to establish a Young Men's Club for Thurles. Its aims were the mutual improvement and amusement of its members. Rev. J. Cantwell Adm. had a great interest in the formation of the club. Its formation reflects an improving social climate in Thurles towards the end of the nineteenth century. The idea was initiated by: Charlie Culhane, J. Stapleton, J.R. Molony, W. Mullaly, T. O'Loughlin and E. Cooney.[35] By 1889 the club had progressed well, having one hundred members, a house, and hall on The Mall. Library, reading, and billiard rooms, were popular and members paid a subscription of ten shillings. Rev. Thomas Fennelly Adm. was president, P. Kirwan and James Butler secretaries and P. Finn treasurer. James Butler was also Thurles G.A.A. club's first secretary.[36]

---

[32] Construction work on Thurles Workhouse started in July 1840. The contract price was £5,840 and the building contractor was Denis Leahy of Cabra and East Main Street, Thurles. He was brother of Patrick Leahy, a future Archbishop of Cashel and Emly (1857-1875).

[33] Anne Lanigan, 'The Workhouse Child in Thurles 1840-1880', in W. Corbett & W. Nolan, (eds). *Thurles – The Cathedral Town* (Dublin, 1989), p. 65.

[34] Note – In 1922 the building was known as the *County Home* and later, in 1954, North Tipperary County Council assumed responsibility, re-naming it the *Hospital of the Assumption*. This building was demolished and the newly constructed – Community Hospital of the Assumption and was officially opened in February 2007.

[35] *Tipperary Leader*, 6 Oct. 1883.

[36] Bassett, p. 375.

SPORT

Townlands of Thurles, bearing such names as Bowling Green and Racecourse give us an indication of the sports that took place in the town in former times. At the end of the nineteenth century sport played a big part in the lives of Thurles people.

In 1889, the local G.A.A. club had nearly two hundred members, who participated in regular games of hurling and football.

Tennis was growing in popularity among the 'well–to-do' in the 1880s. While excellent facilities were available at the Trant Estate in Dovea, a new club – Thurles Lawn Tennis Club was established in 1884. The subscription was £1 with family membership for thirty shillings and the club boasted four grass courts. Croquet was also played on the lawns of many of the 'Big' houses of the locality.

Thurles Cricket Club c1894.

At the time of the G.A.A. foundation, cricket was growing in popularity in Thurles. A new club had been formed in 1869. By 1875 the town landlord, Count de Jarnac, had become its patron.[37] Their colours were blue and white and games were played on the Glebe lawn (Dublin Road), Maryfield (Ballinahow), Monadreen (Clongour) and at Ballycurrane. The membership was approximately fifty and matches were played against Templemore Garrison, Thurles College, Dundrum, Rock (Cashel), County Limerick and Tipperary Town.

---

[37] *Tipperary Free Press*, 19 Mar. 1875.

Indeed, Thurles could be regarded as a stronghold of the game as evidenced by the number of clubs based there during the 1870s and '80s:-

Thurles Ormondes C.C.	Clongour C.C.
St. Patrick's College C.C.	Thurles G.S.W.R., C.C.
Turtulla C.C.	Emerald C.C.
Mr. S. W. Boyton XI	Mr. T. H. Stackpool XI
Thurles C.C.	Mr. Tennant XI[38]

Boxing gave Thurles a hero to be proud of in 1880, when bare-knuckled fighter Paddy Ryan hit the headlines. Paddy, from The Quarry (Mitchel Street), had won the American Heavyweight boxing champion-ship in his first professional fight. Known as 'The Trojan Giant',[39] he defeated forty-two year old Joe Goss at Vancouver in eighty-seven rounds.

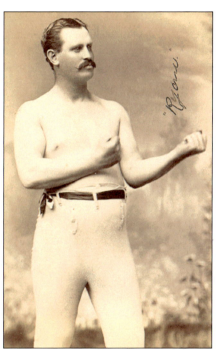

Paddy Ryan

Horseracing, in former times the prerogative of the 'ascendancy class', has a long history in the Thurles area. The townland of Racecourse, to the west of the town is named after a racecourse which has been established there as far back as 1732, where a successful three-day meeting was held in June of that year. Lisnagonoge, near Beakstown in the neighbouring parish of Holycross, was also a popular venue for horse racing from the 1890s to the first decade of the twentieth century. By this stage tenant farmers were very much involved in racing. Racing also took place at Thurles Show Grounds (now Semple Stadium). For the St Stephen's Day meeting in 1910 the organisers had a new stand erected, a carnival atmosphere prevailed and Thurles Brass and Reed Band attended. Eighty horses contested five races.[40]

For most of the nineteenth century foxhunting was the preserve of the landlord class, although the love of the chase became popular with some better off farmers towards the end of that century. There are many references to packs

[38] Patrick Bracken, *"Foreign and Fantastic Field Sports"*, *Cricket in County Tipperary* (Thurles, 2004), pp. 169-171.
[39] Martin O'Dwyer, *A Biographical Dictionary of Tipperary* (Cashel, 1999), p. 375.
[40] *Tipperary Star*, 31 Dec. 1910.

of hounds being kept at several 'Big' houses throughout mid Tipperary. Master of the Tipperary Fox Hounds at the time of the foundation of the G.A.A. was J.M. Langley.[41]

Hunting of deer as well as foxes and hares was practiced. Gerald Knox of Brittas, Thurles, was responsible for the revival of the Templemore Staghounds that hunted the surrounding countryside in the early 1900s. The kennels and deerpark were then situated at Brittas.[42]

The Thurles Harriers were also very active, meeting twice weekly during the season. National newspapers of the mid nineteenth century name meeting places such as: Bachelor's Hill, Brownstown, and Turtulla.[43] Owen Mansergh was master of a pack of harriers that hunted the hinterland of Thurles in the 1870s.[44]

Tommy Johnston, in 1864, became the first Thurles owner of a bicycle known as the "boneshaker". It was a machine of two wooden wheels of equal size. The first race organised by the Thurles Cycling Club was to the Horse and Jockey and back to Thurles via Littleton. Charles Molloy of Beakstown was mounted on a high wheel (Penny Farthing) and though given a good handicap was defeated in the race by J.L. Johnston on a "safety", which was a successor of the Penny Farthing. The modern (safety) bicycle made its first appearance in the 1880s. The introduction of such refinements as gears, pneumatic tyres and brakes made for a more serviceable bicycle and cycling grew rapidly in popularity among the middle classes. In 1893, among the officials in charge of the Thurles ten mile handicap cycling road race were: Charles Culhane, D.H. Ryan, Hugh Ryan, Andrew Callanan and William Delahunty.[45] All of these were active members of Thurles G.A.A. Club. Membership totalled about fifty and successful cyclists of the time were Denis O'Keeffe[46] and Rody Delaney.[47] Both these men were later Thurles G.A.A. club officers.

Mid nineteenth century maps[48] of Thurles show "ball courts", one to the rear of Black Castle and another to the rear of houses between Croke Street and Friar Street. One can but surmise at the games played here, probably an early version

---

[41] Bassett, p. 37.

[42] W.J. Hayes, (ed.) *Moyne-Templetuohy, A Life of its Own, Vol. 2* (Templetuohy, 2001), pp 317-18.

[43] *Irish Times*, 20 Dec. 1859, p.3.

[44] Ibid, 14 Feb. 1871, p.2.

[45] *Nationalist*, 23 Aug. 1893.

[46] Ibid, 25 July, 1894.

[47] Ibid, 19 Sept. 1894.

[48] Manuscript Maps OS 1841.

[49] J.W. Stubbs, *The History of the University of Dublin from its Foundation to the End of the Eighteenth Century* (Dublin, 1889) pp.144-5.

of handball or perhaps the game of "fives" favoured by college students[49] and common in English public schools. In fives, a ball is propelled against the walls of the court using gloved or bare hands as though they were a racquet. Also common in these schools and played in mid-nineteenth century Tipperary was the game known as rackets. Racket matches were played with a wooden racket by two or four persons in a plain four-walled court. To add interest to the games, large sums of money were staked and betting was common.[50] It is highly likely that handball was imported to Ireland by successive generations of English troops during the late Middle Ages although a French influence cannot be dismissed. Handball was common in Ireland in the mid nineteenth century. Tipperary man William Baggs, acknowledged by many as the "father of the modern day handball", was in his prime. He is remembered for his pioneering of dodging tricks, curved balls, low drives and screw tosses.[51] A handball club existed in Thurles in the 1890s with tournaments and competitions being played against Ballingarry, Cashel etc.[52] William Flynn, Jack Ryan (Building) and Pierre Maher played for Thurles in 1893.

Coursing has a long tradition in this area. The Thurles and Templemore Coursing Club was formed in 1871. Their second meeting was held at the residence of Captain Carden at Barnane, Templemore. A very successful meeting, with a Mr. Thompson as judge, and a large number of dogs entered.[53]

Amateur athletics was also growing in popularity in the second half of the nineteenth century. This began in Dublin at Trinity College, where the newly-founded Dublin University Athletic Club held its first sports meeting in 1857. The famous College Races became one of the most fashionable events in Dublin's sporting calendar. Interest in codified athletics slowly spread to other parts of the country, especially to Munster, where a large number of athletic meetings took place from the 1860s. In time it became common for nearly every town and village to hold at least one meeting every summer. Organisation of these rural sports meetings depended to a large extent on existing local clubs or interested parties e.g. cricket or rowing club. Frequently the local "Big House" or landlord organised the annual sports and if a unit of the British garrison was stationed in the area, they could be relied upon to supply stewards and musical entertainment. In the early years it was mainly the "genteel" classes that competed but by the 1870's most sections of Irish society were participating in athletics. While these meetings were usually under the patronage of the local landlord class, the physical organisation of the meeting was more often than not in the hands of local interested personnel not

[50] *Irish Times*, 17 Sept. 1862, p. 4.
[51] Séamus Ó Ceallaigh, *The Gael in Action* (Tralee, 1943), p. 39.
[52] *Nationalist*, 30 Aug. 1893, 22 June, 1895.
[53] *Irish Times*, 22 Feb. 1871, p. 3.

particular to any class. While the running of races formed the principal events, popular traditional pastimes such as weight-throwing and jumping were included in the programme. Invariably, there was an anglicised atmosphere about these sports meetings. The inescapable fact could not be concealed that, in the main, control of them rested firmly in the hands of the establishment or unionist community. The ordinary people who came to see the athletes perform had no say in the organising of the meetings. The meetings usually took place in the summer or autumn.

In the mid summer of 1866 there was great excitement on the Mall in Thurles, when a large number of spectators turned out to witness a 'foot-race' between a Mr. Berry of the Post Office and Thomas Maher who worked for the rail company. Extra excitement was generated by the abundant betting on the outcome. Berry timed his finish expertly, won by a mere three yards and claimed his prise of one pound sterling.[54] Another similar race in Holycross, five years later, had the attractive sum of six pounds as prize money. Leugh man Michael Cahill and Michael Leahy from Moycarkey contested the distance of 200 yards with Leahy winning the purse by about three yards.[55] Also on the local scene, an annual athletic sports was held in Littleton (1876-'7) and Thurles (1878-'9). These events were well organised with many competitors in all events. Thurles Sports was held in the College Field (later the site of Erin Foods Processing Factory) on 15 July 1878 with an attendance of about 20,000. Twenty events were contested – races from 100 yds. to one mile, running, high jump, long jump, hurdle races, walking races, donkey derby, putting the 42lb weight etc. Unusual events included a canoe and a tub race on the Suir and a 'tug of war' between ten officers of The Royal Fusiliers and ten men of Thurles.[56] The regimental band of The 7th Royal Fusiliers from Templemore entertained the large attendance. A special carriage enclosure and a reserve promenade were provided for the "more respectable portion of the community"[57]. Among the competitors of note was Charlie Culhane, who competed in the 100 and 220 yards flat races, winning both. Culhane was present at the foundation of the G.A.A. in 1884. R. Dunbar of the "Irish Sportsman" Dublin was handicapper and referee. At the banquet in the evening, he spoke of the success of the meeting saying that it was one of the largest gatherings he had seen and so orderly and well conducted as to change his opinion very much regarding County Tipperary people.[58]

Such was the interest in the Thurles athletic sports of June 1879 that an

[54] *Tipperary Advocate*, 14 July 1866.
[55] *Nenagh Guardian*, 29 July 1871.
[56] Programme – *Thurles Athletic Club Sports*, 15 July 1878.
[57] *Tipperary Advocate*, 13 July, 1878.
[58] Ibid, 20 July, 1878.

application for reduced rail fares was made to G.S. & W.R. The rail company agreed to this, with return tickets at the single fare for groups of ten or more.[59]

IRISH IRELAND – CULTURAL REVIVAL

During the 1890s and into the first decade of the twentieth-century many forms of cultural nationalism took shape all over Ireland. This saw expression through a national revival of interest in the Irish language and Irish culture including sports, folklore, music, arts etc. Among the most influential of these, Irish-Ireland movements were the Gaelic Athletic Association, founded in 1884, and the Gaelic League – Conradh na Gaeilge, founded in 1893.

Eoin MacNeill and others established the Gaelic League-Conradh na Gaeilge. At the time, the Irish language had diminished as a spoken tongue and English was becoming the dominant language of the majority. The object of the league was to encourage the use of the Irish language in everyday life, so as to counter the ongoing anglicisation of the country. Branches of the Gaelic League were springing up all over Tipperary and G.A.A. members were the backbone of many of them. On the last Thursday in October 1901, a meeting was held in the Confraternity Hall, Thurles, for the purpose of founding a branch of The Gaelic League. Rev. J.J. Dwan Adm. presided at the meeting, which was very well attended. The gathering was addressed by Patrick Dwyer, who outlined the aims and objectives of the league, finishing with the words, "And so gentlemen, let us do our share towards the realisation of that glorious dream, which true Irishmen have never ceased to dream, a dream when the Gael shall walk his native soil, free as the air he breathes and the land he

St Patrick's Day 1900, unveiling of the 1798 Memorial.

---

[59] Albert Maher, *Signalman's Memories* (Thurles, 1998) p. 57.

Thurles Working Men's Club Band 1885. Photo taken in the grounds of St Patrick's College.

treads, the songs of his native country swelling in his heart, and the language of his forefathers enthroned up on his lips".[60] While Archbishop Croke supported the language revival he lamented that he had reached the age, when the acquisition of another language was beyond his powers. His successor, Archbishop Fennelly encouraged and supported the cultural revival. In his 1903 pastoral letter he urged parents to give their children 'every opportunity' to join the Gaelic League and the G.A.A. 'Association with the Gaelic League', he declared, 'will spread knowledge of the old tongue, a love for the old land, and lead to activity in the discharge of the duties of patriotism'[61]. In Thurles C.B.S. those interested in learning the language were accommodated, as a teacher in the school offered voluntary classes to boys, who wished to learn the language.[62] In the following years the Gaelic League – Conradh na Gaeilge organised the celebration of St. Patrick's Day in fine style with a Feis in the town. Irish music, song, and dance, thrilled the large attendances of clergy and laity. Plans were laid for the provision of Irish language classes in the town. A *'múinteoir taistil'* (travelling teacher), who was a native Irish speaker, conducted these classes.[63]

Prior to the foundation of the G.A.A., its founder, Michael Cusack, had become disillusioned with the social exclusiveness of existing sporting bodies

[60] *Nenagh News*, 2 Nov. 1901.
[61] Christy O'Dwyer, 'Pobal Ailbhe' in *Nationalist, 1890-1990, Centenary Supplement* (1990), p. 114.
[62] Risteárd Mulcahy, *Richard Mulcahy 1886-1971* (Dublin, 1999), p. 17.
[63] *Bláith Fhleasg Ó Thiobraid Árann* (1943), p. 77.

and was convinced that the spread of English games was destroying national morale. The G.A.A. from the start attracted substantial I.R.B.[64] (Fenian) support. The fundamental policy of the I.R.B. with regard to sport was that an Irish-controlled organisation would help to make the youth of the country Gaelic in heart and spirit and would motivate them to work for the freedom and welfare of their own country. It also aimed to woo the young generation from the prevalent alien influences, to mould them into a disciplined nationalist force, and eventually to channel physical courage and achievement into physical force.[65] A majority of the founding members of the G.A.A. were members of the I.R.B. and in the early years of the association there was a constant struggle by the I.R.B. to gain control of the new association's executive. The case was similar in Thurles where police reports of that time, state that 'Thurles, in particular, holds solid for the I.R.B.'[66] and 'the I.R.B. and the G.A.A. are carried on in conjunction, as far as the leading men are concerned'.[67] Local Thurlesmen present at the foundation of the G.A.A., Michael Cantwell[68] and Charlie Culhane[69] were under police surveillance for I.R.B. involvement, as were Hugh Ryan,[70] James Butler[71] and Andrew Callanan[72] first chairman, secretary and treasurer respectively of the Thurles G.A.A. Club.

The Land League, founded by Michael Davitt in 1879 to "get the land for the people" and the Home Rule movement[73] are also intertwined in the growing Irish revival of the time.

The steady growth of nationalism and an interest in 'Irish Ireland' among G.A.A. members is evident in the Thurles club during 1907. Regarding a proposed excursion to Dublin in July, a motion was passed at the club's monthly meeting encouraging members not to visit the Irish International Exhibition, recently opened by the lord lieutenant, as it was, in their opinion, a foreign show injurious to Irish industries, trade and to national prosperity. Later in the year, the purchase of a foreign manufactured football caused considerable discussion, resulting in a successful proposal, by James M. Kennedy, club secretary, 'That in future the footballs must be of Irish

---

[64] I.R.B., The Irish Republican Brotherhood was a secret oath-bound organisation founded in 1858. It aimed to overthrow British rule and create an independent Irish republic by means of force.

[65] Tomás Ó Ríordáin, *P.N. Fitzgerald* (Cork, 2004), p. 33.

[66] NAI, C.B.S. 11921-S.

[67] NAI, C.B.S. 11876-S.

[68] NAI, C.B.S. 12958-S.

[69] *Tipperary Star*, 9 Jan. 1926.

[70] NAI, C.B.S.13114-S.

[71] NAI, C.B.S. 1890-1360/s

[72] NAI, C.B.S.13114-S.

[73] Home Rule was the demand that the governance of Ireland be returned from Westminster to a domestic parliament in Ireland.

Dovea House, residence of John Trant in the 1880s.

manufacture and, as far as possible, everything else which is required by the club be of home manufacture'.[74]

The Irish Literary Revival (also called the "Celtic Twilight") stimulated a new appreciation of traditional Irish literature and Irish poetry in the late 19th and early 20th century with Irish writers including William Butler Yeats, Lady Gregory, "AE" Russell etc., while the Abbey Theatre, founded in 1904, provided a stage for Irish plays and playwrights. The Feis Ceoil was founded in 1896 to counteract the neglect of music development in Ireland.

Other events in Thurles that gave expression to the growing nationalist sentiment included the funeral of Charles J. Kickham in 1882, the annual remembrance ceremony for the Manchester Martyrs, the outbreak of the Boer War, the centenary commemoration of the 1798 Rebellion culminating in the unveiling of the 1798 Memorial in 1900, at Liberty Square.

This idealistic nationalism influenced and attracted the youth of Ireland, stimulating intellectual activity and directing attention to the wealth of Irish culture and traditions, which were in danger of being swamped. In Thurles, the fact that the G.A.A. was founded in the town, and was under the patronage of Archbishop Thomas Croke, stimulated a unique loyalty in the townspeople to the ideals of its founding fathers. Young men such as Tom Semple and his team-mates of 'The Blues' era found membership of the association attractive and meaningful and they, in their time, assumed the G.A.A. mantle, and handed on a proud heritage to their successors.

---

[74] Thurles Sarsfields Club Minutes 1907.

CHAPTER 3

G.A.A. – The Early Years in Thurles

BIRTH AND REBIRTH – A BRIEF RETROSPECTIVE

WHEN THE Gaelic Athletic Association was founded at Miss Lizzie Hayes's Commercial Hotel, Thurles, on 1 November 1884, Tom Semple was five years of age. That meeting in the billiard room of the hotel was to have a profound effect locally and nationally in the years that followed. Its purpose, as stated in the circular letter which announced the meeting, was:-

> 'to take steps towards the formation of a Gaelic association for the preservation and cultivation of our national pastimes and for providing rational amusements for the Irish people during their leisure hours'.[1]

| *Charlie Culhane* | *Archbishop Thomas Croke* | *William Delahunty* |

[1] T.F. O'Sullivan, *The Story of the G.A.A.* (Dublin, 1916), p. 6.

The main convener was Michael Cusack, a schoolmaster from Carron, County Clare.

Present along with Cusack were Maurice Davin, the champion athlete from Deerpark, Carrick-on-Suir, John Wyse Power, a journalist from Waterford, J.K. Bracken, a monumental sculptor from Templemore, Joseph O'Ryan, a solicitor in both Callan and Thurles, William Foley, from Carrick-on-Suir, John McKay, a Belfast journalist, and Thomas St. George MacCarthy, an R.I.C. inspector stationed at Templemore. Also present and from the Thurles locality, were Charlie Culhane, Main Street (now Liberty Square), William Delahunty, Cathedral Street, Michael Cantwell, Main Street (now Liberty Square), John Butler, Ballyhudda, Moycarkey, and T.K. Dwyer, Ballyvinane, Littleton.[2]

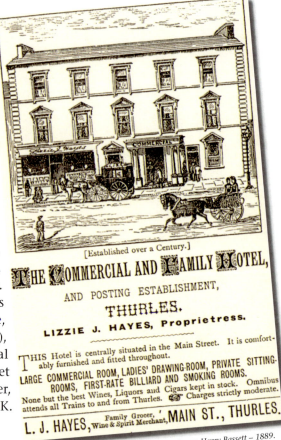

[Established over a Century.]

THE COMMERCIAL AND FAMILY HOTEL,

AND POSTING ESTABLISHMENT,

THURLES.

LIZZIE J. HAYES, Proprietress.

THIS Hotel is centrally situated in the Main Street. It is comfortably furnished and fitted throughout.
LARGE COMMERCIAL ROOM, LADIES' DRAWING-ROOM, PRIVATE SITTING-ROOMS, FIRST-RATE BILLIARD AND SMOKING ROOMS. Omnibus
None but the best Wines, Liquors and Cigars kept in stock. Charges strictly moderate.
attends all Trains to and from Thurles.

L. J. HAYES, Family Grocer, Wine & Spirit Merchant, MAIN ST., THURLES.

From "The Book of County Tipperary" by George Henry Bassett – 1889.

Maurice Davin, was elected president, while Cusack, McKay and Wyse Power were elected secretaries. Notable Irishmen were invited to become patrons on the fledging association and by the end of the year such invitations were accepted by Charles Stewart Parnell, then leader of the Irish Parliamentary Party, Michael Davitt, the founder of the Land League, and by Archbishop Thomas Croke, then the leading nationalist member of the Catholic hierarchy, who gave the G.A.A his unqualified approval.

Regarding the foundation of Thurles G.A.A. Club, sources which might reveal the exact date and location of the foundation are not available, but oral tradition gives the year of its inception as 1884. The first meeting was held in a room up Mixie O'Connell's Lane,[3] most likely in Thomas Ryan's Hotel (McGlades) on Main Street, later McLoughney's, Liberty Square and now House of Elegance.

---

[2] *Tipperary Leader*, 7 Nov. 1884. Note: See also Appendix II – The Foundation of the Gaelic Athletic Association: A Local Perspective.
[3] Interview with Tomás Ó Baróid, Clongour, Thurles (26 Jan., 1998).

| *Hugh Ryan* | *James Butler* | *Andrew Callanan* |

The presence of locals, Charlie Culhane, William Delahunty, and Michael Cantwell, at the foundation of the G.A.A. in Hayes's Hotel, would suggest that they would also provide the impetus necessary for the formation of a local club. It is reasonable then to conclude that the Thurles Club was formed very shortly after the foundation of the G.A.A. The first club officers were:- President (Chairman) – Hugh Ryan, West Gate, a native of Clonoulty, Secretary – James Butler, Friar Street, and Treasurer – Andrew Callanan, West Gate.

The original club colours were green and gold. These were the colours worn in the first championship of 1887. Pantaloons (knee-breeches) in green[4] were also worn. Sometime towards the end of the nineteenth century the club adopted blue and white as its official colours. Oral tradition, regarding this change of colours, points to a special local devotion to the Blessed Virgin Mary, with whom the colour blue is associated. Evidence of this devotion is seen in the naming of the local Roman Catholic cathedral as The Cathedral of the Assumption, the Church of Ireland church as St Mary's, local hospitals as St. Mary's District Hospital and the Hospital of the Assumption. Lady's Well, on the banks of the Suir, beside Thurles Golf Club is also part of this tradition. The 'Lady' is undoubtedly the Blessed Virgin Mary also commonly referred to as 'Our Lady'. This devotion has its roots in the Middle Ages, when an annual pattern was held, on 15 August, at Lady's Well.[5]

---

[4] *Tipperary Advocate,* 1 Oct. 1887.

[5] Note – On July 8th 1432, Richard O'Hedian, Archbishop of Cashel, received from James Butler, Earl of Ormond and Lord of the Liberty of Tipperary, safe conduct for all pilgrims who visited Thurles three days before the three days after the feast of the Assumption. The celebration of Mass and other ceremonies were conducted in the open around the Mass Tree. The pattern went into decline after 1798, when the Archbishop disapproved of the practice due to excesses and the abandonment of conventional Christian morality.

Daniel Maher, Thurles, local history notes – (unpublished).

The blue and white colours became synonymous with Thurles G.A.A. Club and the far-famed title 'Thurles Blues' became a reality.

It was also customary in the early years of the G.A.A. to name teams within a club in memory of saints or Irish patriots – thus the Thurles club's senior hurling team was named Thurles Sarsfield recalling the Jacobite leader, Patrick Sarsfield (c.1655-1693). Other hurling teams within the club honoured the United Irishman Robert Emmet (1778-1803) and the national patron – St Patrick. Thurles G.A.A. club's football team was called Thurles Mitchels at this time, recalling the Young Irelander John Mitchel (1815-1875).

It may be a surprise for some readers to learn that, in the early years, the G.A.A. was more associated with athletics than with the games of hurling or Gaelic football. Until 1887 these games were usually subsidiary events at athletics meeting.[6] In 1885, the rules for hurling and football, drafted by Maurice Davin, were adopted as the formation of new clubs continued and the first competitions in these games were organised.

1886 – Thurles G.A.A. Club undertook the onerous task of organising the first Gaelic tournament at Easter, 1886. The idea of bringing clubs together to compete in friendly rivalry, in hurling and football, was new at the time and originated with the Thurles club.[7] Upon the shoulders of Hugh Ryan, James Butler, Andy Callanan, Denis Maher, James Stapleton and John Gleeson rested the responsibility for the tournament, which attracted national attention[8] and an attendance in the region of 15,000.[9] It is interesting to note that the Thurles club, famed for its hurling and hurlers, entered a football team in this and other tournaments in 1886. Thomas Hackett's field on the Turtulla road was the venue and taking part were:- Davitts, Faughs (both Dublin clubs), Dun Laoghaire, Two-Mile-Borris, Bray, Thurles, Nenagh, Moycarkey, Templemore, Holycross, and Central Tipperary. Games in both hurling and football were played and the pitches for the tournament were in two linked fields marked out by Hugh Ryan, Thurles and John Manning, Ballymoreen, Littleton. Hugh spent much of the day on horseback, stewarding the sidelines and keeping the crowds back.[10] Such was the status of the occasion that when the games began every important official connected with the G.A.A. was on the field, the patron, Archbishop Thomas Croke, the president, Maurice Davin, the vice-presidents, J.K. Bracken and Frank Moloney, the secretaries, Michael Cusack, John McKay and John Wyse Power.

---

[6] Marcus de Búrca, *The G.A.A.: A History* (Dublin, 1980), p. 23.
[7] St Patrick's College, Thurles. Philip Fogarty, research notes (unpublished).
[8] *Tipperary Star*, 16 Oct. 1909.
[9] *Sport*, 1 May 1886.
[10] St Patrick's College, Thurles. Philip Fogarty, research notes (unpublished).

Overall it was a wonderfully successful day, a day that paved the way for many a G.A.A. gathering in Thurles, in the decades that followed. In the evening, when the dust had settled and the crowds were drifting home and the 'special' trains had left the station, Archbishop Croke addressing supporters that had gathered at 'The Palace' on Cathedral Street, concluded with the words "You have today safely planted the G.A.A. and your magnificent tournament will ever constitute the premier page of Irish Gaelic history".[11] In the years that followed, the Easter Gaelic Tournament at Thurles became an annual event.

On Monday 27 December 1886 the first Tipperary G.A.A. County Board was formed at a convention held in the Literary Institute, Nenagh. The first officers were:- chairman – J.K. Bracken, Templemore, vice-chairman – Pat Hoctor, Nenagh, secretary – E.M. Walsh, Nenagh and Treasurer – F.R. Moloney Nenagh.[12] Hugh Ryan, chairman of the Thurles club was elected to the committee.

1887 – The year 1887 was the first year that county championships were organised in Tipperary. Teams were composed of twenty-one players and in their first game of the football championship, Thurles were drawn against Loughmore. The game was unfinished due to a dispute over a forfeit point. Loughmore won the refixture at Borris-Ileigh and Thurles in disgust gave up football for hurling[13]. Jim Maher's version of this game includes the following, 'Keeping order at the game, astride a horse, was J.K. Bracken. Near the end of the match when Thurles were pressing hard and a winning goal seemed imminent, Bracken charged in onto the field to clear off some spectators. The ball on its way to what appeared a certain goal hit his horse, was deflected and Loughmore cleared to finish victors.

Following the controversial and brief sojourn in football circles, the club affiliated a team in the inaugural hurling championship. The first game was against Two-Mile-Borris and played at Holycross on Sunday 3 April and resulted in a Thurles victory. The semi-final against Borris-Ileigh was played at a venue known as the "Stone Jug Field", on the Turtulla Road, Thurles, with the locals winning by a forfeit point[14]. A forfeit point was awarded to the opposition when a defender struck the ball over his own end line. North Tipperary's defeat of Moycarkey left Thurles favourites for county honours. Borris-Ileigh was the venue for the semi-final and final to be played on the same day, 24 July. The location of the field was down the "ould bog road" on land owned by Martin Ryan (Boula) and now in the possession of Séamus Kennedy, Lower St.,

[11] *Tipperary Star*, 16 Oct. 1909.
[12] *Sport*, 1 Nov. 1887.
[13] Philip Fogarty, *Tipperary's G.A.A. Story* (Thurles, 1960), p. 27.
[14] *G.A.A. Annual 1910-'11*, pp. 62-3.

Tipperary, Thurles selection – Inaugural All-Ireland Hurling Champions 1887
Back row (l.-r.): Denis Maher (R), Jim Sullivan, Ned Murphy, Jim Ryan, Matty Maher (M), Ned Lambe, Tom Bourke, Con Callanan, Dan Davoren, Matty Maher (L). Middle row (l.-r.): Pat Ryan, Denis Maher (L), Jim Stapleton (Captain), Tom Maher, John Leamy, Ger Ryan, Tim Dwyer. Front row (l.-r.): Mick Carroll, Martin McNamara, Tom Butler. (Photograph taken in 1910)

Borris-Ileigh.[15] North Tipperary defeated Holycross by a forfeit point in the semi-final and after a short break lined out against Thurles in the final. The teams were scoreless at half-time but then the North began to weaken and had to give way to the fresher Thurles team. The final score was three points and two forfeit points to nil. The victorious Thurles

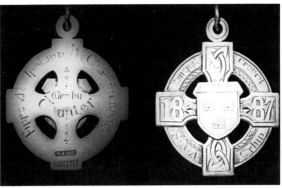

All-Ireland medal 1887 (front and back).

team in their green and gold jerseys, which won the first Tipperary hurling championship, was: Denis Maher (Captain), Andy, Tom and Matty Maher, Jim Stapleton, Ned Murphy, Jer Dwyer, Jack, Dinny, Ned and Matty Maher, Con Callanan, Tom Burke, Dan Davern, Jim Sullivan, Pat Ryan, Stephen Purcell, Dick Butler, Ned Flanagan, Martin McNamara (Mack) and Jack Bannon.

Five counties contested the first All-Ireland hurling championship:- Galway, Wexford, Clare, Tipperary and Kilkenny. Though drawn against Dublin in the first round, Dublin provided no opposition to Tipperary. The next game was against Clare at Nenagh on 25 September. The score in Nenagh was Tipperary (Thurles) one goal and eight points to four points for Clare (Smith O'Brien's). The All-Ireland semi-final against Kilkenny's Tullaroan, was played on Thursday, 27 October, at Urlingford[16] and F.R. Maloney, Nenagh, was referee. The final score read: Thurles four goals and seven points to nil[17]. Thurles had to wait over five months for the final against Meelick/Eyrecourt of Galway.

1888 – On Easter Sunday, 1 April 1888 Thurles, representing Tipperary, had the proud distinction of winning the first All-Ireland hurling championship, played at Birr, County Offaly. At three o'clock, the teams lined up and the red, leather hurling ball was thrown up by Patrick White, Birr. He was a native of Blakefield, Toomevara and was working in Birr at the time. It was a very close encounter until late in the second-half when a goal by Tommy Healy, Two-Mile-Borris, separated the sides. His shot was a dexterous left-hander sending the ball flying from the middle of the field, under the tape. At the call of time, the final score was:- Thurles, Tipperary 1 goal, 1 point and 1 forfeit point, Meelick/Eyrecourt, Galway nil.

Disputed travelling arrangements for the game explains the absence of team

---

[15] *A Century of G.A.A. in Borris-Ileigh* (Borrisoleigh, 1986), p. 11.
[16] *Sport*, 29 Oct. 1887.
[17] Ibid, 29 Oct. 1887.

Jim Stapleton

captain Dinny Maher and six of the original team[18] from the team that contested the All-Ireland final. The twenty-one players were: Jim Stapleton, Capt., Cathedral St. and Bohernamona, Ned Murphy, Cathedral St. and Mill Rd., Martin McNamara, Garryvicleheeheen, Tom Burke, Bohernamona and Rossestown, Matty Maher 'Little', Killinan Cross, Tom Maher, Killinan Cross, Andy Maher, Killinan Cross, Jer Dwyer, Brocka, Rossmore and Cassestown, Tommy Carroll, Moyneard, Moyne, John (Jack) Dunne, Urard, Gortnahoe, Pat Leahy, Fennor, Gortnahoe, Mick Carroll, Rosmult, Drombane, John Leamy, Roskeen, Drombane, Ned Lambe, Hammond's Lot, Drombane, Ned Bowe, Leigh, Two-Mile-Borris, John Mockler, Newhill, Two-Mile-Borris, Tommy Healy, Coolcroo, Two-Mile-Borris, Tom Stapleton, Ballydavid, Littleton, Tim Dwyer, Ballyvinane, Littleton, Ger Ryan, Ballybeg, Littleton, Danny Ryan, Ballybeg, Littleton.

Incidentally, the winners did not get their championship medals until over a quarter of a century later. Munster Council of the G.A.A. decided that only the twenty-one players that played in the final should get medals. Tom Semple, who was representing Tipperary on the Munster Council at the time, had informed the council that more than the twenty-one players involved in the final had played in the earlier games of the championship and were entitled to recognition. Munster Council only supplied twenty-one medals and suggested that Tipperary County G.A.A. Board would supply the remainder. The Board was not in a position to do this at the time.

Also in 1888 the idea was fostered of sending to America the best of Ireland's hurlers and athletes. It aimed to help foster the games among the exiled Irish. It was also hoped that the trip would prove financially worthwhile for the G.A.A. In order to facilitate the tour, the 1888 inter-county championships in

---

[18] Note – The seven players that did not play in the final were:- Denis Maher (L), Ned Maher, Denis Maher (R), Jack Maher, Matty Maher (M), Con Callanan and Pat Ryan.

American 'Invasion' Team 1888
Both these photographs were taken outside St Patrick's College, Thurles, on Friday, 14 September 1888,
before the departure of the 'Invasion' team of hurlers and athletes on tour to the United States of America.
Maurice Davin, first president of the G.A.A. stands on the left holding a hammer. The Tipperary
personnel along with Davin in the group were:- Tom O'Grady and John O'Brien (Moycarkey), Jim
Stapleton (Thurles), Thady Ryan (Clonoulty), Dr. J.C. Daly (Borrisokane), Pat Davin and P. O'Donnell
(Carrick-on-Suir), James S. Mitchel (Emly), Bob Frewen (Aherlow) and William Prendergast (Clonmel).
John Cullinane (Bansha) left for America in advance of the main group to make arrangements
for the athletic and hurling contests.

hurling and football were abandoned. This project became known in time as
the American 'Invasion'. Thurles, as All-Ireland champions, were allowed to
nominate one player for the tour and they selected their team captain, Jim

Stapleton. He played in all the games on the tour. While the tour was a sporting and cultural success, it was a financial disaster and at least seventeen of the traveling party did not return to Ireland, taking up permanent residence in the United States.[19]

1889 – The aftermath of the All-Ireland success should have bred harmony in Thurles G.A.A. but the disquiet felt regarding team selection in that success led to "a parting of the ways". In the first round of the 1889 hurling championship at Clonoulty, Thurles defeated the Racecourse (Cashel) by 2-4 to one point. The second round against Moycarkey was played at Holycross. It was a very close first half with the only score being a pointed free by O'Brien for Moycarkey. Thurles equalized early in the second half when Andy Maher, Doran and Murphy combined to score a point. The issue was decided in the final minutes when the Moycarkey captain Tom O'Grady sent the leather whirling through the Thurles goalposts. Moycarkey had won by 1-1 to one point for Thurles.[20]

Thurles was not alone in misfortune. For the G.A.A. nationally, storm clouds were gathering. A deteriorating financial situation coupled with power struggles within the association was tearing it apart. The real root of the trouble lay in renewed efforts by the Irish Republican Brotherhood (I.R.B.) to dominate the G.A.A., which caused the Catholic hierarchy and clergy to be extremely critical of the association. Up to then the clergy had been enthusiastic supporters of the G.A.A. but now they left the association in large numbers. One notable exception was Archbishop Croke who continued to encourage and assist the G.A.A.[21]

1890 – But worse was to befall the G.A.A. during the following year, 1890, with the Parnell split. Captain William H. O'Shea was granted a decree nisi in his suit for divorce from Katherine O'Shea, a case which named Charles Stewart Parnell as co-respondent. The Catholic hierarchy, with the support of the majority of the priests, called on the Catholic people of Ireland to repudiate Parnell.[22] Archbishop Croke was dismayed by the news of the divorce proceedings. The bust of Parnell, that held an honoured position in the hallway of Croke's residence in Thurles, got a quick exit.[23] The Parnell split tore the country apart and almost split the G.A.A. The Central Council of the G.A.A. placed their support unequivocally behind Parnell.[24] This was defying the

[19] *Cashel Sentinel*, 10 Nov. 1888.
[20] *Sport*, 18 May 1889.
[21] Marcus de Búrca *The G.A.A.: A History* (Dublin, 1980), p.52.
[22] Paul Bew, *C.S. Parnell* (Dublin, 1980), p. 118.
[23] James A. Feehan, *An Hour Glass on the Run* (Cork, 2000), p. 164.
[24] Séamus Ó Riain, *Maurice Davin* (Dublin, 1994), p. 198.

majority view of nationalists and also the opposition to Parnell by the Catholic hierarchy. Thurles G.A.A. sided with Parnell. Tipperary county championships were a fiasco in 1890. Even though the competitions were started they ended in failure. This was also the fate of the championships in Tipperary for the next four years. But Thurles G.A.A. club continued to play challenge and tournament games. Because the club remained active, it was to play a vital role in the rejuvenation of the G.A.A.

Thurles Working Men's Club banner supporting Charles Stewart Parnell in October 1891. Thurles G.A.A. also sided with Parnell.

1893 – A meeting was convened at Dobbyn's Hotel in Tipperary town in 1893 and Thurles G.A.A. was represented by D.H. Ryan, Denis Maher, Hugh Ryan, Willie Butler and Jack Ryan. Michael Cusack and Maurice Davin were also present and a provisional county committee was selected, with the task of organising clubs and arranging challenge games. D.H. Ryan was to the forefront of this committee. This initiative by Tipperary triggered other units of the association, throughout the country, to re-organize. Thurles took part in tournaments throughout the country in both hurling and football and organised their own Gaelic tournament at Easter. Their aim in organising such an event was to send a clear signal to the Gaels of the country that the G.A.A. was alive in the town and county of its birth.

The same impetus continued the following year and a new Tipperary county board was elected. The influence of Thurles on the proceedings is seen in the election of officers to the new board. D.H. Ryan and Hugh Ryan, both of the Thurles club, were elected chairman and treasurer respectively, while John Bourke, Tipperary town was elected secretary. County championships were organised at the first meeting and Thurles contested in both hurling and football. In the county hurling final played at Holycross on 25 November, Drombane were excellent on the day defeating Thurles by 2-2 to nil. All the scores were got by the Riordans Jim and Pat, with the latter being the hero of the day. Teams were now seventeen aside.

Drombane – Fergus Moriarty (Captain), Jim Riordan, Paddy Riordan, Mick Carroll, Ned Leamy, John Leamy, Pat Leamy, Ned Lambe, Jim Ryan, Ned Nugent, Jim Shortt, Jim Corbett, Jim Purcell, Paddy Purcell, Ned Long,

Paddy Harrrington and Jim Gleeson.[25] Field Umpire: Hugh P. Ryan.

Thurles – Denis Maher (Captain), Tom Healy (goal), Matty Maher, Denis Maher (R), Jack Maher, Mick Maher, Jack Maher (B), Paddy Maher, Andrew Maher, Denis O'Keeffe, Jim Sullivan, Tom Bourke, Mike Wall, Jim Stapleton, M. Cahill, Matty Feehan, Ned Murphy. Field Umpire: Jack Ryan.

1894 – During this year, we find the first reference to Tom Semple in a sporting context, not wielding the ash, but competing at the Two-Mile-Borris sports, almost five miles from Thurles. He ran in the half-mile and although he got a twenty-five yard start, he was not listed among the winners.[26]

1895 – The strength of the Thurles club was also seen early the following year, 1895, when the replayed All-Ireland football final, between Cork (Nils) and Dublin (Young Irelands) was played in Thurles. This was the first All-Ireland final to be played in the town. An excellent field had been obtained about a mile at the southern side of the town, beside the railway line,[27] at Ballycurrane. Archbishop Croke, who was celebrating the silver jubilee of his episcopal consecration, was present along with his secretary, Canon Arthur Ryan, and a number of priests. It was the largest attendance to date at a Gaelic football game, approximately 10,000 present. G.A.A. secretary, Dick Blake, was referee but the attendance proved uncontrollably large and finally spilled all over the ground. With a few minutes left, the game was abandoned with Cork ahead by 1-2 to five points. At the time one goal equalled five points.

In the Tipperary hurling championship of this year, Thurles were drawn against Boherlahan (Pike) in the first round. This was to be contested on 28 July at Horse and Jockey. The Boherlahan team, mainly from the Ballytarsna area, turned up, as did the referee Hugh P. Ryan, Roskeen, but there was no sign of the Thurles team. A fair crowd had turned up, their hopes of seeing Thurles beaten were shattered and with drooping spirits they started for home.[28]

The parish of Boherlahan fielded three teams in this year's championship, Suir View Rangers, Tubberadora Rovers, and Boherlahan. Two of the teams, Tubberadora and Suir View, contested the county final. Hugh Ryan, Thurles was the referee. Extra time had to be played to decide the verdict, which went in favour of Tubberadora. They now represented Tipperary in the inter-county championship, defeating Limerick in the Munster final and Tullaroan (Kilkenny) in the final, at Jones's Road, Dublin. This game was not played until 15 March 1896. This was the beginning of a 'Golden Era' for Tubberadora and Tipperary.

---

[25] Philip Fogarty, *Tipperary's G.A.A. Story* (Thurles, 1960), p. 56.
[26] Moycarkey Newsletter, 1999.
[27] *Irish Daily Independent*, 23 Apr. 1895.
[28] St Patrick's College, Thurles, Philip Fogarty, research notes (unpublished work).

CHAPTER 4

Tom Semple's First All-Ireland – 1900

1896 – During 1896 the revival in the fortunes of the G.A.A. continued. In Thurles, early in the year, D.H. Ryan and others were unhappy with the state of the G.A.A. in the town. A great deal of apathy prevailed; the association had declined and was heading for oblivion. They decided to appeal to the young men and Gaelic minded people of the town for support. Posters were circulated calling a public meeting of interested Gaels to take place on the last Sunday in March, with the intention of reviving the association. There was a very positive response, as an enormous collection of young blood assembled. The newly elected officers were:- Chairman – D.H. Ryan, Hon. Secretary – Rody Delaney and Treasurer – James Keogh. Willie Bourke, J. Brereton, Jack Maher and Matty Maher formed the committee.

The club decided to arrange a tournament as soon as it was possible. This proved very successful, with all local clubs taking part and Thurles and Two-Mile-Borris contesting the final. D.H. Ryan's call on the young men of Thurles to join the ranks of the G.A.A. was not in vain and among those who responded was Tom Semple, now a tall strapping black-haired seventeen year old.

D.H. Ryan, Thurles G.A.A.

In the Tipperary hurling championship Thurles were drawn against the reigning county champions, Tubberadora, at Thurles on 12 July. Thurles made a brave though ill-fated stand against their star opponents, whose sweeping onslaughts were the principal feature of this struggle. The Mahers of Killinan: Ned, Dinny and Matty, Con Callanan, Jim Sullivan, Mick and Tom Butler, Paddy Condon, Tom Semple, Jack and Tom Bourke, Jack Maher (Furze), Paddy and Jack Stapleton, Paddy McNamara were all on the Thurles team. This was Tom Semple's championship debut for Thurles, and what a baptism of fire. The final score was:-Tubberadora 4-6, Thurles 2-0. Tubberadora went on to win the county final. They later led Tipperary to a comprehensive All-Ireland victory over Dublin Commercials. This was their second All-Ireland success and Tipperary's third.

Many of the officers and members of the Thurles G.A.A. club were politically active during these years. Their support for the secret oath-bound society, the Irish Republican Brotherhood (I.R.B.), was well known to the British authorities. The I.R.B. aimed to overthrow British rule in Ireland and to create an Irish Republic. Police intelligence reports state:- 'Thurles, in particular holds solid for the I.R.B'[1] and 'The I.R.B. and the G.A.A. are carried on in conjunction, as far as the leading men are concerned'.[2]

1897 – Neighbours, Two-Mile-Borris, opposed Thurles in the first round of the county hurling championship, on 24 October. One score separated them after a titanic struggle. Final score: Two-Mile-Borris 0-7, Thurles, St Patrick's 0-6.[3] However, the championship was won by Suir View, from the Boherlahan/Dualla parish. Reigning champions, Tubberadora withdrew from the championship at semi-final stage, due to an unfortunate injury to one of their hurlers. For Tom Semple the experience gained in these games would stand to him in good stead in the years ahead. His performances were being noted and before the year's end he had represented Tipperary for the first time. This was in the Croke Cup inter-county competition, which was initiated the previous year. To mark his Episcopal Silver Jubilee in

Tom Semple

[1] NAI, C.B.S. 11921-S.
[2] NAI, C.B.S. 11876-S.
[3] *Cashel Sentinel*, 30 Oct. 1897.

1895, Archbishop Thomas Croke had presented two silver cups to the G.A.A., one each for hurling and football. However, the Croke Cup of 1897 was won by Limerick (Kilfinane selection). Thurles had three players on the Tipperary team in the competition:- Bill Ryan, Tom Semple and Jim Sullivan.

1898 – The first round of the Munster hurling championship was not played until July 1898. Suir View Rangers, being county champions, had charge of the selection. The only club that assisted Suir View was Thurles, and Tom Semple, Jim Sullivan and Bill Ryan were selected to play Cork, Blackrock selection.[4] The Suir View players, mentors and supporters assembled in Gooldscross on the morning of Sunday, July 31st, having attended 8.00 a.m. Mass in Boherlahan. The special train would arrive in Cork at 11.00 a.m. This would provide plenty of time for refreshments before taking the field at 1.30 p.m. The train duly arrived in Gooldscross at 9.30 a.m., but it was, surprisingly, already packed. Because of the Thurles players' involvement, there was added support, especially from the Thurles area. The journey proceeded with stops at Dundrum and Limerick Junction to take on more passengers. By this time the train was carrying an immense crowd, possibly five thousand passengers. When an incline was encountered between Emly and Limerick Junction, progress was halted as the engine was unable to haul the carriages over it. A number of the carriages had to be detached and the engine started the painfully slow process of hauling them, a few at a time, over the incline. This task had been completed by the time a second train engine arrived to assist. All the while, players and supporters sat or stood in the cramped carriages, which at that time consisted of small single compartments with no connecting corridors. Most of the hurlers would have risen very early that day, partaken of a light breakfast, and then headed for Mass and the train. It was nearly 3.30 p.m. by the time they disembarked in Cork and the entire company had to rush to the Athletic Grounds, without any refreshment, to play a game that was already two hours late in starting. The teams eventually took the field at 4.00 p.m. An attendance of fifteen thousand awaited the outcome, many of whom had entered free of charge, when an angry section of the crowd broke down the gates before the scheduled start of the game. Many waiting outside felt that they were missing the contest, in fact, they would wait a further three hours to see it.

This was poor preparation for a Munster championship game, the players being exhausted even before the action commenced. Consequently, it was a very one-sided game from the beginning, with Blackrock piling up the scores. Some of the Tipperary players were brilliant and more than matched their opponents, but as a team they were well beaten, despite the heroics of Heaney between the Tipperary posts. The Thurles men on the team were wearing their

---

[4] Peter Meskell, *Suir View Rangers 1895-1898* (Tipperary, 1997), p. 25.

Tipperary, Tubberadora selection – All-Ireland Hurling Champions 1898
Back row (l.-r.): Watty Dunne, Bill Devane, Ned Brennan, Mikey Maher Captain, E.D. Ryan, John Ryan, Tim Condon.
Middle row (l.-r.): Thomas Leahy, Phil Byrne, John Connolly, Jack Maher, Denis Walsh, Jim O'Keeffe, Dick O'Keeffe, Michael Conlon.
Front row (l.-r.): Tommy Ryan, Jack Maher, Ned Maher, Johnny Walsh.

own club jerseys of green and gold and one of them is recorded as having an exceptional second-half performance. The match report stated, 'A player dressed in green stationed himself in front of the Suir View goal and succeeded in repelling many attacks'. This was possibly a youthful Tom Semple getting his first taste of Munster championship hurling, another baptism of fire for him, being hammered by Cork's Blackrock selection, by 4-16 to 0-2.[5]

1898 – In the 1898 county hurling championship, Thurles St Patrick's were drawn against Cashel King Cormacs. This was fixed for 7 August in Clonmel but Cashel withdrew from the competition, so Thurles had a straight run to a county semi-final meeting with Tubberadora. As with many competitions, this game was not played until the spring of the following year. The venue is recorded as, Thurles 'on the Mall', where the locals, led by Tom Semple, suffered one of the most demoralizing defeats of their history, losing to the eventual county champions by 5-15 to nil.[6] Best for Thurles were: Jim 'Hawk' O'Brien, Tom Semple, Rody Berkery, Bill Ryan, John Kirwan, Jer Hayes, Jim Sullivan, Lant Doran, Dick and Dan Dwyer and Pat McGrath.[7]

This is the first reference to Tom Semple as captain of the Thurles team. For a nineteen year old this was no mean achievement. Defeat has been his lot in his hurling career to date but from watching successful teams in action, and with an innate determination to succeed, his time would come.

Having won the county championship, Tubberadora now had the county selection, but did not select any Thurles hurlers. They progressed to the All-Ireland final against Kilkenny's Tullaroan, on 25 March 1900, and won convincingly. This was their third All-Ireland victory and Tipperary's fourth.

1899 – Games being abandoned because teams didn't show up was causing havoc to the organisation of championships and Tipperary County Board were determined to stamp it out. Early in 1899 they resolved, 'That in the event of a team failing to attend at the place and on the date appointed to play in the county championship, such a team will forfeit the match'.

Thurles were the first to suffer under this new rule, when they failed to turn up for their match with Two-Mile-Borris. A letter from the Thurles secretary, James M. Kennedy, to the county board, stated that some of the team were unable to play and looked for a re-fixture. Following a brief discussion at county board, the match was awarded to Two-Mile-Borris. Later in the year, Horse and Jockey beat Two-Mile-Borris in the county final, played at Hackett's field,

[5] Peter Meskell, *Suir View Rangers 1895-1898* (Tipperary, 1997), p. 26.
[6] John G. Maher, *Tubberadora – The Golden Square Mile* (Boherlahan, 1995), p. 10.
[7] Philip Fogarty, *Tipperary's G.A.A. Story* (Thurles, 1960), p. 82.

Clongour, Thurles and their selection went on to win the All-Ireland final, without any Thurles representation on the team.

1900 – The Thurles club made a better effort than the previous year in championship competition. The power-house of hurling in Tipperary this year was in the hinterland of Thurles, where Horse and Jockey, Moycarkey, and Two-Mile-Borris were a step ahead of the rest. Their close proximity to one another and natural rivalry raised the standard of the game and produced many a hurling spectacle. Thurles were drawn against Carrickbeg in the first round, played at Clonmel. This they won, following a very closely contested game, the final score reading:- Thurles 2-5, Carrickbeg 2-3. This win boosted the Thurles confidence and put them in the county semi-final against Moycarkey. This game was expected to match the traditional close encounters between these near neighbours but it turned out to be a damp squib as Moycarkey waltzed to a convincing victory. The score told its own story: Moycarkey 2-3, Thurles 0-2. The Thurles side included six players from the disbanded Suir View club. The friendship that had developed between these two clubs in 1897 was standing the test of time. The names of the Suir View six are not definitely known, but it is almost certain that they came from the following list: Peter Maher, Con Maher, Con Dwyer, Tommy Dwyer, Tom Ryan, Phil Fogarty, Will Dwyer and Simon Moloney.[8] Another source gives the Thurles team as follows:- Tom Ryan, Bill Ryan Vice-captain, Paddy Stapleton, J. Stapleton, M. Mahony, W. Walsh, M. Butler, Lant Doran, Tom Semple, Danny Morrissey, Peter Maher, Con Maher, Jack Fogarty, Tom Ryan, Paddy Dwyer, D. Dwyer, J. Ryan.

Amazingly Moycarkey failed to field against Two-Mile-Borris in the county final. 'Borris were now county champions, having played only one championship game. As county champions they now had the honour of county selection. To strengthen their forces for the Munster and All-Ireland championships, 'Borris selected players from neighbouring clubs:- Thurles, Moycarkey and Tubberadora. Tom Semple and Paddy Stapleton from the Thurles club were among the cream of hurling stalwarts selected.

In the Munster championship, Tipperary defeated Cork (Redmonds) by 0-12 to 0-9, Clare (Tulla) by 6-11 to 1-6 and Kerry (Kilmoyley) in the Munster final by 6-11 to 1-9. Kilkenny (Mooncoin) were next to fall in the All-Ireland semi-final. This match was played at Deerpark, Carrick-on Suir, on the lands of Maurice Davin, the G.A.A.'s first president. Mooncoin had also the pick of hurlers from Three-Castles and Tullaroan and were a formidable side and led at half-time by 1-6 to 0-4. The second-half was a much different story as the Tipperary boys strove to level and then lead in an exhilarating

---

[8] Peter Meskell, *Suir View Rangers 1895-1898* (Tipperary, 1997), p. 27.

Tipperary, Two-Mile-Borris selection – All-Ireland Hurling Champions 1900

Front row (l.-r.): Tom Allen, Matt Ryan, Ned Maher, Ned Hayes (Captain), Mikey Maher, Paddy Maher (Best), Jack Gleeson, M.F. Crowe (Referee), Denis O'Keeffe. Second row (l.-r.): Tom Duggan, Paddy 'Berry' Stapleton (Thurles), 'Big' Bill Gleeson, Paddy Hayes, Tom Semple (Thurles), Jack Maher, Tom Cantwell, David Cantwell. Third row (l.-r.): James Bowe, Johnny Walsh, Mick Purcell, Billy Maher, Mike Wall, 'Little' Bill Gleeson, Tommy Ryan, James O'Keeffe. Back row (l.-r.): —, Tom Fanning, Billy Maher, Jim Skehan, Ned Bowe, Charlie Maher, —.

contest. The final score had them ahead by 0-14 to 1-8.

In the 'home' final, played at The Gaelic Park, Terenure, Dublin, Ardrahan of Galway were well beaten, 6-13 to 1-5, in a very one-sided contest. Tom Semple was one of the stars of this 'Borris selection, scoring points in both halves and finishing a great goal from a pass by Mikey Maher. Galway were completely outclassed by the sheer strength and skill of this 'Borris selection. The famed and daring Tipperary headlong charges, and their excellence in shoulder to shoulder contests, upset the opposition. As regards hurling skill, Galway waited for the ball to touch the ground before striking while the Tipperary lads caught it in mid-air, whirled with the impetus of the catch and had the ball out of danger in quicker time.[9]

P. D. Mehigan, 'Carbery', recalled this game:-

> 'I had heard much of Tom Semple's prowess with ashen blade before I first laid eyes on him in action in the 'home' final of the 1900 championship, played at Terenure Gaelic Park against Ardrahan, Galway. Two-Mile-Borris represented Tipperary that year and they called on the choicest hurlers of mid-Tipp. I think Tom Semple was the only man called from Thurles town. I took a particular notice of him that rich September day-a glorious antelope of a man.

> Tom Semple stood six feet two inches in hurling togs, long limbs beautifully turned; whippy body, good hips and shoulders, powerful arms and the head of an Adonis, fresh complexion, glowing with health; straight Grecian features crowned with a mass of close brown curls. He had an immense stride; his swing of ash was long and graceful. He was a stylist if ever there was one, yet he had typical Tipperary fire and spirit in the close clashes, then a feature. He hit balls half the field's length from his post on the left wing and helped materially to build Tipp's score.'[10]

The All-Ireland final proper against London (Desmonds) was not played until 26 October 1902, at Jones's Road (later Croke Park). The Tipperary hurlers travelled to Dublin by train from Thurles and were due to arrive at Kingsbridge (later Hueston station) at 11.55 a.m. but the train was delayed by one hour and they had to quickly make their way to Jones's Road arriving there at 1.45 p.m. for a game originally timed for 12.30 p.m.

[9] Jimmy Fogarty (ed.), *Two-Mile-Borris 1900, All-Ireland Winners – A Souvenir Booklet* (Two-Mile-Borris, 2000), p. 16.
[10] P.D. Mehigan, 'Carbery', 'Five Great Hurling Captains' *in Carbery's Annual 1943/44*, p. 22.

After a stormy passage across the Irish Sea, the London team arrived at the North Wall, Dublin at 2.00 a.m. on the morning of the match and were met by a few faithful friends, who made them comfortable at their hotel. But they had little sleep as they were excited to be back in the 'ould' country and the thrill of the All-Ireland occasion.

The attendance of over ten thousand stood patiently in the dull weather conditions. Eventually, at 2.10 p.m. the game was underway and before long it was obvious that this would be no canter in the park as the London skill and determination gave a rude awakening to the Tipperary lads. London matched them in skill and fitness. Points were exchanged and as half-time approached a Tom Semple point left the score, 0-5 to 0-3 in favour of Two-Mile-Borris, as they trudged to the dressing rooms for a deserved break. The stunned attendance gave London a well-deserved stirring ovation. They had played against the wind and shrewd observers gave the exiles every chance.

London grabbed the initiative early in the second-half and went ahead. The crowd rose to them and every neutral bellowed encouragement. Tipperary's might was challenged as the railing around the pitch was broken by the swaying throng as stewards strove to gain crowd control. The contest was hotly but sportingly contested and it looked as if the title would

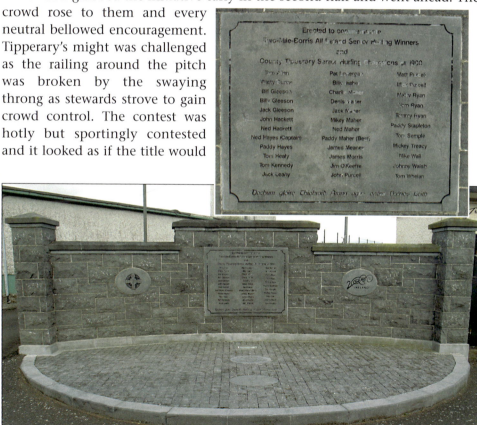

On 26 August 2000, G.A.A. President Seán McCague unveiled this memorial in Two-Mile-Borris, celebrating the centenary of the 1900 All-Ireland hurling victory. Tom Semple was a member of the team.

cross the Irish Sea. With five minutes remaining, London were ahead by 0-6 to 0-5. A free was given in rather unusual circumstances – the ball got stuck in a wheel track near the perimeter of the pitch, where the Hogan Stand is now. The London captain, Danny Horgan, failed to rise the ball with his hurley and so put his finger under it.[11] The resultant free

Tom Semple's Munster Championship medal 1900. Note: Pin added when medal was worn as a brooch.

taken by Ned Hayes resulted in a Tipperary forward charge led by Mikey Maher, which carried the ball over the goal-line. Another goal followed from a weak puck-out, leaving the final score, a Tipperary (Two-Mile-Borris) victory, by 2-5 to 0-6. This was also Tom Semple's first taste of All-Ireland success. Paddy Stapleton, Thurles, was listed among the substitutes. 'Carbery' recalled:- 'This was the day that Tom Semple hit the railway wall from the left wing, one hundred yards away – a flying catch and mighty sweep of long arms'.[12]

After the game, the teams were entertained by the Lord Mayor of Dublin, Right Hon. T.C. Harrington in the Round Room of the Mansion House. The Tipperary hurlers travelled home on the mail-train, leaving at 8.35 p.m. and were greeted with great enthusiasm in Thurles and particularly in Two-Mile Borris.

On Sunday 22 February 1903, the medals for the 1900 All-Ireland Hurling Championship were presented at Two-Mile-Borris. The medals were described as being of gold and silver and as "works of art in themselves". The presentation was organized by David Cantwell, 'Borris secretary[13] and Gaels, numbering about two hundred, assembled, in Skehana, at the residence of Tom Fanning – a noted athletic enthusiast. Thomas Duggan, chairman of the 'Borris club, presented the medals to the players, which included Tom Semple and Paddy Stapleton of the Thurles club.[14]

Two-Mile-Borris selection 1900:- Ned Hayes Capt., Matty Ryan, Billy Maher, Tom Allen, Mick Purcell, Paddy Hayes, Paddy Maher (Best), all Two-Mile Borris, Mike Wall, Bill Gleeson, Jack Gleeson, Billy Gleeson, Jim O'Keeffe, all Moycarkey, Mikey Maher, Ned Maher, Johnny Walsh, Tommy Ryan, all Tubberadora, Tom Semple, Thurles. Substitutes:- Jack Maher (Horse and Jockey), Tom Kennedy, John Hackett, Ned Hackett, Tom Whelan, (Two-Mile-Borris), Wattie Dunne (Ballytarsna), Paddy Stapleton (Thurles). Trainer: Mike Fanning.

---

[11] *Moycarkey-Borris G.A.A. Story* (Thurles, 1984), p. 23.
[12] Note – The hurling ball used weighed eight ounces. 8 ounces = 226.80 grams.
[13] Philip Fogarty, *Tipperary's G.A.A. Story* (Thurles, 1960), p. 107.
[14] *Sport*, 28 Feb. 1903.

CHAPTER 5

The New Century Unfolds 1901-1905

1901 – Tom Semple, as a Tipperary delegate, attended the annual Congress of the G.A.A., which convened in Thurles on 22 September. This time the venue was the new Confraternity Hall. Only forty delegates and officers from eleven counties were present and the future looked bleak for the association. They elected a new president, James Nolan, Alderman of Kilkenny Corporation. The election of a secretary was not as smooth. Former secretary Dick Blake of County Meath was proposed but rejected, on the grounds of non-participation in recent G.A.A. affairs. Next, the name of Michael Cusack, G.A.A. founder, was proposed by T.F. O'Sullivan of Listowel and seconded by Tom Semple from the local club.[1] The reason for Semple's action is unclear. At this time Semple was a hurler of some note in his early twenties, yet to reach his administrative potential, but the fact that he was given this role shows recognition of budding leadership qualities. Was his seconding of Cusack preplanned or was it simply his support for the well-known founder of the association? There is no doubt but that, since the foundation of the association in the town, Michael Cusack had a special affection for Thurles. It may have been the friendship between the Thurles G.A.A. club and Cusack, particularly as he had been a close acquaintance of Jim Maher, New Street (Parnell St.), for some years. In a letter to the inaugural meeting of the North Tipperary Board, in the Literary Institute Hall, Nenagh, on 30 June, Cusack wrote, "Tipperary is ever dear to me. Thurles is my capital for the G.A.A. In November 1884 North and South Tipperary joined me in a 'no surrender' of Gaelic ideals."[2]

However, in the election, Luke O'Toole, a prominent G.A.A. reformer from Wicklow, narrowly defeated Michael Cusack for the position of secretary, by nineteen votes to seventeen.

---

[1] Marcus de Búrca, *Michael Cusack and the G.A.A.* (Dublin, 1989), p. 169.
[2] Philip Fogarty, *Tipperary's G.A.A. Story* (Thurles, 1960), p. 97.

Denis O'Keeffe, G.A.A. Trustee.

At this Congress also, Denis O'Keeffe of the Thurles club was elected trustee of the association. Denis, a native of the Horse and Jockey, had a thriving drapery business at West Gate, Thurles and had thrown in his lot with the local G.A.A. club. At this year's congress, Denis had successfully proposed a motion which stated that no future convention would be called until the accounts of the association were properly prepared and audited.[3] This reflected a growing concern regarding the financial standing of the G.A.A. It could also have been moved on the instigation of the Thurles club's chairman, D.H. Ryan, who was again elected auditor. The influential position of the Thurles club on national G.A.A. affairs is evidenced by the election of O'Keeffe and Ryan to positions of trust at a perilous time for the association.

Only three teams affiliated in hurling:- Ballytarsna, Carrick and Thurles. Two-Mile-Borris, the reigning county champions, did not compete due to an internal dispute. Carrick lost to Ballytarsna and Thurles met the winners at Littleton, in, what turned out to be, the county final. This game was played on 13 April 1902 and it is one that Thurles would rather forget as they went down by 7-11 to one point. The referee was John Cummins of Cashel. The Ballytarsna side was very strong and included players from Horse and Jockey and Tubberadora.[4]

In the Munster Championship, Ballytarsna, representing Tipperary, beat Waterford in round one by 7-12 to nil, but in the semi-final, Cork (Redmonds) received a 'walk-over' and went on to win the Munster championship. There was no Thurles representation on the Ballytarsna selection.

1902 – While Thurles entered a team in the Tipperary championship, they failed to compete in the competition, for one reason or another. They were due to play Ballytarsna in the first game, which was fixed for Ballingarry on 27 July 1902. Because of the death of Archbishop Croke on 22 July, all games fixed for the 27th were postponed as a mark of respect to the association's first patron. The game was re-fixed for 24 August again at Ballingarry, but was not played. The county board was losing patience with the teams but re-fixed the game

---

[3] T.F. O'Sullivan, *The Story of the G.A.A.* (Dublin, 1916), p. 148.
[4] Jimmy Fogarty (ed.), *Two-Mile-Borris 1900, All-Ireland Winners – A Souvenir Booklet* (Two-Mile-Borris, 2000), p. 21.

for 9 November at the same venue. As both Thurles and Ballytarsna were unhappy, they refused to play in either Ballingarry or Glengoole. The county board had enough at this stage and they suspended both clubs for twelve months. This action proved the death-knell for the Ballytarsna team.[5]

The most striking event

Above and right: Archbishop Thomas Croke's funeral procession in Thurles.

in 1902 for G.A.A. followers, at home and abroad, was the death of Archbishop Thomas Croke on Tuesday, 22 July. His name was interwoven with the association since its very inception in 1884. His support was vital particularly during the 'dark days' and it ensured the survival of the movement, keeping it on an even keel. His letter, of 18 December 1884, accepting patronage of the G.A.A. is often referred to as the 'charter of the association' and has been included in every rule-book of the G.A.A. to this day.

Croke's biographer, Mark Tierney, captured the very essence of the man when he wrote, "Perhaps the real strength of Croke's personality lay in the fact that people saw in him a typical Irishman. A big man, he spoke with a slight Irish brogue and he was prepared to stand up to the landlords and to the Dublin Castle authorities. He loved a good fight, especially if it was with words and he did not fear anyone. Unconsciously, he gave others a share of his strength and taught them to stand on their own feet. He became something of a bridge

---

[5] Philip Ryan, *The Tubberadora-Boherlahan Hurling Story* (Thurles, 1973), p. 26.

between the old and the new Ireland. His sights were definitely set on a new Ireland, "free and unfettered".[6]

> Weep ye in sainted Cashel,
> Weep ye in Ormond's Vale,
> Ye shall not find his equal,
> The Prelate and Prince of the Gael.
>
> *Rev. James B. Dollard*

The G.A.A. Congress was back in the new Confraternity Hall on 30 November and during an interval in proceedings a deputation from the meeting went to meet the new archbishop, Most Rev. Dr. Thomas Fennelly. Later, they would remark on the warm friendliness of the archbishop who received them, wearing his black soutane. The deputation invited him to act as patron in succession to Archbishop Croke. To this he gladly consented, adding that he also wished to subscribe to the funds of the G.A.A. On 8 December 1902 he wrote a letter to Luke O'Toole in which he stated, "I have much pleasure in becoming a patron in succession to my illustrious predecessor, the late Most Rev. Dr Croke."

Thurles, since the foundation of the G.A.A. in 1884, had been at the hub of G.A.A. activity in the country. Major games had been played there and Thurles was the accepted venue for the annual congress and other major meetings of the association. The new G.A.A. secretary, Luke O'Toole wanted to change this situation. At the adjourned Congress in 1903, he proposed that, in future, Congress would meet at different venues throughout the country. His proposal was defeated by 21 votes to 16.[7] But O'Toole wouldn't let the matter rest there. Before the year was out, he would try again! Such an attitude annoyed Tom Semple and members of the G.A.A. in Thurles, who always believed and promoted the primacy of Thurles in the life of the association. This may have been another reason why Tom Semple voted against the election of O'Toole as secretary, at the recent congress.

1903 – Congress of the G.A.A. was again in the Confraternity Hall, Thurles, on Sunday 8 November. The financial state of the association was on a sounder footing now, as the balance sheet for the year showed a profit situation and old debts were gradually being reduced. The overseeing and scrutiny of the accounts by D.H. Ryan, auditor, and Denis O'Keeffe, trustee was bearing fruit. Both Nowlan and O'Toole were re-elected president and secretary respectively.

---

[6] Mark Tierney, 'Archbishop Croke's Legacy to Tipperary' in W. J. Hayes, (ed.) Tipperary Remembers (1976).

[7] *Sport*, 17 Jan. 1903.

G.A.A. Secretary, Luke O'Toole seemed to be hell bent on getting the venue for the annual Congress moved from Thurles, as again at this congress he proposed such a motion. His motion read, "That the annual Congress be held alternately in different centres in the four provinces". He had good support but was narrowly defeated by 28 votes to 25.

The 1902 hurling championship, played mostly in 1903, was well contested in North Tipperary, but as it was unfinished, Lahorna De Wets[8], represented them in the county final. South Tipperary, which included the present Mid and South divisions, was in disarray. No team from the present Mid Tipperary area contested the championship and Carrick-on-Suir beat Farranrory in the South final. The county final of 1902, played at Thurles was refereed by Denis O'Keeffe, Thurles, and De Wets defeated Carrick by 7-10 to 1-2. In October 1903, the county championship draws were made. There was no mention of Thurles as contesting in either hurling or football during 1903.[9]

1904 – Planning started early in January 1904 for the Thurles Grand Gaelic Fete, which would take place on St Patrick's Day. Archbishop Fennelly actively encouraged the event particularly as the proceeds would go towards the clearing of the debt on the Confraternity Hall. The new hall, built on the site where once stood the local jail, was completed in the spring. Fr. Bannon, Adm., Thurles, played a major role in the organising of the tournament during the springtime. The venue for the fete, which included two hurling games and one football contest, would be the Thurles Agricultural Society Grounds (now Semple Stadium). The field had the reputation of being one of the finest in the country and always in splendid condition, whatever the weather. Special low train fares were negotiated to Thurles from all the major stations e.g. Dublin – three shillings return, Nenagh – two shillings return.[10]

The tournament proved to be one of the greatest successes to date in the country, with over ten thousand spectators thronging the town. A local newspaper correspondent reported that the debt on the Confraternity Hall must have been considerably reduced, if not totally wiped out. The programme for the day and the final scores was as follows:- Football: Lees (Cork) 1-4, Kickhams (Dublin) 0-3. Hurling: Redmonds (Cork) 3-6, Faughs (Dublin) 3-1.[11] Thomas Semple, Thurles, refereed both finals. The final game had been advertised as *Unconquerable Lahorna against Unconquered Tubberadora*. The Tubberadora team came out of retirement for this game, appearing for the first

---

[8] Note – Lahorna De Wets represented the parish of Cloughjordan, later to be renamed Kilruane MacDonaghs.
[9] *Sport*, 7 Nov. 1903.
[10] Ibid, 30 Jan. 1904.
[11] *Nenagh News*, 19 Mar. 1904.

Tubberadora (including Tom Semple) 1904

Front row: Tom Ryan, Ned Maher, 'Big Bill' Gleeson, Tim Condon, Watty Dunne, Joe O'Keeffe, Dick O'Keeffe. Middle row: Phil Byrne, Johnny Walsh, Paddy Hayes, Tom Semple. Back row: Tom Leahy (President), Mike Wall, Jim O'Keeffe, Jack Maher, Mikey Maher, 'Little' Bill Gleeson, Jack Gleeson, Mike Conlon (Secretary).

time since the 1898 All-Ireland final. Tom Semple hurled with Tubberadora against De Wets. He was the only Thurles player ever to wear the Tubberadora jersey and this was the one occasion it occurred. The day also had a special significance in that it was the last time a team bearing the name Tubberadora lined out in a hurling game. The final score was:- Tubberadora 10-13, Lahorna De Wets 0-3.

The hurling championship of 1904 was unusual in the fact that Thurles joined with Two-Mile-Borris and Horse & Jockey. Neither Two-Mile-Borris nor Horse & Jockey had sufficient players to form a team on their own.[12] Together they looked a talented and formidable bunch. They were better organised than before and they eagerly awaited the championship.

Bishopswood (Dundrum) fell to them at the first hurdle of the Tipperary championship. In the second round Borris-Ileigh gave them a walk-over. The South Tipperary final against Inch was played at Borris-Ileigh on 15 January 1905, Thurles winning convincingly by 4-8 to 0-8. The referee was Mikey Maher of Tubberadora who described the contest as the finest county match he had seen up to that time.[13]

Lahorna De Wets, who had won the North Tipperary final, provided Thurles with a reputable opposition in the Tipperary county final. Roscrea was the

Lahorna De Wets 1902
Front row (l.-r): James O'Meara, Tom Ryan, Jack Dwan Captain. Middle row (l.-r.): Mick McLoughney, Tom Ryan, Tim O'Connor, Pat Williams, Tim Carr, Con Brewer, Martin Darcy. Back row (l.-r.): Jim Darcy, John O'Meara, M. Kennedy, Michael Conway, Dan Ryan, Rody Nealon, Paddy Behan. Officials: Michael Gaynor (Secretary), George O'Leary (Chairman).

---

[12] Jimmy Fogarty (ed.), *Two-Mile-Borris 1900, All-Ireland Winners – A Souvenir Booklet* (Two-Mile-Borris, 2000), p. 22.
[13] John G. Maher & Philip F. Ryan, *Boherlahan and Dualla, A Century of Gaelic Games* (1987), p. 55.

venue with the renowned footballer, Bob Quane, Tipperary Club, as referee. A packed arena greeted both teams as they took the field, on the afternoon of 23 April 1905. De Wets won the toss and played the first half with the aid of a strong breeze. They used this advantage to good effect, leading at half time by eight points. The second half was a different story with the 'Blues' slowly and steadily eating into this lead and eventually drawing level. The Thurles men were now growing in confidence as they sensed victory. The hurling was virile and thrilling and Semple's men could not be stopped. They won a gallant victory with the score reading, Thurles 5-8 De Wets 3-9. De Wets were unhappy after the game. They claimed that the time was up when Thurles got their last score, but their claim fell on deaf ears.

Thurles: Tom Semple (Captain), Jim 'Hawk' O'Brien, Paddy Connolly, Hugh Shelly, Jer Hayes, Martin O'Brien, Rody Berkery, Paddy Stapleton, (Thurles), Paddy Hayes, Tom Allen, Mick Purcell, Paddy Maher (Best), Billy Maher, (Two-Mile-Borris), Jim O'Keeffe, Billy, Jack and Bill Gleeson, (Horse and Jockey).

This was the first county final success for Thurles since 1887. No doubt it brought great satisfaction to Tom Semple, who captained the team. But he also knew that less than half his team was from Thurles and that without the hurlers from Two-Mile-Borris and Horse and Jockey success was doubtful. He was also disappointed that only two hurlers from Thurles were selected to represent Tipperary, even though the Thurles club had the selection of the team. He knew that he needed to mould more local players for future contests.

The Munster inter-county championship of 1904 beckoned with Semple at the helm. Waterford were defeated in the first round by the landslide score of 8-21 to 0-4. Things were much more difficult against Limerick at Tipperary town, as it took a last minute surge to escape defeat. The score was Tipperary (Thurles) 2-12 Limerick (Cappamore) 3-8. This victory put Thurles in a Munster final against St Finbarr's, Cork. Dungarvan was the venue and the game was not played until 17 December 1905. Semple lost the toss and had to face the full force of the elements in the opening half. Ash crashed and there was fire in the air. The 'Barrs led narrowly by 1-6 to 2-2 at the break. In the second-half, when Thurles should have been forging ahead, it was the younger, faster and fitter Cork men who swept them aside and won by 3-10 to 3-4. It was evident that many on the Tipperary side were past their summer glory.

Tipperary, Thurles Selection: Tom Semple (Captain), John C. Maher, Thurles, Tim Condon, Joe O'Keeffe (Goalkeeper), Billy, Jack and Bill Gleeson, Horse and Jockey, Mikey and Ned Maher, Phil Byrne, Johnny Walsh, Watty Dunne, Tubberadora, Paddy Hayes, Mick Purcell, Tom Allen, Two Mile Borris, Paddy

Riordan, Drombane, Con Brewer, Ballymackey. Subs. Jer Hayes, Jim 'Hawk' O'Brien, Thurles, Ned Hayes, Paddy Maher (Best), Two Mile Borris, Mick Wall, Horse and Jockey, Jack Doherty, Ballytarsna.

1905 – At Tipperary G.A.A. Convention held in Walsh's Hotel, Thurles, in early August, Denis O'Keeffe of the Thurles club was elected chairman following the resignation of Dick Cummins, Fethard. The Thurles delegates present were Denis McCarthy and Thomas Semple.[14]

Thurles stood alone in the hurling championship of 1905. Their successful partnership with 'Borris and 'The Jockey was short lived but their confidence was growing following the previous year's success. The first game of the championship was played in Cashel against Knockgraffon. This was a very uneven contest with Thurles having all the play and winning by 7-13 to 1-0.

In the next round Thurles found themselves pitted against former partners and great traditional rivals Two-Mile-Borris. Thurles Show Grounds was the venue, the game was billed as the sporting event of the year and it lived up to all expectations. It was the most vital clash of the championship and the players knew it. The game was bitter and vigorous with both sides showing their traditional inclination not to yield easily. The hurlers knew each other very well, having hurled together in 1904. The result was in doubt right up to the last minute with the final score – Two-Mile-Borris 1-5, Thurles 0-6.[15] Thurles were best served by the veteran Paddy Connolly, Jack Mockler, Hughie Shelly, Tom Kenna, Jer Hayes, Mickie Gleeson, "Hawk" O'Brien and Jack Cahill.[16] 'Borris progressed successfully through the championship. Their county final game versus Lorrha was never played due to disagreements regarding the venue, which resulted in the county board awarding Two-Mile-Borris the game.

Thurles: Tom Semple Captain, Jack Stapleton, Paddy Stapleton, Jer Hayes, Paddy Connolly, Michael Haven, Michael Gleeson, Hugh Shelly, Rody Berkery, Denis Berkery, P. O'Dea, Jack Mockler, Thomas Kenna, James 'Hawk' O'Brien, Martin O'Brien, Jack Cahill, W. Dwyer.

A 'long puck' competition was organized by Tipperary County Board during the year. This was as compensation for the non-playing of the county hurling final. It was open to all the hurlers in the county and these were the top three in the competition:-

---

[14] *Sport*, 12 Aug. 1905.
[15] Ibid, 21 Apr. 1906.
[16] Philip Fogarty, *Tipperary's G.A.A. Story* (Thurles, 1960), p. 119.

1. Mick Purcell, Ballydavid, Littleton – 90 yards.
2. Paddy Maher 'Best', Ballybeg, Littleton – 89 yards.
3. Tom Semple, Thurles – 87 yards.[17]

Hayes's Hotel, Thurles, early in the twentieth century.
(Image courtesy of the National Library of Ireland)

In 1905, Two-Mile-Borris had the county selection and their first game in the Munster championship against Cork at Kilmallock had more controversy. A dispute arose in the second half with 'Borris leading Cork (St Finbarr's) by 2-4 to 2-3 and the game was unfinished. Tom Semple was the only Thurles player on the 'Borris selection that day. Munster Council ordered a replay, which was fixed for Fermoy. 'Borris refused to travel and Cork got a walk-over.[18]

Tom Semple was also part of the Munster team in this year's interprovincial competition, the Railway Shield, which lost the semi-final to Leinster by 3-10 to 1-7.[19] This was the inaugural year of this competition which was contested in both hurling and football. It was decided that if the shields were won twice in succession or three times in all, they could be kept by the successful county. The Great Southern and Western Railway Company presented the shields, worth £50, and proceeds of the competition went to players injured in the All-Ireland championships.[20]

In late October, a tournament, in aid of the Confraternity Hall was played at Thurles Agricultural Society Grounds. Archbishop Thomas Fennelly was present along with a large number of clergy. The local club, particularly county hurler John C. Maher, popularly known as "Foxy Jack", was in charge of the arrangements and the day was most successful. Most of the teams taking part were local except for Faughs of Dublin. The tournament winners were Two-Mile-Borris beating Faughs by 1-7 to 1-2 in the final. Tom Semple refereed all the games and his handling of his responsibilities was entirely faultless. Teas and entertainment were provided in the Confraternity Hall later in the evening.[21]

---

[17] Philip Fogarty, *Tipperary's G.A.A. Story* (Thurles, 1960), p. 120.
[18] Jimmy Fogarty (ed.), *Two-Mile-Borris 1900 All-Ireland Hurling Winners* (Two Mile Borris, 2000), pp 22-3.
[19] *Sport*, 19 Aug. 1905.
[20] Philip Fogarty, *Tipperary's G.A.A. Story* (Thurles, 1960), p. 122.
[21] *Sport*, 4 Nov. 1905.

CHAPTER 6

1906 – Semple leads Tipperary to All-Ireland Glory

CHAMPIONSHIP fixtures were running a year behind schedule, with the Tipperary, Munster and All-Ireland hurling championship of 1906 being played entirely in 1907. The officers in charge of the Thurles club were: Denis O'Keeffe – chairman, James M. Kennedy – secretary, Phil Molony – treasurer. Tom Semple was a Tipperary representative on the Munster Council.

The unexpected death of Michael Cusack on 28 November 1906 shocked the G.A.A. Cusack, the principal architect of the association, had a chequered career within the organisation he had founded. His death, some months short of his sixtieth birthday, unified the membership, who turned out in force to swell the cortege to Glasnevin cemetery in Dublin, on Sunday, 2 December. The hurlers of Munster, all Tipperary (Two-Mile-Borris selection) including Tom Semple and Jim 'Hawk' O'Brien and Leinster were in Dublin that weekend for the Railway

Michael Cusack (1847-1906), G.A.A. founder.

Shield semi-final replay. They took a formal part in the funeral. Wearing mourning rosettes and with their camáns draped and reversed, they formed a bodyguard around the hearse and later marched alongside it all the way from the Pro-Cathedral[1] to Glasnevin cemetery.

---

[1] Marcus de Búrca, *Michael Cusack and the G.A.A.* (Dublin, 1989), p. 183.
  St Patrick's College, Thurles, Philip Fogarty, research notes (unpublished work).

RAILWAY SHIELD 1906

Even though it was the day of Cusack's funeral, this game was played. It resulted in a Munster victory by 4-10 to 4-4. Thurles men Tom Semple and Jim 'Hawk' O'Brien played a leading role. This team, captained by Ned Hayes, went on to win the Railway Shield, defeating Connacht at Ennis on 17 February 1907, by 9-14 to 1-5. The victory was of special significance for Tom Semple, winning his first Railway Shield medal, while an employee of Great Southern & Western Railways, who sponsored the trophy.

The selection included:- Ned Hayes (Captain), Tom Allen, Paddy Hayes, Jimmy Bourke, Mick Purcell, Billy Maher, Paddy Maher 'Best' (Two-Mile-Borris), Jim, Joe and Dick O'Keeffe, Jack, Bill and Billy Gleeson, Tim Condon (Horse and Jockey), Watty Dunne, Jack Doherty (Ballytarsna), Tom Semple, James 'Hawk' O'Brien (Thurles), Con Brewer (Ballymackey), Paddy Riordan (Drombane) and Tim Gleeson (Rossmore).

It was agreed, at Tipperary G.A.A. County Convention, held in Thurles on 12 May 1907, that in future, for championship competition, the county would be divided into three divisions: North, South and Mid.

It was obvious to Tom Semple that a great deal of

Railway Shield Medal

Munster, Two-Mile-Borris selection – Railway Shield Champions 1906
The panel included: -Ned Hayes (Captain), Tom Allen, Paddy Hayes, Jimmy Bourke, Mick Purcell, Billy Maher (Two-Mile-Borris), Jim O'Keeffe, Joe O'Keeffe, Dick O'Keeffe, Jack Gleeson, 'Little' Bill Gleeson, 'Big' Bill Gleeson, Tim Condon (Moycarkey), Watty Dunne, Jack Doherty (Ballytarsna), Con Brewer (Ballymackey), Tom Semple, James 'Hawk' O'Brien, Tom Kerwick, Hughie Shelly, Jack Mooney (Thurles), Paddy Riordan, Tim Gleeson (Drombane).

groundwork needed to be done to build up a Thurles team that would be competitive, not just in the Tipperary championship, but at the national level. While he captained his first Thurles team at the age of nineteen, leading them when they were defeated certainly taught him a lesson. Further, the lean years in 1902 and 1903 showed that much work needed to be done.

As noted earlier, as the son of the maternity nurse for the Thurles area, Tom Semple knew every family in the town and not just who they were and the children in the family, but he knew their heritage and their character. There is no question that he was involved, in those early years of the twentieth century, persuading the young men that he knew to get involved in the G.A.A. and the Thurles hurling team. His own formidable reputation as a hurler, his persuasive skills and leadership qualities were obvious to his contemporaries and the end result was a group of young men he gathered in 1904 and 1905 that would become the famed Thurles Blues, including Jack Mockler, Hughie Shelly, Paddy Brolan, as well as the "Hawk" O'Brien who was well established.

Recruiting talented and eager youth would not be enough, Semple clearly understood the need for not just hurling skill and discipline in the team, but a training regime that would ensure that his 'Blues' would be the fittest players on the field and could play at full steam up to the final whistle. He incorporated those concepts in the training programme that he developed and implemented. Nicholas Mockler, the son of Jack Mockler recalled that his father often told him that when the 'Blues' were in training they would form up outside the Confraternity Hall in Thurles and set off on a march of four or five miles to The Ragg, march back again to Thurles and spend an hour or two skipping and working at punch ball.[2]

Thurles, in preparation for the season's action, bought new hurling balls, three from Dunne and the same number from Bermingham. These cost three shillings each and to fund the purchase subscriptions were collected weekly. Team captain, Tom Semple, was concerned about the fitness of his hurlers and discussions took place regarding the provision of a gymnasium in which the club members could train. The Confraternity Hall was identified as being suitable for the purpose and the hall authorities were willing to give use of the hall and light free of charge, if those attending would become members of the hall. This seemed agreeable and plans were made to provide training equipment. Punch-bags and boxing gloves were purchased and four hooks were to be installed from which to suspend rings etc. It was also agreed that a weekly levy of two pence be collected from members using the gymnasium. Gymnasium accounts were to be kept separate from the games account.[3]

[2] Raymond Smith, *The Clash of the Ash* (Dublin, 1972), p. 171.
[3] Thurles Sarsfields Minute Book 1906-7.

SEMPLE – ALL-IRELAND LONG PUCK CHAMPION

The All-Ireland athletic championships, under G.A.A. rules, were held in the Agricultural Showgrounds, Thurles (later Semple Stadium), on 28 July 1907. This was the second time the town had hosted the event, the first being in 1899. There were many champion athletes present, some that would become household names in the years that followed: T.F. Kiely of Carrick-on-Suir and Paddy Ryan, Pallasgreen among them. Thurles G.A.A. club were very active in the organisation of the day, which was an outstanding success. Much local interest was generated by the presence of local hurlers among the

Long puck championship medal.

competitors. Paddy Maher 'Best', Ballybeg, Littleton, described by onlookers as a 'marvel', came second in the one mile race, in a time of four minutes twenty nine and two fifth seconds.[4] Later in the year Paddy would be a vital cog on the Thurles selection that won the All-Ireland hurling crown. Tom Semple was also successful, winning the event known as 'rising and striking the hurling ball'. The hurling ball weighed nine ounces and the distance was recorded at ninety-six yards, approximately eighty-eight metres.[5]

TIPPERARY CHAMPIONSHIP 1906

The mid Tipperary division of the G.A.A. was formed at a meeting in Walsh's Hotel, Thurles on Sunday, 9 June 1907.[6] The clubs represented were Cashel, Drombane, Racecourse, Templetuohy, Holycross, Rossmore, Thurles, Two Mile Borris and Horse and Jockey. The Thurles delegates were Michael Gleeson and Denis O'Keeffe. John Cahill of Cashel was elected first chairman of the board, while Andy Mason, Drombane, was appointed honorary secretary. Mikey Maher, Tubberadora was agreed as treasurer and trustee.

In the Tipperary hurling championship, twenty teams affiliated, Thurles beat Gurteen in the first round by 5-20 to 1-5, at the Thurles Showgrounds. The weather was most favourable but the attendance was the smallest ever seen in the town. Gurteen were altogether outclassed and Thurles had an easy task set them. Gurteen played a very loose and uncertain game, while the home team showed up in excellent form and played with great dash and precision, their forwards scoring whenever the opportunity offered. Referee: Michael Maher, Tubberadora.

Thurles: Tom Semple (Captain), Jack Mockler, Tom Kenna, Paddy Bourke,

[4] Jimmy Fogarty (ed.), *Two-Mile-Borris 1900, All Ireland Hurling Winners* (Two-Mile-Borris, 2000), p. 32.
[5] *Nenagh News*, 3 Aug. 1907.
[6] Note – Walsh's Hotel was situated at 55 Main Street next door to Hayes's Hotel, Thurles.

Hugh Shelly, Mickey Gleeson, James O'Brien, Martin O'Brien, Paddy Brolan, Jack Mooney, Mickey Ryan (Mack), Jack Cahill, Philip Molony, Tom Dwan, Joe McLoughney, Tom Kerwick, Mick Flynn.

Holycross provided the opposition for the south Tipperary semi-final, played at Thurles Showgrounds on 4 May 1907. The 'Blues' were in sparkling form and had a 'hey day' winning by 5-12 to 1-5. Best for Thurles were Mikey Gleeson and Hughie Shelly.

Stiffer opposition faced Thurles next in the championship as neighbours, Moycarkey, lined out against them in the South final. This was advertised as the year's classic and the Thurles Showgrounds was the venue. Much respected hurler, Tim Gleeson, Drombane, was the referee and when he blew for half-time Moycarkey led by two goals 3-3 to 1-3. Thurles made a good start to the second-half and this gave them the confidence to level the match. Indeed, they were pushing hard for the lead when the long whistle sounded. Their finish surpassed anything in living recollection of Thurles hurling. The verdict was a draw, 3-9 aside.[7] At the next meeting of Tipperary county board there was a heated discussion in connection with the charging of sixpence as admission for this match. Over £16 had been collected on the gate and many felt that such a charge was very high-handed.[8]

The replay was refereed by Denis O'Keeffe, county chairman and Thurles clubman, but Moycarkey native. This fixture was the major topic of conversation among the hurling aficionados of Tipperary. With youthful fire and fervor, and with everything original about their methods the 'Blues' slowly crept to safety. A victory for Thurles on the score of 3-13 to 2-3 brought the 'Cathedral Town' the brightest day it had known since 1887 and the joy was unbounded. Through good and ill, the towering Semple had nurtured and tutored the winners and waited long and patiently for their maturity.

Thurles: Tom Semple (Captain), Jim 'Hawk' O'Brien, Martin O'Brien, Jer Hayes, Jack Mockler, Tom Kenna, Jack Mooney, Hugh Shelly, Tom Kerwick, Mickey Gleeson, Jack Cahill, Joe McLoughney, Paddy Bourke, Jack and Paddy Stapleton, Rody Berkery and Paddy Brolan.[9]

The 1906 county final venue went north to Nenagh on 25 August 1907, where the men of Cloughjordan under the title of 'Lahorna De Wets' stood between Thurles and county honours. Special trains were organised from Thurles via Ballybrophy to Nenagh. Admission to the field was six pence, while

[7] Philip Fogarty, *Tipperary's G.A.A. Story* (Thurles, 1960), p. 126.
[8] *Nenagh News*, 1 June 1907.
[9] Ibid.

the stand cost one shilling. It had been agreed that the expenses of the Thurles team would be paid from gate receipts.[10] There was a large attendance and two bands, Nenagh Brass and Reed and Shamrock Fife and Drum, entertained the crowd. De Wets had trained hard for the final and had high hopes of success. However, the Thurles lads proved their bogey team once more. Thurles had also great confidence from the Tipperary victory over Cork on the previous Sunday. It was a very fine game, each side displaying much craft and skill. The ballad maker recorded the event thus:

"In the final tie at Nenagh, it was a stirring scene,
To view those men in neat attire do battle on the green.
The dash and skill amazed the crowds – the 'Blues' brought Ormond down,
And raised their name again in fame with Gaels around Thurles town."

The final score read: Thurles 4-11, Lahorna De Wets 3-6. Referee: James O'Riordan, Commercials club, Limerick.

Thurles: Tom Semple (Captain), James 'Hawk' O'Brien, Jer Hayes, Tom Kerwick, Hugh Shelly, Michael Gleeson, Paddy Bourke, Paddy Brolan, Jimmy Bourke, Jack Cahill, Joe O'Keeffe, Tim Gleeson, Tim Condon, Paddy Maher 'Best', Tom Allen, Paddy Riordan, Jack Mockler.[11]

De Wets later objected unsuccessfully to the Thurles team, on the grounds of illegal constitution.

MUNSTER CHAMPIONSHIP 1906

As county champions, Thurles had the selection of the team of hurlers to represent Tipperary in the Munster championship. This was a responsibility that Tom Semple took very seriously.

In his hurling career to date, he was often the only Thurles man selected, as in 1900 or one of two for the Tipperary teams in the early 1900s. He certainly recognised how critical it was to use the talent and experience from the other Tipperary teams to ensure that the best possible 'Blues' selection played in the provincial and national championships. He set aside local or parochial rivalries to present the strongest possible team representing the county. His own experience taught him that he needed to ensure that the great players from the other clubs would be happy to play with and feel welcomed on the 'Blues' selection. This was a new era for Tipperary and for hurling nationally. Semple was the recruiter, selector, trainer and manager in his role as captain of the

[10] *Nenagh News,* 10 Aug. 1907.
[11] Ibid, 31 Aug. 1907.

'Blues' and he set the standard and framework for the successful county teams of the future.

Caherline of Limerick provided the first round opposition at Cork on 23 June '07. The boys from the mid Tipperary capital did not disappoint and gave a display that was an omen for the future. Friends of the team came home confident that a new epoch had opened up for the county and that Tipperary could look to Semple for future successes. Caherline faltered under the constant Thurles pressure.[12]

Final score: Tipperary (Thurles) 2-12, Limerick (Caherline) 0-4. Referee: J. Harrington, Cork.

The Munster semi-final was played at the Market's Field, Limerick on 21 July 1907. The Clare representatives were soundly beaten by 5-10 to 0-7. The Dalcassians defied the enemy for twenty minutes or so, but finished poorly. The playing surface was very poor and the game was played in intense heat and sun.

The British military authorities had been, for some time, busy in Thurles making the necessary arrangements in connection with their summer military manoeuvres. It was planned that six thousand British troops would camp near the town in late July and all proceed to Kilcooley. Here a mock battle would take place against another similar sized group.[13]

However, another type of battle occupied the minds of the Thurles hurlers. The duel for Munster honours took place in Tipperary town on 18 August 1907. Cork were represented by their county champions, St Finbarr's. The challenge to Semple's men was great, as Cork teams had dominated Munster since 1901 or as a Tipperary G.A.A. historian wrote, 'Cork hurlers had built a wall around the Munster championship and held it intact'.[14] The attendance was exceptionally large, as was shown by the gate receipts, which amounted to £133,[15] the biggest yet taken in the province of Munster. Special trains ran from Cork, Fermoy, Tralee, Nenagh, Thurles, and other centres, all of which were patronised to the fullest extent. Munster Council provided three pounds and five shillings to Thurles to cover expenses.[16] The gathering was by far the largest ever at this venue. The best of order was maintained and the ground was specially prepared for the occasion. Clare man, J. Roughan, was referee. The game started one hour late, partly due to the heavy showers and also to an

[12] Philip Fogarty, *Tipperary's G.A.A. Story* (Thurles, 1960), p. 128.
[13] *Nenagh News*, 23 Mar. 1907.
[14] Philip Fogarty, *Tipperary's G.A.A. Story* (Thurles, 1960), p. 129.
[15] *Nenagh News*, 24 Aug. 1907.
[16] Thurles Sarsfields Club Minutes 1907.

Tipperary, Thurles Blues selection – All-Ireland Hurling Champions 1906
Back row (l.-r.): Tom Allen, Jack Cahill, Jack Gleeson, Tom Kerwick, Paddy Maher 'Best', J.M. Kennedy (Secretary).
Middle row (l.-r.): Denis O'Keeffe (Chairman), Paddy Bourke, Jimmy Bourke, Paddy Riordan, Jer Hayes (Vice-Captain), Martin O'Brien, Phil Molony (Treasurer).
Front row (l.-r.): Jack Mockler, Joe O'Keeffe, James 'Hawk' O'Brien, Tom Semple (Captain), Tom Kenna, Michael Gleeson, Paddy Brolan.

objection by Cork that some of the Tipperary team were wearing blue jerseys, the colours of the Cork team on the day. The jerseys complained of were changed.[17]

Cork won the toss and defended the town goal. The first-half was keenly contested with both sets of back men keeping the scoring low. The half-time score read Thurles 1-3, St. Finbarr's 0-4. During the interval the Leeside faces were long but their hearts were undismayed. Thurles opened the second half aggressively and within a minute had another point to their credit. Shortly after, resulting from a Thurles free, Semple's puck struck the posts and rebounded leading to a neat goal, which was received with an extraordinary demonstration by the followers of the Premier county. Cheers and compliments were showered on the Tipperary men, they were 'the real thing', well trained, too well coached to be brushed aside or lightly overthrown. Two points for Cork in quick succession, around the fortieth minute, kept them in the game. Up and down the field was the order of events and a fierce onslaught on the Cork posts got a goal by Riordan, which was later questioned. The game was now fast and furious, the defence on both sides being splendid. At the final whistle the score was:

Tipperary (Thurles selection) 3-4, Cork (St Finbarr's) 0-9. When the whistle sounded, Semple's vow was fulfilled, he had changed the line of succession to the Munster throne and his men had written the first epic event in their history.

Tipperary (Thurles): Tom Semple (Captain), Jer Hayes, Jim 'Hawk' O'Brien (Goal), Tom Allen, Tom Kerwick, Tim Condon, Paddy Bourke, Tim Gleeson, Joe O'Keeffe, Paddy Maher 'Best', Jimmy Bourke, Jack Mooney, Jack Mockler, Hugh Shelly, Jack Gleeson, Mickey Gleeson, Paddy Riordan. Substitute: Paddy Brolan.

Thurles hurler, Paddy Brolan recalled, 'What pulling the Tipperary lads did in that hour! In the air or on the ground we pulled on every ball. But the Cork boys, they tried to lift on every occasion and they paid for that policy, it goes without saying. Such a game was of no use against us, pulling first time every time as we were'.

The All-Ireland semi-final was really a non event with Tipperary defeating Galway in Limerick by 7-14 to 0-2, on 8 September. The expenses involved in traveling to Limerick were as follows:- train fares – £1-5-0, car hire – Burroughs, seven shillings and Mulholland, eight shillings and dinners costing £2-10-5. Refreshments at Jim Maher's, Thurles cost six shillings and six pence.[18]

---

[17] *Nenagh News*, 24 Aug, 1907.
[18] Thurles Sarsfields Club Minutes 1907.

ALL-IRELAND FINAL 1906

Sunday, 27 October 1907 was the red-letter day chosen for the All-Ireland hurling final of 1906, between Tipperary (Thurles selection) and Dublin (Faughs). St James' Park, Kilkenny was the venue and at 3.15 p.m. upwards of five thousand were in the enclosure. Special excursion trains began arriving in Kilkenny from early morning. Canon M.K. Ryan accompanied D.H. Ryan to the match in the latter's pony and trap. The Cashel Brass Band were there displaying a fine banner of support for the Tipperary men. They joined the huge crowd that had journeyed from Thurles and the immense number of Tipperary supporters was headed by the band and all marched from the railway station to the stirring strains of well rendered national airs. The Tipperary hurlers were also in the procession and the playing of 'The Gallant Tipperary Boys' was loudly cheered. The weather was unkind with continuous rainfall right through the game, which made the sod heavy and slippery but this did not in any way detract from the brilliant exhibition of hurling. All the arrangements for the final were in the hands of a local committee, under the supervision of James Nowlan, Kilkenny man and president of the G.A.A. Tom Irwin, secretary Cork county board was the referee. The Tipperary team was composed of eleven Thurles men, three from Two-Mile-Borris, two from Horse and Jockey and one from Drombane.

Tipperary won the toss and had the slight advantage of ground, but it was Dublin that had the better start with a goal, after five seconds, by Willie Leonard. Half-way through the half this player added another goal. The Dublin defence was proving impregnable for the Tipperary lads. Eventually Hughie Shelly opened the Tipperary account with a welcome point from the wing. Another from Brolan and later Kenna and the Tipperary machine was in motion. Points from Mockler, Semple, Gleeson and Riordan followed, but it was Kenna's goal that really set the 'Blues' motoring. All the while Dublin were picking off points, leaving the score at the interval: Dublin 2-7, Tipperary 1-7. Tipperary's good progress continued in the second-half and at the three quarter stage the sides were level, following Leonard's third goal for the Liffey men. The puck out finds Shelly and Mockler well placed. The veteran Reardon receives a grand pass from Kenna, which he readily avails of by bringing off a beautiful goal and Tipperary are ahead. A point from O'Keeffe and from the puck out Brolan is away, picking up possession just inside the half-way line and coming along the left wing at terrific pace, he eludes opponent after opponent passing no less than eight Dublin players and finishes up with a truly brilliant piece of play by shooting a marvelous point. The Dublin backs are weakened now and the Tipperary forwards are masters of the situation. Kenna, Tipperary's crack right winger, sends in a beautiful cross to Riordan and the old warrior is at home and makes no mistake in sending up the white flag. The puck out is fielded in fine style by Maher 'Best', who sends the leather out to Shelly and the latter gives Riordan another opportunity to raise a white flag. Riordan is now in his element and pops over two more points and Tipperary are ahead by seven points. The forward combination play of Best, Shelly and Riordan is now unstoppable and as the long whistle sounds 'Magnificent Tipperary' are champions. Tom Semple is carried, shoulder high, by crowds of enthusiastic admirers and heartily cheered. Final Score:- Tipperary (Thurles selection) 3-16, Dublin (Faughs) 3-8.

Tipperary (Thurles): Tom Semple (Captain), Jer Hayes (Vice Capt.), Jim 'Hawk' O'Brien (Goal), Paddy Bourke, Martin O'Brien, Paddy Brolan, Tom Kerwick, Jack Mockler, Tom Kenna, Hugh Shelly, Paddy Riordan, (Thurles), Tom Allen, Paddy Maher (Best), Jimmy Bourke, (Two Mile Borris), Jack Gleeson, Joe O'Keeffe, (Horse and Jockey), Tim Gleeson (Drombane). *Substitutes:* Jack Mooney, Joe Moloughney, Mickey Gleeson, Jack Cahill, Rody Berkery (Thurles), Tim Condon (Horse and Jockey).

It is interesting to note that eleven of the Dublin players that played that day were native Tipperary men. The press commenting, 'It would have been a Tipperary victory no matter what the result'.[19]

The return from the 'Marble City' of Kilkenny on that memorable and murky Sunday evening was marked by much jubilation in the old town. A well-deserved hero's welcome awaited the team all over Tipperary and particularly in Thurles. There was great satisfaction and good feeling among all associated with the hurlers. When the huge excursion train steamed into the station at Thurles, a vast crowd with the band had assembled and cheers were repeatedly given for gallant Tipperary. As the All-Ireland champions filed out from the railway, followed by the crowd, tremendous cheers were lustily given and the local bands played them to the town. There was great rejoicing on every side.

In the week following the victory a special meeting of the Gaels of Thurles was called by Denis O'Keeffe. In congratulating the team he especially congratulated Tom Semple to whose unceasing efforts, energy, and perseverance, the success of the team should be attributed. He was also glad to know that the victory on Sunday was having a good effect and he looked forward to an influx of new members into the club to do their part in popularising the grand old pastime of hurling. He begged to propose – 'That the warmest thanks of the Thurles team and the Gaels of the locality be tendered to the Cashel band for the encouragement given by them, and for their splendid display, which had a stimulating influence on all the Tipperary men in Kilkenny'. Tom Semple, in seconding, said he was very proud of the team.

---

[19] Philip Fogarty, *Tipperary's G.A.A. Story* (Thurles, 1960), p. 130.

They had worked hard for the success and he could say that they deserved it. As for himself he stated that O'Keeffe had given him too much credit. 'I did what I could to have the club on a sound foundation. We have reaped the reward of years of perseverance. I hope the members will remain staunch supporters of our Gaelic pastimes. Being true to the club, in failure and success, will lead to the "Blues" doing their part in keeping up the old reputation of Tipperary as the premier hurling county'. Semple stated that he now had a pleasing duty to perform, to propose – 'That we beg to thank most sincerely those Gaels from 'Borris, Horse and Jockey and Drombane whose valuable assistance was given to us freely and willingly and whose abilities contributed much to the success of the team'.

Tom Semple (Captain).

Hughie Shelly seconded this proposal, which was passed unanimously. Players were asked to assemble at the Confraternity Hall to have photographs taken. A sub-committee was also formed for the purpose of organising a suitable presentation to Tom Semple in recognition of his role in the All-Ireland victory. It comprised Denis O'Keeffe – president, James M. Kennedy – secretary, and both Hugh Ryan and Joseph Butler –hon. treasurers.[20]

Tom Semple's statement in that motion: "I hope the members will remain staunch supporters of our Gaelic pastimes" was not just a heartfelt sentiment, but a theme that he constantly emphasised and that was a guiding light in his own life. Born just as the new Gaelic Athletic Association was founded in the town that would become his home, he recognised the importance of the Gaelic games as a critical heritage and the source of development of both physical and mental wellbeing, the teams could bring communities together and foster a true pride in their Irish character.[21]

Many letters of congratulations were received by the club regarding the All-Ireland victory. Fethard native Patrick O'Dea, secretary of the Tipperary Men's Association in Boston writing on 14 November included the lines: 'Of course it is needless to say that Tipperary men at home and abroad feel themselves sharers in the honour your team has been instrumental in bringing to the old county. Tell the boys that their exiled Tipperary men ask them to cling together and by so doing, it will be safe to say that it will be a wonderful team that can win from them the title of champions of Ireland.'

[20] *Sport*, 7 Dec. 1907.
[21] Note: Tom Semple's 1906 All-Ireland medal is on display at Lár na Páirce – The museum of Gaelic Games, in Thurles.

CHAPTER 7

1907 – Munster Final Disappointment

TIPPERARY CHAMPIONSHIP 1907

A T A MEETING of mid Tipperary board in Walsh's Hotel, Thurles, on Sunday, 17 November 1907, it was suggested by Andy Mason, secretary, that in order to bring the championship matches up-to-date, and as no matches had been played so far, that it would be advisable to drop the 1907 championship and proceed in January or February with the 1908 competitions. He further stated that the recent success of the Thurles team had caused this backward situation and that they should be nominated winners for 1907. Tom Semple said that Thurles were not anxious to proceed in the manner suggested, unless there was unanimity among the clubs on the matter. This was agreed by the delegates and Thurles were declared Mid Tipperary hurling champions for 1907, without striking a ball.

The 1907 Tipperary county hurling final was played at Cashel Rock athletic club on 17 February 1908. Thurles and Lahorna De Wets, who had faced each other so many times in recent years, were again locked in combat. Cashel Brass Band and Nenagh Temperance Fife and Drum Band provided the attendance with a varied selection of national airs. The final score read Thurles 3-14, Lahorna De Wets 1-6. The match was a very keenly contested, although a glance at the scoreline would suggest otherwise.[1]

Thurles: Tom Semple (Captain), Jer Hayes (Vice-Captain), Hugh Shelly Jack Mockler, Martin O'Brien, Jack Mooney, Paddy Bourke, Tom Kenna, Jack Cahill, Joe McLoughney, Mick Flynn, Tom Kerwick, Paddy Brolan, Mickey Gleeson, James 'Hawk' O'Brien, Mick Ryan, Paddy Stapleton.[2]

---

[1] *Nenagh News*, 15, 22 Feb. 1908.
[2] *Freeman's Journal*, 18 Feb. 1908.

Lahorna: Jimmy Meara, Pat Reddin, Mick Conway, Pat Williams, Dan Ryan, Murt Darcy, Din Whelan, Rody Kennedy, Joe Salmon, Tom Ryan, Jack Dwan, Mick Conway, Jack Meara, Jack Nolan, Pat Kennedy, Mick McLoughney, Martin Brien.

MUNSTER CHAMPIONSHIP 1907

In the 1907 Munster hurling championship Thurles, once again, had the responsibility of the Tipperary selection. They felt confident of continuing their successful run, having been crowned so recently with All-Ireland honours. Waterford, represented by Ballyduff, were their semi-final opponents at Carrick-on-Suir on Sunday, 15 December 1907. There was a large attendance present, in miserable weather conditions. The Carrick venue was on Davin's land at Deerpark and Cork man, Tom Dooley, was referee. The first-half was all Tipperary who had 1-6 scored after ten minutes. This was the pattern for the rest of the half which left the interval score: Tipperary 2-10, Waterford 1-0. The second-half saw a changed Ballyduff side eat into the Thurles lead and although they really never threatened an upset, they restored pride in their county. Semple at midfield played in his normal clever style, well supported by Jack Gleeson and Paddy Maher (Best). All the forwards played well while Tim Gleeson, Tom Allen, and Paddy Bourke, were the pick of the backs. It was also the first taste of inter-county hurling for Joe McLoughney, Jack Mooney, Mickey Gleeson, Mick Flynn and Bob Mockler.[3]

Tipperary 3-15, Waterford 3-5.

Tipperary: Tom Semple (Captain), Paddy Bourke, Jack Mockler, Jim O'Brien, Martin O'Brien, Joe Moloughney, Hugh Shelly, Mickey Gleeson, Tim Gleeson, Tom Kerwick, Paddy Brolan, Joe O'Keeffe, Tom Allan, Jack Mooney, Paddy Maher (Best), Mick Flynn, Bob Mockler.

The 1907 Munster hurling final was played at Dungarvan on 26 April 1908. Thurles led by Tom Semple faced Cork's powerful Dungourney, captained by Jamesy Kelleher. The hurling was the 'star' item and with the teams in sparkling form and in full striking force, the contest was of All-Ireland flavour and took place amid thrilling scenes.[4] While Thurles were first to score in a low scoring game, it was Dungourney who led at half-time by 1-2 to 0-2. The second half was very keenly contested with both defences excellent. With ten minutes to go a Thurles goal had them within one point of their opponents. The play now was desperately fast and a head injury to Martin O'Brien did not help the Tipperary recovery.[5] A free was awarded to Thurles and a mighty puck by

---

[3] Philip Fogarty, *Tipperary's G.A.A. Story* (Thurles, 1960), p. 134.
[4] Ibid.
[5] Jim Cronin, *Munster G.A.A. Story* (Limerick, 1986), p. 77.

Dungourney, Cork, All-Ireland Hurling Champions 1902
Back row (l.-r.): J. Quirke (President), M. Shea, W. Daly, W. Fitzgibbon, D. McGrath, J. Daly, J. Shea,
W. O'Brien (County Board), E. Aherne (Secretary). Middle row (l.-r.): J. Desmond, P. Leahy, S. Riordan,
James Kelleher (Captain), T. Coughlan, W. O'Neill, T. Mahony. Front row (l.-r.): J. Ronayne,
W. Parfrey, J. O'Leary, D. O'Keeffe.

Semple did not result in a score, as Jamesy Kelleher saved the day for Cork. However, Thurles kept up the pressure and played their best hurling as the game came to a close, but were unable to overtake the Leesiders. Even when defeated, that training and discipline regime allowed the 'Blues' to maintain their effort to the very last minute of the game.

Cork 1-6, Tipperary 1-4. Referee: M.F. Crowe.

Tipperary-Thurles selection: Tom Semple (Captain), Jer Hayes, James O'Brien, Martin O'Brien, Hugh Shelly, Paddy Bourke, Paddy Brolan, Jack Mooney, Tom Kenna, Tom Kerwick, Jack Mockler, Joe O'Keeffe, Jimmy Bourke, Tom Allen, Elias (Bud) O'Keeffe, Jack Gleeson, Tim Gleeson.[6]

Players and officials felt despondent after the defeat but got together on the following Wednesday and agreed to work loyally together and to do all they could to atone for the disappointment. James M. Kennedy, Thurles club secretary, reported that Fr. M.K. Ryan had given him a pound for club funds, as a symbol of his confidence in the club's ability to come out on top again.[7] Team captain, Tom Semple, added, 'In hurling

James Kelleher,
Dungourney Captain

[6] *Nenagh News*, 2 May 1908.
[7] Thurles Sarsfields G.A.A. Club-Minute Book, 1908.

as in everything else in life, one must expect disappointment, but I would remind you that when Cork were beaten last year they did not sit on the ditch in despair, but they worked with a will and now they have the reward for their perseverance. Many people think that the defeat will demoralise the G.A.A. in Tipperary, and that it will be some time before we take the field again. I can assure you that that will not be the case. This disappointment will stimulate us to work loyally together with earnestness and determination. I want to thank our allies from The Jockey, 'Borris, Drombane and Templetuohy. They did all they could for victory on the field and always responded to the call'.

THRO' THE THATCH

During these years, the jerseys worn by the Thurles team included an interesting new crest, designed in the main by club secretary, J.M. Kennedy. It was circular in shape and included a shamrock in blue on a white background and containing the words – 'Thro' the Thatch'. The shamrock, with its traditional Christian and Irish symbolism acts as a background to the crest. G.A.A. founder, Michael Cusack, who always held Thurles in high regard, added an extra dimension to the significance of the three-leafed shamrock. At the foundation meeting in Hayes' Hotel in 1884, he sought to place the new association under the patronage of Archbishop Thomas Croke, Charles Stewart Parnell and Michael Davitt. As Cusack put it, 'Three names, as the three-leafed shamrock that go to the heart of every true son of the green isle'.

The origin of the legend 'Thro' the Thatch' comes from the late eighteenth century, a time when hurling was flourishing partially due to its association with the landed gentry. They were openly and actively involved in the promotion of the game as players, team captains, trainers and powerful patrons. The newspapers of the time leave us in no doubt as to the influence of the landlords or the popularity of hurling, with several references to game played at Brittas, Thurles, Galbertstown, Loughmore etc. e.g.:-

> The grand Hurling Match so long intended betwixt Upper and Lower Ormond Boys, and those of Thurles and Kilnamanagh, will be played at Brittas near Thurles, on Saturday, the 1st of September; 27 men on each side; when great sport is expected, as the most, superior and elegant players in Europe will appear on a delightful Green properly corded and cleared and in every respect conducted with the greatest regularity. And at night will be an elegant Assembly in Thurles, for which the best Music is engaged and every material to render the Entertainment pleasing to the Ladies.[8]

_____

[8] *Finn's Leinster Journal*, 29 Aug, 1770. Note: It is likely that this match was organised by Henry Grace Langley, who was proprietor of Brittas at this time.

About this time, Lord Mathew, Earl of Llandaff, whose residence was in Thurles, had a celebrated team of hurlers. In a match with a neighbouring team controlled by Baron Purcell of Loughmore, one of the most famous of the Thurles team struck the ball with such force that it went clean through the thatch of a nearby cottage and broke some household utensils inside. Ever since *'Thro'*

Loughmore Castle, residence of Baron Purcell, who in the eighteenth century had his own private hurling team and a hurling ground situated between the main road and the present railway line, on the Templemore side of his castle.

the Thatch' has been a rallying cry of the Thurles hurlers.

Recalling the era of the Thurles 'Blues', old hands remember that, during a game, whenever the tan (hurling ball) reached the forwards, the cry would go up, 'Now lads, 'Thro' the Thatch'. It was invariably the signal for an all-out Thurles onslaught. During the era of the 'Blues', supporters of the team also wore a cardboard badge, similar to the crest. Luckily, some of these have survived to the present day and are treasured memorabilia of that bygone era.

TRAVEL AND TRANSPORT

When travelling to matches at venues such as Horse and Jockey, Holycross or Drombane, the Thurles club usually hired a 'break', a horse-drawn four-wheeled carriage, to transport players and officials. Return journey to the Horse and Jockey cost the club twelve shillings, Templetuohy, one pound and Drombane cost eighteen shillings. Burrough's, Kett's and Mulholland, all from the town, usually provided the transport. Side cars were also procured as required.[9] On some occasions, players walked to local venues such as Two-Mile-Borris or Horse & Jockey. On these occasions, one car would be provided to bring the camáns (hurleys) and jerseys.[10] The road users of Thurles, had something brand new to contend with. Motorcars were making an appearance for the first time. The town now had two registered owners of motor vehicles: Rev. Canon Wilson, the Rectory, Thurles and A. G. W. Cooke, Newtown House, Thurles.[11] Cooke was a noted cricketer and hurler with local clubs. Family saloon cars were costing between £300 and £500 at the time, a prohibitive price which represented the entire salary of a railway man for ten years.[12]

MEMORIES OF BYGONE DAYS

Jack Ryan, a tailor by trade, was born at Garryvicleheen St. (now Abbey Road) on 31 December 1894, and hurled with Thurles. Remembering his youth,

This sketch from the 'Illustrated London News', November 1879, is of a mail car which travelled twice daily from Kilkenny to Thurles. Four passengers could be accommodated and the fare was two pence per mile.

Jack recalled, 'in those early days, teams travelled to matches in wagonettes, which were four wheel carts drawn by two horses. They were capable of holding about thirty passengers and they usually left town for the match after Mass and didn't return again until 2.00 a.m. on Monday morning. Many the times, when they called for me I'd be off hiding in the fields, all because I didn't have a penny in my pocket and was ashamed to go without any money. I remember one day in the Square, they made a collection among the passengers and all they came up with was eighteen pence; some had a penny, some a half-penny but most had nothing at all! Wagonettes were usually hired from Hickeys or Leahys of Borris for the trips. Often we didn't get a bit to eat from the time we left town until we returned home the following morning. When we togged out for the game there was never any shelter for our clothes and often these were soaking wet, when we had to dress again, after the match. If you got injured they dragged you to the sideline and you stopped the blood yourself – as best you could. They didn't have as much as a sticking plaster or even a rag in them days. There were big crowds at the matches and it cost three pence to get in and if you didn't have it, they'd let you in for nothing'.[13]

[9] Minute Books of Thurles Sarsfields G.A.A. Club, 1907.
[10] Ibid.
[11] *Tipperary Historical Journal*, 1994, p. 66.
[12] Tony Gray, *Ireland This Century* (London, 1994), p. 29.
[13] Brigid (Biddy) Condon, *An Droichead*, Vol.3, Copy 13, 4 Sept. 1982.

CHAPTER 8

1908 Railway Shield Success – A Controversial Tipperary Championship

THURLES LOSES STATUS

THE ANNUAL G.A.A. Congress was back in the Confraternity Hall, Thurles, on Sunday, 24 February 1908, but sadly this was the last congress to be held in Thurles for many years. G.A.A. secretary Luke O'Toole had been endeavouring for some time to get the venue moved from Thurles, the birthplace of the association. At this congress O'Toole got his way as a motion stating that congress be held in each of the four provinces, in turn, was carried on a vote of 57 to 46.[1] For Tom Semple this decision was deplorable and difficult to accept. He always held the primacy of Thurles in G.A.A. affairs and this dilution of its status was not to be welcomed.

RAILWAY SHIELD 1908

Tipperary (Thurles, selection), being Munster champions, were

Three Tipperary Captains photographed in 1910. Dinny Maher (Killinan), Jim Stapleton (Cathedral Street) and Tom Semple (Fianna Road).

---

[1] Philip Fogarty, *Tipperary's G.A.A. Story* (Thurles, 1960), p.136.

asked to represent Munster against Leinster in the Railway Shield final on 8 March 1908 at Thurles Showgrounds. To date, Leinster had two wins, 1905, '07, to one for Munster – 1906. If Leinster won this game the shield was theirs. Thurles saw this as both a great honour and challenge and they prepared well. Practice matches were arranged for the Sundays prior to the fixture and the players met at 8.00 p.m. every evening 'for a run'. Ticket sellers were organized and ten men were chosen to mind the walls, to ensure that all patrons paid the entry fee. The proceeds, after paying expenses, went to players injured in the All-Ireland championship. Semple's team included twelve from Thurles, three from 'Borris and Moycarkey and one each from Drombane and Templetuohy. The Leinster team included players from Dublin and Kilkenny. Fully five thousand people, including Most Rev. Dr Fennelly, archbishop of Cashel and Emly, attended, and special trains were arriving all morning. The high wind that prevailed in the course of the match made matters unpleasant and good hurling almost impossible.

Munster had wind advantage in the opening half and took full advantage of it, piling on the pressure and leading by 7-4 to Leinster's 0-2 at half time. The high score was mainly due to Shelly, Semple, Kerwick, Brolan, and O'Keeffe. Even though Leinster made some progress in the second-half they were well beaten on a final score of 8-9 to 1-8.

Munster-Thurles selection: Tom Semple (Captain), Hugh Shelly, Jack Mockler, Martin O'Brien, Joe Moloughney, Paddy Bourke, Tom Kenna, Tom Kerwick, Paddy Brolan, Jer Hayes, Joe O'Keeffe, Jack Gleeson, Tim Gleeson, Jimmy Burke, Anthony Carew, Elias (Bud) O'Keeffe, James 'Hawk' O'Brien.

A local correspondent wrote, 'Munster fielded a magnificent combination, whose stamina and tact proved together too much for their adversaries. The Leinster seventeen lacked the precision, determination and dash of their opponents. This is not to be wondered at, when one considers the strict course of systematic training the Thurles players undergo at the hands of their painstaking captain, Tom Semple. They completely outclassed their opponents, creating quite a record by scoring seven goals in the first twenty minutes . . . I say again all honour to Tipperary, all credit to Tom Semple and the 'Boys in Blue'.'

As both Munster and Leinster had now won the Railway Shield on two occasions, the final contest to decide possession of the valuable trophy took place at St James's Park, Kilkenny on 17 July 1908. Among the supporters of the Thurles club were the thirty members of the Holycross Band and the fifteen strong Ballagh Warpipe Band.[2] Seldom in the memory of inhabitants of the

---

[2] Ibid.

'Marble City' had such a throng of visitors been witnessed there. Three special trains boosted the crowd and the paling enclosing the playing area was lined with supporters seven or eight feet deep in most places. As vantage points, the two corrugated iron sheds surrounding two sides of the ground had their quota of anxious spectators, filled with the prospect of gaining a special view. Their hopes were dashed as the frail structures collapsed immediately prior to the game. Although no one was seriously injured, many a bicycle stored inside was damaged to varying degrees of severity.[3]

Playing with the wind, Tom Semple opened the scoring with a great point for Munster and this pattern continued for the

The Railway Hurling Shield – now held in Nowlan Park, Kilkenny.

opening half, leaving them ahead at the break by 2-3 to Leinster's 0-6. Early in the second half it was all Leinster, who levelled and went ahead with just ten minutes remaining. The home venue was paying dividends as Leinster sensed victory. Try as they might Munster's attacks on the Leinster citadel were repelled and hustled aside. The final score was: Leinster 0-14, Munster 2-5. It was Kilkenny's first significant victory over Tipperary since the foundation of the G.A.A. twenty four years earlier.

Munster-Tipperary: Tom Semple (Captain), Hugh Shelly, Jack Mockler, Martin O'Brien, Paddy Bourke, Tom Kenna, Tom Kerwick, Paddy Brolan, Jer Hayes, Anthony Carew, James 'Hawk' O'Brien (Thurles), Jack Gleeson (Horse and Jockey), Tim Gleeson (Drombane), Mick Purcell, Jimmy Burke (Two-Mile-Borris), Jack Doherty, Watty Dunne (Cashel).

Munster objected to the awarding of the game to Leinster on four points:

1.   The illegality of the fixture.
2.   The referee's decision regarding a free against Mr. Semple.
3.   The encroachment of spectators onto the field.
4.   The assault on three players by outsiders during the game.

The objection was ruled out-of-order. Leinster took outright possession of the Railway Shield, which is now held in Nowlan Park, Kilkenny.

---

[3] *Irish Independent*, 20 July 1908.

WILLIAM McCARTHY

Early in the spring of 1908, Jimmy Kennedy, Thurles G.A.A. secretary, received a letter from William McCarthy (Liam Mac Cárthaigh), president of London G.A.A., inviting the Thurles team to visit London. McCarthy felt that such a visit would give an impetus to the G.A.A. in that city and would infuse enthusiasm among the Irish exiles. The Thurles club accepted this invitation and the costs involved in such a venture were explored. The City of Dublin Steam Packet Company offered rates via the North Wall, Dublin, and Liverpool for twenty-one passengers at £1-8-6 each.[4] All quotations were sent to William McCarthy but the trip never went ahead. The reason is unclear, whether the

Liam McCarthy Cup

costs were prohibitive or whether the many championships commitments for the 'Blues' influenced the cancellation. The William McCarthy mentioned was a Londoner of Irish descent. He gained a unique position in the history of the G.A.A., when, in 1920, he donated £50 for the purchase of a silver trophy, to be presented to the winners of the All-Ireland Senior Hurling championship. The Liam McCarthy Cup now bears his name.

A CONTROVERSIAL TIPPERARY CHAMPIONSHIP

The Mid Tipperary senior hurling championship of 1908 was keenly contested. A total of eight teams entered the competition. Thurles beat Templetuohy in the first round played at the Turnpike and met Two-Mile-Borris in the Mid semi-final. Templetuohy was the venue and Gaels were encouraged to come in their thousands on 17 May and 'witness as fine an exhibition of hurling as has ever been seen in the county'[5]. Thousands did turn up but the game was not played as Two-Mile-Borris objected to the appointment of Tim Condon as referee. This game was re-fixed for Cashel on 7 June, where a great throng assembled and few among them would risk a bet on the outcome. Thurles needed to put all their skill on display to outwit the brawny 'Borris men and they ran out convincing winners on the score of: Thurles 6-8, Two-Mile-Borris 2-10.

Thurles: Tom Semple (Captain), Jer Hayes Vice-Captain, Hugh Shelly, Rody Berkery, Martin O'Brien, Jack Mooney, Jack Mockler, Tom Kenna, Anthony

---

[4] Thurles G.A.A. Club Minutes, 25 Mar. 1908. Note:- In today's values, £1-8-6 would be worth €150 approximately.
[5] *Nationalist*, 16 May 1908.

Cartloads of turf for sale beside the 1798 Memorial on Main Street, now Liberty Square, Thurles, early in the twentieth century. Note the business premises in the background – Edward Dunne, Cornelius Molony and the Munster and Leinster Bank.   (Image courtesy of the National Library of Ireland)

Carew, Jack Cahill, Joe McLoughney, Mick Flynn, Tom Kerwick, Paddy Brolan, James 'Hawk' O'Brien, Michael Ryan (Mack), Jack Stapleton.[6]

But 'Borris were not happy with the outcome and duly lodged an objection on the grounds that the ball used in the game was under weight and not the regulation size.[7] The objection failed, but the whole affair led to disunity and the forthcoming Tipperary games were to suffer the consequences. The Mid final was not played until 1909.

Thurles played Cashel in the 1908 Mid hurling final at Rossmore on 16 May 1909. Cashel had a very wide area from which to select players, as one reporter put it, "From Tullamaine to Tubberadora". Cashel were confident of lowering the colours of Thurles. On the throw in the Cashel men, capturing the ball and brooking no opposition, carried it into the Thurles territory and scored a point. But when the Thurles men settled down to work the Cashel lads could make no show against them.[8] Thurles had a very comfortable victory with the scoreline reading, Thurles 2-12, Cashel 0-3.Tim Condon, Horse and Jockey was referee. Tim Dwyer and Anthony Carew appeared in their first championship for Thurles.[9]

---

[6] *Irish Independent*, 20 July 1908.
[7] Ibid.
[8] *Sport*, 22 May 1909.
[9] Philip Fogarty, *Tipperary's G.A.A. Story* (Thurles, 1960), p. 138.

Thurles were now in the Tipperary hurling and football semi-finals against teams from north Tipperary, De Wets in the hurling and Roscrea in football. These games were advertised in the local press as being the 'County Final'. This fact would have a bearing on subsequent happenings in this championship. The games, with an admission charge of six pence, were arranged for Nenagh Showgrounds on 25 July.[10] To the disappointment of the large attendance at Nenagh, these games did not take place. The size of the ground and the fact that the playing area was not enclosed from the spectators was objected to by the Thurles contingent and the match was abandoned. At the next county board meeting, the referee, Tim Conlon, reported on the abandoned county final[11] and as no team had lined out the match was refixed. The new venue was Roscrea on 26 September, a town where a co-operative bacon factory had recently opened. Extra carriages had to be attached to the special train in Thurles to accommodate players and supporters. A Fife and Drum Band was in waiting, heading the visitors down Bunkers Hill into the historic town of the abbey. The orderly march of the crowd, keeping step to the band was a sight to behold. The Thurles hurlers were on the field early – with the blue showing out from under their open coats. The result was a dual victory for the Thurles lads. Tom Dwan, taking over from 'the Hawk',[12] played in goal for Thurles and was brilliant. The press report on the hurling sets the scene, 'It is questioned if the Tipperary arena has ever witnessed so utterly depressing a scene. Visibly beaten from the beginning, and late on the field, De Wets display had neither heart nor earnestness in it. In unconcealed disgust, they left the pitch before the hour had run its course leaving Thurles to do as they pleased'. Thurles 5-13, De Wets 1-4.

Thurles: Tom Kerwick (Captain), Paddy Bourke, Hugh Shelly, Paddy Brolan, Jer Hayes, James 'Hawk' O'Brien, Martin O'Brien, Jack Mockler, Jack Mooney, Joe McLoughney, Anthony Carew, Mick Mulcaire (Thurles), Tom Dwan, Tim Gleeson (Holycross), Pat Fitzgerald (Glengoole), Jimmy Bourke (Two Mile Borris), Bob Mockler (Horse and Jockey).

The football semi-final between Thurles Mitchels and Roscrea was played after the hurling. This was late starting owing to a delay at the start of the hurling match. Most of the Thurles players had already played in the hurling and were first on the field. Thurles ran rings around their opponents and had all their own way, all the time. The game was best described as a farce. As one commentator stated, 'Hurling is the game of North and Mid'. It was almost dark when the final whistle sounded, leaving the score Thurles Mitchels 0-11, Roscrea 0-0. Larry Walsh of Cashel was referee. There was consternation, at the end of the game, when the players learned that the long journey back to the

---

[10] *Nenagh News*, 17 July 1909, 3 Oct. 1909.
[11] Ibid, 7 Aug., 25 Sept. 1909.
[12] *Tipperary Star*, 2 Oct. 1909.

Glengoole – Tipperary Senior Hurling Finalists 1908
Back row (l.-r.): T. Cahill, R. Fitzgerald, J. Fitzgerald, Pat Fitzgerald (Captain), T. Hickey, M. O'Dwyer, Pat Duggan,P. Meighan.
Middle row (l.-r.): Stephen Walsh, Tom Delaney, R. Kerwick, Willie Fogarty, Jack Delaney.
Front row (l.-r.): J. Gilbert, John Fitzgerald, Jim Fitzgerald, Pat Fogarty.

railway station had to be done in record time. This would leave no margin for dressing or for dinner. Many of the players, some having played two matches, were to be seen racing up to the station with their clothes and hurleys under their arms. Hungry, strapped, harassed men, who could be excused for the harsh things they said!

At a subsequent meeting of Tipperary County Board, De Wets were suspended for three months, for late appearance and for leaving the field before the final whistle.

The 1908 Tipperary hurling county final was the sensation of the year. Glengoole stood between Thurles and another county victory. So confident were the Thurles lads that they agreed to travel to Glengoole to play the final and did not bring their full complement of first team players with them. The gate only realised four pounds and eight shillings, the lowest ever for such a match[13]. There was a small attendance in Cormack's field, on Sunday, 24 October 1909, as most expected that the result was a foregone conclusion. Tom Semple did not take the Glengoole challenge seriously and only brought a makeshift team[14]. But the Glengoole hurlers had other ideas and saw the almost impossible become a reality. Thurles were over confident lacking the commitment and drive to succeed and consequently lost.

The local newspaper reported, 'It was a poor crowd that gathered around the gate at New Bermingham...The day from the financial point of view was, as in other respects, a great loss. Though it was anything but pleasant in the bitter cold, the Thurles men were on the field for a considerable weary time waiting for the home team. It was long after the appointed hour when the referee succeeded in having the game started. From the beginning, the play was extremely dull and uninteresting, so much so that the few spectators huddled together at one of the sidelines gave no indication of enthusiasm. There was missing and fumbling 'go leor'. From start to finish there was an entire absence of good play, both teams playing a very poor game. The Thurles men seemed, during the greater part of the hour, to play without a heart in the game. There was no such thing as a general exertion. There was a dead-and-alive kind of spirit which made one long for the time to be up. The New Bermingham men, with the exception of two, were a mediocre lot, their superior strength and weight was the determining factor. They were able to push their weaker opponents as they wished. In the last few minutes Thurles woke up to the sense of danger, but too late and with consternation rallied around the referee to hear him proclaim the astounding, sensational result that New Bermingham had won by three points'. According to Glengoole hurler, Pat Fitzgerald, 'It

---

[13] *Tipperary Star,* 30 Oct. 1909.
[14] Raymond Smith, *Decades of Glory* (Dublin, 1966), p. 70.

was the saddest day Tom Semple saw in his hurling career'.[15]

Glengoole (New Bermingham) 4-3, Thurles 2-6.

Glengoole (New Bermingham): Pat Fitzgerald (Captain), John Fitzgerald, Jim Fitzgerald, Tom Dinneen, Ned Brophy, Michael McCarthy, Pat Fogarty, Tom Delaney, Stephen Walsh, Pat Duggan, Bill Brophy, Tom Navin, John Norton, James O'Keeffe, Willie Fogarty, Pat Fogarty, Jack Delaney[16]. The Glengoole line-out for the final clearly showed that there was scant regard for parish boundaries in those far off days.[17]

Thurles: Tom Semple (Captain), Anthony Carew, Hugh Shelly, Martin O'Brien, Paddy Brolan, James 'Hawk 'O' Brien, Tom Kerwick, Willie Smee, 'Toss' Mockler, Mick Ryan (Mack), Jerry Fogarty, Tim Hyland, Joe McLoughney (Thurles), Tim Gleeson (Drombane), Pat and Tom Dwan, Patrick Ryan (Holycross).[18]

'Sitting on the bridge below the town' – Suir Bridge and the Ursuline Convent, Thurles.
(Image courtesy of the National Library of Ireland)

In the county football final, which was played after the sensational hurling decider, Cloneen from south Tipperary were the opposition and Thurles almost caused a major upset. Because of the hurling, the game was late starting, close

[15] Raymond Smith, *Decades of Glory* (Dublin, 1966), p. 70.
[16] *Tipperary Star*, 30 Oct. 1909.
[17] John Guiton, (ed.), *The History of Gortnahoe/Glengoole G.A.A. 100 Years* (1984), p. 10.
[18] Philip Fogarty, *Tipperary's G.A.A. Story* (Thurles, 1960), p. 141.

on a quarter to five when the teams lined up, and it was agreed to play twenty minutes aside. But the south lads, boosted by Johnny Tobin's only goal of the game, held out to win. The game concluded 'by the light of the silvery moon'. Thurles scorers were: O'Leary and Hugh Shelly. Tom Kerwick had a good game between the posts for Thurles, while Mahoney, Skehan, O'Brien and Moloney were most prominent.

Cloneen 1-2, Thurles 0-2. Referee: Larry Walsh, Cashel.

G. A. A.

A MONSTER HURLING & FOOTBALL
TOURNAMENT
WILL BE HELD
AT TEMPLETUOHY,
ON SUNDAY, MAY 17TH.

HURLING (County Championship):
THURLES (present All-Ireland Champions)
and TWO-MILE-BORRIS.

FOOTBALL:
TEMPLEMORE (Grattans) and RATH-
DOWNEY.

Come in your thousands and witness as fine an Exhibition of Hurling as has ever been seen in the County. Both teams have been practising hard for the contest, so the game is sure to be a most interesting one. "When Greek meets Greek then comes the tug-o'war." 516

The Nationalist, 16 May 1908

The outcome of the county hurling final caused much discussion, debate and dissension. Thurles objected on the grounds that the Glengoole team was illegally constituted. They held that Pat Fitzgerald had played with two clubs, Thurles and Glengoole, in the one championship. At a subsequent county board meeting, held in the Confraternity Hall, Thurles, Jack Mockler, Thurles G.A.A., stated that his club had withdrawn this objection. However, he questioned the fixture, and after a very prolonged argument, the chairman ruled that the match between Thurles and De Wets was properly the county final, that the Glengoole fixture was due to a mistake of the county board, and was illegal, not according with rule regarding draws. Accordingly he declared Thurles Sarsfields as 1908 county hurling champions.[19] Glengoole, to this day, hold that, 'the county title was taken from them in the Confraternity Hall'. The matter got another airing at the county board meeting in December. It was hoped that the teams would replay the game to solve the crux. While Thurles were amenable to this, the New Birmingham delegate, J. Delaney, said that his club had not considered this. The meeting decided to let the imminent county convention, on 12 January 1910, rule on the dispute. Convention ruled that in view of the difference between the clubs concerned and the county board, to drop the 1908 hurling championship.[20] G.A.A. history books have consistently credited Thurles with this county final,[21] particularly as it was a Thurles selection that represented Tipperary in the 1909 Munster and All-Ireland championships. Thurles always claimed that the De Wet game was the county final, as advertised by the county board. Adding to the confusion was the fact that this year was the first year that the recently formed South Tipperary Board (1907) produced senior hurling champions.

---

[19] *Tipperary Star*, 13 Nov. 1909.
[20] Ibid, 15 Jan. 1910.
[21] Philip Fogarty, *Tipperary's G.A.A. Story* (Thurles, 1960), p. 368.

CHAPTER 9

1908 – All-Ireland Glory for 'The Blues'

I N THE first round of the 1908 Munster hurling championship, Tipperary (Thurles selection) met Waterford at Fermoy, on 27 September. It was a facile victory for Tipperary on a score of 7-16 to 0-5. One of the most prominent hurlers was Tom Semple. Anytime the ball came his way, if he did not score his action led to one. Having their first game in the 'Blue' were Pat Fitzgerald (Glengoole) and Bill Harris (Horse and Jockey).

Thurles were even more organised as they prepared for the next championship match, which was against Cork's Blackrock. Training sessions were nightly with a special practice on Sundays. Fermoy was the venue on 25 October and, as expected, many trains were booked for the game. The estimated attendance was four thousand.[1] Blackrock had the Cork selection and were first on the field. Tipperary were led out by the Ballycahill Fife and Drum Band. Semple won the toss and decided to play into the sun. It was tit for tat all through the first half and the sides were level at half time, 1-4 each. Immediately after the re-start Anthony Carew broke through for a point for Tipperary. The fielding of the 'Rockies' was now faulty and the Tipperary forwards took advantage of the extra possession. Semple passed to Gleeson for another point. Both defences were not as tight as usual and the scores were coming thick and fast on both sides. Teams level or a point ahead was the story of the day and luckily for Tipperary a goal by Bill Harris, late in the game made all the difference. The score presented by the referee at the close of play was: Tipperary 2-11, Cork 3-7.

Tipperary (Thurles selection): Tom Semple (Captain), Hugh Shelly, Jack Mockler, Martin O'Brien, Paddy Bourke, Jack Mooney, Tom Kenna, Tom

---

[1] *Nenagh News*, 31 Oct. 1908.

Kerwick, Paddy Brolan, Joe McLoughney, Anthony Carew, James 'Hawk' O'Brien (Thurles), Joe O'Keeffe, Bill Harris, Bob Mockler, Jack Gleeson (Horse and Jockey), Tim Gleeson (Holycross).

Photographs taken at the Munster semi-final at Fermoy on 25 October 1908. Note the musicians entertaining the crowd and money being collected.

Best for Tipperary were Paddy Brolan, Tom Kerwick, Anthony Carew, Tom Semple, Tim Gleeson, Jack Mockler and 'Hawk' O'Brien between the sticks. It is interesting to note that the Cork team on that day included Paddy Mehigan. Paddy is better remembered as the famed G.A.A. writer 'Carbery'. Some years later, in 1926, he was hurling's first match broadcaster on radio.[2] Interviewed about the game, Tom Semple said, 'We won by no fluke. We should have won by at least four points, as I consider Cork decidedly lucky to score their last goal. Then, again, Cork got four frees, three of which were materialised, whereas we got no free. Our team all round was splendidly balanced, and played throughout a good combined game. We had few weak spots. Our fullbacks certainly played up brilliantly, and bested Cork's forwards on several occasions when our posts were in jeopardy; in fact I never witnessed better all-round play from the team.'

In a letter dated 30 October 1908, the Blackrock secretary, P. Twohig, wrote objecting to the match being awarded to Tipperary. Most of his case was based on, what he saw as poor refereeing decisions. However the Tipperary hurlers did not escape comment, as Twohig wrote: 'This match was the most glaring case of rough and foul play yet witnessed on a Gaelic field, from start to finish.' The

---

[2] Note:- P.D. Mehigan broadcast on 2RN the first field game (hurling) not only in Ireland but in Europe on 29 Aug. 1926. Patrick P. Gutrie, *The GAA and Radio Éireann 1926-2010* (Dublin, 2013), p. 38.

Ballintemple man further claimed that five of their players were seriously injured through this rough and foul play.[3] However, the Munster council upheld the referee's report.[4]

Tipperary were now in another Munster final but this game proved a real fiasco in Cork Athletic Grounds on 6 December 1908. Kerry, who had beaten Clare two years in a row, failed to muster a team. A mixed match between players from both sides was played for thirty minutes, just to entertain the crowd.[5] Later Tipperary were declared Munster hurling champions.

Hugh Shelly not alone starred on the hurling field this year but also showed his undoubted talent on the athletic track. At the Nenagh Athletic Club sports in early August, Hugh, with a handicap of nine yards, was first in the 100 and 440 yards sprints.[6]

SEMPLE HONOURED

As this very busy year drew to a close, a special night of celebration was held in the Confraternity Hall, Thurles. Focus of attention was on Tom Semple, Thurles and Tipperary's hurling captain, who was presented with a testimonial, initiated by the Thurles club, and subscribed to by Gaels throughout the country and in America. This was in recognition of his achievements as a hurler, a captain, and an organiser. Rev. M.K. Ryan C.C., Thurles and patron of the Thurles G.A.A. club, made the presentation.[7] Among the attendance were: Denis O'Keeffe – club president, J.M. Kennedy – hon. sec., D.H. Ryan, Philip Molony, Joseph Butler, Jack Mockler and Charles Culhane. In making the presentation, Rev. M.K. stated that this was a well deserved testimonial and continued, "We knew that before he left his boyhood years, he took a foremost part in some of the most prominent teams Ireland ever put on the field and then as he grew into manhood had a bigger work before him, he captained a team of his own. When the teams in the locality were being dissolved he gathered around him a few very old veterans and put a county team on the field. But when clubs were resuscitated in the locality he founded a team, he gathered to his side a number of gallant beardless youths taken from the town of Thurles and Tom's 'gorsoons' in the end won the county. He was the Achilles of the team, invincible on the field, their officer and counsellor and their trainer". Rev. M.K. then presented a cheque to Tom who replied that his efforts were simply 'a labour of love'.[8]

[3] Thurles Sarsfields G.A.A. Club-Minute Book, 1908.
[4] Irish Independent, 26 Oct. 1908.
[5] Jim Cronin, Munster G.A.A. Story (Limerick, 1986), p. 79.
[6] Nenagh News, 15 Aug. 1908.
[7] T.F. O'Sullivan, The Story of the G.A.A. (Dublin, 1916), p. 192.
[8] Sport, 2 Jan. 1909.

Tipperary, Thurles selection – All-Ireland Hurling Champions 1908

Back row (l.-r.): Mick Mulcaire, Michael Ryan (Mack), James 'Hawk' O'Brien, Michael O'Brien, Paddy Bourke, Tim Gleeson, Martin O'Brien, Tom Kerwick, Jimmy Bourke, James M. Kennedy (Secretary). Middle row (l.-r.): Jer Hayes, Joe Kavanagh, Pat Fitzgerald, Jack Mockler, Tom Semple (Captain), Rev. M.K. Ryan, John Fitzgerald, Tom 'Gaffer' Kenna, Mikey Maher (Tubberadora). Front row (l.-r.): Denis O'Keeffe (Chairman), Paddy Brolan, Jack Mooney, Hugh Shelly, Joe McLoughney, Anthony Carew. (Photograph taken at the replay at Athy).

At the Tipperary county convention at Thurles in January 1909, Tom Kerwick, Thurles G.A.A. club, was elected chairman. Tom, at this time, was a noted All-Ireland hurler with Thurles. He succeeded Frank Moloney, Nenagh. Tom Semple was elected Tipperary's representative on the Munster Council.[9]

The 1908 All-Ireland semi-final was played on 14 February 1909 at the Markets' Field in Limerick. A one-sided affair left the final score Tipperary 5-15, Galway 1-0.

The All Ireland hurling final was played at Jones' Road (now Croke Park), Dublin, on 25 April 1909. Tipperary met foemen worthy of their steel in Dublin Kickhams. The facilities at the ground, for both player and spectator, had been greatly improved in recent times. Attended by between six and seven thousand spectators the match was one of the best finals for years, Dublin's masterly display surprising even their own supporters. T. Irwin, the referee, threw in the ball at 12.45 p.m. and Tipperary, having won the toss and favoured by the wind, hurled into the loopline (railway) goal. A free, awarded to Tipperary close to the end line, was centered by Semple and after a scramble in front of the Dublin goal Carew finished the ball to the net for the only goal of the first half. The half time score was: Tipperary 1-3, Dublin 0-3.

Early in the second-half the players, on both sides, seemed tired and sluggish and the play was slow. Dr Russell attended to an injured Tipperary player and this break in play afforded a welcome rest for the jaded hurlers. Following this, the game sprang to life as both teams suddenly seemed to realise that they were in an All-Ireland final and that they were capable of winning it. Tipperary were ahead coming to the final whistle but points by Boland and Leonard for Dublin left the sides level.

Final score: Tipperary 2-5, Dublin 1-8.

Tipperary (Thurles selection): Tom Semple (Captain), Jack Mooney, Tom Kerwick, Martin O'Brien, Jack Mockler, Tom Kenna, Hugh Shelly, Paddy Bourke, James 'Hawk' O'Brien, Paddy Brolan, Anthony Carew, Joseph McLoughney, (Thurles), Joe O'Keeffe, Jack Gleeson, Bill Harris, Bob Mockler, (Horse and Jockey), Tim Gleeson, (Drombane).[10]

Thurles G.A.A. were in no doubt about the magnitude of the task that faced them as they prepared for the replay. The training schedule under Semple was disciplined and rigorous and no stone was left unturned in the preparation. A challenge game with Dungourney was played at Thurles Showgrounds on the

---

[9] Ibid, 30 Jan. 1909.
[10] *Sport*, 1 May 1909.

last Sunday in May. The absence of the Horse and Jockey players is unexplained. The Cork team were heavier than the Tipperary men but the latter played a better ground game right through. The visitors gave a great display and really tested the locals. However they were not as sharp as their opponents in getting possession and delivering effectively. A lucky Thurles goal, when the Dungourney goalkeeper slipped, gave Tipperary victory on the scoreline:- Tipperary (Thurles) 3-9, Cork (Dungourney) 2-8.

The training schedule by the Thurles hurlers had also to be adjusted to take account of the local parish mission, in the first week of June. Full attendance at the mission in the cathedral as well as at training was Semple's 'order of the day'. The mission attracted a huge congregation. Were a stranger to visit Thurles on any one of those evenings, he would be inclined to exclaim like Napoleon at Moscow, 'This town is a desert'. The streets were practically empty from 7.00 to 9.30 p.m.[11]

The replay of the All-Ireland was fixed for Jones' Road on 27 June. There was a concerted effort by Thurles to play the replay at a venue other than Dublin. They felt that Kickhams had the advantage there, so they suggested Kilkenny or Thurles as venues.[12] However, the agreed venue was the Agricultural Society's ground at Athy, Co. Kildare, with J. McCarthy of Cork as referee.

There was much turmoil in Thurles in the days before the final. This all stemmed from a riot that occurred at Friar Street in the town on the previous Monday, after the races. A sergeant and three policemen were attacked and badly beaten. Fr. Bannon and Fr. M.K. Ryan were called and they tried to pacify the people, advising them to go home. The land agitation in Holycross was the source of the aggravation.[13]

Michael O'Dwyer played brilliant hurling in the replay.

Many special trains were booked for the replay in Athy and the attendance was much the same as for the drawn game. It was a splendid day for hurling and an attendance of between six and seven thousand had assembled. The Thurles selection showed many unexplained changes from the drawn game. The twelve from Thurles were unchanged while the remaining included Jimmy Bourke (Two-Mile-Borris), Tim Gleeson, Michael O'Dwyer, (Holy-cross), John and Pat Fitzgerald (New Birmingham). Dublin

---

[11] *Nenagh News*, 12 June 1909. Note:- A mission is usually a week long parish retreat for members of the Roman Catholic faith. It consists of morning Masses and evening services linked to contemporary issues of faith and life in Ireland.
[12] *Nenagh News*, 5 June 1909.
[13] Ibid, 26 June 1909.

Thurles goalkeeper, James 'Hawk' O'Brien, in action at the 1908 All-Ireland final replay at Athy. At this time point posts were in operation. Goal posts were similar to those used for soccer, while there was a post on each side through which a point was scored.

won the toss and were first to score with a point from Kelleher. Semple levelled with a fifty yard free some minutes later. Generally, the first half was close with Tipperary having the better of the exchanges and leading 1-6 to 1-1 at the break. Fitzgerald had passed the ball to Shelly, who scored the goal, while most of the points came from Semple.

The second-half was a completely different story with McLoughney and Carew in fine scoring form, while Jack Mockler scored two points from seventies. The speed of Hughie Shelly often had the Dublin defence at sea and while scoring 1-1 himself, he had a hand in most of the other scores. Hurling balls seem to have been scarce on the day as an unusually long break in play occurred when Carew sent the ball 'out of bounds' and it took some time before it was recovered.[14] In a much-lauded team, Mick O'Dwyer of Holycross stood out. He was then a clerical student at St Patrick's College, Thurles. The game finished rather one-sided, a goal by Carew sealed Dublin's fate.

Final score: Tipperary (Thurles) 3-15, Dublin (Kickhams) 1-5.

When all was over, the players were carried off the field by a joyous throng of supporters. One of the greatest of these supporters was Paddy Maher 'Best', who cycled all the way to Athy and was there before the train arrived. This was Tipperary's eighth All-Ireland success in hurling and the third by a Thurles selection. The victory was celebrated on both sides of the Atlantic. In Washington, Edward Murphy, a native of Emly, penned these lines:

All-Ireland medal 1908.

'Two stauncher teams did never camáns wield,
Than in Athy for higher honours met,
Dublin's athletes marched proudly on the field,
Tipp's matchless sons composed the other set.'[15]

The quiet way the news was received in Thurles was characteristic. All-Irelands were often won in Tipperary. The crowd rapidly dispersed without any jubilation worth mentioning. The match in Athy was the All-Ireland Home Final. Glasgow-Gaels were now entitled to play Tipperary in the All-Ireland Final but as one commentator wrote, 'They shirked the ordeal'.[16]

---

[14] *Sport*, 31 July 1909.
[15] Ibid.
[16] Philip Fogarty, *Tipperary's G.A.A. Story* (Thurles, 1960), p. 143.

CHAPTER 10

1909 – A Flight of Pigeons

MUNSTER CHAMPIONSHIP 1909

THURLES GOT very little time to celebrate their 1908 All-Ireland success, as they were on the field again the following Sunday, 4 July 1909, in Fermoy, defending their title, while playing Kerry (Kilmoyley) in the first round of the 1909 Munster hurling championship. This was an easy victory for the All-Ireland champions, whose hurling was very impressive.

Final score: Tipperary (Thurles) 5-18, Kerry (Kilmoyley) 0-8. Referee: J. Egan (Cork). After the game Tom Semple, on behalf of the team, presented Jack Mockler with a beautiful gold watch and chain as a token of appreciation of his services to the club.[1] The Munster semi-final was against Clare at Limerick's Market Field, on 8 August. Thurles arrived in the city heralded by the Ballagh Pipers Band. Willie Walsh, Waterford, was referee and Tipperary had a good win on the score line 4-10 to 2-9. There was great hurling in this game, Clare (Kilnamona) making an admirable effort and having the sympathy of the greatest number of the large attendance. At the interval Tipperary were ahead by 2-6 to 1-4. Tom Semple was well held by Willie Considine. In fact, for three quarters of the game, they played with a zeal bordering on the heroic.[2] The goalkeeping display by James 'Hawk' O'Brien was widely praised, with his excellent saving and transferring of play to the centre.[3]

Tipperary: Tom Semple (Captain), Jack Mooney, Tom Kerwick, Martin O'Brien, Jack Mockler, Hugh Shelly, Joe McLoughney, James 'Hawk' O'Brien

---

[1] *Sport,* 10 July 1909.
[2] Philip Fogarty, *Tipperary's G.A.A. Story* (Thurles, 1960), p. 150.
[3] *Nenagh News,* 14 Aug. 1909.

(Goal), Paddy Brolan, Anthony Carew, Frank O'Meara, Tim Dwyer, Willie Smee, Pat Fitzgerald, John Fitzgerald, Tim Gleeson, Paddy Bourke.

Tipperary Town was the venue for the Munster hurling final, on 28 August, between Tipperary (Thurles) and Cork (Dungourney). The Tipperary team and supporters travelled together on the train from Thurles and before they set out, Archbishop Thomas Fennelly arrived in his back-to-back trap with grey mare, driven by his right-hand man, Dave Dee. After words of encouragement to the team, the archbishop gave everyone his blessing as the train began its journey to Tipperary. This was the clash that all hurling lovers dreamed about. Anxiety was written on many faces and here and there groups discussed the prospects of the rival contenders. It was a day of most unfavourable weather as the rain poured in merciless and continuous fashion. Cork won the toss and their Dungourney captain, Jamesy Kelleher, was in fine scoring form. A stiff wind and 'the fall of ground' favoured Cork in the first half.[4] It was all Cork at this period and their confidence grew as their lead increased. Tom Semple had a good first-half scoring two points. Coming close to the interval, Semple's great pass to Jack Mockler saw the green flag, indicating a goal, being waved, amid the increasing excitement. The score at the break was: Cork 1-6, Tipperary 1-2 and it was generally reckoned that Cork were now favourites for victory.

During the interval, Semple having collected his hurlers around him said to them, "Now lads, listen! Cork can't play without the ball, so don't let 'em have it. They must not get possession in this half." Semple and the Tipperary hurlers were also annoyed and insulted by the fact that, at half-time, the Cork supporters were letting off the pigeons, carrying the news to the banks of the Lee that the prized Thurles scalp was theirs. The towering Thurles captain, pointing at the disappearing pigeons remarked:- 'Look at the carrier pigeons flying south to the banks of the Lee with the news that we are beaten. There they go, Cork think it's all over'.[5] The hurt spurred the Tipperary boys to prove their worth. The Thurles effort turned from a dying flame into a raging fire, fanned by the

Semple's finest hour

---

[4] Raymond Smith, *Decades of Glory* (Dublin, 1966), p. 65.
[5] Ibid, p. 66.

Tipperary, Thurles Blues selection – Munster Champions and All-Ireland Finalists 1909

Back row (l.-r.): Tim Gleeson, John Fitzgerald, Martin O'Brien, Bob Mockler, Jimmy Bourke, Jack Mooney, Jack Mockler. Middle row (l.-r.): Ter Lawlor, Tim Dwyer, Joe Kavanagh, J.M. Kennedy (Secretary), Paddy Brolan, James 'Hawk'O'Brien, Tom Kerwick, Anthony Carew, William Bowe (Treasurer), Jer Hayes, Ed Fitzgerald. Front row (l.-r.): Mick Mulcaire, Hugh Shelly, Joe McLoughney, Tom Semple (Captain), Rev. M.K. Ryan, Fr. Russell, Michael O'Dwyer, Pat Fitzgerald, Paddy Bourke.

urgings of the crowd who caught the surging excitement of the moment. Play resumed and Semple's words were taken to heart and had effect. He was prominent, himself, in the early stages of the second period and the tide seemed to be turning in Tipperary's favour. There was a shock for the local supporters, when Semple raised his hand to indicate that he was hurt but luckily his injuries were apparently trivial. A bloodied and bandaged Semple returned to the play and dragged the "Blues" back into the game nearly single-handedly. Anyhow, play was stopped and the ball, which was heading menacingly for the Tipperary goals, was brought back. Semple scored a goal, which gave Tipperary the lead by one point.[6] A point from Gleeson and two from Carew made the outcome certain. At this stage some supporters, overcome with enthusiasm, got the better of the stewards and began to encroach on the playing area. Excitement was now at fever pitch as the crowd brimmed over with enthusiasm nearing hysteria. There was a desperate attack on the Tipperary backs, which was cleared and proved the final shot from the Cork men, as Tipperary surged ahead. This was the famous Tipperary rally, which made the 'Blues' such a much-feared combination. All the Tipperary players were chaired off the field, after the victory. No victory was sweeter for Tom Semple than this. It was possibly his finest hour as Tipperary's captain, and his inspirational leadership had won the day. Pat Fitzgerald recalling the day and the inspirational words of Semple at half-time said, 'His words put new life into us. We were like so many children; he has such command over us. With one wave of his arm, he could make anyone do his bidding. We became a new side and nothing could halt us in the second-half...I never played in a match of such passionate fury'.[7]

The ballad maker penned the lines:

> Tipp's gallant captain worked things through,
> James Bourke was there and Brolan too,
> And to crush Cork in rushed Carew
> And piled up score on score.[8]

Final Score: Tipperary (Thurles selection) 2-10, Cork (Dungourney) 2-6. Referee:- D. Roughan (Clare).[9]

Tipperary (Thurles selection): Tom Semple (Captain), Jack Mooney, Tom Kerwick, Martin O'Brien, Jack Mockler, Hugh Shelly, Joe McLoughney, Paddy Burke, James 'Hawk' O'Brien (Goal), Paddy Brolan, Anthony Carew, (Thurles),

---

[6] Pat Courtney, *Classic Munster Finals* (Galway, 1993), p. 5.
[7] Raymond Smith, *The Hurling Immortals* (Dublin, 1969), p. 81; *Decades of Glory* (Dublin, 1966), p. 66.
[8] Jimmy Smyth, *In Praise of Heroes* (Dublin, 2007), p. 129. Ballad composed by Edmund Murphy.
[9] *Nenagh News*, 4 Sept. 1909.

Bob Mockler (Horse and Jockey), Jimmy Burke (Two Mile Borris), Mick O'Dwyer (Holycross), Pat and John Fitzgerald (New Bermingham), Tim Gleeson (Drombane).[10]

Some, usually reliable, reports of the game include these names among the players: Willie Smee and Frank O' Meara, while omitting Bob Mockler and Pat Fitzgerald.[11]

There was great delight and celebrations in Thurles and surrounding areas. In much demand was a postcard photograph of the team, which had been specially taken in Tipperary town. These were available from E. Shanahan, Main Street, Thurles, whose window displayed the photograph with the following words:- 'Possess a souvenir of Ireland's Premier Hurling Team'. Regarding the result, Dungourney objected unsuccessfully to the Munster G.A.A. Council.[12]

The All-Ireland semi-final was against Galway at Limerick's Markets Field, with Charlie Holland, the noted Limerick Gael, as referee. Galway wore the Croughwell colours. Thurles really got a good fright from the western combination and were within 'the pick of a robin' of being on the ditch. Half-time score:- Tipperary 3-6, Galway 3-2. The attendance was amazed with Galway's great display. The Tipperary players, although almost at full strength, failed to hurl to form and nearly stumbled to defeat. The high number of matches that the team was playing this year was beginning to militate against good performance. However, they won by one goal 6-7 to 5-7, but the result and the display augured badly for the final.

Tipperary (Thurles): Tom Semple (Captain), Tom Kenna, Tom Kerwick, Martin O'Brien, Jack Mockler, Hugh Shelly, Joe McLoughney, Paddy Bourke, James 'Hawk' O'Brien (Goal), Paddy Brolan, Tom Dwan, Anthony Carew, (Thurles), Bob Mockler (Horse and Jockey), Mick Dwyer (Holycross), Pat and John Fitzgerald (New Bermingham), Tim Gleeson (Drombane).[13]

ALL-IRELAND FINAL

Delighted with the result were some emigrant Irish in Washington. They decided to show their appreciation for the exploits of the 'Blues', in a tangible way, by organizing a 'whip around' and the proceeds, $22 and 50 cents, arrived safely from Edmund Murphy to Thurles secretary, J.M. Kennedy. In the

[10] Philip Fogarty, *Tipperary's G.A.A. Story* (Thurles, 1960), p. 151.
[11] *Sport*, 4 Sept. 1909; *Nenagh News*, 4 Sept. 1909.
[12] *Nenagh News*, 25 Sept. 1909.
[13] Philip Fogarty, *Tipperary's G.A.A. Story* (Thurles, 1960), p. 151.

Tim Gleeson – a brilliant All-Ireland display.

accompanying letter, Edmund noted that most of the subscribers were twenty-five years or more in the United States and had never seen a hurling match under G.A.A. rules. When the letter was read at the November meeting of the Thurles club, Tom Semple stated that the letter was a great encouragement to them, proving that the Tipperary exiles in America eagerly followed the fortunes of the team. The following week, a $20 draft arrived from The Tipperarymen's Association in Boston – 'to the Sarsfields, in recognition of the splendid work they have done in maintaining Tipperary's superiority on the hurling fields'.[14]

The 1909 All-Ireland hurling final between Tipperary (Thurles) and Kilkenny (Mooncoin) was played in Cork's Athletic Grounds, in the depth of winter, on 12 December. The conditions were cold and wintry and the playing surface was soft and boggy. The near-waterlogged pitch didn't suit the 'Blues' ground hurling style. Thousands poured into the Leeside city for the game. This was the first occasion, in G.A.A. history, in which the All-Ireland final was played in its own calendar year. Tipperary bore the brunt of this change, having to contest two national finals and a replay, those of 1908 and 1909, in twelve months. Tipperary supporters were there in plenty. The attendance was in the region of eleven thousand and as expected the day was far from favourable for good hurling and Thurles lacked their old fire and dash. Tipperary were first to take the field, the royal blue with white stripe, showing up well.[15] From the start it was obvious that Tipperary were up against a determined and well-prepared adversary. Kilkenny had two goals scored in the first three minutes and another shortly afterwards which put them ahead by 3-4 to 0-3 at half-time. They had been completely dominant in that opening period. Tipperary settled better early in the second-half, scoring some points. Another Kilkenny goal and the game was over as a contest. Kilkenny's individual play was a rich treat for the spectators, but Tom Semple, who had often steered Tipperary's colours to victory, had a versatile and courageous opponent who tackled the Tipperary stalwart at every movement and with success. Kilkenny had their homework done regarding Tom Semple and knew that if his influence on the game could be curbed and diminished that they were in with a chance of success. The

[14] *Tipperary Star*, 20 Nov. 1909.
[15] Ibid, 18 Dec. 1909.

victory for Kilkenny was significant as it marked Tipperary's first ever defeat in an All-Ireland final, having won their previous eight final appearances. It must be stated that the Noresiders fully deserved victory with their sterling defence keeping the Tipperary forwards goal-less for the hour. Even at half-time the writing was on the wall for Tipperary with the scoreline: Kilkenny 3-4, Tipperary 0-3. In the second-half, Tipperary put on the pressure, scoring nine more points and staging a great recovery but poor shooting cost them dearly as they sent fourteen wides in twenty minutes. All the old 'Blues' fire and dash was missing, never did they, never could they, strike their old form and even the 'Hawk' belied his name. But at the close of play the Kilkenny goals were the real winners for the Mooncoin selection. Tim Gleeson's brilliant play cannot be ignored. He was far and away the best man, not alone for Tipperary, but among the thirty four players. However, Tipperary lacked their traditional dash and fire, their appetite for the battle had eluded them. Lack of proper training was very noticeable as was blundering inaccuracy. The loss of Michael O'Dwyer, Skeard, Holycross, was very significant. He had a great game in the Munster final but had returned to studies at Maynooth before the All-Ireland final. At this time, and for many subsequent years, clerical students were not allowed to play for club or county, except during holiday periods. The Thurles players were tired, this was their thirteenth championship game, club and county for that year – and their third All-Ireland final appearance in one year, a record in itself.

Writing in the *Cork Sportsman*, the well-known G.A.A. journalist 'Kinalea' had this to say, 'It was not perhaps of that great swiftness and brilliancy that might be expected in an All-Ireland final. It was powerful hurling just the same, all the time high-class. The chief points that struck us were – the deadly accuracy of the Kilkenny scorers, the wild shots of the Tipperary forwards, the magnificent wing-play of Gleeson (Tipperary) and Doyle (Kilkenny), the cool confidence of Dunphy in the Kilkenny goal, the grand blocking and returning of Burke, the speed of Shelly…the penetrability of 'Hawk' and the failure of Semple'[16].

Final score: Kilkenny 4-6, Tipperary 0-12.[17] Referee:- M. F. Crowe (Dublin).

Tipperary (Thurles): Tom Semple (Captain), Jack Mooney, Tom Kerwick, Martin O'Brien, Jack Mockler, Hugh Shelly, Paddy Bourke, James 'Hawk' O'Brien, Paddy Brolan, Anthony Carew, Joseph McLoughney, (Thurles), Bob Mockler, (Horse and Jockey), Tim Gleeson, (Drombane), Jimmy Bourke, John Hackett (Two-Mile-Borris), John and Pat Fitzgerald (New Birmingham).

This was the only championship match the 'Blues' had played without

---

[16] Phil O'Neill, *History of the G.A.A. 1910-1930* (Kilkenny, 1931), p. 15.
[17] *Sport*, 18 Dec. 1909.

scoring a goal. This defeat heralded the decline of the glory days for Thurles. The heyday for this gallant band of hurlers had run its course and their gifted leader, Tom Semple, retired from inter-county championship hurling. As the years went by the legend of the 'Blues' and their awesome, indelible impact on the hurling world, would make them immortal.

Commenting on Tom Semple's retirement from inter-county championship hurling, G.A.A. historian Philip Fogarty wrote, 'One has to regret that the heyday of this gallant band of hurlers, the 'Blues', had run its course so unexpectedly, but the master brain of the team – the gifted and immortal Semple – definitely retired. Had he remained, history would likely continue. Captain Tom has left behind him an enviable career in the service of Tipperary; he was inseparably connected with the hurling activities since the days of Tubberadora. From his first appearance to the date of his retirement, he was akin in feeling with 'Mat the Thresher', enthusiastic as the winter tempest on our heather-clad hills, and had an

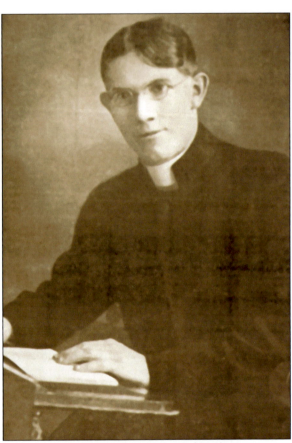

Canon Philip Fogarty, G.A.A. historian.

innate genius for leadership. Since he left the arena, and to the date of his death in 1943, Tom Semple's name was a household word all over Tipperary, indeed all over Gaelic Ireland'.[18]

---

[18] Philip Fogarty, *Tipperary's G.A.A. Story* (Thurles, 1960), pp 152-3. Note – 'Mat the Thresher' was the hero in C.J. Kickham's novel *Knocknagow*.

CHAPTER 11

Tipperary Championships 1909-1910

THE CUFFE SHIELD

IN THE 1909 Mid Tipperary championship, the senior hurling contenders were Moycarkey, Thurles, Holycross and Cashel. Moycarkey faced Thurles at Holycross in the semi-final. These rivals of old battled for supremacy and local pride, with Moycarkey ahead at the break by 0-5 to 0-3. A Thurles goal early after resumption was to be the game's deciding score in a low-scoring game. Final score:- Thurles 1-9, Moycarkey 0-7. For the Mid Tipperary title, Holycross opposed the 'Blues' in Thurles Showgrounds, on 5 September. Because of the strife in Holycross, due to the Clarke land trouble, they were ill-prepared for the final. Thurles led by 1-5 to 1-1 at the interval, Joe McLoughney scoring the Thurles goal. Even though they lost, Holycross put up a credible performance. Tom

James M. Kennedy,
Thurles G.A.A. Club Secretary.

Kerwick was injured during the game and was replaced by Jer Hayes. Final score: Thurles Sarsfields 3-10, Holycross 2-3.[1] The interval in this game was enlivened by an exhibition by a well-known local long distance runner. Also a ballad singer drew a good portion of the crowd around him with a song about the Munster final and an allusion to the objection.

Thurles: Tom Semple (Captain), Tom Kerwick, Anthony Carew, Jack Mockler, Jack Mooney, Paddy Brolan, Martin O'Brien, James 'Hawk' O'Brien, Hugh Shelly, Joe McLoughney, Tim Dwyer, J. Dwyer, Tom Dwan, Paddy Dwan, Toss Mockler, Mick Ryan, J. Carroll.

---

[1] *Nenagh News*, 11 Sept. 1909.

The Mid Tipperary senior football final, between Thurles Mitchels and Castleiney, was played at Thurles on 21 November, with Mikey Maher as referee. This was the first time that the Mid Board organised a football championship. The attendance was two hundred and fifty and Thurles were winners by 3-10 to 1-0. The game was fairly good but the number of fouls on both sides robbed the spectacle of any continuity. The gate receipts were fourteen shillings.[2]

Thurles Mitchels:- Paddy Hunt (Captain), Tom Kerwick, Hugh Shelly, Anthony Carew, Michael O'Brien, Jack Mooney, Bill Moloney, Toss Mockler, Tim Gleeson, J. Quinn, Willie Smee, Pierce Purcell, Michael Graydon (Goal), Joe McLoughney, Dan Mahoney, Tom Semple, John O'Brien.

Thurles were now in both hurling and football county semi- finals, but they would have to wait until the following year, for those games to be played. The 1909 county semi-finals were fixed for Templemore on 12 June 1910. Thurles were drawn to play Youghalarra in hurling and Templemore in football. There was no hurling played, as there was no sign of the north champions. Despite the best efforts of Templemore Brass Band, it was a tedious and irritating wait of two hours. Finally, Mikey Maher, Tubberadora, the referee awarded the match to Thurles. Later on, the Youghalarra team arrived, having been delayed by a breakdown on their journey.[3] Many among the attendance were very disappointed and urged the Thurles team to hurl, but Thurles refused.[4]

The football game was poor but was well contested, even though the standard was low. Final score was:- Thurles Mitchels 0-10, Templemore 1-3.

Thurles Mitchels: Padraig Hunt (Captain), Michael O'Brien, Seán O'Brien, Michael Graydon, Jack Mooney, Hugh Shelly, Anthony Carew, Morris Kelleher, Toss Mockler, Pierce Purcell, Bill Moloney, Thomas Kerwick, Liam Smee, J. O'Keeffe, Justin McCarthy, J. Curtis, Paddy Brolan.

Thurles were now in both county finals, against the champions of south Tipperary. Fethard was the venue for both games which took place on 21 August 1910. Even though the weather was pleasant the attendance was poor. A recent rule change had abolished the old point posts. Thurles Sarsfields played Racecourse-Grangemockler in the hurling. The odds were a million to one on Thurles for an easy victory and the forecasters got it right. The combination of the Racecourse-Cashel-Boherlahan, led by Dan Delaney, was trounced by double scores, 10-4 to 5-2.

---

[2] Philip Fogarty, *Tipperary's G.A.A. Story* (Thurles, 1960), p. 146.
[3] Ibid, p.149.
[4] *Nenagh News*, 18 June 1910.

Thurles: Tom Semple (Captain), Jack Mooney, Tom Kerwick, Martin O'Brien, Jack Mockler, Hugh Shelly, Joe McLoughney, Tom Dwan (Goal), Paddy Brolan, Anthony Carew, Jerry Fogarty, Tim (Thady) Dwyer, Willie (Bill) Smee, Ned McGrath, 'Toss' Mockler, Mike Brien, Andy Callanan.

In football Grangemockler proved too big an obstacle for Thurles Mitchels. Their skill and experience were too much for the Thurles players, many of whom were tired, having contested the hurling county final earlier in the day. The score was: Grangemockler 4-7, Thurles 0-4. Best for Thurles were Pat Hunt, Mick Graydon and Bill Moloney.[5]

MID TIPPERARY HURLING CHAMPIONSHIP 1910

In the 1910 Mid Tipperary senior hurling championship Thurles played Boherlahan in the first round. Boherlahan were under the guidance of the well-known Tubberadora stalwart, Mikey Maher. The game was played at Holycross but the result was not encouraging for Boherlahan.

Thurles 3-13, Boherlahan 0-1. Referee: Ned Hayes, Two-Mile-Borris.

Thurles: Jack Mooney, Tom Kerwick, Martin O'Brien, Hugh Shelly (Captain), Joe McLoughney, Tom Dwan (Goal), Paddy Brolan, Anthony Carew, Jerry Fogarty, Tim Dwyer, Ned McGrath, 'Toss' Mockler, Mike Brien, Andy Callanan, Jack Cahill, Paddy Corbett, Jack Dwyer.

The Mid Tipperary semi-final was fixed for Moloney's field in Holycross and old rivals Two-Mile-Borris were there in strength. Thurles were also at full strength with the exception of Tom Semple, whose loss was sorely missed.

What with bicycles and cars, it was no easy task for the pedestrian to maneuver his way on the road from Thurles. The hospitable home of Tom Moloney, the Green, was crowded when the 'Blues' arrived to avail of the chance of dressing under slates rather than under the downpour. There was a heavy growth of grass on the field, due to much recent rain. Thurles were first away and scored twice, but Gleeson replied with a goal for 'Borris. The game was fought inch by inch. Jack Mockler received a nasty blow on the head, but played on, following bandaging. The ball was never allowed to rest and travelled up and down the field at speed. 'Borris were more fortunate in scoring goals, while Thurles notched the points. Paddy Brolan had to retire in the second half and was replaced by Andy Callanan. Reporting on the hurling, the local correspondent was getting worried. 'Men crashed into opponents with recklessness, which is so perplexing to those not familiar with the game and

---

[5] Philip Fogarty, *Tipperary's G.A.A. Story* (Thurles, 1960), p. 149.

so alarming to those who prefer the timid rheumatic games of golf, hockey, cricket etc.'[6]

The half-time score was: Two-Mile-Borris 5-3, Thurles 1-7, while at full-time it read: Two-Mile-Borris 6-5, Thurles 1-14.

Thurles: Hugh Shelly (Captain), Toss Mockler, Jerry Fogarty, Bill Smee, Martin O'Brien, James O'Brien, Jack Mooney, Tom Kerwick, Paddy Burke, Paddy Brolan, Paddy Corbett, Jer Hayes, Jack Cahill, Joe McLoughney, Anthony Carew, Jack Mockler, Thady Dwyer.

A boardroom tussle followed. Thurles objected to Jack Doherty of Ballytarsna, who played for 'Borris – asserting that he was illegal, when there was a senior club in Boherlahan, his native parish. 'Borris claimed that he had been a member of their team for six years and would be illegal only if Boherlahan applied for and were given his transfer. The Mid chairman refused to rule on the objection and looked for propositions. An Upperchurch delegate proposed that the match be given to Thurles. This was seconded by a Thurles delegate and passed. Protesting that the honours won on the field were grabbed from them in the hall, the 'Borris delegate left the meeting and would give no assistance in the Munster championship semi-final against Cork fixed for Limerick, ten days later. However, at the eleventh hour, the 'Borris hurlers agreed to travel on the agreement that Thurles would withdraw for the county championship.[7] Tipperary lost the semi-final to Cork by 5-7 to 3-4. The team was picked by a committee owing to the Thurles/Two-Mile-Boris dispute.

Tipperary: Tim Gleeson (Captain), Tom Kerwick, Anthony Carew, Paddy Brolan, Jack Mockler, Hugh Shelly, Jack Mooney (Thurles), Michael O'Dwyer (Holycross), Bob Mockler, Dick Buckley, Jack Gleeson, Jimmy Murphy, Jack Leahy (Two-Mile-Borris), Pat, John and Dick Fitzgerald, Tom Cahill (Glengoole).

Thurles secretary, James M. Kennedy, informed the Mid board, at their August meeting, that his club had relinquished all claim to the championship.[8]

THE CUFFE SHIELD 1910

Another inter-county hurling festival was being launched, known initially as the Ring Shield tournament, but better remembered as the Cuffe Shield. This most impressive shield was on display in Denis O'Keeffe's drapery shop, on West Gate, Thurles. It had been presented by Otway Cuffe, Kilkenny, to the Irish

---

[6] *Nenagh News; Tipperary Star,* 11 June 1910.
[7] Philip Fogarty, *Tipperary's G.A.A. Story* (Thurles, 1960), p. 162.
[8] *Tipperary Star,* 27 Aug. 1910.

College in Ring, Dungarvan, (Coláiste na Rinne) to be put up for competition in a tournament to reduce the debt on the college. Tom Semple was a member of the organising committee. The shield, with a circumference of seventy-five inches, was designed from a bronze disc found in Co. Kildare. It included over one hundred ounces of silver inlaid with amethyst and crystals from Achill Island. It was made by Messrs. Hopkins and Hopkins of Dublin and weighed fifty-six pounds.

Otway Cuffe, who presented the shield for the tournament.

Tipperary beat Limerick in the first game of the tournament by 2-14 to 2-10. Kilkenny were their next opponents, which were overcome at Dungarvan in late September by 5-3 to 4-3. Tipperary (Two-Mile-Borris) had a runaway victory over Wexford (Castlebridge) in the tournament final, played 9 April 1911, to become holders of the Cuffe Shield for the first time. Tipperary 7-2, Wexford 2-1.

Two-Mile Borris: Jimmy Burke (Captain), Bob Mockler, James Murphy, Jack Gleeson, John Hackett, Jack Doherty (Two-Mile-Borris), Jack Mooney, Jack Mockler, James O'Brien (Hawk), Hugh Shelly, Martin O'Brien, Tom Kerwick,

Johnny Ryan (Cusack), Ballybeg, Paddy Bourke, Rathcunikeen (son of Jimmy Bourke who twice captained the winning Cuffe Shield team), Paddy Ryan (Sweeper), Ballybeg and Sam Melbourne, Curraheen (all Moycarkey-Borris) – photographed with the Cuffe Shield in 1979.

Tipperary, Two-Mile-Borris selection – Cuffe Shield Winners 1911
Back row (l.-r.): T. Cahill, Hugh Shelly, Jack Mockler, Joe Fitzpatrick, Jack Mooney, Paddy Maher 'Best',
Jack Doherty, Tom Semple. Middle row (l.-r.): Ned Hayes, Joe McLoughney, Martin O'Brien, John
Fitzgerald, Tom Kerwick, Jack Gleeson, Anthony Carew. Front row (l.-r.): Pat Fitzgerald, Bob Mockler,
Jimmy Bourke (Captain), Tim Gleeson, James 'Hawk' O'Brien.

Anthony Carew (Thurles), Tom Cahill, John and Pat Fitzgerald (Glengoole) and
Tim Gleeson (Rossmore). Paddy Brolan (Thurles) played in some of the games.
Proceeds of the tournament amounted to £230, which were gratefully received
by the Ring College Committee.

A misunderstanding on the conditions for the competition having arisen, the
dispute was not settled until 1914, when the second series of games was
advertised. Two-Mile-Borris, captained again by Jimmy Bourke, defeated Limerick
to retain the shield. Otway Cuffe, the generous benefactor and supporter of
various Irish-Ireland movements died in 1911.

Coláiste na Rinne, Ring College, Dungarvan, was the beneficiary of the tournament.

CHAPTER 12

Pan Celtic Congress – Trip to Brussels 1910

T HE G.A.A. Central Council granted permission for two hurling teams from Ireland to visit Brussels in September. A session of the Pan-Celtic Congress was being held there in connection with the Universal and International Exhibition (Exposition Universelle et Internationale)[1] and the Gaels of Europe were there to voice their aspirations.

The Pan-Celtic Congress was a cultural organisation that sought to promote and perpetuate the culture, ideals and languages of the Celtic peoples of Ireland, Scotland, Wales, Brittany, Cornwall and the Isle of Man. The first such congress was held in 1838 in Abergavenny, Wales. So as to provide an ideal platform to promote their ideals they linked the 1910 Pan Celtic Congress with the year's Brussels Exposition Universelle. These congresses were held triennially and this was the first time that the game of hurling was included among the exhibits. It was indeed the first time that the game of hurling was played on the European mainland since the foundation of the G.A.A.

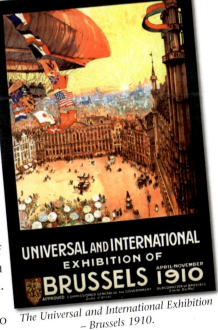

The Universal and International Exhibition – Brussels 1910.

It was the start of a historic journey to

---

[1] Exposition Universelle et Internationale was a world's fair held in Brussels in 1910, from 23 April to 1 Nov.

The Tipperary hurling team, Thurles selection, photographed outside Clonmel Railway Station on Friday, 26 August 1910, on tour to Brussels. Back row: William Butler, Thady Dwyer, James Kennedy, John Fitzgerald, Joe Cormack, Martin O'Brien, Eddy Flynn, William Carroll, Jack Mooney, Jimmy Bourke, Tom Kerwick. Middle row: Joe McLoughney, Richard O'Hanrahan, Tom Semple (Captain), Fr. Michael O'Dwyer, Tim Gleeson, Jack Mockler. Front row (l.-r.): Pat Fitzgerald, Paddy Brolan, John Ryan-Lanigan, Jim Bourke, Paddy Bourke, Anthony Carew.

Brussels for exhibition games in the Belgian capital. Thurles, representing Tipperary, and Cork's Dungourney were the teams selected. The congress was to be a great union and uplifting of the Celtic nations, while the Gaelic pastime of hurling would be among the many exhibits. The novel idea was the brain-child of J.J. Walsh, chairman of Cork G.A.A. Board.[2]

Thurles captain, Tom Semple, was asked to select the team to represent Tipperary. There were many letters received promising financial support for the trip and local G.A.A. bodies loaned the following amounts:- Munster Council £100, Tipperary County Board £10 and Mid Tipperary Board £10. The patron of the association, Dr. Fennelly, Archbishop of Cashel and Emly, gave £5, Archdeacon Ryan P.P., Fethard, subscribed £2 and there were other smaller contributions but Central Council declined giving any support. The cost per person for rail and hotel was fixed at £5. It was agreed that each member of the team travelling to Brussels provide himself with a handbag to bring jersey, togs, hurling boots and personal outfit. A new blue jersey, with a white star, was selected for the trip. Players were expected to bring two hurleys each, strapped together and to assemble at Thurles railway station at 5.00 p.m. on Friday 26 August.[3]

The following was the Tipperary contingent:- Tom Semple (Captain), Jack Mooney, Paddy Burke, Martin O'Brien, Anthony Carew, Tom Kerwick, Paddy Brolan, Jack Mockler, Tim (Thady) Dwyer, Joe McLoughney, William Butler, Joe Cormack, James M. Kennedy (Thurles), Michael O'Dwyer (Holycross), Tim Gleeson (Drombane), Bob Mockler (Horse and Jockey), Jack (John) and Pat Fitzgerald (New Birmingham), Jimmy Bourke (Clonakenny), Jack Ryan-Lanigan, William Carroll, Eddy Finn (Borrisoleigh), R.M. (Dick) O'Hanrahan (Fethard) and Pat McGrath (Munster Council Sec.).

The Cork party included:- T. Irwin (Redmonds), J. Walsh, W. O'Neill (Sarsfields), Jim Kelleher (Captain), M O'Shea, W. Cronin, T. Garde, M. Collins, J. Ronayne, W. Hennessy (Dungourney), J. Williams (Midleton), E. O'Neill (Kinsale), Cotter (Shanbally), T.P. Forde (St Finbarr's), D. Barry, S. and T. Riordan and W. Mackessy (Blackrock).

In charge of the Tipperary team were Messrs. Semple, Kerwick and Kennedy, while Messrs. Kelleher and Mackessy took charge of Cork.

The excitement in Thurles was palpable as an enthusiastic crowd gathered at the railway station to wish them a hearty *bon voyage*. When the train stopped

---

[2] *Tipperary Star*, 2 Sept. 1950.
[3] Ibid, 20 Aug. 1910.

Pipers and hurlers at Fontenoy in 1910.

in Clonmel, the team and officials were photographed at the railway station. This historic photograph shows the care and attention that players and officials took in presenting themselves in appropriate fashion for the tour. They are dressed in suits, ties and waistcoats, again reflective of the pride and discipline of the team. Some are wearing their hard won hurling medals, as was customary at the time. It is obvious that, regardless of their regular jobs or backgrounds, they recognised the significance of this event in Europe, the historic nature of the trip, exhibiting the ancient Celtic game of hurling under the newly formed Gaelic Athletic Association. They are looking dapper, strong and proud, surrounded by admirers and onlookers. They were ambassadors for the G.A.A. and Ireland and they knew it.

Having changed trains, they travelled on to Waterford where the Cork team joined the train, then on to Rosslare and boarded the 'St David' for the crossing to Fishguard. As they steamed out of Rosslare Harbour, there were cheers and good wishes from those on shore and the singing of the 'Boys of Wexford' and 'Gallant Tipperary' was taken up simultaneously by the two teams of hurlers on board. Having arrived at Fishguard at about 5.00 a.m., they continued onward by train to London, where they were entertained by many Irish exiles. The day was spent sightseeing in London, followed by an evening train journey to Dover at 9.00 p.m. They travelled aboard the 'Princess Clementine' from Dover to Ostend, arriving at 3.25 a.m. and onward by train to Brussels, which was reached at 6.00 a.m. on Sunday morning.[4] Even at that hour, there was a large crowd to greet them and warnings were given more than once in broken English, by some railway officials to *'beware of ye pick-pockays'*. Having arrived at their hotel, the party had some linguistic difficulties to overcome before they could make their needs known but then 'steaming pots of tea with plates of bacon and eggs were brought to the dining room table to everybody's delight.[5]

One of the principal items on the Pan Celtic programme was a reception by his Eminence Cardinal Mercier, Primate of Belgium and he had expressed the

---

[4] *Tipperary Star*, 20 Aug. 1910.
[5] P.J. Lyons, 'On the Fields of Fontenoy' in *Tipperary Star*, 2 Sept. 1950.

desire that the members of the teams should participate in it. In the afternoon, the group journeyed out to the quaint old town of Mechelen (in French – Malines). The cardinal manifested his feelings of regard for the visitors

Locals and some of the touring party at Fontenoy.

with unmistakable warmth. He recalled the racial and historical connections between Ireland and Belgium. He paid great tribute to the steadfast devotion of the Irish, gave a blessing to all and bade them a hearty good-bye. Musical selections were enjoyed and the function concluded by His Eminence blessing the banners.

For the general body of people in Malines, the main attraction was the exhibition of hurling to be seen on the grounds of the Racing Club de Malines. At four o'clock the teams mustered in the large square in front of the railway station. They were in playing gear and with hurleys on shoulders, they marched two deep through the town, headed by the O'Neill Pipers' Band from Armagh, which F.J. Biggar M.R.I.A., had brought over at his own expense. The green jerseys of the Cork men were side by side with the blue of Tipperary. A green flag with its emblazoned harp floated bravely from the stalwart shoulders of a Tipperary man.[6] Every street was lined with curious spectators and one heard flattering comments in three languages on the splendid physique and appearance of the teams and groups of locals raised a hearty cheer for 'Les Irlandais'. When the teams arrived at the grounds, a soccer match was in progress, watched by about 20,000 spectators. The hurlers watched the game with interest until their turn came to take the field. Some of those present at the soccer game remained to watch the hurling.[7] The attendance included Charles Page Bryan, the American ambassador, Shane Leslie – the Irish-born diplomat and writer, Count and Countess Plunkett[8] and the antiquarian Joseph Biggar.

To the air of 'God Save Ireland' the teams took the field. The large attendance of approximately two thousand, were mainly interested in the manner in which the game impressed those who were viewing the game of hurling for the first time. The preliminaries were quickly got through and Mr.

---

[6] Eamonn O'Neill, 'With the Hurlers to Belgium' in *Mungret Annual* 1911, pp.374-7.

[7] R. M. O'Hanrahan, *Tipperary's Annual*, p.83.

[8] Count Plunkett (1851-1948) was a biographer and Irish nationalist, and father of Joseph Mary Plunkett, one of the leaders of the Easter Rising 1916.

Quinlan, Limerick, was in charge of proceedings. The length of the field militated against a proper contest. Another factor was that the players had no sleep on the previous night. The teams confined themselves almost completely to ground play and when they warmed to the task they exerted themselves to effect, particularly the forwards, who pressed hard whenever they were in possession. About thirteen hurleys were smashed whilst the game was in progress and to the spectators it seemed that a battle royal was in progress. The demeanour of the onlookers was a flattering testimony to the impression it created. Bad misses were laughed at or criticized, good strikes applauded, but the feature which seemed to appeal most to the crowd were the puck outs delivered by the goalkeepers on both sides. The game was far from championship fare, both teams exhausted from the long journey. At half-time they were level at two goals each but in the second-half Tipperary (Thurles) pulled away and won by five goals to three.

Tipperary: Tom Semple (Captain), Jack Mooney, Paddy Burke, Martin O'Brien, Anthony Carew, Tom Kerwick, Paddy Brolan, Thady Dwyer, Jack Mockler, Joe McLoughney, (Thurles), Michael O'Dwyer (Holycross), Tim Gleeson (Drombane), Bob Mockler (Two-Mile-Borris), Jack and Pat Fitzgerald (New Birmingham), John Ryan-Lanigan (Borris-Ileigh), Jim Bourke (Clonakenny) goal.[9]

And so it was on to famed Fontenoy, where on 11 May 1745 the French army, spearheaded by the Irish Brigade (Wild Geese), won a notable victory over the British and Dutch.[10] A wonderfully enthusiastic crowd greeted the Irish contingent. For Thurles Sarsfields hurlers, it must have been a poignant occasion, conscious as they were of Patrick Sarsfield's historic link with the 'Wild Geese'.

So general and so deep were the expressions of welcome that one instinctively felt that these wielders of the camán were regarded in the light of the descendants of those heroes, who snatched victory from the embrace of defeat at the Battle of Fontenoy.

---

[9] *Tipperary Star*, 3 Sept. 1910.

[10] *Note:-* The Battle of Fontenoy was a key moment in the War of the Austrian Succession (1740-8), when France and Prussia wrangled with Britain and the Netherlands over who would succeed Charles VI of Austria. The French were led by Marshal Maurice de Saxe and met the combined army of British, Hanoverian, Dutch and Austrian, led by the Duke of Cumberland, at Fontenoy. Marshal de Saxe had a master trick up his sleeve. Hiding near the wood of Barri, were the Irish Brigade, around four thousand men in five regiments. At a critical moment of the battle Marshal De Saxe unleashed this reserve, which enveloped the flanks of the British. The Irish Regiments advanced to the cry: *'Cuimhnigh ar Luimneach agus ar feall na Sasanach'*, which translates as 'Remember Limerick and the English treachery.' They turned the tide of battle, bringing victory to the French. These Irish soldiers were the 'Wild Geese', exiled from Ireland after the Treaty of Limerick in 1691, serving in continental European armies in the 16th, 17th and 18th centuries.

'Thrice at the huts of Fontenoy the English column failed,
And twice the lines of Saint Antoine the Dutch in vain assailed.'[11]

The scene presented as the hurlers entered the village of Fontenoy on Tuesday, 30 August was qualified to draw ineffaceable lines on the minds of those who witnessed it. The whole village turned out. Young and old joined in the welcome, which was so exuberant and so whole-hearted that it recalled the land which gave the hurlers birth. Welcoming mottoes and welcoming cheers were everywhere and audible. The progress of the players and their friends through the streets was a triumphal march. Perhaps the most impressing and inspiring feature of the reception at the Celtic Memorial Cross, was the singing by the school children of the Irish anthem 'God Save Ireland', in both French and Irish. The Celtic Cross commemorates the contribution of the Irish Brigade, Wild Geese, to the French victory at Fontenoy in 1745.

The Memorial Celtic Cross at Fontenoy 2015. (© Photo Pierre Peeters)

The greasy and sloping nature of the ground did not admit of anything but a mere exhibition of the game of hurling, but it highly pleased the spectators present. The brilliant play of Les Verts and Les Bleus was loudly applauded and the game was as spirited and dashing as could be expected. The match itself was a grand exhibition, captains Tom Semple and James Kelleher playing with marvelous skill and coolness. Cork, in the end, retrieved their fame, winning 2-4 to 2-3.[12] Billy O'Neill of Cork Sarsfields was injured during the game and as his wound was being dressed, made the remark, 'I'm not the first Irishman to shed blood on this plain'.[13] Sadly it was not the last blood to be shed here. It is worth noting that within four or five years of this hurling exhibition by the 'Blues' and Dungourney, the very field where they played at Fontenoy was the site of another bloody battle with huge loss of life in the First World War.

---

[11] *'Fontenoy'*, by Thomas Davis.

[12] *Tipperary Star*, 3 Sept. 1910; Tipperary's Annual, *Belgian Gaelic Tour* by R.M. O'Hanrahan, pp 83-90; *Tipperary Star*, 2 Sept. 1950.

[13] P.J. Lyons, 'On the Fields of Fontenoy' in *Tipperary Star*, 2 Sept. 1950. Note:- Lyons was a Cork man, living in London at the time and was carried away by the romantic nature of the tour. He simply bundled up his knapsack, including his uileann pipes, and went on the trip. When the party arrived at Ostend, Lyons piped them ashore.

The players had visited the International Exhibition on Monday and went there again on Wednesday, the last day of the tour. They also played their final game. It was supposed to start at 3.00 p.m. but, due to objections by the Irishmen over the flying of a British flag on the

Some of the touring party at the Memorial Celtic Cross.

playing ground, did not get underway until three hours later. Programmes, printed in Irish, English and French were on sale and visitors to the exhibition were thrilled as they viewed the game, which was won by Tipperary.[14]

On 31 August, the touring party left Brussels for home, while a number remained over to visit Paris, Ostend, Antwerp etc. A tumultuous welcome was afforded them on arrival in Thurles on 2 September. The railway station was thronged with cheering crowds and the Confraternity Band played 'See the Conquering Heroes Come'.

The exhibition games received little publicity in Belgium. There was a brief mention in the French language 'Le Soir' on 30 August 1910 and a short account in the Dutch language 'De Staal' on 31 August. The most extensive report appeared in 'La Vie Sportive', a newspaper published in Brussels, on 1 September 1910.[15]

Even though the tour was not as successful financially as it was hoped, mainly because the arrangements at the Belgian end were faulty, for those who travelled it was a memorable occasion and a highlight of their sporting lives.

On 9 March 1913 a tournament game was played at Thurles Sportsfield, between Tipperary and Cork, so as to defray the costs incurred in the Brussels tour. Over six thousand attended and saw Tipperary, captained by Hugh Shelly, lose by 6-3 to 2-3. Tom Semple refereed the game and Tipperary's top scorer was Elias 'Bud' O'Keeffe with 1-2.[16]

> 'On Fontenoy, on Fontenoy, like eagles in the sun,
> With bloody plumes the Irish stand – the field is fought and won!'[17]

---

[14] *Tipperary Star,* 31 Dec. 1994.
[15] S.J. King, 'On the fields of Fontenoy' in *Tipperary Star,* 31 Dec. 1994.
[16] *Tipperary Star,* 15 Mar. 1913.
[17] *'Fontenoy',* by Thomas Davis.

CHAPTER 13

Tom Semple
– The Family Man

I N FEBRUARY 1910, Tom Semple, now aged thirty-one, married Mary Devitt. The ceremony took place in the St John the Baptist Church, Cashel, presided over by Fr James Byrne. Best man was Tom's hurling colleague, John (Jack) Mockler, while Hanna Devitt was Mary's bridesmaid. Mary, aged twenty-six, was the daughter of Thomas and Katherine Devitt from the Racecourse, Cashel. Mary's father was a cattle-dealer and she had five brothers: Tom, Jack, Dan, Pat and Mick. It was through the hurling that they met. Apparently, Tom Semple was friendly with the Ryans, Mike and Jack of the Racecourse, Cashel, noted hurlers and rugby players of the time.[1] Tom would occasionally visit at Ryans and since they lived virtually across the road from Devitts, he got to

Tom Semple and Mary Devitt on their wedding day in February 1910.

---

[1] Mike Ryan was capped seventeen times for Ireland between 1897 and 1904, and Jack fourteen times over the same period. Both played on the Triple Crown team in 1899, when Ireland defeated England, Scotland and Wales for the first time.

know Mary.[2] Mary's brother Pat was also on some Thurles selections of this time.

Following their marriage, they lived at Deerheen Mall (later called Fianna Road), Thurles, a property rented from Edmond O'Flanagan.[3] Tom and Mary had five children that survived to adulthood:- Thomas b.1911, John b.1912, Patrick b.1919, Michael b.1920 and Joseph b.1921. Three children died as infants:- Michael b.1915-d.1918, James b. 1918 and James b.1923.

Tom Semple's eldest son, Tommy, spent his schooldays at Thurles C.B.S. and following his Leaving Certificate examination, he took up a position with Royal Liver Assurance Company Ltd. In later years he held the position of store-keeper at Thurles Sugar company. Tommy was an accomplished hurler, winning a minor All-Ireland with Tipperary in 1930 and many county championships with Sarsfields. A noted referee at club and inter-county level, he is remembered as a successful county selector. Tommy was Sarsfields club secretary from 1942 to 1947.

Tommy Semple with his linesmen and umpires. Back row (l.-r.): Jos and Michael Connors, Louis Sheehan, Joe Moloney, Joey Kavanagh. Front row (l.-r.): Jimmy O'Connell (Pip), Gerry Loughnane, Tommy Semple, Danny Loughnane and Tom O'Neill.

[2] Interview with Kitty Devitt, niece of Mary Devitt, Racecourse, Cashel, by Seamus J. King (20 Dec. 2013).
[3] NAI, Census of Ireland 1911.

Recalling memories of his father Tommy said, 'He was a very strict man from a family point of view, everything had to be done to time-time for dinner, time for tea and supper etc. He was very dedicated to the hurling. We could give all night and all day at it, so long as we were hurling, he didn't mind. When we were small fellas down in Fianna Road, we had a great bunch that hurled in the street leagues in the twenties:- Rody, Paddy and Johnny Curran, Dick Ryan, Bunny Murphy, Joe Ryan, Jerry Murphy, Willie Kennedy, Mick Phelan and the Dorans-Séamus, Timmy and Mikey from Croke Street. My father was very interested in the leagues and great players came through those leagues, under the auspices of Fr John Meagher. One of my greatest memories is of having a few pucks with Hughie Shelly above in the field. I also remember seeing Hughie and Paddy Brolan playing hurling beyond in 'The Jockey. Hurling is very different now to my father's time. It's probably faster now but the main reason for that is that the ball now is half the weight of the ball they played with. There are fewer stoppages now too, but the hurling was tougher and the players were of bigger physique then and the opposition were also older'.[4]

Tommy was married to Josephine, née Kennedy, Liscrea, Bouladuff, Thurles. Her brother Mick was a member of the famous Limerick team of the thirties.[5] Tommy and Josephine set up home at 11 Butler Avenue, Thurles. Tommy and Josephine had a family consisting of one daughter – Mairín and three sons – T.J., Conor and Eamonn. Tommy, who was an excellent singer, was a member of Thurles Musical Society for many years. He died on 4 June 1984, aged seventy-three and is buried in St Patrick's Cemetery, Thurles.

Tommy's son, T.J. Semple, won All-Ireland inter-mediate hurling honours in 1963 with Tipperary and played at senior level with the county in 1969/'70 . He captained Thurles Sarsfields in 1970 and won four county senior hurling championships with them, 1962,'63, '64 and '65. T.J. and his wife, Anne, live in Thurles. They have one son, Thomas. T.J., who spent his working life with the production team at the *Tipperary Star* newspaper in Thurles, is now retired. Both Conor and Eamonn played hurling with Thurles C.B.S. Eamonn also played soccer with U.C.D., Thurles Town and Kilkenny League teams, becoming an international player with Irish universities.

T.J. Semple captained Thurles Sarsfields in 1970.

---

[4] Interview by Paddy Doherty, Ardnacrusha, Thurles, with Tommy Semple, Butler Ave., Thurles (12 Aug. 1980).

[5] Mick Kennedy (1911-1977) was a native of Bouladuff, Thurles. Playing at left full-back, he won three senior hurling All-Irelands with Limerick-1934, '36 and '40. At club level Kennedy played with Young Irelands, Limerick.

Tom Semple's grandson, Paddy's son, Michael Thomas Semple visited Thurles in January 1989.

Tom Semple's second son, John, was known locally as 'Skint', due to his slim build. He was a good hurler and lined out with Thurles Sarsfields in all their

Josephine and Tommy Semple, Butler Avenue, Thurles, in the early 1980s.

championship games between 1935 and 1943. John, who usually played at

Thurles advertisement, 1916.

wing-back, was on the Tipperary minor hurling team that won the All-Ireland in the 'Triple Crown' year of 1930. John, like his father, worked with the rail company, Córas Iompair Éireann (C.I.E.) and was based at Thurles station. He emigrated to the U.K. in 1957 and took up residence in Bristol. John, having been ill for a few months, died on 3 September 1970, aged fifty-

Tommy Semple's Family Celebrates (l.-r.): Eamonn Semple, Máirín Semple-Thomas, Josephine Semple, Conor Semple and T.J. Semple.

eight. He was interred in Holy Souls Cemetery, Bristol. At his funeral a guard of honour of hurleys was formed over the coffin at both his removal and burial.

Michael was born at Fianna Road, Thurles, in 1915 and like his brothers hurled with Thurles C.B.S. and Thurles Sarsfields. In the late 1930s Michael emigrated to Wales and settled in the Cardiff area. During World War II, he took part of the Allied forces invasion of Normandy on 6 June 1944, a day best remembered as D-Day. This was the largest seaborne invasion in history and led to the Allied victory in the war. It was a fateful day for Michael, who became casuality in the action, losing his sight. Michael was married to Rose and had a number of children.

Thomas Semple, great-grandson of Tom Semple.

Patrick, always referred to as Paddy, was born in 1919. Following his schooldays at Thurles C.B.S., he finished his apprenticeship as a carpenter. In the late 1930s he emigrated to England and later settled in Bristol. Paddy married Gwen and they had one son named Michael. Michael is now living in New Zealand. Paddy's brother, John (Skint), lived with them, when he moved to Bristol.

Joseph, affectionately called Joby, the youngest son of Tom and Mary Semple, was born in 1921. In his youth he enjoyed Gaelic games, particularly hurling, and played with Thurles Sarsfields until he emigrated to Liverpool in the early 1940s. Before he left Thurles, he had completed his apprenticeship as an electrician. During the Second World War, Joby joined the R.A.F. and was stationed at Cairo, Egypt, where he maintained aircraft for the Allies. After the war, he lived with his wife Edna in the Sutton Coalfield region. They had one son, Alan. Some years later he lived in Litchfield. Joby worked until his retirement in the rates department of Birmingham City Council. He died in Staffordshire, England, aged 79, on 6 December 2000. He is buried in St. Mary's cemetery, Thurles.

Joseph (Joby) Semple.

Tom Semple's father, Martin, died on 5 July 1915, at Cashel Hospital, aged seventy-six years. Expressions of sympathy were received from Thurles G.A.A. club, Thurles Urban Council, Cashel Sportsfield committee, and Cashel G.A.A. club.[6]

Three generations of Semples (l.-r.): Thomas Semple (great-grandson), Anne Semple-Gunning (daughter), Josephine Semple (daughter-in-law), T.J. Semple (grandson).

[6] *Tipperary Star*, 10, 17 July 1915.

CHAPTER 14

1911 – Another Championship for the 'Blues'

MUNSTER FINAL WOES

THE CHALLENGE

IN JANUARY Tipperary fielded two teams on the same day. One, captained by Ned Hayes, Two-Mile-Borris and it included some of the more noted of the Thurles hurlers, Jack Mooney, Tom Kerwick, Hugh Shelly, Anthony Carew and 'The Hawk' O'Brien. The other was in the charge of Tom Semple and Tim Gleeson. Both teams had been successful, one defeating Kilkenny, the other accounting for Limerick.

> *Dear Sir,*
>
> *We, the undersigned, on behalf of the team that defeated Limerick, hereby challenge the Two Mile Borris combination that defeated Kilkenny for the Cuffe Shield. The match to take place at Thurles Sporting Grounds on New Year's Day. A reply to the 'Star' or to either of us will bring the matter to a head.*
>
> > *Signed: Tom Semple, Thurles*
> > *Tim Gleeson, Drombane*
>
> *Dear Sir,*
>
> *Permit me space in your valuable paper to reply to the challenge sent to my team. On behalf of the Two Mile Borris team, I accept the challenge, and will be happy to meet Messrs. Semple and Gleeson, on any day they name, to arrange a suitable venue and the sooner the better.*
>
> > *Signed on behalf of the Two Mile Borris team,*
> > *Ed. Hayes (Captain).*[1]

---

[1] *Tipperary Star*, 7 Jan. 1911.

Much of the talk during the Christmas season and into the New Year concerned this challenge match between Thurles and Two Mile Borris. Following last year's defeat in the championship, and the fact that two different teams had lined out for Tipperary, Thurles hurlers were anxious to set the record straight and when Tom Semple issued the challenge, there was no going back.[2] The date agreed was 21 January and Thurles Sporting Grounds the venue, with Tom Irwin, Cork as referee. It was a very exciting and vigorously fought game with Semple and Thurles making no mistake this time. The lighter Thurles 'Blues' were more active from the beginning, while the Two-Mile-Borris hurlers were slower on the ball. Final score:- Thurles 5-3, Two-Mile-Borris 2-1.

Semple's Team:- Tom Semple, Tim Gleeson, Martin O'Brien, Bill Smee, Jack Mockler, Thady Dwyer, Tom Mockler, Jerry Fogarty, Andy Callanan, Mick Brien, Ned McGrath, Joe McLoughney, Bill Ryan, Paddy Brolan (Thurles), J. Ryan, T. Ryan, Mick Hammond (Borris/Ileigh).

Hayes's Team:- Ned Hayes, Paddy Maher (Best), Joe Fitzpatrick, Phil Leahy, Mick Leahy, Jimmy Bourke, Bob Mockler, Jack Gleeson, Jimmy Murphy, Tom Allen (Two/Mile/Borris), Tom Cahill, Pat Fitzgerald (New Birmingham), Jack Mooney, Tom Kerwick, Hugh Shelly, Anthony Carew, James O'Brien (Thurles).[3]

At the Tipperary County Convention, held in the Confraternity Hall on 12 February, the election of officers produced an unusual and unique result in that the chairman, secretary and treasurer elected were all from the Thurles G.A.A. Club. These were respectively Tom Kerwick, Anthony Carew and Denis McCarthy. Ned Fitzgerald, Thurles G.A.A. was elected vice chairman of the Mid Tipperary Board at their convention.

1911 TIPPERARY CHAMPIONSHIP

In the Mid Tipperary championship, Thurles Sarsfields were drawn against Boherlahan in senior hurling and to everyone's surprise Two-Mile-Borris did not affiliate a team. From early in the year Tom Semple had picked his panel, as follows:- Tom Semple (Captain), Jack Mooney, Jerry Fogarty, William Ryan, William Smee, Anthony Carew, Ed McGrath, Martin O'Brien, Andy Callanan, Paddy Brolan, Toss Mockler, Joe McLoughney, Hugh Shelly, Jack Mockler, Tom Dwan, Mick

Hugh Shelly, Tipperary Captain 1911.

[2] *Tipperary Star*, 12 Dec. 1910.
[3] Ibid, 28 Jan. 1911.

Hammond, Thady Dwyer, Mick O'Brien and Tom Kerwick.

Thurles had a very successful year in senior hurling. They got a walk over from Boherlahan in the first round and defeated Rossmore 5-6 to1-1 in the semi-final at Borris-Ileigh. The attendance was good and the game started about one hour after the advertised time, 'as is usual locally'.[4] Jack Cahill replaced the injured Anthony Carew. Only sixteen players were listed in the match report.

Thurles Sarsfields:- Jack Dwyer, Ned McGrath, Bill Smee, Thady Dwyer, Tom Dwan, Mick O'Brien, James 'Hawk' O'Brien, Hughie Shelly, Anthony Carew, Jerry Fogarty, Andy Callanan, Tom Kerwick, Toss Mockler, Paddy Brolan, Mick Hammond, Joe McLoughney.

The Mid final against Borris-Ileigh was played, at Rossmore, on 2 July. According to a brief preview of the game in the local newspaper:- 'Borris-Ileigh is a young, most enthusiastic and very ambitious team and as such is keen on practice. They beat good opposition along the way and these successes would be crowned by beating the 'Blues'.

In contrast there was an ominous quiet from the Thurles camp 'which betokens that the team will not lightly enter into the struggle without being prepared to exert themselves with all the great ability which, on many a hard-fought field, shed lustre on the far-famed 'Blues'.'[5]

Thurles secretary and player, Anthony Carew, a Rossmore native, was instrumental in fixing the game for Rossmore. The field was owned by a relation of Carew's.

The game was a poor affair and failed to live up to its pre-match expectations. It was late starting because of the failure of Thurles captain, Tom Semple, to arrive. It appears he was expected but failed to tell anybody he would not be there. Thurles had a problem because they had the bare seventeen players and the absence of

1798 Memorial on Liberty Square.

Semple left them short. Nobody was forthcoming to take his place until eventually Jack Cahill was pressed into service and, 'though out of practice for years, got through the game with considerable credit.'

Playing against the breeze in the first half, Thurles scored heavily in the first quarter and easily overcame the Borris-Ileigh defence to lead at half-time by 6-2 to nil. The second half was uninteresting as Thurles won with unexpected ease on a scoreline of 8-2 to 1-1.

Thurles Sarsfields:- Hugh Shelly (vice-captain), Jack Mooney, Thady Dwyer, Joe McLoughney, Ned McGrath, Jim O'Brien (Hawk), Martin O'Brien, Tom Kerwick, Andy Callanan, Anthony Carew, Jack Cahill, Jack Dwyer, Paddy Brolan, Tom Mockler, Jerry Fogarty, Bill Smee, Mick Hammond. Referee: Tim Gleeson, Drombane.[6]

Sarsfields as Mid Tipperary winners had a bye into the county final at Cashel. Thurles were in both hurling and football county finals, played on 3 September. As the Mid Football championship had not been completed, Thurles Mitchels were nominated to represent the division. In hurling, Sarsfields were pitted against the previous year's champions Toomevara, led by Wedger Meagher. In football Thurles Mitchels faced Nenagh Institute.

A special train from Nenagh, calling at intermediate stations, brought a good number from the north of the county It was consoling for the 'Blues' that the old stalwart Tom Semple was there to lead them against the 'Greyhounds'. From the throw-in the outcome was evident, Semple in his element and scoring at his ease. This was perhaps the finest result in their successful era. The 'Blues were once more the hurling champions of Tipperary, for the seventh time.

Final score:- Thurles Sarsfields 4-5, Toomevara 1-0.

Thurles Sarsfields:- Tom Semple (Captain), Jack Mooney, James 'Hawk' O'Brien, Jerry Fogarty, Anthony Carew, Jack Dwyer, Ned McGrath, Martin O'Brien, Andy Callanan, Paddy Brolan, Toss Mockler, Joe McLoughney, Hugh Shelly, Mick Hammond, Thady Dwyer, Mick Brien and Tom Kerwick. Referee – John McGrath, Youghalarra.

The county football final against Nenagh Institute was played immediately after the hurling, with many of the same players lining out again for Thurles. It was a mediocre contest with an absence of first-class football. There was no clever play and combination was non-existent. Following the scientific and

---

[6] *Tipperary Star*, 18 July 1911.

vigorous hurling match, the football was a total disappointment. The result was a draw. The Thurles men invited the Nenagh lads to play a further half-hour, but the invitation was unheeded. The Thurles followers were naturally jubilant at the great achievement of fielding two teams in the county championships and almost winning the double. The Thurles goal came in the second-half, from the boot of Hughie Shelly. In the final minutes C. Connors got the equalising score for Thurles.[7]

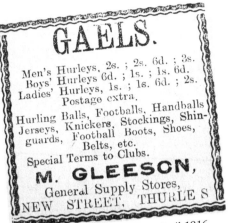

Old Thurles Advertisement – April 1916.

Thurles Mitchels:- Pádraig Hunt (Captain), Tom Kerwick, J. Curtis, E. Dillon, J. Quinn, Joe McLoughney, Anthony Carew, James O'Brien, Michael O'Brien, Paddy Brolan, Toss Mockler, Hughie Shelly, C. Connors, William Moloney, Jack Mooney, J. O'Brien. Note: Only 16 players listed.

For the replay, Templetuohy represented Mid Tipperary, having subsequently won the divisional title, beating Thurles Mitchels by 3-0 to 2-1. However, Templetuohy failed to score against Nenagh Institute at Borrisoleigh. The final score was:- Nenagh Institute 2-3, Templetuohy Nil.

As they celebrated their hurling victory in Thurles, little did they know that eighteen years would pass before the Tipperary senior hurling title would return to the 'Cathedral Town'.

MUNSTER CHAMPIONSHIP 1911

Junior Hurling

The Munster junior hurling championship was again won by Tipperary. Thurles secretary, James M. Kennedy, acted as marshal to the team, which included fellow clubmen Willie Smee, Tom Mockler, Andy Callanan, Tim Dwyer and Ned McGrath. They defeated Cork at Kilmallock by 5-4 to 0-4 and Limerick in the Munster final at Waterford by 6-4 to 2-2. At this time, the junior championship was confined to the province.

Senior Hurling

At senior level, the clash with Cork at Dungarvan, on 23 July, was a great topic for discussion for weeks. On the day, the inhabitants of Thurles were up and about early; the attendance at first Mass was proof that there was

---

[7] *Tipperary Star*, 9 Sept. 1911.

something on somewhere. At Thurles station there was a struggling stream of humanity besieging the ticket office. Even though there were not enough carriages, standing room was availed of gladly. Cooped up in the uncomfortably packed space, with the tobacco laden atmosphere adding to the unpleasantness, it was almost impossible to play a good game after five hours in the train. While Cork favoured Dungarvan as a venue, it was unpopular with Tipperary. Goals from Anthony Carew and Tim Gleeson set the Tipperary supporters at their ease as they led 2-2 to 0-1 at half-time. 'Hawk' was at his best, cool and consistent, between the sticks and the backline of Ryan, Kerwick, O'Brien and Burke could not be broken. Tom Mockler's speed on the wing was greatly admired. Jack Mooney was probably the best trained of the seventeen, and the mainstay in the centre, always on the ball and doing the right thing with it. Paddy Brolan was a star and definitely the best hurler on show. Up front, Hughie Shelly's speed and Carew's dash were invaluable. The second half was barely on when Hughie had another goal bagged. Carew was not to be outdone and before the long whistle blew he had rattled the Cork net twice. Joe McLoughney had a great game and even after a severe cut was a formidable opponent. Semple got great praise for his efficient training of the team.

Final score:- Tipperary (Thurles) 5-2, Cork (Blackrock) 0-3.

Tipperary (Thurles):- Hugh Shelly (Captain), Paddy Brolan, Jack Mooney, Mick Ryan, Anthony Carew, Tom Kerwick, Martin O'Brien, Joe McLoughney, Andy Callanan, James 'Hawk' O'Brien, Toss Mockler, Jerry Fogarty, (Thurles), Tim Gleeson (Rossmore), Bob Mockler, Phil Leahy, Joe Fitzpatrick (Two-Mile-Borris), Paddy Burke (Borris-Ileigh).

A Waterford correspondent wrote, 'If the Blues stay true to this form they should annex the 1911 All-Ireland. The new men fully justified their selection. 'Kid' Mockler is the best winger I have ever seen, his display was a treat. Watch the little red fellow, he is great and will be greater. All the old hands were in great form and appeared trained to the ounce. The team is a credit to Semple whose judgment in selection will be acknowledged to be very accurate'.

The match was over at 5.40 p.m. and the players had to run from the field to the hotel, scurry through dressing and leave the dinner on the table untasted. It required one to be a marathon runner to arrive at the station at 6.15 p.m., the time the train was scheduled to leave. A jaded hungry crowd waited and waited and the train left for the return journey one hour and a quarter late. At Clonmel the passengers had to change to another train, which eventually arrived in Thurles at 12.30 a.m.[8]

---

[8] *Tipperary Star,* 29 July 1911.

The Munster final took place at the Cork Athletic Grounds on 19 November, under the whistle of Willie Mackessy. Limerick supporters greatly outnumbered their Tipperary counterparts. John 'Tyler' Mackey led a powerful Limerick side (Castleconnell) and though the field was soft and slippery, the game was worthy of the occasion and enjoyed by the six thousand attendance. Tipperary was captained by Hughie Shelly and led 2-1 to 0-2 at the break and were seven points to the good with as many minutes remaining. An unexpected score, completely

Old Thurles advertisement – 1915.

against the run of play, set the whole Limerick camp on fire. 'Tyler' Mackey tore in from the wing to collect the puck out and for the second time in as many minutes, the 'Hawk' was picking the leather out of the net. Limerick went on to finish winners by 5-3 to 4-3. Tipperary, through Tom Semple, who trained the team, objected to Limerick claiming that they played John Mackey, who was at the time suspended. This was later over-ruled by the Munster G.A.A. Council. Semple was also unhappy with the state of the pitch, saying 'Tipperary will not ever again play in a swamp and will give a 'walk-over' unless the field is a proper one for the game'.

Tipperary (Thurles):- Hugh Shelly (Captain), Paddy Brolan, Jack Mooney, Jack Mockler, Anthony Carew, Tom Kerwick, Martin O'Brien, Joe McLoughney, Andy Callanan, James 'Hawk' O'Brien, Toss Mockler, Jerry Fogarty, (Thurles), Tim Gleeson (Rossmore), Bob Mockler, Phil Leahy, Joe Fitzpatrick (Two-Mile-Borris), Jack Kennedy (Toomevara).[9] Tom Dwan (Thurles) replaced the injured Jerry Fogarty.

Limerick, having beaten Galway in the All-Ireland semi-final, qualified to meet Kilkenny in the final. There were many difficulties in fixing this final, which dragged into 1912. Limerick's continued refusal to play, led to their suspension and Kilkenny were awarded the title. The loss of revenue from the un-played All-Ireland was sorely felt by the G.A.A.'s Central Council. In order to atone for this, they organised a substitute All-Ireland final, in which the

---

[9] *Tipperary Star*, 25 Nov. 1911.

Munster Council were asked to nominate a team to play Kilkenny. Tipperary took Limerick's place and faced Kilkenny at Dungarvan on 28 July 1912, for set of medals valued £20. It was a hard fought tie, which lacked the glamour and finesse of a 'real' final. A more strenuous test could not be imagined. Whatever the game lacked in technique, it made up for in dash and determination. Tipperary captain, Hughie Shelly, opened the scoring with a goal. Kilkenny replied with two points. Just on the stroke of half-time, Anthony Carew got Tipperary's second goal to leave the score:- Tipperary 2-0, Kilkenny 0-2 at the break. It was all Kilkenny in the second half, with Tipperary's only score a pointed free by Tim Gleeson. Towards the end, Tipperary had a Carew goal disallowed, which was seen by Kilkenny as a real 'let off'. Final score:- Kilkenny (Tullaroan) 3-3, Tipperary (Thurles) 2-1.

Tipperary (Thurles):- Hugh Shelly (Captain), Paddy Brolan, Jack Mooney, Anthony Carew, Tom Dwan, Pierce Purcell, Tom Kerwick, Martin O'Brien, Joe McLoughney, Andy Callanan, James 'Hawk' O'Brien, Toss Mockler, (Thurles), Tim Gleeson (Rossmore), Bob Mockler, Jimmy Bourke, Joe Fitzpatrick (Two-Mile-Borris), Pat 'Wedger' Meagher (Toomevara).

TOM SEMPLE – A RAILWAY GUARD

Tom Semple, Railway Guard

By 1911, Tom Semple has gained promotion with the rail company and was now a railway guard.[10] This was a position of greater responsibility with Tom no longer confined to Thurles station. This responsibility would have been taken very seriously by Tom, who valued punctuality, order and discipline, traits that come to the fore in all aspects of his life. The position of railway guard also afforded him also the opportunity of getting to know the country and he could see at first hand the importance of Thurles as a central location. As a passenger guard, Tom worked mainly on the Dublin/Cork line and also on the Thurles/Waterford line. This latter service that has been long since discontinued. During the 1920s the weekly wage of a passenger guard was three pounds and two shillings, but due to the economic state of the country in the thirties the wage was reduced by four shillings.

---

[10] NAI, Census of Ireland 1911.

CHAPTER 15

1912 – *Semple leads Tipperary to Croke Cup Success*

END OF A GLORIOUS ERA

AS Thurles Emmets had won the previous year's Mid Tipperary junior hurling championship, they were promoted to senior hurling for the 1912 competitions. So, Thurles G.A.A., for the first time, had two teams in the Mid Tipperary senior championship-Emmets and Sarsfields. Emmet's term as seniors was short-lived, losing to Emly in the first round by the narrowest of margins, 2-2 to 2-1.

Thurles Emmets:- Mick Leahy (Captain), M. O'Meara, J. Carroll, J. Kavanagh, E. Ryan, D. Ryan, Justin McCarthy, P. McCarthy, D. Bourke, J. Shelly, William Moloney, J. Maher, T. Maher, John Devane, E. Purcell, J. Shelly, J. Maher.[1]

Sarsfields were drawn against Horse and Jockey and following a fierce and virulent struggle in Thurles Sporting Grounds, the referee declared the result a draw 2-2 each. 'The Jockey had led by 2-1 to 1-2 at half-time, Hughie Shelly scoring the Thurles goal. It was a good hard and fast game, with no unseemly outbursts. Tom Semple though injured played on wearing a large bandage on his head. The Sarsfields team was strengthened by the transfer of Tim Gleeson, Drombane, to the club.

Thurles Sarsfields:- Tom Semple (Captain), Hugh Shelly, Tim Gleeson, Jack Mockler, Toss Mockler, Paddy Brolan, Joe McLoughney, Jack Mooney, Tom Kerwick, James 'Hawk' O'Brien, Martin O'Brien, Mick Hammond, Anthony Carew, Tom Dwan, Andy Callanan, Jerry Fogarty, Willie Smee.

The Thurles hurlers had to head to the 'Jockey for the replay. From every corner of the Premier County, the light-hearted sons and daughters of Tipperary

---

[1] *Tipperary Star*, 13 Apr. 1912.

poured into the venue for the re-play. For miles around the 'Jockey, on every side, the roads were absolutely congested with every sort of vehicle: motors, waggonettes, side-cars, bikes, motor-bikes and drays. At Horse and Jockey cross, a surging, swaying, good-humoured, well-conducted mass of about ten thousand, eager to see two of the best teams in Ireland do battle with the camán, converged. There was great disappointment when it was heard that Tom Semple, Tom Kerwick, Joe McLoughney and Jack Mockler were unable to line-out due to injury. They were replaced by Eddie McGrath, Jer Hayes, Mick Hammond and Pierce Purcell. In the first-half Thurles opened the scoring when Toss Mockler passed to Carew for a point. A goal followed by a point from Andy Callanan and a Shelly goal left the half-time score Sarsfields 2-2, Horse and Jockey 1-0. The 'Jockey started the second period in great style with a point, but the tide started to turn against then when Toss Mockler goaled. A fierce dash for goal by the 'Jockey resulted in an exciting tussle around the Thurles posts. An altercation occurred between some of the players and things looked threatening. Great credit was due to the crowd for not invading the pitch at this time. The referee came up and ordered Jack Gleeson of the Horse and Jockey team to leave the field. Gleeson persisted in his refusal and the referee concluded that he had no option but to award the match to Thurles on the score:- Thurles Sarsfields 3-3, Horse and Jockey 1-0.[2] Jack Gleeson, Templemore, was in charge of the whistle. Thurles were later awarded the game by the Mid Tipperary board.

Boherlahan had beaten Emly in their semi-final but provided little opposition to Sarsfields in the final at the Horse and Jockey. This game was played in torrential rain. A goal from Toss Mockler and another from Willie Smee, along with a Brolan point, left the half time score: Sarsfields 2-1 to nil at half-time. Hugh Shelly had the green flag waving again early in the second-half and two from Anthony Carew secured the title for Thurles. The 'Hawk' was brilliant throughout.

Final score:- Thurles Sarsfields 5-1, Boherlahan 1-0.[3]

Thurles:- Hugh Shelly (Captain), James 'Hawk' O'Brien, Anthony Carew. Pierce Purcell, Mick Hammond, Eddie McGrath, Toss Mockler, Tom Kerwick, Willie Smee, Thady Dwyer, Joe McLoughney, Paddy Brolan, Jack Mooney, Jerry Fogarty, Tom Dwan, Martin O'Brien, Jer Hayes.

In the county semi-final Sarsfields played Toomevara at Nenagh. The game was originally fixed for Cashel, but Toomevara were not agreeable to travel there. In a letter to the *'Nenagh News'* they stated that they would let Thurles

---

[2] *Tipperary Star*, 1 June 1912.
[3] Philip Fogarty, *Tipperary's G.A.A. Story* (Thurles, 1960), pp. 175-6.

have a walk-over, rather than go to Cashel again, as they had done last year. The county board eventually agreed to refix the game for Nenagh. Because of the difficulty in fixing the game, it was not played until 16 February 1913. Thurles were favourites and there was great interest in the game, with over two thousand spectators attending the Showgrounds. The railway company had to be given a guarantee of £18-15-0 to run a special train from Thurles. The Toomevara 'Greyhounds' were now a more formidable team, anxious to uphold their reputation for hurling and to regain former glory. Toomevara had trained well for the final and were anxious to prove that there were hurlers in north Tipperary equal to those in the other divisions. Thurles were but a shadow of themselves, going down to rampant 'Toome'. Final score: Toomevara 4-5, Thurles Sarsfields 0-1. This defeat of Thurles marked the end of a long period of dominance by 'The Blues' of Tipperary hurling.

CROKE CUP 1912

This was a competition for the runners-up in the previous year's provincial finals. Tipperary, as defeated finalists from 1911 and represented by Thurles played Dublin (Faughs) in the final. In preparation for the game, Tom Semple organised a challenge game among the club's hurlers. He captained one side and Mick Leahy led the other.

Dr Croke Cup Medal 1912

Dr Croke Cup

Thurles No.1 Team:- Tom Semple, Hugh Shelly, Jack Mockler, Toss Mockler, Paddy Brolan, Joe McLoughney, J. Mooney, T. Kerwick, M. O'Brien, J. O'Brien, M. Brien, E. McGrath, A. Carew, Tom Dwan, Thady Dwyer, Andy Callanan, Jerry Fogarty, Willie Smee, Jack Cahill.

Thurles No. 2 Team:- Mick Leahy, M. O'Meara, J. Cleary, T. Quinn, P. McCarthy, J. McCarthy, T. Ryan, S. Ryan, W. Shortt, T. Maher, J. Maher, M. Dwyer, M. McCarthy, P. Purcell, J. Purcell, D. Burke, J. Kavanagh, E. Purcell, E. Ryan.

The Croke Cup final was a home fixture for the 'Blues' and Thurles Sports Ground was packed to capacity on 21 April 1912. Because of the poor weather only one hundred supporters travelled on the special train from Dublin. Tom Semple was there to lead his men and this would be his last appearance in an inter-county contest. Sarsfields, in a phenomenal rally, covered themselves in glory and won the trophy by 6-3 to 4-3.

Tipperary (Thurles Selection):- Tom Semple (Captain), Tom Dwan (Goal), Hugh Shelly, Paddy Brolan, Jack Mockler, Anthony Carew, Martin O'Brien, Joe McLoughney, Andy Callanan, Toss Mockler, Mick Hammond, Jerry Fogarty, Ned McGrath, Tim Gleeson (Thurles), Bob Mockler, Phil Leahy, Joe Fitzpatrick (Horse and Jockey).

MUNSTER CHAMPIONSHIP 1912

Tipperary (Thurles) played Clare at Ennis on 18 August and were lucky to survive a fearless onslaught from the Bannermen. Tipperary 3-3, Clare 2-3. In the Munster final on 27 October, captained by Hugh Shelly, Tipperary faced the old enemy, Cork, in Dungarvan. The attendance of 17,681 witnessed a hard struggle. Disappointment was Tipperary's fate in an unusual game, in which they failed to score in the second-half. Goal scoring was the order of the day, but Cork scored most of them. The final score was:- Cork 5-1, Tipperary 3-1.

Tipperary lined out as follows:- James 'Hawk' O'Brien (Thurles), Martin O'Brien (Thurles), Tom Kerwick (Thurles), Tom Dwan (Thurles), Johnny Leahy (Boherlahan), Jack Doherty (Boherlahan), Tim Gleeson (Thurles), Paddy 'Wedger' Meagher (Toomevara), Jack Mooney (Thurles), Jimmy Bourke (Horse & Jockey), Andy Callanan (Thurles), Jack Mockler (Thurles), Bob Mockler (Horse and Jockey), Toss Mockler (Thurles), Jack Gleeson (Horse and Jockey), Paddy Brolan (Thurles), Hugh Shelly (Captain).

This game was filmed by Gaumont Films for showing in Ireland and to Irish exiles in the U.S.A. The film was first shown at the Assembly Rooms Picturedrome, Cork, the following Wednesday and then moved on to Limerick and Wexford.[4] There, loud and frequent applause was heard at intervals during the performances, which testified to the great enjoyment that was derived by all present.[5]

Following the game, the legendary goalkeeper of the 'Blues', James 'Hawk' O'Brien, announced his retirement. He had given sterling service to Thurles and Tipperary and the memory of his 'saves' lived long in the local folklore of the town. Among the people of Thurles, there was a warm desire to provide a testimonial through means of a tournament or otherwise, to give a suitable send-off to the 'Hawk', on the occasion of his retirement. A collection of subscriptions was organized.[6]

Munster Final 1912 was filmed by Gaumont Film Company.

Kilkenny went on to win the All-Ireland, defeating Cork. Commenting on the game, Tom Semple said, 'Kilkenny are the luckiest team in Ireland today or any other day. They are All-Ireland champions now and that is the thing that matters'. James M. Kennedy added, 'Cork were most unlucky and were winners on the play'.[7]

The year 1912 marked the end of an era in more senses than one. It was the last championship contested by seventeen-a-side teams and the year saw the last appearance of Tom Semple on the inter-county scene, but he would play at club level for a time. This was the last fling for the great 'Blues' combination, as the balance of power in Tipperary hurling moved northwards to Toomevara's 'Greyhounds'.

Tipperary, Thurles selection, captained by Hugh Shelly, won the Croke Cup on 30 March 1913. The final against Laois was fixed for an earlier date but owing to poor weather conditions, Tipperary were unable to travel and Laois were awarded a walk-over, but declined to take it. The match was re-fixed for Maryborough (Portlaoise) and was a fairly even contest with Tipperary ahead by four points at half-time. A lucky second-half goal kept them ahead and there they stayed. Tipperary 5-3, Laois 3-2. Six Thurles 'Blues' were on the team:- Hugh Shelly (Captain), Tim Gleeson, Tom Kerwick, Tom Dwan, Thady Dwyer and Mick Hammond.[8]

---

[4] *Evening Echo,* 28 Oct. 1912, 14 July 1913.
[5] *Note:* G.A.A. matches drew the attention of several local picture house owners, most prominently James T. Jameson – who ran the Rotunda, Dublin and a circuit of provincial venues – and Alex McEwan, a Cork-based impresario, who operated from the Assembly Rooms Picturedrome.
[6] *Tipperary Star,* 8 Aug. 1912.
[7] Phil O'Neill, *History of the G.A.A. 1910-1930* (Kilkenny, 1931), pp. 62-3.
[8] Ibid, p. 69.

Toomevara, captained by Pat 'Wedger' Meagher, won Tipperary hurling championships in 1910, 1912, 1913, 1914 and 1919. Tipperary had their first outing in the 1913 Munster championship with an easy victory over Waterford, 6-0 to 2-2. Congress had issued a new rule that each county must wear a distinctive jersey in inter-county championships. Initially Tipperary had decided on black and amber but then referred the matter to James. M. Kennedy of the Thurles club. He suggested the adoption of colours based on the arms of the kings of Cashel. These featured gold cross keys on a circular shield of crimson red. Kennedy's suggestion of a crimson jersey with gold neck and arm bands and the crossed keys of the kings of Cashel on the centre was adopted. These new colours were first worn in the 1913 Munster final. The jerseys were supplied by Thurles draper, Denis McCarthy. Cork appeared in blue and saffron. The game was hot and furious and resulted in a famous win for the 'Toome' selection with people disbelieving the final score of – Tipperary 8-2, Cork 4-3. Two of the goals came from the stick of Hugh Shelly in the first-half.

Tipperary, Toomevara selection – All-Ireland Finalists 1913
Front row (l.-r.): Bill Kelly, Jim Murphy, Hugh Shelly, Elias 'Bud' O'Keeffe. Middle row (l.-r.): Ned Guilmartin, Jack Harty, Frank McGrath, Patrick 'Wedger' Meagher (Captain), Stephen Hackett. Back row (l.-r.): Jack Kennedy Jack O'Meara, Ned Cawley, Jack Raleigh, Mick Ryan, Jim O'Meara, Paddy Kennedy.

However, Tipperary (Toomevara selection) lost the All-Ireland final to Kilkenny (Mooncoin selection) by 2-4 to 1-2. Toomevara won the Thomond Feis tournament in 1915 and 1916. Some Thurles 'Blues' were regulars on the Toomevara selections, including Hugh Shelly, Paddy Brolan, Tim Gleeson and Mick Hammond.

CHAPTER 16

The Croke-Fennelly Cup

THE Fethard tournament was first contested in October 1908. This inter-county tournament was organised by Archdeacon Innocent Ryan, the pastor of Fethard, for the purpose of paying off a parochial debt, due to the renovation of the local church and the building of a parochial residence.[1] This hurling and football[2] tournament was to attain a status, seldom achieved by such a competition. This was mainly due to the fact that the trophy for the winners in hurling was of an exceptionally historic nature. Made of solid silver and lined with the finest porcelain, it had been presented to Archbishop Thomas Croke in 1886 by three exiled Irish in America. The inscription on it reads:

The Croke-Fennelly Cup

---

[1] *Tipperary G.A.A. Yearbook 1971*, p.41.

 T. F. O'Sullivan, *The Story of the G.A.A.* (Dublin, 1916), p. 192.

[2] *Note:* The trophy for the football tournament was the Burke Tally-Ho Challenge Cup. This was presented by Richard Burke of Grove, Fethard, who was master of the Tipperary foxhounds. It was Irish made of solid silver and bore Celtic design.

The Unchanged and Unchangeable
Archbishop and Patriot
The Joy and Pride
Of
The Sea-divided Gael
This slight tribute
From
Three of them
1886

No information is available on the 'three of them'. The trophy was in the form of a large silver jug, swinging on silver uprights, with two silver gilt-lined goblets on the sides and a silver ewer beneath. The uprights terminated in a flexible artistic handle.[3]

Following the death of Archbishop Croke in July 1902, the silverware passed into the possession of his successor, Archbishop Thomas Fennelly. In 1908 he gave the trophy to Archdeacon Innocent Ryan for the purposes of the Fethard tournament. The trophy became known as the Croke-Fennelly Cup and could be won outright by any club winning the tournament on two occasions.[4] Tipperary, Kilkenny, Limerick and Cork participated in the tournament.

In the semi-final of the tournament Tipperary, Thurles selection, played Redmonds of Cork. Thurles were very determined to win, particularly as their defeat in James's Park, Kilkenny had hurt their pride and they wanted to make an emphatic statement that in Tipperary they would never brook

Archdeacon Innocent Ryan, Fethard.

Archbishop Thomas Fennelly (1845-1927)

---

[3] T.F. O'Sullivan, *The Story of the G.A.A.* (Dublin, 1916), p. 192.
[4] *Note:* The Croke-Fennelly Cup is on display at Lár na Páirce – The Museum of Gaelic Games, Thurles, Co. Tipperary.

defeat. The Cork side was not at full strength, as some of their prominent players missed the train. Thurles had their full team and wasted no time in showing their determination as their first dash ended in a goal. It was all Thurles in the first half, notching up 2-8, while Redmonds failed to score. They did not fare much better in the second half, Thurles having their own way in all quarters. Final score: Thurles 4-12, Redmonds 0-3.

Tipperary (Thurles): Tom Semple (Captain), Hugh Shelly, Jack Mockler, Martin O'Brien, Jack Mooney, Tom Kenna, Tom Kerwick, Paddy Brolan, Joe Moloughney, Anthony Carew, James 'Hawk' O'Brien (Thurles), Joe O'Keeffe, Bill Harris, Bob Mockler, Jack Gleeson (Horse and Jockey), Tim Gleeson (Holycross), Pat Fitzgerald (Glengoole).

The final of the prestigious tournament was contested by the Thurles selection and Limerick's Young Irelands on 12 September 1909. The venue was Flynn's field on the Cashel road. Admission to the final was four pence and for an extra two-pence access was allowed to an exclusive enclosure and for prime viewing of the proceedings the Grand Stand was available for one penny extra.[5] It was a great day in Fethard with bands from Ballinonty, Cassestown, and Littleton, entertaining the gathering and Archbishop Fennelly was present to throw in the ball. The Shannonsiders had high hopes of success and by half-time this was justified, as they led by 1-4 to 0-5. The game re-started with the 'Blues' at once clamouring for position but Limerick fought back obstinately and heroically, and showed no signs of surrender. A free taken by Semple was blocked. Coming in with a rush Carew got the ball from Shelly and scored the deciding goal.[6] Towards the close however the tables turned. The Mid Tipperary men broke their bonds and mounted into a prominence that gave them victory, and the treasured cup for the first time.

Final score: Thurles 1-11, Limerick 1-7.

Thurles: Tom Semple (Captain), Jack Mooney, Tom Kerwick, Martin O'Brien, Jack Mockler, Tom Kenna, Hugh Shelly, Paddy Bourke, James 'Hawk' O'Brien, Paddy Brolan, Anthony Carew, Mickey Ryan (Mac) and Tim Dwyer (Thurles), Jimmy Bourke (Two-Mile-Borris), Pat and John Fitzgerald (Glengoole) Tim Gleeson, (Drombane).[7] Referee: M. J. Fielding, Mooncoin.

The famous trophy was presented to Tom Semple by Archbishop Fennelly and in the weeks and months following the victory, the Croke Fennelly Cup was on display in Anthony Carew's window, South Main St., Thurles.

---

[5] Micheál Aherne(Ed)., *Fethard, Coolmoyne and Killusty G.A.A. Story* (Fethard, 1988), p. 262.
[6] *Sport*, 18 Sept. 1909.
[7] Philip Fogarty, *Tipperary's G.A.A. Story* (Thurles, 1960), p. 145.

CROKE-FENNELLY CUP 1913

As holders of this trophy, Thurles G.A.A. were invited in 1913 to defend their title. The 'Blues' were determined to repeat their initial success over Limerick and thus win the Croke-Fennelly Cup outright. Tipperary (Thurles) and Limerick (Caherline) were fixed to meet at Fethard on 10 August 1913. Special trains ran from Limerick, Kilmallock, Clonmel and Nenagh. Two bands were in attendance – Clonmel War Piper's Band and Thurles Confraternity Brass and Reed band. Despite the torrential rain, there was a very good attendance. Thurles had a large contingent of supporters present. The tournament trophies were on display and much admired. Because of the weather and the fact that many Limerick hurlers did not travel, there was much speculation as to whether the game would take place at all. Following much discussion J. O'Neill, secretary of Caherline hurling club, declared against playing and offered a 'walk over'. The referee then awarded the match to Tipperary (Thurles) without a ball being struck. And so the Croke-Fennelly Cup, became the property of Thurles Sarsfields G.A.A. Club.[8]

The inscription on the cup reads: -

Presented by Most Rev. Dr. Fennelly,
Archbishop of Cashel,
To the Best Hurling team in Ireland.
Played at Fethard, Co. Tipperary.
Won by Thurles Blues.

Anthony Carew, Thurles G.A.A. Secretary

Tom Semple, Thurles G.A.A. Chairman

[8] *Tipperary Star*, 9, 16 Aug. 1913.

James Maher, Thurles G.A.A. Treasurer.   *Rev. J.J. Meagher P.P., Tipperary G.A.A. Chairman.*

This historic cup had been in the possession of the Thurles club, since they won it outright in 1913. Anthony Carew, the 'Blues' famed full-forward, who was also the club's secretary at the time became the custodian of the Croke-Fennelly Cup. Early in 1930, a fire occurred in Carew's licensed premises on Lower Main Street (Liberty Square), Thurles. Carew's premises and the adjoining building, a drapery owned by Eddie Flynn, were gutted. During the course of the fire, Flynn, perturbed for the safety of his own business, was in the ruins of Carew's and noticed the famous trophy engulfed by flames in the attic. He was successful in rescuing it, in a tarnished condition. The wooden base was completely burned away. Knowing the history of the cup, Eddie informed club treasurer, James Maher, who in the presence of Garda Laurence Kinsella, took possession of the cup. Club chairman, Tom Semple and treasurer, James Maher, were instrumental in having the cup restored to its original condition.[9] A new base was fashioned by Michael Power, a skilled craftsman who worked at Thurles Sugar factory, while the renowned Dublin firm Hopkins and Hopkins refurbished the silverware.

From 1930, the trophy was in the possession of James Maher, Parnell Street, on behalf of the Thurles club. During the G.A.A. jubilee celebrations in 1934, the trophy was put on display in the presbytery on Cathedral Street, at the request of Rev. J.J. Meagher, Thurles, who was then chairman of Tipperary County Board.

In August 1942, when Rev. J.J. Meagher was appointed parish priest of

---

[9] John Lanigan, *Tipperary G.A.A. Yearbook* (1971), p.39.

Anacarty, he brought the cup with him from Thurles to the west Tipperary village. Here in the parochial house it remained until the mid 1940s, when James Maher collected it and returned it to Thurles. It was put on display in the Sarsfields trophy case in Glenmorgan House, Parnell Street, Thurles.

In February 1948, it was decided by Thurles Sarsfields Club, to return the cup to the archbishop's house in Thurles. Archbishop Jeremiah Kinane accepted the cup and the following inscription was added to the wooden plinth:-

Receiving the Croke-Fennelly Cup from Archbishop Dermot Clifford for Lár na Páirce, Thurles, in 1994 (l.-r.): Seamus J. King, Chairman, Lár na Páirce; Archbishop Dermot Clifford; Liam Ó Donnchú, Chairman, Thurles Sarsfields Club.

Coiste Chumann Iomána agus Peile na Sáirséalach, Dúrlas Éile,
a bhronn an corn seo ar a Ghrásta, An Dochtúir Sároirmhidhneach
Ó Cuinneáin, Árdeaspag Chaisil agus Imleach Iúir, i Mí Feabhra 1948.
Coiméad an corn sa Phálás, Dúrlas Éile feasta.[10]

In 1994, with the opening of Lár na Páirce – Museum of Gaelic Games, in Thurles, Archbishop of Cashel and Emly, Dr Dermot Clifford felt that this was the ideal location for the historic trophy and with the agreement of Thurles Sarsfields Club presented it for display to the new museum.

---

[10] Ibid, p.41.

CHAPTER 17

The Croke Memorial and Croke Park

EVER SINCE the death of Archbishop Croke in July 1902, it was the wish of the Gaelic Athletic Association that the memory of its first patron and valued mentor would be suitably perpetuated. At the annual Congress of the association which assembled in the Confraternity Hall, Thurles, on 8 January 1905, the following motion was passed unanimously – 'That the Gaels of Ireland erect a memorial or some token, to the memory of the late Archbishop of Cashel'. It was proposed by Martin Brennan, Ballingarry, who was Tipperary county secretary, and was greeted with acclamation by the delegates.[1]

No progress was made in the following two years and when congress met at the same venue in Thurles on 24 February 1907 the delegates authorized Central Council to appoint a sub-committee to

Archbishop Croke Memorial in Thurles

[1] T.F. O'Sullivan, *The Story of the G.A.A.* (Dublin, 1916), p. 170.

progress their decision regarding the memorial but Central Council failed to take action. It was more or less a similar situation in the years that followed, with congress passing motions and resolutions demanding action, but with little action being taken.

At the G.A.A. congress held on 16 April 1911, on the proposition of James M. Kennedy, Thurles, the Central Council was requested to take immediate steps to bring the Dr Croke memorial to a satisfactory conclusion. Kennedy further proposed that every county board in Ireland should set apart a certain day for the holding of a tournament, the proceeds to be handed over to the memorial committee. This was passed.[2] It was estimated that the fund for this purpose now stood at £138.

CROKE MEMORIAL TOURNAMENTS

By 1913 the funds to hand for the erection of a memorial to Croke amounted to £500. Of this £100 had come from the profit on the visit of the American hurlers, while both Munster and Leinster councils contributed £25 each. With a view to augmenting this sum and following Tipperary's protestations, the Central Council decided to take James M. Kennedy's proposal more seriously and initiated medal tournaments in both hurling and football. These were a great success and became known as the Croke Memorial tournaments. The number of counties taking part was small, five in football and nine in hurling, but these counties were considered the best in the country. Such was the calibre of the tournaments that they were put on a par with the All-Ireland championships.

In the first Croke Memorial hurling tournament, Tipperary had a bye in the first round and their first outing in the tournament was against Galway. Captained by 'Wedger' Meagher they won easily, by 7-3 to 1-4. Tipperary accounted for Cork in the semi-final. They played Kilkenny in the final at Dungarvan on 1 June and Tipperary, now a Toomevara selection, turned on the style for a convincing victory, by 5-4 to 1-1. There was a huge attendance, with the result that many were not able to gain admission. The gate receipts amounted to £437. The Tipperary team officials took the unusual step of bringing the team down to Dungarvan the day before the final and arranged and played a practice match on the morning of the game.[3] Captained by Pat 'Wedger' Meagher, the team included Hugh Shelly, Tim Gleeson and Toss Mockler from the Thurles club. Before the game, Tom Semple's advice to the team was, 'Keep close to your men from the start. Make the pace and the day is yours'. He then sprinkled them with Holy Water.[4]

[2] Phil O'Neill, *History of the G.A.A. 1910-1930* (Kilkenny, 1931), p. 32.
[3] Pádraig O'Toole, *The Glory and the Anguish* (Galway, 1984), p. 75.
[4] Donal Shanahan (ed.), *Toomevara G.A.A. 1885-1985* (1985), p. 8.

The Croke Memorial tournaments were an unqualified success, in particular in football. Kerry and Louth met in the final at Jones' Road, Dublin (later Croke Park) and such was the interest in the match that major improvements had to be made to the grounds by the owner, Frank Dineen, and the Central Council withdrew its usual policy of allowing ladies free admission.[5] The capacity of the venue was now increased by ten thousand. The teams did not disappoint and the game ended in a draw. The replay was watched by thirty-two thousand spectators and many more watched from the railway line. The teams were level at half-time but Kerry went on to win the match by 2-4 to 0-5.

Not in their wildest dreams could the Central Council have envisaged the success of the tournaments. According to the minutes of Central Council, their original target was £1,000 but with expenses paid the total funds amounted to nearly £2,400.

The idea began now to grow among some of the G.A.A. authorities that instead of a statue in Thurles, that a stadium in Dublin might be a more relevant memorial to Croke. Central Council's feeling was that the G.A.A. as a whole should benefit from the substantial fund rather than one local area in Tipperary, even though it was the birthplace of the association and the seat of Archbishop Croke. One could be excused for wondering if the G.A.A. authorities had organized the Croke tournament with a view to purchasing a permanent venue in Dublin, which it certainly needed for holding its principal events. However, the G.A.A. in Tipperary had assumed that all the money collected over the years would be spent on a memorial of some kind in Thurles.

At a Central Council meeting on 6 July 1913, a Galway delegate proposed that the Jones' Road ground be purchased as a memorial to Archbishop Croke. Pat McGrath, Tipperary, objected and said that the funds were collected, not for the purchase of grounds in Dublin, but for a memorial in Thurles. On hearing of this proposal, Tipperary county board launched a bitter attack on Central Council claiming that they had defaulted on the agreement to invest the money totally on a memorial to be sited in Co. Tipperary. Tom Semple further declared that they would accept nothing less than the entire amount collected. 'The idea of buying a field to perpetuate the memory of the illustrious Dr. Croke is ridiculous. We would be unworthy of the name of Tipperary men if they did not fight Central Council.'[6] Dan Fraher, Dungarvan, suggested that as an alternative that £1,000 be given to Thurles, and the balance go towards the purchase of the grounds. No agreement was reached but it was decided to send a deputation, led by G.A.A. secretary Luke O'Toole, to Thurles to meet

---

[5] Tim Carey, *Croke Park – A History* (Dublin, 2004). p. 34.
[6] *Tipperary Star*, 6 Dec. 1913.

Archbishop Fennelly and Fr. Michael Bannon, Adm., Thurles. Due to illness, the archbishop was unable to receive the deputation, but they met Fr. Michael Bannon Adm. O'Toole first sounded the priest on the earlier idea of the Central Council that a new marble altar and stained-glass windows be erected in the cathedral. Fr. Bannon had an answer to this opening move, stating that there was no room for any more altars, and all the windows were already in stained-glass. It was, he firmly told O'Toole, the view of the clergy that a bronze statue of Croke should be erected. He further suggested that a suitable site for the statue was with the one of Archbishop Leahy in front of Thurles cathedral.[7] In addition, a donation of from £500 to £600 to rebuild the Confraternity Hall would be welcome. This hall, had been originally erected around 1900, partly with G.A.A. money, had recently been destroyed by fire; although covered by only £1,000 insurance, it would cost £1,600 to rebuild. According to Tom Semple, Fr. Bannon told O'Toole that it was not up to him to make the decision on what form a memorial to Croke should take and that he should speak with the Tipperary Gaels about the matter.

On 27 July, the Central Council made three important decisions. The bronze statue was agreed on unanimously, £300 would be allocated to Fr. Bannon towards the new Confraternity Hall, on condition that it be called The Croke Memorial Hall, and the rest of the money would be used to purchase a ground in Dublin to be called Croke Memorial Ground. Pat McGrath, Tipperary, proposed that the matter be referred to the next annual congress, but the motion was passed by nine votes to three. This decision outraged Tipperary and sparked off a major row between the Tipperary county board and the Central Council.

At a meeting of the Tipperary county board on 28 September, delegates voiced their anger at the small amount of money allocated to erect the Croke memorial in Thurles. Tom Semple stated, 'It is extraordinary that the officials of the Central Council imagined they could come to terms on the matter with people outside the Gaelic body. What they (Tipperary) wanted was a public monument to Dr. Croke and not one on any private grounds'.

G.A.A. PURCHASE JONES' ROAD

Following their decision to purchase a playing ground in Dublin, Central Council selected three delegates to inspect several grounds to help them decide which one to buy. When the council met in August the three advised that there were but two suitable grounds – Jones' Road which contained 9.25 acres, the asking price being £4,000 and the second property was in Elm Park, which consisted of 15 acres costing £5,000. Since 1896 the G.A.A. were using the

---

[7] St Patrick's College, Thurles, Philip Fogarty, Research notes, (unpublished work).

Croke Park in the early days.

Jones' Road grounds for their games. After the owner of the land, Maurice Butterley, died in 1908, the property was sold by his daughter, Mary, to Francis (Frank) B. Dineen for £3,250. He was a former president and general secretary of the G.A.A.

The council decided to inspect Elm Park, and Frank Dineen, fearing the council might buy it brought down his asking price for Jones' Road to £3,625 and then finally to £3,500. In a vote taken at Central Council on 4 October 1913, by a majority of one vote, eight to seven, it was decided to purchase Jones' Road. The venue was to be known in future as Croke Memorial Park, later shortened to Croke Park. A down payment of £1,500 was made and the balance followed. On 18 December 1913, ownership of Jones' Road grounds passed from Frank Dineen to Daniel Fraher and others, trustees of the G.A.A. and subsequently on 11 December 1914 from the trustees to The Gaelic Athletic Association Ltd. Including legal fees, the total cost of purchase was £3,641. The G.A.A. finally had a home of its own.[8]

While matters seemed solved in Dublin in October, Tipperary G.A.A. were seething with anger as the dispute continued and had serious implications for the Tipperary senior hurlers, Toomevara selection, prior to their All-Ireland final with Kilkenny, fixed for 2 November. Just one week prior to the All-Ireland final, Tipperary county board met and discussed what action could be taken against Central Council. No Toomevara delegates were present. After much debate about what action should be taken, Tom Semple said that a letter be sent to the secretary of the Central Council requesting that the All-Ireland final be

---

[8] Tim Carey, *Croke Park – A History* (Dublin, 2004), p. 38.

postponed until after a discussion on the Croke Memorial funds at the G.A.A. Congress at Easter and that Toomevara be written to and asked to 'fall in line with the decision of the county board'. The Toomevara supporters were naturally slow about falling into line with the proposal regarding strong action. Tom Kerwick added, 'After all, what are medals, what is an All-Ireland championship, compared with a monument to the great Dr Croke'. To the delight of the delegates Andy Mason, Mid Tipperary secretary, said, 'Only for Dr Croke very likely we would not have any All-Ireland or any championships at all.'

What transpired between then and 2 November is not clear. Toomevara at first agreed not to play the final but then changed their minds. The uncertainty and the divided loyalties in the Tipperary camp was in stark contrast to the preparation of the Kilkenny men, who beat Tipperary by 2-4 to 1-2.[9]

LEGAL PROCEEDINGS

The Croke Memorial dispute dragged on and at Tipperary county convention, held at Lambe's Hotel, Thurles, in February 1914, on a vote of fifty-two to thirty; it was decided to initiate legal proceedings against the Central Council to stop them from disposing of the funds prior to the 1914 Congress.

Tipperary county board protested in the names of the following:- Tom Semple, Eamonn Mansfield, James M. Kennedy, Michael Maher, William Butler,

Confraternity Hall, erected in 1901 on the site of the old Bridewell, on Pudding Lane (Jail Street), now O'Donovan Rossa Street. (Image courtesy of the National Library of Ireland)

---

[9] Philip Fogarty, *Tipperary's G.A.A. Story* (Thurles, 1960), p. 187.

Tom Kerwick, Andy Mason, E.D. Ryan, J. Cahill, D. O'Leary, D.B. English, D.P. Walsh and T. McDonnell. Tipperary county board instructed its solicitor, Mr Carrigan, Thurles, to commence litigation to stop Central Council from disposing of the Croke Memorial fund in the manner decided by the council. As Tom Semple put it, 'What object had the teams in view when they competed in the tournament? None, other than the erection of a public monument in Thurles. That has not been done. We have been insulted'. The Central Council had received a writ from Tipperary county board for the recovery of the Croke Memorial funds. The dispute dragged on for some months until Luke O'Toole, encouraged by a £200 grant from the Munster Council, skilfully piloted through Congress a compromise motion, even though some of the Congress delegates were not impressed with the actions of the Tipperary men. The Central Council, along with financing the memorial statue, agreed to increase their donation to £1,000 towards the cost of rebuilding the Confraternity Hall, on the agreement that it be named the Croke Memorial Hall.[10] While Tipperary County Board withdrew its legal action, they had always felt that that the money raised for the Croke Memorial should be used only for a memorial in Tipperary.[11]

SELECTING A SITE

The next difficulty for the G.A.A. in Tipperary was to agree on a site for the memorial. G.A.A. general secretary, Luke O'Toole wrote to Thurles Urban Council requesting a meeting, with a view to selecting a site for the memorial. This was arranged and G.A.A. President Alderman Jim Nolan and Luke O'Toole travelled to Thurles. Messrs. William Butler, John Lambe and J.L. Johnston conducted them to all possible sites for the memorial. The site favoured by the deputation was not acceptable to the urban council. It was agreed that further suggestions would be sent to O'Toole. Long and weary discussions regarding the form and site of the Croke Memorial ushered in the year 1915. These were confined principally to Thurles. Some people favoured the re-construction of the Confraternity Hall for the benefit of Gaels socially. Others were in favour of a monument in Liberty Square, Thurles. The urban council were requested to provide a site on Liberty Square, but they passed the following resolution, at their January meeting: 'That we regret having to refuse the request of the Tipperary County Board for a site on the Square of Thurles for the Croke Memorial, as the Square is already overloaded on fair and market-days and would not admit to further obstruction'.[12] This prompted the Cashel Urban Council to offer a site on their Main Street. This move concentrated the minds in Thurles and the present site, at the western end of Liberty Square, was agreed.

---

[10] Pádraig O'Toole, *The Glory and the Anguish* (Galway, 1984), p. 83.
[11] Marcus de Búrca, *The Story of the GAA* (Dublin, 1990), p. 123.
[12] *Tipperary Star*, 30 Jan. 1915.

Central Council adopted the design of Francis William Doyle-Jones,[13] of London, and gave him charge of the work.[14] His proposal, which was accepted, was a three-sided column in Irish limestone with steps. The chief figure would be eight feet, six inches in height and be made of bronze, bringing the total height of the memorial to twenty-four feet. The protestations of Mid Tipperary secretary, Andy Mason, regarding the commissioning of an Englishman to do the work, went unheeded.

A few years drifted by and there was much disappointment that the progress with the erection of the memorial was so slow. At the 1919 county convention, M.F. Crowe, representing the Central Council, explained that the delay was due to:-

1. The designer, William Doyle-Jones couldn't get bronze as, at the outbreak of the war, the British government prohibited the use of bronze for any purpose other than in the war effort.

2. William Doyle-Jones was commandeered by the British government to carry out work in aviation design.

William Doyle-Jones's working model of the memorial.

3. When conscription was introduced in Britain, the age was raised to 41 years. William Doyle-Jones was thus liable for conscription.

Fr M.K. Ryan, chairman, felt that these excuses were not reasonable, as the war was now over for some time. The money, £1,100, was in the bank to fulfill the contract. It was agreed that if the memorial wasn't erected by 15 October, that the contract with Doyle-Jones would be deemed broken.

In December 1919, Doyle-Jones attended the Central Council meeting. He promised to have the foundation of the monument made for St. Patrick's Day, so that they could organise a ceremony of celebration. He further promised to have the total project completed by August.

---

[13] Francis William Doyle-Jones (1873-1938) was of Irish descent and was born at Hartlepool, Durham, U.K. He produced several memorial statues in Ireland: to John Mandeville at Mitchelstown, Co. Cork (1906), to Canon P.A. Sheehan at Doneraile, Co. Cork, and to Cardinal Patrick O'Donnell at St Eunan's Cathedral, Letterkenny, Co. Donegal (1929). His last Irish monument, unveiled in 1938, the year of his death, was a six-metre tall granite statue of Saint Patrick at Saul, Co. Down.

[14] Philip Fogarty, *Tipperary's G.A.A. Story* (Thurles, 1960), p. 196.

FOUNDATION STONE LAID

On St Patrick's Day 1920, Archbishop Harty laid the foundation stone of the long-awaited memorial to Archbishop Thomas Croke. Bands were present from Thurles, Moyne, Templemore, Moycarkey, and Clonmore. The streets of the town at various points were spanned by streamers, mostly in Irish, and striking mottoes indicated the fervid feelings of the people. One in English stated 'A Nation is a stubborn thing – very hard to kill'.[15] It was known that there had been great British official activity around the town during the preceding twenty-four hours. There was an immense gathering in the town. On the platform with the parochial, college and neighbouring clergy were:- Messrs. James Nolan, Luke O'Toole, President and General Secretary of the G.A.A., Jerry O'Brien and Pat McGrath, Munster Council Chairman and Secretary, Rev. M.K. Ryan, Tipperary G.A.A. chairman and Thurles Town Clerk, James M. Kennedy, who had charge of arrangements. During the proceedings a troop of the 'Black and Tans' were lined up on Main Street (now Liberty Square) with some of their number on the rooftops with the guns directed at the archbishop.

Archbishop John Harty, in a rousing address, recalled the foundation of the G.A.A. in Thurles and the joy and hope it brought to Irish people. He emphasised, 'the fittingness of having the memorial in Thurles, the home of Dr Croke, and the cradle of the G.A.A.' Concluding he stated, 'Our games tell us that we were once a free nation, and to that ideal we should remain firm as the Rock of Cashel. We can be, and we ought to be, Irishmen worthy of our race, worthy of our grand traditions, and worthy of the freedom that, please God, will again return'. Standing shoulder to shoulder with the archbishop as he spoke was Tom Semple. Both Semple and the archbishop knew that they were engaged in an act of defiance in that ceremony, honouring Dr Croke, a champion of nationalist Ireland. Rev. M.K. Ryan,

Archbishop John M. Harty (1867-1946).

chairman of Tipperary G.A.A. board, in the course of his address said,' They tried to kill the G.A.A. but they might as well have tried to keep the Atlantic waves back with a broom'.[16]

---

[15] *Tipperary Star*, 20 Mar. 1920.

[16] St Patrick's College, Thurles. Philip Fogarty, research notes (unpublished work). *Tipperary Star*, 20 Mar. 1920.

After the ceremony of laying the foundation stone, the Archbishop was presented with a silver trowel by Luke O'Toole, on behalf of the Central Council. The crowd then headed to Thurles Sportsfield for a hurling game, between Tipperary and Cork, which was won by the home team by 4-2 to 1-2. Police and military were very evident, viewing all proceedings from a distance. In the evening a banquet was held in Hayes's Hotel and a fitting end was brought to the day with a Céilí Mór. Many commented favourably regarding the arrangements made by James M. Kennedy, Tom Semple, and Andy Mason.

The G.A.A. was now in its thirty-fifth year and it was also fifteen years since the decision was taken to erect the memorial. Other than the disputes already discussed, which delayed the project, the occurrence of the First World War, the 1916 Rebellion, the War of Independence, and the Civil War were all delaying factors.

CROKE MEMORIAL UNVEILED

The saga of the Croke memorial finally came to fruition, when it was unveiled on Whit Sunday, 4 June 1922. A large and representative gathering was present in Liberty Square, Thurles, when the imposing monument was unveiled. The memorial is situated on the western end of Liberty Square and looks towards the Cathedral. The preparations for the unveiling were not on a very lavish scale and the attendance was not up to expectation. The following inscriptions were to be seen on the large platform: 'We want Irish Education, Irish Language, Irish Games', 'God Save Ireland', 'You are not Irish until you are an Irish speaker' and 'Ireland will yet be Free'.[17] Across West Gate, convenient to the memorial, a banner with these words greeted the gaze of all comers:- 'Ireland Will Yet Be Free'.

On the platform were:- Dr John M. Harty – Archbishop of Cashel and Emly, Rev. M.K. Ryan – Tipperary G.A.A. chairman, Dan McCarthy – G.A.A. president, Luke O'Toole – G.A.A. general secretary. Speaking of the foundation of the G.A.A. in 1884, Rev. M.K. Ryan said, 'that but for the vitalising letter, written by Dr Croke, the association would have ended with a few paragraphs in the press. Today the games are flourishing and we have the fruit of the archbishop's labour in the powerful, all-embracing organisation that we behold. Gaelic Ireland has not forgotten and the statue to be now unveiled will be a lasting monument for generations yet unborn to the memory of the Cashel and Emly Prelate, who gave the G.A.A. its immortal spirit'.[18]

---

[17] *Tipperary Star*, 10 June 1922.
[18] Philip Fogarty, *Tipperary's G.A.A. Story* (Thurles, 1960), p. 234.

Croke Memorial through the years.

Croke Memorial today.

Most Rev. Dr Harty was given an enthusiastic reception and having performed the unveiling ceremony said, 'It was a happy day for the country when the G.A.A. was started, and it was a happy day for the association when they appointed the greatest Irishman of the nineteenth century as its first patron. Through Dr Croke's influence, the G.A.A. went bounding along. Small wonder it is proud of him today, and that his memory is still as fresh as it was twenty years ago, when his funeral procession wended its sad way through the streets of his 'Cathedral Town'. Thurles was honoured by the archbishop's presence during his life, now it is honoured, and it appreciates the honour of being given this monument to commemorate him. I can promise you that Gaeldom in Thurles and Tipperary will guard the monument as it would its own life'.

The memorial committee were also present:- Tom Semple, James M. Kennedy, John Walsh, James Maher, William Butler, Michael Russell, Denis McCarthy, Andy Mason, John Lambe, Jerry Dwyer, Daniel H. Ryan and Phil Slattery. However, the committee were very dissatisfied with the arrangements and complained that, 'O'Toole and company made the arrangements and messed them'.[19]

Afterwards, Dublin, the All-Ireland champions, defeated St Finbarr's, the Cork champions, in a challenge game at Thurles Sportsfield, to mark the occasion, on the score 3-2 to 2-2. Former Thurles hurlers Bob Doherty and John Joe Callanan lined out with Dublin.

The memorial, the pedestal of which forms a magnificent structure of limestone, stands on a tapering triangular shamrock-shaped base and is eighteen feet high. This is surmounted by an eight feet high bronze statue of Archbishop Thomas Croke, standing erect and holding a breviary in one hand.[20]

A bronze representation of St. Patrick, with the motto *Ar son Dé* occupies one of the niches on the side of the pedestal. The other niche contains a cloaked figure in bronze with a harp, representing Saoirse (Freedom) and the words agus *Tíre*.[21]

An inscription on the western side reads:-

---

[19] *Tipperary Star* 10, 17 June 1922.
[20] Note:- Tom Semple had high regard for Archbishop Croke and a framed image of the prelate still hangs in the hallway of Tom's home at Fianna Road, Thurles.
[21] Note:- *Ar son Dé agus Tíre* translates as *For God and Country*.

*Do thóg lucht cleas
lúth na hÉireann an
leacht cuimhne seo
Mar chomhartha onóra
Do Thomás Sár-Oirbhidh-
neach Mac Crócaigh D.D.
Árd-Easpog Chaisil
agus Imleach nIubhair.
ceud Phatrún Chumainn
na gCleas Lúth nGaedhlach
Sompla do chách
D'uaisleacht agus de
neart Clanna Gaedhal.*[22]

The designer was F.W. Doyle-Jones, a Londoner of Irish descent and much of the stonework was sub-contracted to William McDonnell, Monumental Sculptors, Templemore.[23]

And so the Croke Memorial stands in the heart of the 'Cathedral Town', where the G.A.A. was founded. It serves as a sermon in stone and bronze to the thousands of supporters of Gaelic Games, who throng in their periodic pilgrimages to Thurles – 'The Mecca of the Gael'.

Portrait of Archbishop Thomas Croke at Lár na Páirce Museum, Thurles. This portrait was for many years in the Ursuline Convent, Thurles.

[22] English translation:- The Gaelic Athletic Association erected this memorial as a mark of respect to Archbishop Thomas Croke D.D., Archbishop of Cashel and Emly. First Patron of the G.A.A. An example to all of the nobility and strength of the Gael.

[23] *Tipperary Star*, 10 June 1922.

Cashel's Patriot Prelate

Though death has stilled the prelate's heart,
His memory fadeth not,
His life work lives to tell the part
He bore in Erin's lot.
For her he stood a champion bold,
When vengeance sought her prey,
A prince, a priest like those of old,
We honour him today.

With croziered hand and mitred brow,
He led with wisdom's eye,
For Ireland then, for Ireland now,
His only slogan cry.
Like flashing fire his matchless tongue,
Inspired the mind with thought,
And woke to life what poets sung
And martyrs died and fought.

And time shall pass and years will roll,
To add unceasing fame,
More lasting than the bronze or stone
Erected to his name,
There graven in the Nation's heart,
Unchanged by blight or shock,
The well-won love, for the patriot's part,
There staunch as Cashel's rock.

– FRANCIS PHILLIPS, Cashel.

Liberty Square, Thurles in the 1940s.

CHAPTER 18

Thurles Sportsfield in Semple's Time 1910-1943

PURCHASING THE GROUNDS

IN OCTOBER 1909, the sale of Thurles Agricultural Society showground was a large topic for discussion around Thurles. The property had belonged to a local Thurles business man, Joseph Molloy and it passed into the possession of his wife, Mary, on his death. On 3 November 1901, it was sold by public auction in two lots of £205 for one and £105 for the other – £310 in total[1] and bought by Thurles Agricultural Show committee.

> 'Whereas by indenture of lease dated the twenty-fourth day of September, one thousand nine hundred and three, William Daly and Denis St. John Daly demised to the Thurles Agricultural Society Ltd., all that part of the lands of Thurles Townparks, known as Castle Meadows and that other part known as Muttonfield adjoining said lands of Castle Meadows both situate in the parish of Thurles … and containing in all eleven acres and thirty-five perches or thereabouts Irish plantation measure as then in the occupation of the lessees together with the rights, members and appurtenance thereunto belonging…'

This venture was a success for the show committee for some years but by the end of the decade, financial difficulties determined that the property be offered for sale. The local urban council had a special meeting of its members convened to discuss the sale, as they had got an offer of the grounds from its directors, for the sum of £1,500. The need for a new burial ground in the town was high on their agenda and many members considered that this property, if purchased, would make an ideal location. They discussed this suggestion and the erection

---

[1] *Tipperary Star*, 1 Feb. 1913.

of a caretaker's house and mortuary chapel on the site.[2] John Walsh, town engineer, submitted a map of the showground at a subsequent meeting and this included proposed alterations for the purposes of a town park and manure depot.[3] The council agreed to send a letter to the Local Government Board for a loan of £1,700, for the purpose of acquiring the ground for the purposes of a graveyard, a public park, and a Gaelic arena.[4] This move angered Thurles Ratepayers Protective Association, who also wrote to the same board asking them not to give the loan on the grounds that:

1. The town has enough public parks and walks – a waste of money to acquire more.
2. The park, if created would not be supported.
3. The housing and sewage conditions of the town were in a more needy situation than this 'wild cat' scheme.[5]

Matthew Butler, hon. secretary of the showgrounds, informed the urban council that if they were not prepared to come to an agreement by the 10 December, that other means would be taken to dispose of the grounds. Among the locals in Thurles it was felt that the grounds should be kept 'for the boys' and a public meeting was organised.

Since G.A.A. competitions began in 1887, Thurles was popular as a venue for major inter-county games in both hurling and football. The centrality of the town with its main-line railway station and the fact that the G.A.A. was well established with capable personnel available in sufficient numbers, to organise and run such events, all added to the demand for Thurles. By 1910, three All-Ireland senior football finals had been hosted by the town.[6] Coupled with this demand, was the desire among Thurles G.A.A. activists, being conscious of the special significance that the town held in the hearts of Gaelic games supporters, for a permanent home for the hosting of Gaelic games in the town.

In early January 1910, a group of local business men had made a move to secure the grounds for the Gaels as a Gaelic field, but when the urban council decided to purchase it, the group withdrew in their favour. But now the Local Government Board had objected to the purchase by the urban council and it

---

[2] *Nenagh News*, 2 Oct. 1909.
[3] Ibid, 9 Oct. 1909.
[4] *Tipperary Star*, 11 Sept. 1909.
[5] *Nenagh News*, 4 Dec. 1909, *Tipperary Star*, 27 Nov. 1909.
[6] April 21st 1895. All-Ireland Football Final 1894 (Replay), at Ballycurrane, Thurles. Cork (Nils) 1-2 Dublin (Young Irelands) 0-5. June 16th 1907. All-Ireland Football Final 1905, at Thurles Agricultural Society Grounds. Kildare (Roseberry) 1-7, Kerry (Tralee Mitchels) 0-5. May 9th 1909. All-Ireland Football (Home) Final 1908 at Thurles Agricultural Society Grounds. Dublin (Geraldines) 0-10, Kerry (Tralee Mitchels) 0-3.

looked that the field would be 'put to the hammer'.[7] By mid April a spirited civic attempt was made to hold the showgrounds for the Gaels and for the good of the town. In his diary, Jim Maher, Parnell Street, wrote, '5 April 1910. Had small meeting in small room of Confraternity Hall, composed of Fr. M.K. Ryan, Denis O'Keeffe,

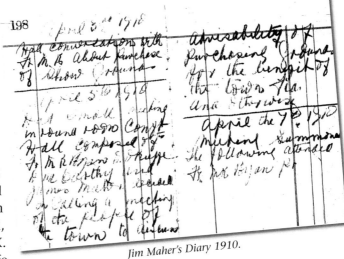

Jim Maher's Diary 1910.

Denis McCarthy[8] and myself. Decided on calling a meeting of the people of the town to discuss advisability of purchasing grounds for the benefit of the people of the town'.[9] An offer of £900 was being gamely backed up.[10] By the end of the month the local press reported:- The Thurles showgrounds are now safe for the Gaels, the show and whatever will help the town – £900 is the purchase price.[11] All legal transactions were completed on 3 June 1910, when Thurles Agricultural Society sold the remainder of its lease to John Walsh, Main Street, Thurles, agent and trustee for a number of persons.

To meet the cost of the purchase, an issue of shares was subscribed to by the townspeople. Shares were on sale, costing £1, from hon. secretaries:- Denis O'Keeffe and William Butler. The first list of shareholders was printed in the *Tipperary Star* on Saturday, 28 May 1910. The grounds are now referred to as Thurles Sporting Grounds. The total collected through the sale of shares amounted to £502 and the balance of £400 was borrowed from a local bank.

The election of the first committee, consisting of twelve members, took place in the Confraternity Hall on 24 May. The voting, which was by ballot of shareholders was open from 7.00 p.m. until 10.00 p.m. Nearly three quarters of shareholders recorded their votes. At 11.30 p.m. the result was declared. Out of forty-one eligible for election it was decided to limit the committee to fourteen members. By a unanimous decision Thurles G.A.A. and Mid Tipperary Division G.A.A. were each entitled to a permanent representative. The voting resulted

---

[7] *Tipperary Star*, 1 Jan. 1910.
[8] *Note:-* Denis McCarthy had a drapery business on Main St., Thurles. Family later moved to Dublin.
[9] Diary of James Maher, loaned by his son Mícheál, Castlemeadows. 15 June 2008.
[10] *Tipperary Star*, 16 Apr. 1910.
[11] Ibid, 30 Apr. 1910.

Thurles Sportsfield 1910 – Some members of the first committee are included.
Back row (l.-r.): J.M. Kennedy, D.A. Butler, Michael Kennedy, J.J. Ryan (Solicitor).
Middle row (l.-r.): John Walsh C.E., Denis O'Keeffe, Hugh Ryan, H. Barry, James Maher.
Front row (l.-r.): Phil Slattery, William Butler, John Lambe C.U.D.C., Denis McCarthy U.D.C.

as follows for the twelve places:- John Walsh 202, James Maher 195, Denis O'Keeffe 195, Edward O'Meara 169, Hugh Ryan 148, Denis McCarthy 141, Thomas Semple 122, John Lambe 122, William Butler 113, D.A. Butler 102, J.J. Ryan 102, L.J. Ryan 98.[12]

Thurles Sports Committee was set up to organise events for the venue:- chairman – Hugh Ryan, secretary – William O'Loughlin, treasurer – E.T. O'Meara, and members:- John Walsh, Denis McCarthy, John Lambe, William Butler, Matthew Butler, D.A. Butler, James Maher, James M. Kennedy, Thomas J. Semple and Denis O'Keeffe.

EARLY EVENTS

The grounds held a very successful first race meeting on 29 August 1910 under the rules of the Irish Racing Association. Many preparations needed to be made. Five races, one confined, were run with prizes to the value of £50 on offer. In October, a major sporting occasion took place on the grounds. Athletics and cycling were to the fore. Prizes were on display in Denis McCarthy's window on Main Street. Cycling was growing in popularity with a new club started in the town in March. Borris/Ileigh native, Mick Hammond, was a prominent cyclist in Thurles at this time.

---

[12] *Tipperary Star*, 28 May 1910.

Horse racing was popular at Thurles Sportsfield in the early days.

At a meeting of the committee, chairman, Hugh Ryan, West Gate, was amazed that some patrons were attempting to gain free entry to events by forcing a way through the galvanized enclosure. 'I am amazed that respectable people would be so lost to self respect as to avoid a small payment'.[13] They decided to appoint a caretaker and prosecute any trespassers.

DRUMS AND GUNS

John Walsh expressed the opinion that it would be necessary to open the grounds with a first class tournament, with proceeds in aid of the grounds. He voiced the view that as the principal teams of Tipperary and other counties had medals 'go leor', there would be a greater struggle for a more esteemed prize. According to him there would be no presentation more acceptable to a team than brand

Terrier coursing at Thurles Sportsfield in 1922.

new valuable double-barrelled guns. Thurles secretary, James M. Kennedy agreed that guns would be most acceptable. The committee agreed that the guns would be purchased and stocked in the field at the first match, so that the public would be satisfied that the tournament was bona fide.[14]

The first game of the tournament took place on 26 June, when the Davis hurling club, Dublin played Tipperary represented by the Thurles club. The local organizers were very anxious that all was in order for the occasion. The prestigious Dublin Fife and Drum band and the local Confraternity band, under the masterly conductorship of a Mr Mears, were on hand to inaugurate the new regime with a special display culminating in a parade of teams in double file. A great hurling game followed, which did justice to the occasion, Dublin winning

---

[13] *Tipperary Star*, 2 June 1910.
[14] Ibid, 11 June 1910.

by the narrowest of margins:- 2-9 to 2-8. During their stay the visitors were most hospitably entertained.

On the last Sunday in June, the only photograph of the 1887 winning Tipperary, Thurles selection, team was taken, at Thurles Sporting Grounds, by Webster Photography, The Mall, Thurles. This photograph would not have been taken except for the exertions of James M. Kennedy, who for years had spoken about the importance of having such a photograph for posterity. The players had to wait over twenty years for the occasion. As could be expected, all the players were not available, three members were dead and one had emigrated. Three captains: Jim Stapleton, Denis Maher and Tom Semple were also photographed together.

Now that the control of the grounds was in their own hands, many improvements and alterations were planned, which when completed would make the grounds the finest in the country. Reviewing their activities at year's end, the committee was delighted with the successes to date and horse racing on St Stephen's day would complete the year's programme. For that meeting, no faraway horses with long pedigrees would be allowed to come in and canter off with all the prizes. Races for the best horse in the parish and best horse in the barony would be run.

THURLES GAELIC ATHLETIC AND CYCLING SPORTS 1911

Thurles Gaelic Athletic and Cycling sports took place at the new grounds in August with the Thurles 'Blues' proving invincible in feats of fleetness. Some results:-

- *Boys Race:* First – Maher, The Mall. Second – Mahony, West Gate.
- *100 Yards (open):* First – Hugh Shelly. Second – Toss Mockler. Winning Time – 10.5 secs.
- *Half-mile Flat Race* (confined to Thurles G.A.A. Club): First – Toss Mockler. Second – James 'Hawk' O'Brien. Winning time: 2 mins. 5 secs. (Off 30 yard handicap)
- *220 Yards:* First – Hugh Shelly. Second – J. O'Brien, Galbally.
- *Composite Race* (A lap each of walking, running, cycling): First – Jack O'Connor, Bansha. Second – J. Mullane, Rossmore.
- *440 Yards:* First – Hugh Shelly. Second – M. Connolly, Thurles. (Off 28 yard handicap)
- *Half-mile (open):* First – William Furlong, Dundrum. Second – E.P. Quinlan, Roscrea.
- *Bicycle Race* (One mile, confined to Thurles and adjoining parishes): First – Mick Hammond, Thurles. Second – T. Gleeson, Ballinahow.

- *Long Jump (open):* First – J. O'Dwyer, Thurles. Second – Bernard Lyons, Turtulla.
- *Five Miles (open):* First – Tim Crowe, Dundrum, Second – Jack O'Connor, Bansha.
- *One Mile Flat (open):* First – J. O'Connor, Bansha. Second – E.P. Quinlan, Roscrea.
- *High Jump:* First – H. Power, Littleton. Second – Bernard Lyons, Turtulla.
- *Bicycle (one mile open):* First – D. Egan, Roscrea. Second – Mick Hammond, Thurles.
- *Putting 28lbs. with follow:* First – W. Murphy, Emly. Second – Bernard Lyons, Turtulla.
- *Slinging 28 lbs. between feet with follow:* First – J. Skehan, Thurles. Second – W. Murphy, Emly.

Thurles annual sports meeting on 2 June 1912 attracted a large attendance to the Sportsfield. In the half-mile race, confined to Thurles G.A.A. club members, John Quinn was first, closely followed by Toss Mockler. Mick Hammond won the one mile bicycle race with Thomas Keane, Thurles, second. Andy Callanan and Mick Leahy also competed. This race was confined to Thurles and adjoining parishes. Not all the cyclists were happy, especially when they saw the prizes offered. Some felt that they were not up to the mark and refused to compete. Fleet footed Hugh Shelly was master of the 100 yards, while Bernard Lyons cast the 28 lbs. weight 31 feet, 3 inches. J.K. O'Dwyer jumped 20 feet and 5 inches to win the long jump event.[15]

THURLES FOR SALE

A strong local topic of discussion during 1912 was the possibility of town tenants being able to purchase their properties from the landlord through the Estates Commissioners. Regarding the sale of Thurles town, a very successful meeting was held in late May with the Estates Commissioners in Dublin. Representing the local interest were Rev. M.K. Ryan C.C., John Hackett M.P. and Dr Ryan solicitor. The death of William Daly J.P., D.L., co-owner of Thurles with Denis St. George Daly, occurred in December 1910, at Dunsandle, County Galway. This accelerated the sale of Thurles. The estate was valued at £50,278-14-11 and the sale was successfully completed. Rev. M.K. Ryan received much deserved credit for his role.

In selling the town to the people, the Daly landlords marked the event by presenting as a free gift to the town, Thurles Sporting Grounds free of rent forever – the annual rent up to then was £37. The urban council was asked to take over the grounds and purchase out the committee. A loan of £1,000 would

---

[15] *Tipperary Star*, 8 June 1912.

be provided.[16] At a special meeting of the urban council Mr. Carroll proposed and Mr. McCormack seconded this motion, which was passed unanimously, 'That we agree to purchase the Sporting Grounds on the terms laid down by the Sports' Committee, subject to the approval of the Local Government Body.'

A meeting of the shareholders of Thurles Sporting Grounds was held in the Confraternity Hall on Sunday evening, 22 September. Hugh Ryan presided and the following motion was proposed by John Walsh and seconded by Denis McCarthy, 'That we being shareholders of Thurles Sporting and Athletic Grounds, resolve, that seeing the landlord, Captain Daly, and the trustees of the Daly estate have offered to give the enclosed grounds, which are at present in our possession, as a public park for the town at the very small purchase price of £5, we now agree to dispose of same to the urban council for this purpose and further agree that the price to be paid to us for same will be the amount which will clearly indemnify our shareholders against loss and we respectfully request the urban council to carefully consider this splendid offer of the fee-simple property as a public park for the town'. This motion was passed unanimously and forwarded to the urban council.[17] Present at this meeting were those above named and D. Mullaney, James M. Kennedy, T. O'Connell, P.W. Dunlop, E. Murphy, J. Dwyer, R. Barry and Anthony Carew. The members of Thurles Sporting Grounds said that they would not stand in the way of the generous offer. All they wanted was that the grounds would not go into private hands and that they be indemnified for the amount they had paid in shares and subscriptions. Hugh Ryan felt that it would be an advantage to the town, if the council acquired the grounds as proposed and especially to have it for nothing. Thurles Urban Council would convert the grounds into a public park and discussions were underway regarding the provision of walks, seats, shelters and the employment of a caretaker. One worry was that the council felt that some of the grounds could be used for housing purposes, though leaving sufficient for a public park. However, the Local Government Board would not advance the money required, approximately £1,000, to buy out the interests of the shareholders and pay

Tipperary Star advertisement 1923.

---

[16] *Tipperary Star*, 21, 28 Sept. 1912.
[17] Ibid, 28 Sept. 1912.

debts due to the bank. The grounds, as a result, remained in the hands of the shareholders.

By 1913, the Munster G.A.A. Council was now beginning to arrange championship games for Thurles Sporting Grounds. During the year the Munster senior football championship game between Tipperary and Waterford was played there, but the main fixture to be staged in Thurles was the Munster senior hurling semi-final between Cork and Limerick, refereed by Tom Semple. Incidentally, Thurles Sporting Grounds are referred to as Daly Park in local press, at this time.[18] Since they had purchased the grounds, the committee had spent a large amount of money on levelling, enclosing the area etc. In preparation for this game, the stand was enlarged and new side-line seats were installed. These developments received much favourable comment. The townspeople of Thurles had responded admirably to the great influx of people to the town. In the days before the game butchers, bakers, caterers etc. were busy in anticipation of the extra business to be transacted. Householders also got in on the act, plain and meat-teas were made available, a whole-hearted 'Céad míle fáilte' was extended to all the visitors and the Thurles tradition of catering for large crowds was enhanced.

Many workmen were engaged at Thurles Sportsfield in 1926 banking the enclosure.

[18] *Tipperary Star,* 5 July 1913.

Admission to ground was six pence, to the stand sixpence extra. The sideline seats cost one shilling. The attendance was estimated at 20,000, gate receipts were £303-2-0, a record for a Munster game. An extra special match programme was on sale for the occasion. 'It was a great pennyworth and a splendid Gaelic souvenir'.

FIRST MUNSTER FINAL

The first Munster senior hurling final to be played in Thurles was that of 1914. It was played, between Clare and Cork, on 20 September. There was a mighty hosting of Gaels from all over Ireland and the match was fought out in the most dexterous and determined fashion. Clare were champions and Tom Semple, who refereed the game stated that, 'It was as hard fought a Munster final, as ever I saw. The issue was in doubt up to the last minute. It was a strenuous game, but nevertheless a sporting one'.[19]

In August 1915, the A.G.M. of Thurles Sporting Grounds took place in Lambe's Hotel, Friar Street. John Lambe presided over this meeting of share-holders in the absence of Hugh Ryan. Audited accounts were presented, income for the period 18 July 1911 to 11 June 1915 amounted to £1,223-13-5, while the expenditure for the same period was £1,013-13-5. The profit margin of £210 pleased the share-holders and testified to good management. Share capital stood at £502 and the bank overdraft amounted to £273-15-2. The following committee of twelve were elected by ballot:- Michael J. Bowe, D.A. Butler, William Butler, Michael Hickey, John Lambe, Denis McCarthy, James Maher, Joseph Maher, Michael Russell, Hugh Ryan, Tom Semple and John Walsh.[20]

A SOLDIER'S SONG – AMHRÁN NA BHFIANN

On 5 August 1917, Boherlahan and Toomevara played an epic hurling game in the county semi-final at Thurles Sportsfield, with Boherlahan victorious. With the top two teams in action, it was of little surprise that a huge attendance gathered. There was a profuse display of the republican tricolour in evidence and for the first time 'A Soldier's Song' was sung at the venue. Written by Peadar Kearney, it was a popular marching song of the Irish Volunteers. This song would within a few years become Ireland's national anthem – Amhrán na bhFiann.[21]

DALY PARK RACES

The 'flapper' meeting, on Easter Sunday 1920, at Thurles Sportsfield (Daly Park) was a great success. M.F. Meagher was judge, Tom Semple was starter and

---

[19] Phil O'Neill, *History of the G.A.A. 1910-1930* (Kilkenny, 1931), p. 94.
[20] St Patrick's College, Thurles. Philip Fogarty, research notes (unpublished work).
[21] Philip Fogarty, *Tipperary's G.A.A. Story* (Thurles, 1960), p. 213.

Willie Hugh Ryan, James Maher, Michael Russell, Anthony Carew and Denis McCarthy were on hand to ensure the success of the day.

BLACK AND TANS

In 1920, a British officer and a military sergeant called on Maurice O'Loughlin, secretary of Thurles Sportsfield committee and warned him that unless the ticket slots in the sportsfield wall were not closed within forty eight hours, that the British military would blow the entire wall away. The Black and Tans did much damage to the stand and fences in Thurles Sportsfield.[22] The gates were flung open, the grounds were made a commonage and woodwork, of every kind they burned to ashes.[23] A claim for compensation, by the committee, resulted in the payment of £200 from the British Treasury.[24]

In 1922, the annual general meeting of Thurles Recreation and Sporting Grounds was held in the Confraternity Hall on 12 February. The accounts were adopted and the meeting gave instructions to the new committee to erect a stand, paling and caretaker's house. The following were the members of the new committee, elected by ballot:- chairman – John Walsh, hon. secretary – William Butler, hon. treasurer – James Maher, Denis McCarthy, John Lambe, Michael Russell, D.H. Ryan, Tom Semple, Jerry Dwyer, Matthew Dowling, Philip Slattery, J.L. Johnston. Representatives from Thurles G.A.A. and the Mid Tipperary board would be added later.[25] Mid Tipperary board agreed not to draw a dividend on their shares in the sportsfield, even though the sportsfield was £250 in credit. The money would go towards the provision of a stand at the venue.[26]

Thurles Terrier Coursing club held its initial meeting it the sportsfield in early February. J. Loughnane, Mitchel Street was secretary, Michael O'Connell – judge, and P. Webster was 'slipper'. Organisers reported a successful outing with thirty-two terriers and sixteen mongrels competing.

MUNSTER FINAL 1923

Jim Bolger, a noted sports journalist recalled, 'My first experience of a Munster final at Thurles was in the summer of 1923 – a year after the Croke Memorial had been unveiled in the town. Tipperary and Limerick were playing for the 1922 championship. The playing pitch as I recall it, even then, was well-nigh perfect; but accommodation for the crowd was not anything like what it

---

[22] Philip Fogarty, *Tipperary's G.A.A. Story* (Thurles, 1960), p. 229.
[23] *Tipperary Star*, 25 Feb. 1933.
[24] Ibid, 21 July 1928.
[25] Account Book of James Maher, Parnell Street, Thurles.
[26] *Tipperary Star*, 18 Feb. 1922.

is at present and there was a good deal of confusion and crushing around the entrances. The clicking of the turnstiles and the regularity and smoothness in the control of greatly increased numbers today is in striking contrast, a tribute alike to the enthusiasm and hard work of the men in charge of that spacious ground and the growing strength and popularity of our national pastimes.

Thurles has ever been noted for efficiency in stewarding; and if a word of praise in this respect is due to no one more that another, it goes to Tom Semple, one of the greatest hurlers of his time. His towering figure commanded respect and he took a pardonable pride in the welfare and improvement of the ground, his aim to ensure the utmost comfort for everybody. I will always remember with gratitude the personal interest he took in the press, seeing that we were adequately seated and that our view from the side-line was not obstructed. Best of all, however, was the cheery greeting. We were always sure of a hearty welcome in Thurles and when the game was over and the day's work done, there was the usual exchange of views on the merits of the teams, invariably merging into recollections of great struggles of the past. As a rock, where firmness is required, yet genial and open in manner, Tom Semple was a grand character; and his passing a few years back, left a void in our after-the-match reunions that cannot be filled.'[27]

NEW STAND

Early in 1926 a fine, roofed stand was completed at Thurles Sportsfield. It was one hundred and twenty-five feet long by twenty-five feet and there were twenty-one commodious tiers. The contractor was Tim Brophy, Thurles, and

This stand at Thurles Sportsfield accommodated patrons from the 1920s until the mid 1960s. It was replaced in 1968 by Ardán Uí Chuinneáin – Dr. Kinane Stand. The small construction to the right of the stand housed the commentator, usually Mícheál Ó hEithir, on big match days. (Photo: Donal Sammon)

---

[27] Jim Bolger, 'Glamour of Thurles', in Séamus Ó Ceallaigh (ed.), *Gaelic Athletic Memories* (Limerick, 1945), pp 85-6.

the iron-work was supplied and erected by E.J. Delahanty, Kilkenny. Beneath were added dressing-rooms and all the most modern adjuncts for the benefit of the players. The committee, responsible for Thurles Sportsfield, were very unhappy with the portion of the 'gate' given to them and were taking steps to improve this. The officers and committee were:- chairman – James Walsh, vice chairman – Tom Semple, secretaries – William Butler and Ed. J. Gorman, treasurer-James Maher, committee – P. Slattery, M. Russell, J. Dwyer, J.L. Johnston, J. Lambe, D.H. Ryan, Stephen Dwan (Thurles G.A.A. club representative), J.J. Callanan (Mid Tipperary board representative).

THURLES MAKES ITS NAME

In 1926, Cork's Athletic Grounds was an amazing scene for the Munster hurling final between Tipperary and Cork, on 12 September. Twenty-six thousand paid for admission, far too large a crowd for the capacity. The match started but had to be called off after sixteen minutes; there was no room to hurl and Tipperary were winning 1-2 to nil. The paling had cracked and the crowd surged through in one surging mass. There was utter confusion, the game had to be abandoned and was refixed for Thurles.

Feverish preparations were made at Thurles Sportsfield. Over one hundred men with twenty-five horses and carts had been busily engaged banking the enclosure. More than ten thousand tons of earth and rubble was moved into position. This new embankment permitted well over 20,000 to watch the game without interference. The fine roofed stand at the venue had been recently named the Canon Ryan Memorial Stand and a new temporary wooden stand was erected for the occasion. Between them, the stands could accommodate

Celebrations as Tipperary draw with Cork at Thurles Sportsfield on 19 September 1926.

6,000. A limited number of side-line seats were also provided. The field was like a billiard table and Tom Semple was in charge of an 'army' of stewards, who were disciplined and strict, yet, courteous to the excited supporters. As journalist Raymond Smith wrote, 'Tom Semple, like Napoleon, had sent out the call for an army of helpers and stewards, and they rallied to the flag of the 'Old Blues' captain. He strode the sideline that Sunday like a general making a final inspection of the barricades, his word was law, the match was watched in comfort and the name of Thurles was made'.[28]

This game, played on 19 September, ranks among the classic finals, and was a treat to witness and brought renewed luster to the ancient game. It was the first Munster G.A.A. match to be broadcast on radio, as Paddy Mehigan, 'Carbery', brought news of the match to many listeners. At half-time Cork led by 2-3 to 1-0 but a spirited Tipperary response in the second period forced a draw, 4-1 to 3-4, amid scenes of wonderful enthusiasm and wild excitement. Sports journalist, Jim Bolger, wrote, 'I have yet to hear a cheer to equal that which greeted Tipperary's drawing level with Cork in the second half hour'.[29] The stewards at Thurles under the leadership of Semple managed the crowd effectively and safely: 'A short time before the teams made their appearance, every portion of the enclosure was filled to its utmost capacity, and it was indeed remarkable the facility with which the spectators were able to secure their seats and positions. Plenty of entrances were available at every point and a hard working staff of stewards, under the capable direction of Tom Semple, a well-known and popular All-Ireland hurler of some years ago, largely contributed to this satisfactory state of affairs.'[30]

Back to Thurles Sportsfield again for the second replay, on 3 October, to a venue that was growing in status for the excellence of its hosting of games. This was due in no small measure to the efficiency of Tom Semple and his team of stewards, who kept perfect order. Thurles was the place to be as seventeen crowded excursion trains, carrying almost 14,000 supporters, steamed towards the 'Cathedral Town'. The Cork Volunteers Pipers' band, which usually accompanied the Cork hurlers, were there entertaining both friend and foe, with their rousing music. Their big drummer was of particular interest, as his antics both entertained and amused the throng.[31]

Tom Semple added to his reputation for leadership and administrative ability, when he personally planned and oversaw the stewarding arrangements

---

[28] Raymond Smith, *Decades of Glory* (Dublin, 1966), p. 133.
[29] Jim Bolger, 'Glamour of Thurles' in Séamus Ó Ceallaigh (ed.) *Gaelic Athletic Memories*, (Limerick, 1945), pp 85-6.
[30] *Southern Star*, 25 Sept. 1926, p. 3.
[31] Pilib Ó Duibhir, Tipperary 1915-1928 (unpublished work).

Munster Hurling Final, Thurles Sportsfield – July 1928

Top: *Archbishop John Harty, G.A.A. Patron, with Munster Council officers.*

Centre: *Archbishop Harty throws in the ball to begin the game.*

Bottom: *A packed stand and sideline enjoy the spectacle.*

(Photos: Irish Examiner)

for these two epic games. Today's health and safety inspectors would raise an eyebrow at the following account of the crowded stand, 'The Canon Ryan Memorial Stand was packed to its utmost capacity. So great was the congestion that at times the entire stand moved as one man and swayed from side to side, as the scene of the game shifted from one end of the pitch to the other. Now and again, too, the pressure on those on top would force the unfortunates below out on the level ground in front of the stand'.

More than 30,000 saw Archbishop Harty throw in the ball and all seemed well for the first ten minutes, and then Martin Mockler, Moycarkey/Borris, was ordered off the field. From then on, Tipperary were playing a rearguard action, struggling tenaciously but yet retreating. 'The Banks' and the Cork shouts of jubilation filled the air, as the Leesiders relished their victory by 3-6 to 2-4.

The traders in Thurles had a great day, 'as good as four fair days', was the comment from a publican on the Square.[32] On Sunday night, the teams were entertained to a civic reception and banquet in the Confraternity Hall, as the guests of the people of the town. Denis Maher and Michael Gleeson were secretaries of the organising committee. Messrs Mills, Dublin were the caterers and Madame Gladys Long's Clonmel Orchestra rendered Irish airs and many of the company contributed songs.

The masses that thronged Thurles for these games were amazed at the ability of the townspeople to cater for all requirements. Throughout every street numerous facilities were arranged to feed the people. The whole town seemed transformed into a gigantic restaurant from the fronts of the shops and ordinary dwelling houses to the haysheds at the rear. Signs with inscriptions such as 'Plain or Meat Teas', 'Luncheons' and 'Dinners' etc. caught the eye everywhere. The name and fame of Thurles for its ability to cater for large crowds was made and affirmed by such days.

Many letters were received acknowledging the wonderful occasion. Archbishop J. M. Harty wrote, 'Now that the capabilities of Thurles and the suitability of its sportsfield are recognised, we hope that many gatherings of a similar kind will take place in our midst'. J.J. Walsh, Minister for Posts and Telegraphs, 'In our brightest dreams, none of us expected to see the day when public patronage would out-grow the capacity of our extensive Munster grounds.'[33] Thurles Urban Council also passed a resolution of congratulations.

The reputation of Thurles as a popular hosting centre was enhanced and

[32] Interview with Bobby Mockler, Mathew Ave., Thurles (16 Jan. 2011).
[33] *Tipperary Star*, 9 Oct. 1926.

Thurles Sportsfield Committee 1928
Front row (l.-r.): Tom Semple, John Walsh, James Maher, William Butler, Phil Slattery.
Back row (l.-r.): S. Dwan, Ed. O'Gorman, John Lambe, Michael Russell.

with the games gaining in strength and appeal, the committee in charge went on improving their ground. 1926 marked a big uplift in the fortunes of the G.A.A. Stewarding was tested as perhaps never before, but the crowds behaved splendidly and the games were thoroughly enjoyed. Tom Semple's son, Martin, recalls, ' My mother told me that Archbishop Thomas Morris discussed with her a number of times his recollection of my father on the sidelines at the Thurles grounds directing and controlling crowds with a wave of what the Archbishop described as an 'ash plant'; my mother corrected him that Tom always carried a blackthorn stick'.

THE MUNSTER FINAL 1932

Clare won the Munster hurling final, at Thurles Sportsfield on 31 July, with a classic performance. A capacity attendance saw an epic struggle, with the 'Rebels' going down, by 5-2 to 4-1. No wonder Clareman, Joseph Senan Considine, penned the lines:-

> 'Oh, to be in Thurles, when the final there is played,
> A sight to cheer the hearts of all, who wield the ashen blade,
> A hosting of the Gaelic clans from districts far and wide,
> Where age and youth and beauty fair foregather side by side'.[34]

---

[34] *Tipperary Star*, 23 July 1932.

Jack Mockler was in charge of the stewarding that day, ably assisted by Joe Purcell, James 'Hawk' O'Brien, Ned O'Gorman, Con Keane and many more. They were in their places at 12.30 p.m., having entered the sportsfield through a designated gate on Hayes's boreen, at the rear of the stand. The after-match atmosphere downtown was enjoyed by Phil O'Neill (Sliabh Rua) who recalled, 'After the game, we had a pleasant evening in Jim Maher's. We had several drops of conversation water and we played old games and mentioned old names of men who had played with ash'. Many of the old brigade were present:- Tom Semple, Charlie Murphy, Jerry Beckett of the Old Lees, Paddy 'Best' Maher of the old 'Blues', Willie Aherne 'the mighty atom' of the old Cork team, Con Deasy from Kinsale and many others. Then the Clare boys came in and the order was repeated. We drank their health and victory in the true spirit of sportsmanship... Tom Semple insisted on a 'deoch an dorais'. The order must be carried out to the letter. No excuse! We clink our glasses to victors and vanquished, to our hosts and their hospitality. The day is over. The field is fought and won.'

PLANNING THE GOLDEN JUBILEE CELEBRATIONS

In the 1933 Munster championship semi-final, Limerick, selected by Ahane, swamped the Leesiders, by 2-9 to 1-6, at Thurles Sportsfield. Thousands

Refreshments on the sideline at Thurles Sportsfield during the Munster semi-final, Cork v Limerick, in 1934.

(Photo: Irish Examiner)

200

1934 – G.A.A. Golden Jubilee Year. Workmen busy extending the embankment at Thurles Sportsfield. Tom Semple is on the left.

attended and further thousands had to be turned away, disappointed through lack of accommodation. From reading Thurles Sportsfield committee reports, it is obvious that the committee were almost certain that the 1934 All-Ireland final would be played in Thurles, as part of the association's golden jubilee celebrations. But they also knew that to host such an event successfully, that the grounds would need major investment. Since April 1932, the sportsfield was now registered as a Friendly Society, the official title of the grounds now being:- Thurles Gaelic Sportsfield Society Ltd. A letter to the Munster Council, signed by John Walsh, Tom Semple and Edward G. Gorman, included the following, 'The Gaels of Ireland will decide at Congress to have the jubilee of the association celebrated in the cradle-land by a demonstration in keeping with and worthy of the founders...' Johnny Leahy spoke on behalf of Thurles at the Munster Council meeting, seeking financial support. The council agreed to match whatever sum was raised by the sportsfield committee, the Thurles traders and the friends of Gaelic sport in Mid Tipperary. All Munster counties favoured Thurles, as the venue for the 1934 All-Ireland final, although Cork had reservations. Thurles traders called a special meeting to organise the raising of funds. Estimated costs were £1,500 to £2,000. Subscriptions could be given to:- James Maher, Parnell Street, W.H. Ryan, West Gate, Ed. Flynn, Liberty Square and Denis Maher, Liberty Square.

In anticipation of a favourable response to the request to have the All-Ireland played at Thurles Sportsfield, the committee was busy upgrading the venue. Accommodation for an attendance of sixty thousand was the ambitious target. Between two and three thousand pounds would be expended on new stands and enlarged embankments. The two new stands would be erected on either side of the existing covered stand. In March 1934, work was concentrated on enlarging the existing bank. Many lorries were hired and numerous workers were employed in moving thousands of tons of material from a refuse dump at the railway to the sportsfield.[35]

A significant event of the golden jubilee celebrations was the hosting of the G.A.A. annual Congress at the Confraternity Hall, Thurles, on Easter Sunday. Of bitter disappointment to Thurles G.A.A. and Tipperary was the decision taken by Congress not to stage the All-Ireland hurling final in the town.

LEGAL STATUS SECURED

A general meeting of the shareholders was held in the Confraternity Hall, in February 1935, for the purpose of securing the legal status of the property. It was proposed that Thurles Gaelic Sportsfield Society Ltd. would purchase the property from the present shareholders. The purchase money would be accepted in fully paid up shares of the society - three fully paid up £1 shares in respect of each £1 originally contributed. If the offer was accepted, it was further proposed that the existing debt of £515, due to the National Bank, would be taken up by the new society.[36] Tom Semple, chairman of the society, presided at the meeting, attended by about forty people. He explained that the original committee was not a legally established body, not registered under any Limited Liability Company or Friendly Society and that the proposal under discussion, if accepted, would secure the ownership of the grounds. Following a brief discussion, acceptance was proposed by William Carroll, seconded by Gerard Connaughton and carried unanimously. Later in the year, Tipperary county board unanimously approved this decision.[37]

The sportsfield committee was busy finalising the provision of accommodation for an extra ten thousand people. The embankment had been extended; thousands of tons of material had been drawn from houses recently demolished in the town and further material was made available by the Irish Sugar Co., Thurles. A new stand had been erected, constructed of timber on concrete supports and galvanized roof and would accommodate over eleven hundred patrons.[38] Thirty thousand supporters saw Limerick out-class Cork, the extra accommodation, though very welcome, was not sufficient to cope with the attendance. The local press was very critical of the Sportsfield committee, in this regard.[39]

---

[35] *Tipperary Star,* 3 Mar. 1934.
[36] Ibid, 23 Feb., 2 Mar. 1935.
[37] Ibid, 9 Sept. 1935.
[38] Ibid, 27 July 1935.
[39] Phil O'Neill, 'Slieve Ruadh' in *Tipperary Star*, 3 Aug. 1935. Henry Martin, *Mick Mackey – Hurling Legend in a Troubled County* (Cork, 2011), p. 21-2.

THE POWER OF PRAYER

Limerick played Cork in the Munster semi-final at Thurles Sportsfield, on 28 July 1935. Limerick won well by 3-12 to 2-3 but the game left two abiding memories. Mick Mackey's display for Limerick is regarded as one of the most brilliant and spectacular individual displays of hurling ever seen. The other concerns an accidental injury suffered by Cork hurler, Tommy Kelly. For a time his condition appeared so grave that the 'Last Rites' of the Catholic Church were administered, as players and spectators knelt in prayer. Rumour quickly spread around that he was dead. 'As I knelt in prayer with thousands of others for the happy passing of this young soul, I feared greatly in my heart for the future of our Gaelic games'[40]. The player was later removed to Thurles District Hospital, where he quickly recovered and was discharged on the following day.

EXPANSION 1936-'38

In 1938, the following committee members of Thurles Gaelic Sportsfield Society Ltd. were elected by ballot, at a special meeting held on 28 September:- M.J. Bowe, Thomas Semple, William Dwan, Rev. Philip Fogarty, James Maher, Philip Slattery, William Leahy, William Bowe, D.H. Ryan, Jeremiah Dwyer, Sylvester Butler and Loughlin Scully. Ed. O'Gorman was re-appointed secretary as was Tom Semple chairman and William Dwan treasurer. The solicitor to the society was E.T. Ryan, Cathedral Street. Title to the property, formerly held by Messrs Daly, has now been secured by the society.[41]

New sideline seating, eight rows, and a new embankment were added in 1938.

40 Phil O'Neill *Tipperary Star,* 3 Aug. 1935.
41 *Tipperary Star,* 10, 31 Oct. 1936.

There was an important meeting in the town, at the end of October to discuss plans for the improvement of Thurles Sportsfield. The traders and townspeople heard Rev. Philip Fogarty C.C. and Mid Tipperary chairman, talk about plans to expand the capacity of the field to cater for attendances of fifty thousand people. The first part of the expansion would cost £4,000 and the Munster Council had agreed to contribute £2,000. He hoped that the townspeople would contribute the remainder and in this way help to make the venue the 'Croke Park' of Munster. A resolution in favour was passed and the following committees were formed:- Material committee (chairman – Fr. Philip Fogarty), concert and plays committee (chairman – Br Lynam), whist drive committee (chairman – Willie Joe Moloney) and the dance committee (chairman – Joe Dan Fitzpatrick).

A joint committee, consisting of six members of Thurles Gaelic Sportsfield Society Ltd. and six members of Munster Council was appointed to investigate means of developing the venue. By the end of November, T.J. Hyland B.E., town surveyor, had plans to erect a wall around the pitch at an advanced stage. Regarding the provision of material for extending the embankments, it was agreed to ask the railway company, after the sugar campaign in Thurles was over, to give their lorries at an agreed reduced rate to draw the cinders from Thurles sugar factory to the Sportsfield. The Board of Works would be asked to provide an excavator to help with the work.

In order to facilitate entrance to the venue, seventeen new turnstiles were provided. They would be used as follows:- two for the side-line, four for the stands and eleven on the roadside.

At the following year's Munster convention, T.J. Hyland gave details of proposed alterations and improvements to the Sportsfield. The estimated accommodation: embankment – 34,000, stand – 10,000, sideline 6,500. The cost was estimated at £8,684. After a long discussion, Hyland was asked to prepare plans for an alternative scheme, costing £4,000.

In April, Hyland presented a revised scheme to the council, which would increase the capacity of the grounds to 40,000 and costing £4,415. This proposal was adopted and the Munster Council agreed to contribute £2,000 of the cost, if the local committee could raise a similar amount.[42]

The field in front of the monastery (C.B.S.) was placed at the disposal of the G.A.A. to hold their fund-raising bazaar and carnival, which lasted thirteen days, in aid of improvements to the sportsfield. The bazaar was a great success

---

[42] *Tipperary Star*, 27 Mar. 1937.

making £564 profit. An inter-club tug-of-war competition, in association with the bazaar, was the highlight for many, with Moycarkey coming out best. It was decided to hold something similar the following year.[43]

By 1938, the refurbishment and development of Thurles Sportsfield, agreed the previous year, had been progressing very well. The support from the townspeople of Thurles for the fund-raising events gave great encouragement to the Sportsfield committee to proceed. By April, the following works had been completed:-

1. Moving the pitch forward from the stand-side, so as to enlarge the sideline accommodation on that side.
2. The embankment on the opposite side had been moved backwards and repositioned.
3. Eight rows of sideline seats were laid on concrete blocks, all around the pitch, curving at the corners. The front rows were sunk below pitch-level.
4. A concrete wall was built all around, behind the sideline seats.
5. Bridge-like entrances had been provided to the sideline with corridors for turnstiles.
6. 30,000 extra tons of material had been acquired to raise and extend the embankment.
7. 2,000 railway sleepers had been purchased to help raise and terrace the embankment.
8. The main entrance had been improved and extra stiles provided.
9. A score-board was installed.[44]

The entire contract was carried out by James Skehan & Sons., Thurles, while Thomas J. Hyland B.E., acted as architect. To date the present works had cost £5,000. £2,000 had been granted by the Munster Council, £500 from Central Council, with the remainder being raised by the traders and townspeople of Thurles. The grounds were now capable of accommodating 50,000 people, in comfort and safety and described as second only to Croke Park. It was the largest embanked playing area in Ireland.

THE STRATOSPHERE GIRL

One of the highlights of the year was the annual carnival and bazaar. For the second year, Thurles Sportsfield Committee organised the carnival as a fundraising event for their major development. This year, the venue was again the monastery grounds and the festivities were officially started by Very Rev. Michael O'Dwyer D.D., the former Thurles All-Ireland hurler.

---

[43] Mid Tipperary Board Minutes-1938, p.187.
[44] *Tipperary Star*, 23 Apr. 1938.

Top attraction at the fundraising carnival in 1938 was Camille Mayer, The Stratosphere Girl.

At the carnival, the 'tug o' war' contests were the stuff of legend as all the surrounding G.A.A. clubs, Garda Síochana, local firms etc. entered teams. Ten shillings was the entry fee per team of ten. Two contests would take place each evening and the ultimate winners would receive a valuable Blarney suit-length each. Eighteen teams entered the fray and by the following week Holycross and Clonmore had won their way to the final, with Clonmore winning the suit-lengths.

Highlighting each evening were performances given by 'The Stratosphere Girl'. This young German, fraulein, Camille Mayer, dressed in a sailor costume, thrilled the crowds with her acrobatics on top of a steel mast, one hundred and thirty-seven feet (42 m) above the ground.

A confined cycle race on the Mall-Mill Road circuit was very attractive, especially to members of the Thurles Cycling Club. There was a large entry and it created great local interest. Sarsfields hurler, Tommy Doyle was so far ahead, going into the last lap and seeing no opposition in sight, eased up his blistering pace. Tommy explains, 'It was a mistake that cost me the race. In the last hundred yards D. Cleary came from nowhere to pip me at the post. Though I lost first place, I nevertheless qualified for the honour of a dance with 'The Stratosphere Girl'.[45] Third in the cycle-race was Neil McNamara.

---

[45] Tommy Doyle as told to Raymond Smith, *A Lifetime in Hurling* (London, 1955), p. 80.

MUNSTER FINAL 1939

The Munster final, the plum fixture of the year, was in Thurles, on 30 July. No less than 40,986 people saw Cork beat Limerick, by 4-3 to 3-4. This was 10,000 more than the previous best. Twenty-two special trains brought much of the crowd to a game described as one of the greatest of all time. One report described the game thus, 'It was a glorious, thrilling all-exciting game, an event that set hearts throbbing madly and blood pulsating madly. Class hurling at any time is the fastest ball game on earth. Sunday last at Thurles it was 'grease lightning' and of such play adequate description is inadequate. On the forty odd thousand that thronged Thurles, it left an indelible impression that can never be erased. Those not present can never get an adequate description'.

Catering for such an influx of people into the town seriously challenged those who had undertaken this task. The local correspondent wrote,' Bread simply vanished in heaps, milk in gallons, tea in streams and meat in cwts.[46] By the time that all demands had been met and those who were catering had time to have a bite themselves, it was none too easy to scrape a meal together. It was the general opinion that this event eclipsed all other occasions in the volume of business done.' It was conservatively estimated that the day meant a taking of £20,000 in the town. The attendance at the All-Ireland final, known

Pre match parade 1940s Cork v Limerick

---

[46] cwt. = centum weight = the hundredweight. It is defined as 112 pounds, which is equal to 50.802345 kg. This is the definition used in the imperial system of measurement.

Mícheál O'Hehir, with plenty of clerical support, broadcasting from Thurles Sportsfield in the 1940s.

popularly as the 'Thunder and Lightning' final, in Croke Park, on 1 September, was over one thousand less than the Munster final attendance in Thurles.

In 1939 also the N.A.C.A. All-Ireland championships were held at Thurles Sportsfield. Star of the show was Garda Ned Tobin, who created two new records at the event.

THE SPORTSFIELD CARNIVAL

The fundraising carnival and bazaar was held again this year at the Monastery grounds. Billed as being better than ever, it lived up to expectation and people travelled from far and wide to enjoy the attractions. Once again the 'tug o' war' competition was a highlight. Two divisions were contested, teams of 112 stone and 120 stone.

Holycross reached the final, of the 120 stone division, but were defeated by Tubbereenmore from Cork. They got the runners up prize of a set of rugs, while the winners received suit-lengths. Kilcommon beat Ballyhackett, Carlow in the 112 stone division. Judges were Guard Charlie Harkins, Sergeant Gerry Reidy and Guard Larry Kinsella.

Not to be missed was the daring nightly performance given by 'Cyclone Danny' and the 'Blonde Bombshell' (Miss Betty Plant) aboard their motor-cycle. Tragedy almost struck on the first night, when a plank snapped as they approached the 'flaming wall'. Both were hurled off the machine and rendered unconscious. Gladly they made a full recovery.[47]

Financially, the carnival was much more successful than the previous year and the debt on the sportsfield was almost cleared.

MUNSTER FINAL 1940

The Munster final between Cork and Limerick was in Thurles Sportsfield on 28 July. After an hour's hurling, the score stood at Limerick 4-3, Cork 3-6. Carbery, the popular correspondent described it thus, 'Thurles was no place for weak hearts in Sunday's broiling heat and excitement...Many of us thought that the 1939 Munster final had reached hurling meridian. Yet this year's memories switched 1939 into limbo of forgotten things and battles long ago. Scribblers are bankrupt of phrases. Our vocabulary is exhausted-we must invent a new language to describe modern hurling. So overwhelming was the closing delirium of surging scores-like a crescendo of brass music-that all spectators were hushed and awestruck. Good men and true, all in action to the stirring finish. And there is more to come for they finished all square.'[48]

The replay was at the same venue, the following Sunday and the game was equally as good. The first thirty minutes produced hurling hardly ever before witnessed. At half-time Cork led by one point to nil. Then in the third quarter Limerick hit a golden patch that brought them ten points in ten minutes. Cork rallied and but for brilliant Limerick back play and unbeatable Paddy Scanlan, between the sticks, they might have succeeded. Limerick 3-3, Cork 2-4. Limerick went on to win the All-Ireland title.

THE 1940s ATMOSPHERE

Local journalist Raymond Smith sets the scene:-

He sits on the footpath that leads to the Gaelic grounds at Thurles on a summer's day that is different from any other day in the sporting calendar. For it is Munster final day. 'Blind from Birth' reads the card across his chest and the voice cries unmistakably to the passer-by: 'Never pass the poor afflicted blind'. His voice mingles with the cries of those selling favours: 'Colours of the match, get your colours', with the shouts of the programme sellers; 'Programmes of the

---

[47] *Tipperary Star*, 17 June 1939.
[48] 'Carbery' – Paddy Mehigan, *Hurling – Ireland's National Game* (Dublin, 1942), p. 97.

match, official programme', and the music of the three blind fiddlers, for whom the pennies pour in.

The turnstiles click merrily and the stands and embankments fill up-a shirt sleeved crowd if the day is hot and colour everywhere. The crowd join in singing 'The Banks of My Own Lovely Lee' or 'Slieve-namon'. There are certain songs as there are certain characters associated with the day and the occasion.

The players come out and walk up the sideline past the main stand. The crowd hums with expectation as the famous faces are recognised, the stars of the present and the great ones, now team mentors, who won renown on this ground in the past.

The teams are parading now and shrewd eyes look out calculatingly from under the lowered cap peaks of the knowing ones on the embankment-the men born and bred in Thurles, 'the cradle of the G.A.A.' These are the most exacting critics in the country and coldly dispassionate in their judgments of hurling men-even their own.

The cheers rise as the teams parade. They swing

Tom Semple at Thurles Sportsfield (now Semple Stadium) after a game in 1934.

210

Left to right: John Walsh, Chairman of Thurles Sportsfield; Phil O'Neill, 'Sliabh Rua'; Tom Semple, Chairman Thurles Sarsfields and Paddy Mehigan, 'Carbery', at Thurles Sportsfield in the late 1920s.

into the centre of the field and now they stand to attention as thousands of voices sing 'Faith of Our Fathers'. How stirring always the moment. You are standing there bare-headed as you look around the ground at the tight-packed crowd, the sea of faces; you feel the tradition built up down the years flowing through your veins. Silence now-the national anthem and then a surging roar as the ball is thrown in and the game is on...

You can die a thousand deaths in the last minute of a typical Munster final as the ball bobs about in the goalmouth and the dust flies in the clash of the ash. The tension becomes almost unbearable as time ebbs away and your team is desperately striving to hold on to a slender lead. And yet in those very moments of nerve-racking tension you live all that is great in our native pastime.

Those who have experienced it know what I mean; those especially, who come from the hurling strongholds of the south, and have been brought up to know that it is in the testing fires of Munster championship hurling that a Munster hurler must establish his reputation, if it is to be a lasting one.

Enjoying the 1928 Munster final at Thurles Sportsfield. The group includes:- Most Rev. Dr Harty – Patron of the G.A.A., Seán Ryan – G.A.A. President, Rev. J.J. Meagher – Chairman Tipperary G.A.A., Rev. M.J. Lee, General Eoin O'Duffy, Major Fitzmaurice, Chief Supt. Hannigan – Thurles, William Myles – Editor Tipperary Star, Rev. T. O'Connor – Thurles, Rev. Dr Doyle – Kilkenny, Rev. M. Maher – Killenaule, Con Browne – G.A.A. Limerick, Dan Morrissey – Dungarvan.

A Munster final etches incidents in the memory that never die. You can talk about them in the glow of the firelight for a lifetime...

Afterwards the crowd flows down like a great tidal wave over the railway bridge and back into town. The pubs spill over. The hotels and restaurants and the private houses with their 'Meat Teas' signs prominently displayed, quickly swallow up the hungry. Many of the spectators have been in the field since midday. Nowhere can they cater as they do in Thurles on big match days, for they have known these big occasions since 1926. There is hurling talk in the air and there is atmosphere-the atmosphere that Thurles alone can evoke on this day.

The trains leave and the cars pull out from the car parks; twilight lengthens into darkness and they gather at 'the school around the corner' to argue about the match. This is the corner in the shadow of the Dr Croke Memorial in Liberty Square sacred to the knowing ones, who have seen them all back in the days of Captain Johnny Leahy and earlier. The banter and repartee, the wit and humour flow in the evening air.[49]

END OF AN ERA

The untimely death of Tom Semple in 1943 was a major loss to Thurles Sportsfield Committee. Tom had been central to all the developments since the grounds were bought in 1910, being on the first ever committee and was chairman of the sportsfield committee at the time of his death. Tom played a major role in the raising of funds for its early development. There is no doubt that Tom Semple was born to lead, a commanding figure, his magnificent physique and easy manner earned the respect of thousands of patrons, as he built up the reputation which Thurles Sportsfield gained for excellent stewarding on the days of major games. His guidance and foresight had ensured that the Sportsfield had kept abreast of developments through the years and had met the growing needs of the association. Thurles Sportsfield was seen as possessing the best playing surface in Ireland, capable of hosting major fixtures and a welcoming and memorable venue for the supporter. No other stadium in the country could compare with its unique atmosphere, especially on a Munster final day.

[49] Raymond Smith, *Decades of Glory* (Dublin, 1966), pp 9-12.

MAJOR GAMES PLAYED IN THURLES SPORTSFIELD 1910-1943

6 November 1904. *Croke Cup Finals* at Thurles Agricultural Society Grounds (now Semple Stadium).
Football – Tipperary (Tipperary Club) 2-4, Dublin (Bray Emmets) 0-4.
Hurling – Cork (Dungourney)1-1, Dublin (Faughs) 0-2.

16 June 1907. *All-Ireland Football Final 1905* at Thurles Agricultural Society Grounds. Attendance – between 15,000 and 20,000.
Kildare (Roseberry) 1-7, Kerry (Tralee Mitchels) 0-5.

9 May 1909. *All-Ireland Football (Home) Final 1908* at Thurles Agricultural Society Grounds. Attendance – 12,000.
Dublin (Geraldines) 0-10, Kerry (Tralee Mitchels) 0-3.

20 September 1914. *Munster Hurling Final* – Clare 3-2, Cork 3-1.
Referee: Tom Semple. Attendance: 20,000.

15 September 1918. *Munster Hurling Final* – Limerick 11-3, Clare 1-2.
Referee: Tom Semple.

28 May 1922. *Munster Hurling Final (1921)* – Limerick 5-2, Cork 1-2.
Referee: Frank McGrath.

1 July 1923. *Munster Football Final (1922)* – Tipperary 1-7, Limerick 0-1.
Referee: W. P. Aherne.

1 July 1923. *Munster Hurling Final (1922)* – Tipperary 2-2, Limerick 2-2.
Referee: Paddy O'Keeffe. Attendance 20,000.

19 September 1926. *Munster Hurling Final* – Tipperary 3-4, Cork 4-1.
Referee: Denny Lanigan. Attendance 30,000.

3 October 1926. *Munster Hurling Final (Replay)* – Tipperary 2-4, Cork 3-6.
Referee: Denny Lanigan. Attendance 30,000 plus.

15 July 1928. *Munster Hurling Final* – Cork 2-2, Clare 2-2.
Referee: W. Hough, Limerick. Attendance 27,000.

29 July 1928. *Munster Hurling Final (Replay)* – Cork 6-4, Clare 2-2.
Referee: P. Walsh, Kilkenny. Attendance 30,000 plus.

31 July 1932. *Munster Hurling Final* – Clare 5-2, Cork 4-1.
Referee: W. Gleeson, Limerick.

2 August 1936. *Munster Hurling Final* – Limerick 8-5, Tipperary 4-6.
Referee: J. O'Regan, Cork.

30 July 1939. *Munster Hurling Final* – Cork 4-3, Limerick 3-4.
Referee: M. Hennessy, Clare.

28 July 1940. *Munster Hurling Final* – Limerick 4-3, Cork 3-6.
Referee: D. Ryan Kilkenny.

4 August 1940. *Munster Hurling Final (Replay)* – Limerick 3-3, Cork 2-4.
Referee: D. Ryan, Kilkenny.

CHAPTER 19

Troubled Times in Thurles – Anglo Irish War

CALM BEFORE THE STORM

THERE IS no doubt but that the second decade of the twentieth century was one the most turbulent in Ireland's history. In Thurles, as the decade began, the Irish/Ireland movements such as the G.A.A., the Gaelic League and others were growing in prominence and had gained a sound foothold in the town. The quest for Home Rule was also gaining momentum. A huge Nationalist demonstration supporting Home Rule was held in Thurles on 18 April 1909.The local press encouraged a full attendance: 'It behoves every Tipperary man worthy of the name, to rally to the call and no matter how far his home may be from Thurles, he should be there to show by his enthusiasm on the great occasion, that the voice of Tipperary rings as true as when her men assembled under Smith O'Brien, John Mitchel, John Martin and John Kenyon.[1]

In the House of Commons, London, the Home Rule Bill was passed in 1912. The Unionist reaction was the formation of the Ulster Volunteer Force (U.V. F.) to oppose Home Rule, which it turn triggered the formation of the Irish Volunteers (*Óglaigh na hÉireann*) in 1913 to support it and Nationalist causes generally. Many G.A.A. members enrolled in the Volunteers. Thurles volunteers trained and drilled at Thurles Sportsfield and many of the local G.A.A. members were involved including most likely Tom Semple. His life-long colleague and best-man at his wedding, Jack Mockler, was to the forefront in the organisation of the Irish Volunteers. Volunteer activity increased as the year progressed with regular parades from the town through Leugh and back to Thurles through Rossestown and the Quarry. Drilling was arranged to take place on four nights weekly and competent military instructors were secured.[2]

[1] *Nenagh News*, 17 Apr. 1909.
[2] *Tipperary Star*, 15 May 1914.

In August, the outbreak of the Great War convulsed Europe. Home Rule was suspended until the end of the war. John Redmond, leader of the Irish Parliamentary Party called for the Irish Volunteers to support the British war effort. This caused a split in the Volunteers; a minority opposed to participating in the war retained their original name-Irish Volunteers. In Thurles and in North Tipperary generally there was no rush to join the British army following Redmond's call for enlistment. In most cases it was economic factors that caused enlistment.[3] The Redmondite majority was renamed the National Volunteers, but less than one sixth of these had enlisted in the British army by February 1917.[4] In October, the Thurles Corps of the National Volunteers used Thurles Sporting Grounds as a rifle range. Three targets were set up with a range of 200 yards.[5]

The reality of the Great War really hit home in Thurles, when tragic news of deaths and casualties began to filter through and the visit of the Post Office boy, with the dreaded telegram, bearing the bad news, was too common. Prayers were said in the Cathedral for the dead, wounded and those missing in action. The names of war zones, such as Gallipoli, Arras, Marne and Ypres became familiar.[6]

The secret military organisation, the Irish Republican Brotherhood (I.R.B.) was also active in Thurles. As seen in a previous chapter, police reports of that time, state that 'Thurles, in particular, holds solid for the I.R.B.'[7] and 'the I.R.B. and the G.A.A. are carried on in conjunction, as far as the leading men are concerned'.[8] Thurles G.A.A. club chairman, Denis O'Keeffe, and secretary, James M. Kennedy were deeply involved in the movement, as were many club members. The successes of the Semple era had enhanced the status of the G.A.A. in Thurles. The rise of the G.A.A. had stimulated a sense of local patriotism, as the club base was the local parish. Pride in parish led to pride in one's native county and this in due course led to a stronger feeling of identity with one's nation. The role played by James M. Kennedy in the I.R.B. cannot be underestimated. Jimmy as secretary of Thurles Sarsfields club and later town clerk was a very close colleague of Tom Semple, a relationship forged to great success on the G.A.A. front would now focus on the struggle for Irish independence.

---

[3] Seán Hogan, *The Black and Tans in North Tipperary*, (Dublin, 2013), p. 109.

[4] *Note:-* Over 93% joined the National Volunteers, leaving the Irish Volunteers with an estimated 12,300 members. Conor Mulvagh, *Irish Independent, Home Rule Supplement*, p. 3, 13 Sept. 2014.

[5] *Tipperary Star*, 10 Oct. 1914.

[6] *Note:-* Seventy-two Thurles men lost their lives in the Great War. One of them, John Cunningham (1890-1917), a native of Stradavoher was awarded a Victoria Cross posthumously for gallantry near Barlin, France.

[7] NAI, C.B.S. 11921-S.

[8] NAI, C.B.S. 11876-S.

In a statement to the Bureau of Military History, Jimmy Leahy, Tubberadora native and Thurles hurler, who was later Commandant of the Second Tipperary Brigade I.R.A., stated, 'In January or February 1916, I was sworn into the I.R.B. by Jimmy Kennedy, the town clerk in Thurles, and the local I.R.B. centre. It was he who was responsible for the reorganisation of the Irish Volunteers in the town in 1915. I was still in Thurles when the Rising occurred in Dublin in Easter 1916. Jimmy Kennedy was in direct contact with the leaders of the rising... A dispatch was received by him on Easter Sunday, or on the previous day, from Dublin. I am not aware or the contents of this dispatch...[9]

Jimmy Leahy, Thurles, in Irish Volunteer uniform in 1917.

Public opinion was utterly hostile to the Easter Rising. However, the execution of the leaders caused a change in the attitude of the Irish people to admiration for the insurgents and support for the nationalist cause. By June, the newsagents in Thurles were selling huge quantities of picture postcard photographs of the executed leaders, and in the drapery shops there was a big demand for republican mourning badges.[10]

Following the 1916 Rebellion, the Sinn Féin Party re-formed itself as the political arm of Irish militant nationalism, in opposition to John Redmond's Irish Party. The steady growth in support for Sinn Féin, particularly in the Thurles area was noted by the police authorities. According to their intelligence reports, the membership of Sinn Féin was synonymous with that of the G.A.A. and the Gaelic League.[11] How to deal with this youthful energetic movement that combined politics, culture and sport would be challenging for the authorities. The newly-formed Thurles (Seán Mac Diarmada) Sinn Féin Club had its first meeting in early June 1917. The following

J.M. Kennedy.

[9] Irish Bureau of Military History, 1913-21, Document No. W. S. 1454. p. 3, Statement by James Leahy, Nenagh, Co. Tipperary.
[10] *Tipperary Star*, 17 June 1916.
[11] Seán Hogan, *The Black and Tans in North Tipperary* (Dublin, 2013), p. 66.

committee was elected:- president – Charlie Culhane, vice president – D.H. Ryan, hon. secretaries – James M. Kennedy and Denis Morgan[12], treasurer – James Butler, committee – Michael Eustace, Pat Hunt, J. Fitzgerald, Tom Kerwick, J. Higgins, W. O'Loughlin, M. Rahill, Joe McLoughney, R.F. Quinn and M. McCarthy.[13] All the officers and most of the committee members were members of Thurles Sarsfields club and close acquaintances of Tom Semple.

Early in July 1918 an order from the British authorities at Dublin Castle prohibited the holding of public meetings without a permit. Needless to say, the G.A.A. refused to apply for permits. The association also requested every unit to organise matches in hurling and football at 3.00 p.m. (old time) on Sunday, 4 August 1918. In every nook and corner of the country, even in jails and prison camps in Ireland and Britain, games took place. Some 54,000 players participated in Gaelic matches in an impressive display of passive resistance. As a consequence, the British ban was rendered useless. Games were to start at 3.00 p.m. The G.A.A.'s decision was published in advance and faced with such a massive act of disobedience, the authorities were powerless to intervene. Tom Semple, chairman of Mid Tipperary Board organised fourteen games, all of which were played.

'From Jones's Road to the craggy hillsides of the Kingdom, the day was fought and won in fields no bigger than backyards, in stony pastures and on rolling plains, on the banks of rivers and on village greens and in the official venues of the Gaels, wherever posts could stick up and places cleared, the descendants of Fionn and the Fianna routed the seal of servitude. In one never to be forgotten tournament, we crossed our hurleys with the lion's claw and emerged victorious.'[14]

ANGLO IRISH WAR – WAR OF INDEPENDENCE (COGADH NA SAOIRSE)

With the ending of the Great War in early November 1918, a general election was called. Polling took place on Saturday, 14 December. Sinn Féin confirmed their popularity, sweeping the boards by getting seventy-three of their candidates elected to six for the Irish Parliamentary Party. Sinn Féin could now claim, with justice, to represent majority opinion in Ireland. Rather than take their seats at Westminster, the newly-elected Sinn Féin representative constituted themselves as Dáil Éireann and proclaimed themselves the parliament of the Irish Republic. The election victory was followed not by peace

---

[12] Dublin native, Denis Morgan, was a teacher in Thurles C.B.S., teaching English, Irish and Mathematics. He also taught Irish to the students at St Patrick's College in the town.
[13] *Tipperary Star*, 9 June 1917.
[14] William Nolan, (ed), *The G.A.A. in Dublin 1884-2,000* (Dublin, 2005), pp 144-'5.

but by the Anglo-Irish War (War of Independence), which began at Soloheadbeg, County Tipperary on 21 January 1919. The Irish Republican Army (I.R.A.), as the Volunteers became increasingly called, through their 'flying columns' conducted ambushes and barrack-burning, which were punished by the proclamation of Martial Law and reprisals. They aimed to make British rule in Ireland impossible. Many players were in jail, others 'on the run', roads were often blocked with fallen trees, bridges blown up and the British military on constant patrol. To train a team was impossible and travel was restricted. All led to championship games being disrupted and few competitions completed. Even the usual monthly fairs and markets in Thurles did not take place, as permits for such were refused by the military authorities.

COLLINS AND SEMPLE

Michael Collins

Tom Semple

The success of the I.R.A. in the Anglo/Irish War depended not alone on the courage and sacrifice of the officers and members of the 'flying columns' but also on the vast silent support network that existed in the background. These networks provided logistic assistance to the fighters, without which they could not succeed. The British military forces often assumed they were fighting a small group of activists, not realising the multiple layers of supporters and sympathisers that made up the resistance to British rule in Ireland. The simple task of carrying messages occupied thousands of forgotten but dedicated activists, both men and women, during the Anglo/Irish War. Michael Collins was appointed the Director of Intelligence of the Irish Volunteers in January 1919. At an early stage he knew how vital it was to their effort to have a better intelligence service than the British and without delay he laid the groundwork for his intelligence network. Collins had penetrated the Irish and English postal, telephone and telegraph systems. Letters and dispatches could be moved to various contacts by certain train inspectors. The railway workers were organised by Michael Collins so effectively that the military frequently had to move troops and stores by road, which would play into the hands of the I.R.A. ambushes as the war intensified. Many railway workers were suspended owing to their refusal to work on trains carrying soldiers or munitions of war[15]. One of Michael Collins' most valued and trusted railway couriers was Tom Semple. He was the direct link to Collins for the Tipperary No. 2 Brigade I.R.A.[16] Tom's knowledge of the transport system, his integrity, leadership qualities and decision making capacity were invaluable to Collins's intelligence structure. Since 1911, Tom Semple was railway guard on the G.S.& W.R.[17] This position was ideal in his capacity as a courier for Michael Collins. He had responsibility for the safety of the train and usually has a purpose-built compartment complete with controls for the brake and communication with the driver and the passengers. It was the guard's duty to see that the doors are properly closed and the train is safe to depart and signal to the driver. The guard was also responsible for seeing that the train ran punctually. Green flags or lamps were used and the guard could also signal with a whistle. The position of railway guard also necessitated that Tom would be occasionally away from home overnight. In the Thurles locality of Fianna Road, Croke Street and Friar Street, he was a familiar figure as he walked to work in uniform. If work demanded that he be away overnight, he carried a large basket containing food and a change of clothing.

Though we have no specific proof of Tom Semple knowing Collins prior to the 1918 or 1920 period, it is likely that their paths would have crossed in G.A.A. circles. When Collins, as a teenager, went to work in London, he became very involved with the G.A.A.[18] In addition to being an active hurler; he became treasurer of the London G.A.A. Board in 1907. It is certain that he would have known of Tom Semple at that time, and they would have had numerous common friends and acquaintances within the G.A.A. circles.

Michael J. Costello (1904-1986), who was later general manager of the Irish Sugar Company, was, during the Anglo Irish War, intelligence officer with the North Tipperary Brigade I.R.A. He was well aware of Semple's involvement in the struggle. Speaking with Seamus Leahy he stressed the importance of the ease of communication between Thurles and Dublin. 'Thurles', he said, 'was

---

[15] Piaras Béaslaí, *Michael Collins and the Making of a New Ireland,* Vol. I (Dublin, 1926), p. 441.
[16] Seán Hogan, *The Black and Tans in North Tipperary* (Dublin, 2013), p. 255.
[17] NAI, Census of Ireland 1911.
[18] Piaras Béaslaí, *Michael Collins and the Making of a New Ireland,* Vol. I (Dublin, 1926), pp 15-16.

nearer to Dublin than to Nenagh and Tom Semple was a vital link in the chain.'[19]

Piaras Béaslaí, in his monumental work, *Michael Collins and the Making of a New Ireland*, Vols. I and II, published in 1926, makes reference to Collins' work with regards to railway communication:- 'On all the lines there were guards and other officials who regularly carried Volunteer messages, even during the time when trains and passengers were systematically searched by the Black and Tans. Among the men he was closely in touch with in connection with this work may be mentioned… and Semple of the Great Southern.'[20] The dispatches carried by Semple were for or from Jimmy Kennedy, later Thurles town clerk, who was Collins's principal activist in Thurles[21].

In 1926, Francis Conlan (1884-1953) of Edward Street, Newbridge, Co. Kildare, a railway porter and I.R.A. member, applied successfully for a military service pension. In his affidavit seeking the pension he stated, 'I joined the Irish Volunteers in 1917. I was in the I.R.A from 1 April 1920 to 30 June 1922. My activities included looking after dispatches and ammunition in Newbridge. Captain Ambrose asked me to report on troop movements from Newbridge and he gave me dispatches to pass to an individual named Semple. I was, on orders from Michael Collins and O'Sullivan, responsible for organising contacts on the railway line. I recruited individuals in counties Kildare, Kilkenny and Tipperary. The majority of Irish Volunteers were recruited from the ranks of the Gaelic Athletic Association and I was a prominent Gaelic footballer. I was a member of the railway intelligence group, reporting directly to G.H.Q.'[22]

Evidence given by, Irish Volunteer, John C. Murphy, Mallow County Cork, to the Bureau of Military History includes:- 'About this time (1919) I joined the staff of the Great Southern and Western Railway as a porter at Mallow station. I was then detailed to do intelligence work regarding the movement of military stores… As a result of reports furnished by me and the other railway employees engaged on this work, several raids were carried out… We were responsible for the safe transit of all dispatches passing through Mallow railway station and post office. We had the handling of all such communications for all units in the southern area. We worked in conjunction with the railway guards and ticket checkers on all trains, amongst them the following:- Tom Mulligan, Peter Brady, Dan Hickey, John Lenehan, Martin Fox, Tom Semple, John Ivors and

---

[19] Interview with Seamus Leahy (6 Oct. 2014). Seamus Leahy's father, Jimmy, was Commandant of the Second Tipperary Brigade I.R.A. during the Anglo Irish War. Note:-In 1914, the Leahy brothers, James (Jimmy) and Mick, natives of Tubberadora, transferred to Thurles Sarsfields. Both brothers had come to work in Thurles soon after leaving school in Gaile N.S.
[20] Piaras Béaslaí, *Michael Collins and the Making of a New Ireland*, Vol. I1 (Dublin, 1926), p. 38.
[21] Interview with John Hassett, Croke Street, Thurles (14 June 2012).
[22] Irish Military Service Pensions Collection, File Ref. 24 SP12102.

Con Buckley. There were several others whose names I cannot recollect'.[23]

Tom Semple's grandson, T.J. Semple recalls, 'In my early days working in the *Tipperary Star*, Friar Street, Thurles, I often met Sarah Kennedy from Drombane. During the War of Independence, she was a member of Cumann na mBan and was well aware of my grandfather's involvement as a courier for the I.R.A., carrying dispatches etc. She mentioned it to me several times. She also mentioned that Tom Semple was regularly searched by the R.I.C. and British military on his way home from the railway station after work.'[24]

TERROR IN THURLES

District Inspector Michael Hunt, R.I.C., aged forty-six, was shot dead in Thurles on Monday, 23 June 1919. The men who actually fired the shots were Jim and Tommy Stapleton, first cousins, and Jim Murphy. The Stapletons came from Finnahy, Upperchurch and Murphy belonged to

British military tank in Liberty Square, Thurles, September 1919.
(Photograph courtesy: Paddy Loughnane, Thurles)

Curreeney, Kilcommon,[25] all I.R.A. volunteers. The shooting happened at the junction of Parnell Street and Liberty Square. It was race day in the town and Hunt was in charge of a body of police and military at the racecourse. Hunt had been to the forefront in the suppression of Irish Ireland activities in the hinterland of Thurles.

Jack Carew

Jack Carew, Parnell Street, recalls, 'I remember the day in 1919, when I was six or seven. It was race-day in Thurles and Gerard, my younger brother, and myself went out to the street. My mother warned us not to go further than the Palisades, which is Dr. Barry's corner. We went towards the Square and crossed over to Denis McCarthy's drapery shop and were both standing on the footpath. The crowds were going by in their hundreds from the races, when we heard two shots – a

[23] Witness Statement, 1217, Bureau of Military History, John C. Murphy, member of Fianna Éireann 1917, I.R.A. Cork 1919-1923.
[24] Interview with T.J. Semple (3 Feb. 2014).
[25] Irish Bureau of Military History, 1913-21, Document No. W.S. 1454. p. 19. Statement by James Leahy, Nenagh, County Tipperary.

man dropped dead right beside us. He was as dead as a door-nail and we were looking down at him. The people went racing here and there and we in our youthful ignorance didn't really appreciate what was going on. We were both grabbed and pulled into the shop. The man who was shot was a policeman, D.I. Hunt. He was shot by a republican from Upperchurch. That was a very long time ago but I remember it, as if it was yesterday'.[26]

Archbishop Harty condemned the killing as a flagrant breach of the fifth commandment.[27] Following the shooting, the Government at once banned Sinn Féin, the Irish Volunteers, Cumann na mBan and the Gaelic League throughout County Tipperary. The Black and Tans,[28] were a force hastily recruited to assist the Royal Irish Constabulary (R.I.C.), in late 1919. Thousands, many of them British World War I veterans, answered the British Government's call for recruits. The R.I.C. in Thurles was reinforced and armed parties of police and military, patrolled the town and surrounding districts, day and night. The extra forces were housed at Thurles Fever Hospital.[29]

On Tuesday night, 20 January, an R.I.C. officer, Constable Luke Finnegan, was shot when entering his house at Thomond Road. His shooting triggered scenes of great disorder in the town, remembered as 'The Sack of Thurles'. The police and military, Sherwood Foresters, rushed through the town shooting up houses and throwing grenades indiscriminately, wrecking and looting several houses. The violent night assault on Thurles by the R.I.C. is generally considered to be the first instance of police reprisals in this increasingly brutal war. The home of Denis Morgan, chairman of Thurles Urban District Council, opposite the Ursuline convent on Cathedral Street, was especially targeted. Many other premises in the town were raided and some wrecked with explosives:- Molloy's Hardware, Jer. O'Dwyer's, McLoughney's drapery, O'Connell's public house, D.H. Ryan's drapery, Benson's drapery, Tobin's Hotel – all on Liberty Square,

Donncha Ó Muireagáin – Denis Morgan – Chairman of Thurles Urban District Council 1920.
(Photograph courtesy: Donagh Morgan)

---

[26] Jack Carew was a jeweller at Parnell Street, Thurles. He was treasurer of Thurles Sarsfields G.A.A. Club for a period in the 1970s.

[27] Seán Hogan, *The Black and Tans in North Tipperary* (Dublin, 2013), p. 131.

[28] *Note:-* The nickname "Black and Tans" arose from the colour of the improvised khaki uniforms they initially wore.

[29] Thurles Fever Hospital, later St Mary's District Hospital, now St Mary's Health Centre.

*Michael (Mixie) O'Connell with his son
Michael, taken c1925.*

'The Irish Independent' – January 22nd, 1920

T. Fitzgeralds, West Gate and the Tipperary Star and the
premises of Charlie Culhane on Friar Street.[30]

On the night of 26/27 March, a young man, James
McCarthy, a close neighbour of Tom Semple and a
baker at Johnston's in the town, was shot dead, by two
policemen, when he answered the door of his house on
Fianna Road. His brother, Michael, was on the urban
council and had sought an inquiry into the events of
20 January, following the shooting of Constable

James McCarthy

Finnegan. This murder was seen by the public as retaliation. On 12 May there
was a further vicious attack on the McCarthy home, when the police were
suspected of arson.[31]

When it became clear that the Black and Tans were insufficient, the British
cabinet authorised the formation of another police organisation, the Auxiliary
Division of the R.I.C., composed of ex-army officers, who enrolled as 'police
cadets'. They were formed on 27 July 1920 to be a mobile strike force and were
known the 'Auxies'.

The shooting of Thomas O'Loughlin, Killinan, on 1 December 1920 by the
R.I.C. while attending a card game at the farmhouse of Michael Leahy in
Mullaunbrack, caused heartfelt grief and shock in the locality. Tom, who was

---

[30] Fr. Colmcille, O Cist., 'Tipperary's Fight in 1920' in *Capuchin Annual*, 1970, p. 266; *Tipperary Star*,
24 January 1920.
[31] *Nenagh Guardian*, 15 May 1920.

twenty four years of age, had died in Thurles hospital, eighteen days after the shooting. Archbishop Harty strongly condemned the outrage and counselled the people to exercise patience and restraint in the face of terrible provocation.[32]

From the beginning of October 1920, the Thurles police began a campaign of violence and terror unequalled by anything previously experienced. Sometimes masked and disguised, they went around the town and district at night to the houses of people whom they suspected of being connected with the I.R.A. If the person was at home, he was shot out of hand. On the night of 1 October several houses were raided by this 'Murder Gang', one of the first being Jimmy Kennedy's home. Luckily Jimmy was not available. Later the same night Michael Cleary, was taken from his home at Drish and shot, but survived. As Piaras Béaslaí recorded:- 'The 'Murder Club' found one of its first centres in Thurles, where the R.I.C instituted a reign of terror. Civilians were held up, beaten and robbed daily in the town and its vicinity... and at night they introduced the practice of 'shooting up' the town – a lesson quickly learned by the Black and Tans. The practice consisted of firing wildly about the streets so as to create terror... They also invented the 'reprisal' which became an established practice of the English Government in Ireland and ultimately was officially acknowledged... These events synchronised with the announcement of the appointment of Sir Hamar Greenwood as Chief Sec. for Ireland and Sir Nevil Macready as commander-in-chief of the British forces in Ireland...[33]

In the last days of February 1921, at Loughtagalla, Thurles, a young I.R.A. volunteer, William Kelly, Mitchell Street, was fired at by the police and shot dead. He had been acting as a scout for Thurles I.R.A. who were drilling in the area. The I.R.A. responded to this and to the arrest of some prominent members among their ranks by executing two suspected spies. Jimmy Leahy stated, 'Reprisals for those executions took place on the night of 9/10 March 1921. Five masked and armed policemen raided the house of Laurence Hickey, aged forty, a vintner and grocer, Main Street, Thurles, and found the owner in bed. He was

Laurence Hickey

ordered out in his night attire and when he reached the head of the stairs he was tripped and thrown downstairs by an R.I.C. man named Jackson. In the fall, Hickey's neck was broken and he was in great pain at the foot of the stairs when

[32] *Tipperary Star*, 4, 18 Dec. 1920.
[33] Piaras Béaslaí, *Michael Collins and the Making of a New Ireland*, Vol. I (Dublin, 1926), p. 433, pp 440-1.

Plaque at the entrance to St Mary's, Thurles.

Willie Loughnane.
(Photograph courtesy Paddy Loughnane)

Sergeant Enright, who was in charge of the raiders, shot him dead, to put an end to his agony. Hickey was a well known republican in Thurles, and a detailed account of his shooting was given to me during the Truce period by Sergeant Enright himself. While the raid in Hickey's was in progress, another party of masked policemen visited the home of the Loughnane family in Mitchell Street, Thurles, and shot dead in bed William Loughnane, a labourer, aged twenty-three. This man along with his father and three brothers were active members of the local I.R.A. company. On the same night, the Barry homestead in Turtulla, a short distance from Thurles, was entered by R.I.C. men in disguise. They were looking for Denis Regan, aged thirty-two, a workman and a prominent I.R.A. man. He had hidden in a couchette in the house and when the police could not find him, they ordered Michael Barry to come with them, as they were going to shoot him instead of Regan. Barry had no connection with the republican movement and Regan overheard remarks made by the raiders. Rather than see his employer suffer on his account Regan left his hiding place and gave himself up. Barry was then released while Regan was led into the yard where the police fired six or eight shots at him. Though very seriously, wounded in the chest and right hand, he survived...[34] The town was in mourning with all normal business practically suspended. Most Rev. Dr Harty, speaking at Mass in the cathedral, on the following Sunday stated, 'We call for, we demand a public inquiry, in which the public can have confidence'.[35]

[34] Irish Bureau of Military History, 1913-21, Document No. W.S. 1454, p. 68. Statement by James Leahy, Nenagh, CountyTipperary.
[35] *Tipperary Star*, 19 Mar. 1921.

Tragedy continued to stalk the town of Thurles. Three I.R.A. volunteers were surprised by a police patrol on 30 March, as they raided the office of the Petty Sessions clerk on Slievenamon Road, in the town. Following an exchange of gun-fire, they fled the town, through the railway yard, pursued by the police and their reinforcements of Black and Tans on foot and in lorries. One of the three, James (Jimmy) McLoughlin, aged eighteen, a native of Croughafoyle, Kilcommon who worked in Thurles, was shot dead at Cormackstown, while the other two escaped. Jimmy was a past-pupil of Thurles C.B.S., having attended there from his aunt's house at Corcoran's, The Heath[36]. During his funeral a group of Auxies, stationed at Templemore, entered the cathedral in Thurles and removed the Sinn Féin flag

Jimmy McLoughlin

from his coffin[37]. The following week, on 2 April, Thurles I.R.A. executed, what they termed a 'convicted spy' in Thurles.

Obviously, Tom Semple was known to both the local R.I.C. and the Black and Tans not only as a leading G.A.A. figure and administrator, but was suspected of being a Collins courier and without question a supporter of the I.R.A. Tom was connected, through his second marriage, with the Loughnane family, which suffered the ultimate reprisal mentioned above. Willie's brother, Jimmy, married Katherine (Kit) Creagh, the sister of Winifred Creagh, who married Tom Semple in 1934.[38]

THE BLACK SPOT

As those who knew Tom well, often recall the black spot on his cheek and its origin is worth explaining. As a railway guard on the Dublin/Cork line, Tom Semple was a regular courier for the republican movement carrying dispatches. When he arrived back in Thurles one evening after his day's work, he received a tip-off from a policeman that he would be stopped on his way home. He

---

[36] *Tipperary Star*, 20 Mar. 1971.
[37] *Nenagh Guardian*, 9 Apr. 1921.
[38] *Note:-* Both Tom Semple and Willie Loughnane are buried in St Mary's cemetery, Thurles. Plaques on each of the two pillars at the entrance to the cemetery commemorate them.

delivered his 'goods' to Ned Hogan, who was his contact at the station and was travelling down on Jimmy Dorney's Munster Hotel bus when he was stopped and taken into the barracks that was on Friar Street at that time.[39] There he was strip-searched but nothing was found except a battered button from a rail-workers uniform. Tom's interrogators maintained that the button was off an Irish Volunteer's uniform. They then stood Semple against a door and started blazing bullets from their revolvers, close to his head, but he did not 'crack'. The outcome of the incident was that some gunpowder became embedded in the skin on his face, accounting for the ever-present black spot. Later that evening, Tom was released.

Tom's only daughter, Anne, recalls, 'Our mother told us the story of our father being picked up by the 'Tans' or the R.I.C. and being taken to the R.I.C. barracks on Friar Street for interrogation. Either on the way or at the barracks our father got rid of the communication by eating the papers prior to being searched'.[40]

U.C.C. historian, John Borgonovo, writing in the *Irish Sword* states, 'Reliable communication between Dublin and Cork emanated from the distribution of the banned Irish Volunteers magazine *An tÓglach*, in 1918. These first editions were smuggled from Dublin to Cork by sympathetic railway workers. Some participating firemen, conductors, guards and office clerks were Volunteers, but many were older unaffiliated sympathisers. The railway network eventually consumed control of I.R.A. communications between Dublin and Cork and later various provincial units. Documents might be hidden in ink-jars and Guinness bottles and left casually in the guard's van. During daylight, workers also placed messages inside tail-lamps. Often workers simply tacked the documents under the floor boards of carriages. Once the train arrived in Cork, dispatches were left at the station office, inside a secret compartment built into the floor.[41] Tom Semple's son, Martin, recalls his mother, Winifred, telling him that Tom normally carried the communications in a secret pocket sewn into his railway uniform overcoat.[42]

It was in this atmosphere of strife that the foundation stone of the Archbishop Croke memorial was laid by Archbishop John M. Harty, on St Patrick's Day, in Liberty Square, Thurles. Croke was always seen by the British authorities as a champion of Irish nationalism and a most influential voice in the success of the Gaelic Athletic Association. The erection of such a monument

---

[39] Mason Mechanical Limited now occupies the premises where the barracks was situated.

[40] Interview with Mrs. Anne Gunning, née Semple (11 July 2014).

[41] John Borgonovo, *The Guerrilla Infrastructure: I.R.A. Special Services in the Cork No.1 Brigade, 1917-1921. The Irish Sword*, Vol. XXVII (No. 108), p. 207.

[42] Interview with Martin Semple (11 July 2014).

to Croke in such a significant position in the town was seen as defiance by the British authorities. Such was the tension in the town that the organisers feared that the event might not go ahead and be proclaimed by the British.[43] As we have seen in the previous chapter, even the menacing presence of the Black and Tans did not deter the proceedings going ahead and the solemn expression of solidarity shown by Tom Semple in standing shoulder to shoulder with the Archbishop did not go unheeded by the authorities.

There was very good reason to believe that Dr Harty might well be at risk by the 'Black and Tans'. Jimmy Leahy recalled, 'I think it was in the last week of October that Sergeant Hurley gave me a list containing twelve names of prominent people who had been marked down for shooting by the Thurles R.I.C. "murder gang", if there were any more of the Crown forces shot in the Thurles district. My own name headed this list and, either second or third was Dr Harty, Archbishop of Cashel and Emly... In the first three was Joe McLoughney, a draper and a staunch republican. On receiving this list, I made a secret visit to Canon M. K. Ryan and informed him of the dangerous position of the archbishop... I assumed that he had no idea that he was marked down for the vengeance of the "Murder Gang" and told all this to Canon Ryan. The canon became very upset on hearing what I had to say. He tried to obtain an assurance from me that nothing would occur around Thurles which might harm the archbishop, but I firmly assured him that considerations of that kind would not cause any lessening in the activities of the men under my command in Thurles or elsewhere...[44]

TRUCE

The War of Independence ended at noon, on 11 July, when a truce was arranged. The order circulated by I.R.A., G.H.Q. was signed by Risreárd Ua Maolchatha (Richard Mulcahy), chief of staff. Mulcahy, who took part in the Easter 1916 Rebellion, was a past-pupil of Thurles C.B.S., a most active member of the Gaelic League and a member of Thurles Sarsfields G.A.A. Club.[45] The announcement of the Truce was greeted with gladness in Thurles and when the appointed time of twelve o'clock was reached on Monday a breath of relief was drawn by everybody in the district. The Anglo

General Richard Mulcahy

[43] St Patrick's College, Thurles, Philip Fogarty, research notes, (unpublished work).
[44] Irish Bureau of Military History, 1913-21, Document No. W.S. 1454. p. 50-50A. Statement by James Leahy, Nenagh, County Tipperary.
[45] *Tipperary Star*, 2, 23 Dec. 1916.

LEFT:
Lancia armoured car and
Crossley Tender leaving Thurles
R.I.C. Barracks, Friar Street,
January 1922.

BELOW:
British forces leaving
Friar Street, Thurles,
January 1922.

Irish Treaty was finally agreed and signed on 6 December. With the Treaty, the Irish Free State came into being and the British forces began to leave the twenty-six counties.

1922 CIVIL WAR, COGADH NA GCARAD

The Anglo Irish Treaty was ratified by Dáil Éireann on a vote of 64 to 57, on 7 January. This narrow verdict divided the Dáil and the country. The evacuation of the town by the R.I.C. was completed by 24 February. The British military, who had occupied Thurles Fever Hospital,[46] had already withdrawn. The forces

---

[46] Thurles Fever Hospital, later known as Thurles District Hospital, now known as St Mary's Health Centre.

so firmly united in the struggle for independence were divided now on the terms of the Treaty. Charlie Culhane, chairman of Thurles Urban Council, left the chair rather than accept the motion in favour of the Treaty, which was passed unanimously in his absence. Old neighbours and old comrades parted company and in a military conflict, lasting about ten tragic months, between June 1922 and May 1923. Ireland was a land of broken hearts and broken hopes.

With the setting up of the Irish Free State, Tom Semple answered Michael Collin's call for those who had participated in the War of Independence to join the newly formed National Army, also referred to as the Free State Army. It was Semple's great sense of duty that spurred him in making this decision. Michael Collins, whom Semple greatly admired, was the army's first chief-of-staff. Tom resigned his position as railway guard on 12 December 1921 and while with the army he was commissioned as a captain in the force. Tom was now forty-two years of age and soon discovered that army life did not suit him. He also realised that his main responsibilities lay in Thurles with his wife and family and so on 26 May 1922 returned to his position with the railway.[47]

1923 SLOW RETURN TO NORMALITY

Although almost all of the military activity had ceased, the political temperature remained high for most of the year. The formal end of the Civil War was declared in April, but a large number of political prisoners, including many hurlers, were still detained and conditions in the country were far from normal. Thurles town clerk, J.M. Kennedy, had been arrested during the year but was released un-conditionally.[48] The Civil War had an impact on the G.A.A. with former team mates now finding themselves on different sides of a bitter conflict. The brutality of the Civil War necessitated extraordinary degrees of reconciliation. It was on the playing fields after the Civil War that the G.A.A. played its part in bringing former enemies together, in the middle and late twenties. Gaelic games gave to a shattered people a reason to unite for a common purpose. As the months went by, young men, who had borne arms against one another were hurling on the same teams and working together as club officials. Irishmen who had viewed each other from opposite camps were back in the same fold and the G.A.A. facilitated the slow process of reconciliation and normalisation of life. Tom Semple was to the forefront in helping unite players from both sides of the Civil War. As a coach, trainer and administrator, he was at the grass-root level of the G.A.A. and was well aware of the deep scars and the broken trust caused by the Civil War. In the years that

---

[47] Interview with Oliver Doyle, Irish Railway Record Society Sec., Hueston Station, Dublin (9 April 2014).
[48] *Tipperary Star*, 28 Apr. 1923.

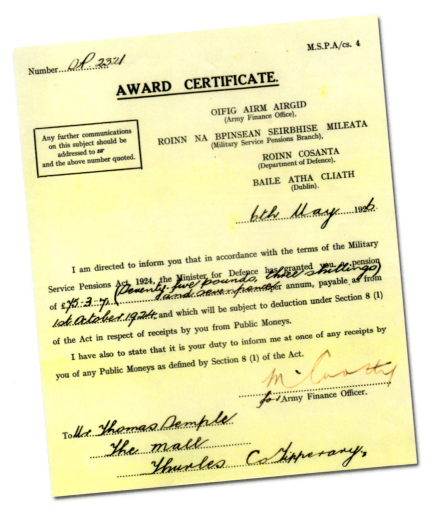

followed, Tom was approached on a number of occasions to stand for the Dáil, but always refused so that he could devote all his spare time to the G.A.A. in his various roles.

Just a few weeks after Tom Semple's death in 1943, his War of Independence service medal was delivered to his home at 3 Fianna Road, Thurles. It is remembered as being a very emotional event for Tom's widow, Winifred. His son, Martin, now holds the medal and it is among his most treasured possessions.

Tom Semple's War of Independence medal.

CHAPTER 20

Tom Semple –
G.A.A. Administrator

MUNSTER COUNCIL

TOM SEMPLE was Tipperary's representative on the Munster Council of the G.A.A. from 1907 until 1917. Holding this position for such a long period is reflective of the high standing Tom had attained among the Gaels of Tipperary. During his early years on the council, Tom was still a very active inter-county hurler. Such a situation would not arise today, where council representatives are usually past their playing days and well-seasoned G.A.A. administrators. But his success on the playing fields and his undoubted leadership qualities gave Tom Semple a status that belied his years in the council chamber. His advice was sought and his opinion valued, not alone in Tipperary but throughout the province. Tom had a proficient knowledge of the G.A.A. rule-book and was formidable in the council chamber as he presented, argued, advocated and debated propositions, resolutions, objections and appeals on behalf of Tipperary. This was all part of the cut and thrust of administration in the association, particularly in the early days, when objections to decisions and appeals were more common than in the modern era.

When Tom joined the Munster Council, it was still in its infancy, having been established in 1901. The main competitions at senior inter-county level were well established and while Tom was on the council, junior football and hurling championships were inaugurated. It was also during these years that Gaelic games were included as organised competitions for schools and colleges. The main impetus for this came from Tipperary G.A.A. and received support from Archbishop John M. Harty, patron of the association, who sponsored a trophy for inter-schools hurling. Thus the Dr Harty Cup competition, for senior inter-college hurling, was inaugurated in 1918. Tom Semple advocated, at

Munster Council, that a similar competition for football should be organised.[1]

The early development of Thurles Sportsfield, with which Tom Semple was so closely identified, gained from his presence on Munster Council. As a member of the council, he was in a prime position to see that Thurles Sportsfield got, at least, its quota of championship matches, thus establishing Thurles as a major venue for hosting games. He was also able to secure grants and loans from the Munster Council so that the sportsfield kept abreast of developments and became the standard-bearer for G.A.A. venues nationwide.

Frank McGrath, Toomevara and Nenagh.

The most contentious issues of the period, that involved Tom Semple, were undoubtedly the dispute involving the Croke Memorial and the purchase of the grounds that are now known as Croke Park. These are dealt with already in this book. Tom was also on the Munster Council during the period of the Easter Rising in 1916 and its aftermath. This was a very tense period for the G.A.A., as its members ran the gauntlet for organising games and activities that clearly were anathema to the British authorities. Incidentally, for many of the years that Tom represented Tipperary on the Munster Council, the other representative from the county was Frank McGrath, Idrone, Nenagh, who was later commandant, Tipperary No. I (North Tipperary) Brigade I.R.A.

To serve on the Munster Council for a decade required a huge commitment from Tom Semple. While some meetings were held in Thurles, most were held in Limerick or Tipperary town, which involved time-consuming travel. He was now a married man with a wife and young family to provide for. He also had the responsibility of his daily work duties on the railway and coupled with this, in his later years on the council, he was chairman of Mid Tipperary Board and deeply involved at Thurles Sportsfield.

MID TIPPERARY G.A.A. CHAIRMAN

The Mid Tipperary G.A.A. Board was formed on Sunday, 9 June 1907 and from its inception, Tom Semple was among its leading lights. Even though his hurling career was now at its height, Tom as captain of club and county, was deeply involved in administration. The role of captain has greatly changed

---

[1] *Tipperary Star*, 13 Jan. 1917.

Mid Tipperary G.A.A. Board c1915
Front row (l.-r.): Tom Semple, Chairman; Very Rev. Fr. Finn P.P., Drom.
Back row (l.-r.): Maurice O'Loughlin, James Maher, Anthony Carew, Daniel Maher N.T.

since Semple's time, when the captain was central to all matters dealing with the preparation and selection of his team, transport arrangements, substitutions during play etc.

In 1911, at the annual convention of the Mid Tipperary Board, Tom Semple was proposed for the chairmanship, but declined and he proposed Mikey Maher, the former Tubberadora hurling stalwart, in his stead. Mikey was elected unanimously, but at the following year's convention, on 11 February 1912, Tom Semple, who at first declined the position, was prevailed upon to take the chairmanship for the following year. Tom, now aged thirty-two, was no stranger to leadership roles, having captained Thurles and Tipperary for almost a decade. Indeed, Tom Semple relished leadership roles, whether on or off the field. He was more a doer than a talker and leadership positions gave him the opportunity to get things done.

In 1913, Tom was re-elected but because of work commitments with the railway company, he could not attend many meetings. This concerned him and in the course of his address to the convention, held on 12 January in the Confraternity Hall, Thurles, he stated, 'I'm in a peculiar position. My business often takes me away from Thurles on Sundays and I could not attend any meeting during the week. Some people might think I am shirking my position but such is not the case. I'd like to see men in the position that could attend every meeting'. Tom wished to resign the chairmanship, but it was the unanimous wish of convention that he remain in office.

The following year, at the annual convention, on 18 January, held in Lambe's Hall, Tom Semple sought to be relieved of the position of chairman but was elected unanimously. In a lengthy address to convention he noted that the financial position had improved and went on the comment on the games, 'The standard of hurling is good, of a high order, both senior and junior. But turning to football, I regret that I cannot compliment them as I do the hurlers. Between two teams in the division there was nothing but objections and objections'.[2] In 1915 Tom Semple was re-elected chairman. This was a year that also saw Tom as a selector on the county senior team. The Forrester's Hall, Thurles, was the venue for the Mid Tipperary convention on 2 January 1916. Tom Semple was unanimously re-elected as chairman, following a proposal by Johnny Leahy, seconded by Paddy Maher (Best).[3] During the year, under the Defence of the Realm Act (DORA), permits were necessary to run G.A.A. games. Under Semple's chairmanship, the Mid Board decided not to apply for permits to run their games and also decided that police be refused admission to their games, unless they paid the admission fee.

Later that month, at the Tipperary county convention on 12 January, the outgoing chairman, Tim Ryan, Newport, did not seek re-election. Tom Semple was nominated for the position of chairman. While thanking those who nominated him, Tom withdrew his nomination intimating his reluctance to seek election to the chair. However, his former team-mate with Thurles and Tipperary, Tim Gleeson, was then unanimously elected.[4]

In his address to the Mid Tipperary convention at the Forrester's Hall on 11 February 1917, Tom Semple congratulated Boherlahan on bringing back All-Ireland honours to Tipperary. He had special praise for vice-chairman and treasurer, E.D. Ryan, for the steps he was taking to introduce Gaelic Games to the schools and colleges in the county. However, Tom was critical of the baneful effect on the association of not playing matches at the advertised time. He stated, 'The board will support any referee who strictly enforces the rule on punctuality. Referees have the power to suspend a team or both teams who are not on the playing pitch, within a quarter of an hour of the scheduled time'.[5] Tom was re-elected chairman unanimously. In proposing his re-election, vice-chairman E.D. Ryan stated, 'We, Gaels, would be little better that ship-wrecked, if we were deprived of Tom Semple's valued guidance'.[6]

---

[2] *Tipperary Star*, 24 Jan. 1914.
[3] Ibid, 8 Jan. 1916.
[4] Ibid, 18 Jan. 1916.
[5] Ibid, 17 Jan. 1917.
[6] Ibid, 17 Feb. 1917.

The Mid Tipperary convention met at the Forrester's Hall on 17 February 1918. Tom Semple wrote resigning the chairmanship of the board. He also wished to thank the members for the courtesy shown him while he was chairman. On the motion of Tom Kerwick, seconded by Jim Maher, both of the Thurles club, Tom Semple was re-elected as chairman.[7] Early in July an order from Dublin Castle prohibited the holding of public meetings without a permit. The intention was to prevent the playing of games and the holding of athletic meetings. The G.A.A. refused to apply for permits. A special meeting of the Central Council, on 20 July, decided to throw down the gauntlet to the authorities by arranging 1,800 games all over the country. Games were to start at 3.00 p.m. on 4 August. This decision was published in advance and faced with such a massive act of disobedience, the authorities were powerless to intervene. Tom Semple and the Mid Tipperary Board organised fourteen games, all of which were played.

During 1918, Tom Semple was unable to be present at most of the meetings of the Mid Tipperary Board. His absence is unexplained, possibly due to work commitments. In his absence his fellow clubman, Tom Kerwick, usually acted as chairman. Tom Semple did not attend the Mid Tipperary annual convention at the Forrester's Hall, Thurles, on Sunday 23 February 1919. He was not proposed for re-election and Tom Kerwick, was elected chairman.[8] Kerwick had been chairman of Tipperary County Board from 1910 to 1914.

REFEREE

When his playing days were over, Tom was in great demand as a referee. His undoubted knowledge of the games, his reputation for fairness and sportsmanship coupled with his strict interpretation of the rules, all ensured that he was kept busy with the whistle. It was a role he enjoyed himself, as it kept him close to the games he loved. He was also a firm believer that former players should stay involved with their club and participate in administration or team preparation. Tom Semple took charge of games at all levels from street-leagues in Thurles to Munster championships in both hurling and football.

Not alone did Tom referee hurling and football games, he also had control of the whistle at some camogie matches. Such involvement is indicative of his encouragement of active participation in sport by women. When the neighbouring camogie clubs of Horse and Jockey and Two-Mile-Borris met in a tournament final on 9 January 1916, it was Tom Semple was in charge of the whistle.[9]

---

[7] *Tipperary Star,* 23 Feb. 1918.
[8] Ibid, 1 Mar. 1919.
[9] Ibid, 2 July 1988.

Among the highlights of his refereeing career, which extended from 1912 until 1920, was his handling of the 1914 and 1918 Munster senior hurling finals. These were the first two Munster hurling finals to be played at Thurles Sportsfield. Tom occasionally combined his role as chief steward with his refereeing duties, as seen by this report from 1914, 'Tom Semple who had refereed the junior event and who also had charge of the whistle in the senior contest performed his duties in a highly satisfactory manner. Previous to the start of the senior event the side line was thickly crowded with spectators, and Tom Semple adopted the wise precaution of insisting on the touch line being cleared before the big contest was begun.'[10]

G.A.A. TRUSTEE

Tom Semple's many spheres of involvement in the G.A.A. were recognised nationally when he was elected trustee of the association at the annual Congress, held in the Mansion House, Dublin, on 1 April 1923. On the day, brisk voting marked the election of the two trustees and eventually Paddy McDonald, Dublin and Tom Semple, Thurles, were selected.[11] This was the first congress to convene since the memorial honouring Archbishop Croke was unveiled in Thurles in June 1922 and Tom's appointment as trustee was an acknowledgement by the association of the leadership role played by him, particularly, in that historic event.[12]

1914 Munster Hurling Final. Referee Tom Semple.

This Congress was held at the end of the Civil War, which formally ended in April, and the delegates recognised that they needed the leadership and commitment of men like Tom Semple to help unify and bring together hurlers and footballers, especially those who had been on the opposite sides in that conflict. The G.A.A., which played a critical role in gaining the newly-won freedom of the Irish State, facilitated the slow process of reconciliation and normalisation of life.

[10] *Cork Examiner*, 21 Sept. 1914.
[11] *Tipperary Star*, 7 Apr. 1923.
[12] *Note:-* Nowadays G.A.A. trustees are known as 'Representatives of Congress'. They serve a three-year term as representatives of Congress on the G.A.A.'s Central Council.

CHAIRMAN OF THURLES SARSFIELDS CLUB

Among his many G.A.A. responsibilities, Tom Semple always saw the fortunes of his local club, Thurles Sarsfields, as being paramount. As captain and player, in his hurling days, he strove might and main to achieve success for his beloved club. He demanded a high standard from himself and from his team-mates. He believed in disciplined preparation for whatever challenge lay ahead and unity of purpose in achieving their goal.

Tom became chairman of Thurles Sarsfields club in 1925, taking over from Canon M.K. Ryan, and he held the position until 1939. The experience he had gained from his years as Mid Board chairman and as a delegate to the Munster Council, made him invaluable to the club. He was a first-class administrator and his years at the helm saw the return of Sarsfields as a hurling power in 1929, winning the Tipperary county championship for the first time since 1911. This pattern was continued in 1935,'36, '38 and '39.

During his years as the chairman of the Sarsfields, he continued to be a major force and the leader in the development of Thurles Sportsfield. The very year after he became chairman, he led the critical stewarding and crowd control at the replayed Munster final that was held in Thurles in 1926, where he established once and for all that the Thurles Sportsfield could safely accommodate the largest crowds and was the ancestral home of Munster hurling.

Membership Card – Thurles Sarsfields 1940.

GOLDEN JUBILEE CELEBRATIONS 1934

At the G.A.A. Congress, in March 1932, delegates were well aware that the golden jubilee of the association would be celebrated in 1934. A suggestion mooted was that the Congress and the All-Ireland hurling final of that year would be held in Thurles. Local correspondents were of the same opinion that the suggestion was fitting and appropriate that the association should honour its birthplace.[13] The following year, at the Congress, in City Hall, Dublin, it was decided that, as part of the forthcoming jubilee celebrations, the congress in 1934 would be held in Hayes's Hotel, Thurles. However, there was much local disappointment, that the decision on the playing of the All-Ireland in Thurles was postponed and was dependant on improvements being completed at Thurles Sportsfield.[14]

'Irish Independent' – Golden Jubilee Souvenir.

From a perusal of Thurles Sportsfield committee reports, it is obvious that Tom Semple and the committee were almost certain that the 1934 All-Ireland final would be played in Thurles. Rev. J.J. Meagher, Club President, speaking at the 1934 annual convention of Thurles Sarsfields club, appealed to the club to help the sportsfield committee to improve the field, so that when representative Gaels would come to Thurles for Congress, on Easter Sunday, they would see that the Gaels of the town were up and doing; and that they meant to have the All-Ireland final played in the sportsfield in the Jubilee Year.[15]

GOLDEN JUBILEE CONGRESS IN THURLES

For Thurles and Tipperary, the highlight of the Golden Jubilee celebrations

---

[13] *Tipperary Star*, 2 Apr. 1932.
[14] Ibid, 22 Apr. 1933.
[15] An tAthair S. Ó Meachair, S.O., *Conventions or A Dozen Years with the Gaels of Tipperary* (Thurles, 1938), p.120.

1934 – G.A.A. Congress memorabilia.

was the hosting of the Congress in Hayes's Hotel, Thurles, on Easter Sunday. The town lived true to tradition, in providing a rallying centre for Gaeldom. Proud of the honour conferred on them, the townspeople spared neither expense nor effort to have everything in keeping with the historic event. Houses were decorated and the streets ornamented with bunting, flags and streamers with appropriate mottoes. To commemorate the occasion, the Minister for Posts and Telegraphs issued a special stamp and the national newspapers published special supplements.

Congress delegates, numbering two hundred, representing every county in Ireland, attended High Mass in the cathedral, at which Archbishop Harty presided. The celebrant was Rev. Philip Fogarty C.C., Thurles. After the Mass, the veteran and youthful members of the association marched in procession through Liberty Square, led by the Cassestown Fife and Drum Band and the Moycarkey Pipers' Band, they circled the Croke memorial and formed up in front of Hayes's Hotel. It was here that Archbishop Harty unveiled a bronze memorial plaque to commemorate the foundation of the G.A.A., on 1 November 1884. Among the attendance were several links with the earliest days of the G.A.A., three members of the victorious Tipperary (Thurles) team in the first All-Ireland of 1887 were present:- Martin McNamara, Tom Burke and Ned Maher. Also present was Michael Cusack's son John.[16] Prior to the unveiling ceremony, the archbishop, having welcomed the delegates to Thurles, paid tribute to the founders and continued, 'The G.A.A. is now beginning a new cycle of years. In the full vigour of its strength and manhood, it tranquilly faces

---

[16] Marcus de Búrca, *The Story of the G.A.A. to 1990* (Dublin, 1990), p. 200.

Delegates to the Golden Jubilee Congress of the G.A.A. photographed with Archbishop Harty outside the Cathedral of the Assumption, Thurles, on 1 April 1934. Tom Semple is towards the right on the front row, with his right arm raised.

the future. I believe that the triumph of the coming years will surpass its past glories. Genuinely Irish and standing for a united Ireland with glorious traditions and cherished customs, it must grow from year to year in the affection of our people. May God grant the fulfillment of this, our dearest prayer.'[17]

G.A.A. president, Sean McCarthy, thanked the archbishop and later at Congress in the Confraternity Hall, he stated, 'the G.A.A. was conceived and sponsored by Tipperary, Clare and Cork. For years, it rocked on troubled waters but it has successfully weathered every storm. Side by side with the revival of Irish games, there arose a greater love for Ireland, evident in the early years,

G.A.A. President Seán McCarthy addresses a thronged Liberty Square, Thurles at the G.A.A. Golden Jubilee celebrations, Easter Sunday 1934.

[17] Philip Fogarty, *Tipperary's G.A.A. Story* (Thurles, 1960), p. 348.

G.A.A. Golden Jubilee Plaque.

when our youth refused to be submerged in waves of foreignism sweeping the country and in later years in the fight for national independence... The future is full of responsibilities but it is safe in the keeping of the Gaels'.[18]

Most Rev. Dr John Harty, Archbishop of Cashel and Emly, Patron of the G.A.A. unveils the G.A.A. Golden Jubilee plaque at Hayes's Hotel, in the presence of G.A.A. President, Seán McCarthy.

Thurles G.A.A. club also presented an address to Congress. It was signed by:- Tom Semple – chairman, James Maher – treasurer, Donnacha Ó Macasa – secretary. It concluded with these lines, 'Come weal, come woe, let us guard the association for above it shines the glory of the Gael ... fifty years hence, may it be as strong, vigorous and Irish as it is today; as unchanged and unchangeable as its first patron. 'Céad míle fáilte' to Thurles, where close to Dr Croke's relics, you will recall the burning enthusiasm alone and unaided of his magnificent plea to rouse the old spirit and to open men's eyes to a true conception of things national. He spoke the message of Ireland unconquered, and he saw hosts uplift again in pride, and strength and beauty, the culture of this historic Irish nation'.[19]

---

[18] Philip Fogarty, *Tipperary's G.A.A. Story* (Thurles, 1960), p. 349.
[19] Ibid, p. 349.

The address that Semple presented on behalf of Thurles G.A.A. Club to the Congress truly reflected his deep beliefs of what the G.A.A. stood for and its critical role in the development of the nation.

ALL IRELAND FINAL FOR THURLES?

1934 Commemorative Stamp.

Of bitter disappointment to Tom Semple, Thurles G.A.A. and Tipperary was the decision taken by Congress not to stage the All-Ireland Hurling final in the town. Semple had moved the motion, 'That Thurles, the birthplace of the association, be honoured with this year's All-Ireland hurling final'. Tom had proceeded but a short distance when Seán Óg Murphy, Cork's G.A.A. secretary, brought the matter to an abrupt halt on a point of order as to the existing rule, by which it was agreed and had become the established usage to have all senior championship finals played at Croke Park. The chairman admitted that the rule was as stated and would need to be rescinded before the Tipperary motion could be entertained. He stated no further discussion could be allowed unless Standing Orders were suspended. A motion to suspend Standing Orders was moved by T. Flood, Meath, but it did not receive the necessary two thirds majority and the matter was closed.[20] Tom Semple had worked assiduously to host the 1934 All-Ireland hurling final in the town where the G.A.A. was founded fifty years before and one of his great disappointments was his failure to persuade the Congress to approve that request.[21]

PRESIDENT OF THURLES SARSFIELDS CLUB

As the 1930s drew to a close, ill-health was becoming a major problem for Tom and he was unable to attend meetings or fulfil his administrative duties, as he would like. He held his position as railway guard until 1940 when, he suffered permanent ill-health and was unable to work.[22] Consequently, he was paid-off by the Great Southern and Western Railway Co. on 3 September of that year.[23]

At the Sarsfields annual convention in February 1940, Tom did not seek re-election, handing over the chairmanship to William (Bill) Leahy, Friar Street. At this convention also, it was the unanimous wish of the delegates that Tom be appointed president of Thurles Sarsfields, a position he held until his death in 1943.

---

[20] G.A.A. Golden Jubilee Celebrations and Minutes of Annual Congress 1934 (Dublin, 1934), pp 18, 19.
[21] An Camán, 7 Apr. 1934, p. 7.
[22] P.D. Mehigan, 'Carbery', 'Five Great Hurling Captains' in *Carbery's Annual 1943-4*, p. 23.
[23] Interview with Oliver Doyle, Irish Railway Record Society Sec., Hueston Station, Dublin (9 Apr. 2014).

CHAPTER 21

1930 – The Ecstasy and the Agony

THE TREBLE CROWN

BEING 1929 county senior hurling champions, the spirit of the Gael was high in Thurles, as the new decade dawned. 1930 is remembered as the most glorious year, to date, in Tipperary's G.A.A. story. Winning the 'Treble Crown', Minor, Junior and Senior All-Irelands, was a feat never before achieved in G.A.A. history. Thurles G.A.A. Club, with Tom Semple at the helm, was the lynch-pin, from which that success blossomed.

The annual convention of Thurles G.A.A. Club was held in the Confraternity Hall on 9 February. The large attendance heard their chairman, Tom Semple, congratulate the senior hurlers on winning the county title even though, 'they entered the contest as a mere bunch of novices'. He complimented the training that had been done by Messrs O'Donnell, Harty and Tierney. He noted that the team had the three qualities for success:- speed, stamina and pluck.[1]

Thurles Sarsfields, as county champions, had the county selection and Tom Semple had undertaken the task of training the team. Tom was also chairman of the selection committee, which included Johnny Leahy, Frank McGrath, James Maher, Michael Gleeson and Paddy Brolan.

Tipperary and Waterford met in the Munster semi-final, at Dungarvan. The Déise had high hopes, following their defeat of Limerick, in the first round. This was a powerful Tipperary outfit, which went to their task early and secured a safe lead. In the second-half the game came to an abrupt end, when Waterford refused to continue. A scuffle had taken place in the Waterford backline between the opposing captains. The referee, Seán Óg Murphy, ordered both

---

[1] *Tipperary Star*, 15 Feb. 1930.

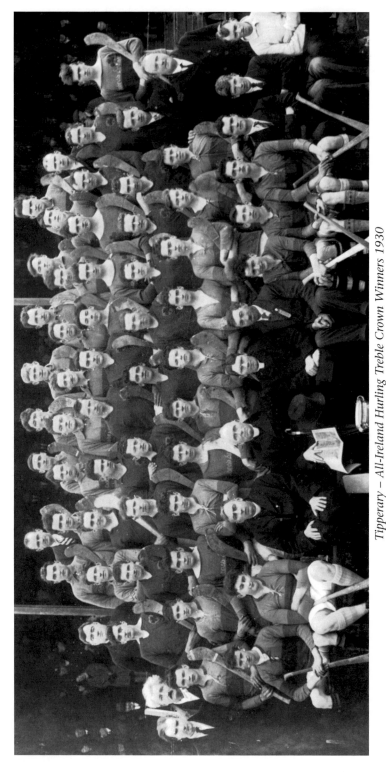

Tipperary – All-Ireland Hurling Treble Crown Winners 1930

Photograph includes seniors, juniors and minors. Back row: Phil Cahill, James Harney, Tommy Treacy, Tom Butler, Jack McKenna, Tom Leahy, Jack Stapleton. 5th row: Jim Lanigan, M.F. Cronin, Jimmy Heaney, Phil Purcell, J.J. Callanan (Senior Captain), Mick Ryan, John Maher, Jimmy O'Loughlin, Dan Looby. 4th row: Rev. M.J. Lee, Tommy Butler, Seán Harrington, Tom Rainey, Paddy Harty (Junior Captain), Jimmy Ryan, Tom Hayes, Tom Power, Martin Kennedy, Mick Ryan, Jack Dwyer, John Connolly. 3rd row: William O'Gorman, Ned Wade, Tom Harty, Tim Connolly, Martin Brown, Mick McGann, William Ryan, Joe Fletcher, Mick Ryan, Paddy Furlong. 2nd row: Frank McGrath, Pat McGrath (Munster Secretary), Paddy Ryan, Tom Kennedy, Joe Dunne, Gerry Heavey, Paddy Ryan, Ned Maher, Timmy Harney, Johnny Semple, John Lanigan, Jim Close, Dinny O'Gorman, Mick Maher. Front row: Peter Flanagan, Jack Russell (Minor Captain), Rev. J.J. Meagher (Co. Board Chairman), Archbishop John Harty, Rev. Philip Fogarty, Johnny Leahy (Tipperary Secretary), Jack Coffey, Jack Quinlan, Tommy Semple, Mick Boland, Willie O'Neill, Jack Gleeson.

men to the side-line. The Tipperary captain left but the Waterford captain refused to go and commenced to argue with the referee. A large number of spectators then entered the pitch. After much effort the pitch was cleared and as the match was about to re-commence, the Waterford team left the field, with Tipperary ahead 2-5 to 0-1. Tipperary were awarded the game.

The Munster title was 'up for grabs' at Cork's Athletic Grounds. Cork were out of the championship, having lost to Clare. This really spurred on the Banner men, as the crowds paid gate receipts of £1,295. Both Tipperary and Clare were at the peak of perfection, and the sequence of scoring in the opening half made it a succession of thrills. The pace was incredible and the hurling top-class. At half-time, Tipperary were barely ahead, 2-3 to 1-5. The goalkeeping of Toomevara's Tom O'Meara was uncanny and he guaranteed Tipperary's victory by 6-4 to 2-8.

The All-Ireland semi-final against Galway, in Tullamore, was a one-sided affair on a wretchedly wet day, with Tipperary victors by 6-8 to 2-4. The final against Dublin, in Croke Park, attracted an attendance of 21,730. Dublin were well in contention at half-time, with Tipperary ahead 1-3 to 1-2. Tom Semple was not happy at the break, as he gathered his men about him and did not mince his words as he gave them the instructions for the second-half. Straight from the resumption of play they got into battle with characteristic fire and determination. There was no going back, typified by Tommy Treacy, with his blood-stained bandage about his head. John Joe Callanan's goal in the second-half clinched the issue. Final score:- Tipperary 2-7, Dublin 1-3.

John Joe Callanan, Tipperary's captain, accepted the Liam McCarthy Cup. For the Thurles club, it was a proud occasion, with players John Joe Callanan, Jim Lanigan, John Maher, Mick Ryan and Jimmy O'Loughlin on the team, while Jack Stapleton, Jimmy Harney, Tommy Butler and Mick Maher were among the substitutes.

The team was accorded an enthusiastic reception, on their arrival in Thurles on the following day. Thurles Brass and Reed and the Moycarkey Fife and Drum bands led the thronged procession from the railway station to the cathedral yard, where Archbishop Harty greeted them. Tar barrels blazed through the town and jubilation prevailed. The archbishop,

John Joe Callanan (Thurles Sarsfields) – Tipperary Senior Hurling Captain 1930.

addressing the gathering, stated, 'We are proud they brought back the cup to Thurles, the home of the G.A.A. We are delighted that the men of Thurles and the men of Tipperary, whom Thurles selected, won such a great victory.'

Tom Semple's contribution to the All-Ireland success is recorded in these lines from the ballad:-

All-Ireland Final 1930

'Hats off to those heroes, this dashing fine pack,
Coached by Leahy and Semple, who stood at their back.
To those two past masters all honours are due,
For the victory they gained when the long whistle blew'.[2]

Jack Russell (Thurles Sarsfields) – Tipperary Minor Hurling Captain 1930. *Patrick Harty (Borris/Ileigh) – Tipperary Junior Hurling Captain 1930.*

The minor All-Ireland was also won, beating Kilkenny in the final by 4-1 to 2-1. Thurles were again in a leadership role. Jack Russell was team captain and Larry Burke, John Lanigan, Timmy Harney, Gerry Heavey, John Semple, and Tommy Semple, all from the Thurles Sarsfields club, on the team. What a proud day it was for Tom Semple, not alone a Tipperary All-Ireland victory but also seeing his two eldest sons, Tommy and John, hurling with the county.

The success of the juniors confirmed that the historic 'Treble Crown' had been realised. They also beat Kilkenny in the All-Ireland final by 4-8 to 3-2. Tim Connolly and Mick McGann were the Thurles club men on this historic junior team.

---

[2] King, Ó Donnchú, Smyth, *Tipperary's G.A.A. Ballads* (Thurles, 2000) p.191.

The action on the Gaelic fields came to a close as Christmas and convention time approached. Tipperary had the 'Triple Crown' and Tom Semple was happy that Thurles had played a pivotal role. Eighteen All-Ireland hurling medals had come to Thurles club hurlers during the year:- 2 Junior, 7 Minor and 9 Senior. The firesides of Thurles were happy; the turkey market on Liberty Square was large and brisk, with turkeys seven to nine pence per pound.

Following the success, Tipperary County Board received an invitation, through Wedger Meagher, sports editor of the *Irish Echo* in New York, inviting the All-Ireland champions to the U.S.A., to give exhibitions of the game of hurling.

Thurles G.A.A. club were to the fore in the organisation of the 'céilí mór' in the Confraternity Hall, Thurles, on Sunday, 15 February 1931, to celebrate the winning of the 'Treble Crown'. Earlier in the day, at Thurles Sportsfield, exhibition games were played, the three All-Ireland winning teams were photographed and Archbishop Harty presented the All-Ireland medals. Tom Semple's absence from the photographs is unexplained, but possibly was due to work commitments or the recent death of his wife.

Later, in the Confraternity Hall, the Siamsa Gael band from Dublin was making things lively with:- The Walls of Limerick, The Siege of Ennis, The Haymaker's Jig, The Fairy Reel and The Rince Fada. From the back of the hall and led by their captains, marched the three victorious teams, to the strains of O'Donnell Abú and formed up at the front of the hall, where they were officially welcomed by Rev. J.J. Meagher. Later, about one hundred and forty couples took the floor and dancing continued with unabated vigour and at intervals there were songs, stepdancing, solos on the pipes, violin and piccolo.

Rev. J.J. Meagher, Tipperary G.A.A. Chairman offered a prize of five pounds for the best poem on the county's success. It was won by Tom Keating, Cloneen, with his poem – 'Tiobraid Árann Abú'. This is the final verse:-

'In the game of the Gael, may our men never fail,
To be faithful to Éire's fair name;
May they ever march on, like the men who are gone,
True to gallant Tipperary's great fame'.[3]

TRAGEDY FOR TOM SEMPLE

The joy of winning the All-Ireland faded into insignificance for Tom Semple when his beloved wife, Mary, became seriously ill. It was a rather protracted

[3] Philip Fogarty, *Tipperary's G.A.A. Story* (Thurles, 1960), p. 296.

illness, to which she succumbed on Saturday, 8 November 1930, at their residence on Fianna Road, Thurles. Mary, who, had been ailing for some months died at the relatively young age of forty-six. She received the last rites of the Catholic Church from Rev. J.J. Meagher C.C., a frequent visitor to the house and a great friend of the family. There was a great outpouring of sympathy for the bereaved and following a well-attended funeral at the Cathedral of the Assumption, Mary was interred in St Mary's cemetery, Thurles.

Many messages of sympathy were received and votes of sympathy were

Mary Semple (née Devitt)

proposed and passed to Tom Semple and family by Mid Tipperary G.A.A. board and Thurles Sportsfield committee. Tom was then chairman of Thurles Sarsfields G.A.A. Club and a special meeting of his old associates and present officers and committee was called and passed the following message of sympathy, all present standing:-

'That we the members of Thurles Sarsfields G.A.A. past and present extend to Thomas Semple, our esteemed chairman, our deepest sympathy in his great loss on the death of his devoted wife and to his young family in the death of a loving mother and we pray that they might find consolation in the thought that she has passed to her eternal reward'. A vote of sympathy was also extended to Thomas, Patrick and Daniel Devitt, Cashel, brothers of Mrs. Semple.[4] The County Tipperary National Teachers Association also voted sympathy to Tom Semple and his family.[5]

Tom, now bereft of the support of a loving wife, had sole responsibility for their five sons, now ranging in age from nine to nineteen. It was heart-breaking for Tom, who took his added responsibility seriously and did his utmost to provide for all their needs. His life-style would change as now life's circumstances did not allow him be as involved in the G.A.A. as heretofore. As the Tipperary team sailed for the U.S.A. on 8 September 1931, they were without their trainer and selector, as Tom had to keep the home-fires burning.

[4] *Tipperary Star*, 15 Nov. 1930.
[5] Ibid, 6 Dec. 1930.

CHAPTER 22

Tom Semple
– Team Trainer

A S A TEAM trainer, Tom Semple achieved greatness at the highest level for club and county. Good hurlers may be plentiful but great trainers and captains are few. Even during his own playing days, it was he who organised and controlled the training sessions, had a major input into the team selection and on match-day had the tactics in place, made changes as required and spurred his players to great achievement. There is no doubt but that he also conducted the post-mortems when defeat was their lot.

There are some common threads through the various accounts of Semple's

Tipperary Senior Hurling Team 1923
Back row (l.-r.): Anthony Carew (Secretary), John Conway, Bill Ryan (K), Jack O'Meara, Frank McGrath, Pat Browne, Tom Semple, Arthur O'Donnell, Stephen Hackett, Martin Ayres, John Cleary, Patrick 'Wedger' Meagher. Middle row (l.-r.): John Darcy, Martin Kennedy, Tom Shanahan, Pakie Spillane, Johnny Leahy, Bill Dwan, Jim Gleeson. Front row (l.-r.): Jack Power, John Joe Hayes, Tom Dwan Captain, Paddy Power, Martin Mockler.

approach to the task of team preparation. Tom has been described as a born leader, a man that players and colleagues respected and responded to. He realised himself that if success was to be secured that he needed men of character to carry out the task, men with backbone that would not shirk when the pressure was great in the heat of battle. Tom knew his players very well, their strengths and weaknesses, their capabilities, their dedication and commitment. He also had the advantage that he was the son of the maternity nurse, who knew the history of the town and certainly knew the lineage of those he played with. Tom was a shrewd judge of men and knew the men he wanted.

Semple had a great knowledge of the game of hurling. He had played the game from a young age and had been always a keen student of the various skills and tactics of the game. A decade before he blossomed as a hurling captain, Semple had watched the men of Tubberadora cast all opposition aside on their glorious track to All-Ireland victory. He saw Cork's Blackrock and Dungourney, Kilfinane and South Liberties of Limerick and the famed Kilkenny hurlers of Tullaroan and Mooncoin and many more. Tom became a very shrewd judge of

Thurles Sarsfields 1925
Back row (l.-r.): Eddie O'Gorman, Joe Campbell, John O'Gorman, Tom Semple, Willie Ryan, Paddy Brolan, Mick Maher, M. O'Flynn, Mick Ryan, James Maher. Middle row (l.-r.): Hugh Shelly, Willie Harney, Jack Gleeson, Jimmy O'Loughlin, Jim Cullagh, Tom O'Meara. Front row (l.-r.): Eddie Campion, Staphen Dwan, John Joe Callanan Captain, Tommy Butler.

Thurles Sarsfields Senior Hurling Team 1933
Back row (l.-r.): Paul Keane, T. Morris, Mixey Kennedy, Pat Lanigan, Denis Maher, Tom Maher.
Third row (l.-r.): James Maher, Dan Breen, John Joe Callanan, Michael McGann, Tommy Butler,
Denis 'Bunny' Murphy, Fr. Denis Finn, Michael Doran, Matty Maher, Jim O'Loughlin, Michael Craddock,
Paddy Bermingham, Jim Lanigan. Second row (l.-r.): John Maher, Paddy Mulhall, John Lanigan,
Jack Stapleton, James Harney, Con Keane, Denis Max, Mick Ryan, James Maher, William Bowe,
Tom Semple (chairman and trainer). Front row (l.-r.): Mick Maher, Paddy Callanan (mascot),
Bill Harney, John Tierney (masseur).

hurling and hurlers. He saw their hurling skills, their tactics, commitment and determination and he wanted to develop that successful ethic in his own club and county.

In all facets of Semple's life, a strict, disciplined approach was emphasised. He was strict because he knew that without discipline the full striking force of a team was lost. When John Power of Piltown, Kilkenny, an old hurler just a hundred years old, was asked, 'What was so special about Tom Semple?' He replied in one word 'Discipline'. He explained, 'Semple demanded discipline. He was the captain, the trainer, the father-figure, the man in control, the one who believed that victory, on and off the field would come from discipline'.[1] There were no half-measures with Tom Semple. He was a strict disciplinarian whose word was law.[2] As Canon Fogarty recalled, 'Literally he towered high on

[1] *Tipperary Star*, Tales of the Gaels, 10 Apr. 1993.
[2] Raymond Smith, *Decades of Glory* (Dublin, 1966), p. 64.

Thurles Sarsfields – Tipperary Senior Hurling Champions 1935

Back row (l.-r.): Tom Butler, Jim Maher, Jimmy O'Loughlin, Paddy Brolan, William Leahy. Third row (l.-r.): Joe Campbell, John Joe Ryan, John Maher, Jer Cornally, Denis 'Bunny' Murphy, Dan Mackey, Mick Murphy, Paddy Berninghram, Pat d'Arcy Russell, William Bowe. Second row (l.-r.): Tommy Max, Denis Max, Br. Ryan, Tom Semple (chairman and trainer), Jim Lanigan Captain, Fr. I.I. Meagher, Br. Lynam, Rody Curran, John Lanigan. Front row (l.-r.): Michael Callanan, Mick Maher, John Semple, Paddy Bowe, Dick Ryan, Tommy Lanigan, Tommy Butler, Paddy Maher (W), Tommy Semple, Paddy Connors, Seamus Bowe, Dermot Butler (mascot).

the field and his fine athletic figure caught the eye, but it was as a captain he excelled. He dominated his team; his discipline was rigid but never disputed'.[3] His instructions were clear and unambiguous. The players went on the field with a clear knowledge of what they were expected to do.

One of Fr. Jim Semple's favourite memories of his father gives a classic example of the great disciplinarian. Jim's brother ,Martin, recalls, 'Jim revelled in telling the story about our brother John, known to his friends as "Skint" because of his light stature, and Ger Cornally sitting on the windowsill of our home on Fianna Road. Cornally was the fullback for the Tipperary county team that won the 1937 All-Ireland hurling championship, and both he and John played on a number of championship teams for the Sarsfields. They both worked on the railway and were in their mid to late twenties at the time. Cornally was smoking a cigarette when suddenly our father came around the corner from Slivenamon Road. Of course Cornally tried to immediately cover the cigarette. Our father came over to the two of them and immediately said "Cornally, do you expect to play for Tipperary on Sunday?" Ger's response was "I do, Mr. Semple." Then our father said "Well if you do Cornally, you will take that cigarette out of your mouth and never let me see it in there again." "Yes, Mr. Semple" was the response.'[4] A story certainly from another era, emphasising that to be a member of a team that was either captained or trained by Tom Semple, you had to accept his leadership and direction without question.

Tom Semple had an uncanny ability of getting the best out the talent at his disposal. The classless nature of Thurles Sarsfields over the years may have been established during the Semple era. Tom moulded individuals together into a team, from whatever walk of life they came, whether the work-shop or the farm, the main street or the back street.

Tom Semple believed that the key attributes required by a successful hurler were skill, speed and speed of action on the ball. Physical fitness was a vital key to success and to achieve this end Semple demanded that his players undergo a strenuous fitness programme. As early as 1904, Semple had identified the Confraternity Hall in Thurles as a suitable venue for indoor training. Tom arranged with the club for the purchase of training equipment for his gymnasium. Skipping ropes were supplied as well as a punch-ball and boxing-gloves. Four hooks were installed from which to suspend rings etc.[5] Such innovative training methods were new to the G.A.A. at this time. Nicholas Mockler, son of Jack who hurled with Semple, recalled that his father often told him that when the 'Blues' were in training they would form up outside

---

[3] Philip Fogarty, *Tipperary's G.A.A. Story* (Thurles, 1960), p. 372.
[4] Interview with Martin Semple (10 July 2014).
[5] Thurles Sarsfields Minute Book, 1906-7.

the Confraternity Hall in Thurles and set off on a march of four or five miles to
The Ragg, march back again to Thurles and spend an hour or so skipping and
working the punch-ball.[6] Other evenings were spent in the practice field,
perfecting the hurling skills and playing practice matches. Tom's son, Martin,
recalls, 'That training regimen was reflected in the Semple household, even
long after Tom's playing days were over; I remember that there were boxing
gloves and weights in our home at 3 Fianna Road, that were used by my father
and my stepbrothers when they were playing for the Sarsfields.[7]

Semple's team favoured a ground hurling style and worked hard to perfect
it. This required anticipation, speed, concentration and great hand/eye co-
ordination. It also required great courage to contest the 'clash of the ash' when
closely marked by an opponent or opponents, or when your opponent had the
advantage in contesting the ball. The aim was to deliver the ball with the
minimum delay. Semple himself is remembered as having a strong ground
stroke off either side and using it to good effect. Meeting the ball in the air,
doubling on it overhead, was greatly encouraged. The rising and handling of
the ball was kept to a minimum. As Paddy Brolan, one of Semple's star hurlers,
recalled:- 'And he (Semple) would drive a ball over the bar from sixty yards out,
off the ground, if he got half a chance. If he saw you stopping a ball he would
shout, 'Go home, if you won't pull'.

Tactically Tom was brilliant. He could read the situation well, whether it was
going badly or going well, could identify a weakness in his own team or spot a
flaw in the opposition. He could turn disadvantage into advantage as was seen
in Tipperary town in the 1909 Munster final. That day Cork's Dungourney were
ahead at half-time and sensing victory released the pigeons bearing the news
southwards to Cork that Thurles and Tipperary were a spent force. Even though
Thurles were 'on the rack' that day, Semple appealed to their strength of
character, used the sight of the pigeons to get his hurlers to dig deep within
themselves, feel the hurt that they were being disregarded and to respond
with a match winning second-half. On that same day, Semple stressed the
importance of possession of the ball and keeping that possession. He stressed
the simple truth that the opposition was powerless if they did not have the ball.
Incidentally, when Tom Semple was asked, 'Who was the greatest hurler of
them all?' his reply to P. D. Mehigan was, 'I saw them all and I give Jim Kelleher
of Dungourney the brush'.[8]

Remarkable also was Semple's longevity as a trainer. It stretched almost forty

---

[6] Raymond Smith, *Decades of Glory* (Dublin, 1966), p. 64; *The Hurling Immortals* (Dublin, 1969),
p.111.
[7] Interview with Martin Semple (7 Nov. 2014).
[8] P.D. Mehigan (Carbery), *Carbery's Annual 1961/'62*, pp 78-9.

Tipperary – All-Ireland Senior Hurling Champions 1937
Back row (l.-r.): Tom Semple, Jim Maher, Jimmy O'Loughlin, Willie O'Donnell, —, John Maher,
Joe Campbell, Jer Cornally, Johnny Ryan, Paddy Brolan (trainer), Willie Wall, Philly Ryan, Jim Lanigan
(Captain), Jimmy Cooney, Paddy Connors, Bill Leahy, Tom Collins, Johnny Leahy.
Middle row (l.-r.): Willie Bowe, Dinny Max, Martin Maher, Jack Gleeson, Fr. Phil Purcell, Jimmy Coffey,
Denis 'Bunny' Murphy, Tommy Treacy, Tommy Kennedy.
Front row (l.-r.): Dinny O'Gorman, Gerry Doyle, Tommy Doyle, Paddy 'Sweeper' Ryan, Tommy Butler,
Willie Barry, Paddy Maher (W), Dan Mackey.

years from his early days as captain of the 'Blues' to the late 1930s, just a few years before his death. After the 1930 Treble Crown, his front line involvement in selection and training continued through Tipperary's All-Ireland victory in 1937. Tom was a selector, having guided Thurles Sarsfields to county championship success the previous year. Johnny Ryan, Moycarkey/Borris, a member of the Tipperary team, recalled the tactics of Tom Semple and Johnny Leahy in preparing them for the Munster final against Limerick and their analysis of the play and style of the legendary Mick Mackey. He stated, 'They insisted that first-time pulling must be the motto. We in the half-line tried to get out in front of our men and beat them to the ball rather than play them from behind. That is how I played John Mackey. One of the things noticed by Semple and Leahy was that Mackey, after trapping the ball, tipped it some yards to either side, then pounced on it and away with him through the centre. We planned our tactics accordingly. It was decided that while John Maher held the centre, the wing-backs should watch for the break of the ball from Mackey's stick and clear it first-time before he could make his gambit.' The tactic worked and Tipperary recorded a memorable victory.[9]

Tom Semple usually played at centre-field or in the half-forward line and controlled the area, calling the shots. This was the area of the pitch where the puck-out from the opposing goal usually dropped. Watching the flight of the

[9] Raymond Smith, *Clash of the Ash* (Dublin, 1972), p. 243.

ball, Tom would shout the name of his man that was to contest that ball, saying 'Mooney that's your ball' or 'Shelly that's your ball' and so on.

Regarding players having a few drinks after the game, this was acceptable to Tom but there was to be no drinking between matches, no exceptions. As Jack Murphy, Iona Ave., Thurles, recalled, 'If a player broke this rule, he was off the team. When the team was named, he was not on it. No one questioned it. That was the discipline they had.[10]

On 20 April 1913, Tipperary, Toomevara selection, played Cork in the Croke Memorial Cup semi-final at Waterford. Their famous captain, Patrick 'Wedger' Meagher asked Tom Semple to talk to the team before the game. The local press reported:-

> "Big Tom Semple was there and though his muscles may have somewhat stiffened, his brain was as clear and his heart as warm for the old pastime as when as captain for Tipperary, he led his men through many stubborn fields to victory. And as the young enthusiasts under captain 'Wedger' Meagher prepared for the fray, the wary old Gael stepped up to them. 'Keep close to your men boys, from the start; keep close to them to the end. Make the pace and the day is yours' Such was the advice of the veteran, and then, having arranged the men, and given a cheering word here and there to the players, he suddenly produced a little bottle from his pocket – not the whisky flask or the black porter bottle, for the courteous, noble, young Gaels of Tipperary touch it not. It was simply a little bottle of Holy Water and the brave handsome young heads were for a moment bent, their talk was hushed, as reverently the Gaelic chieftain sprinkled them. 'God bless you boys', he said, 'may you win and may all of you and every player escape unhurt'. A quiet murmur of prayerful assent came from those noble, muscular young men and then their eyes sparkled and the gay talk and laughter burst forth. Priests who stood near and watched felt a thrill of pride and joy as this gleam of Catholic faith and fervour flashed forth and mentally thanked God that the young Gaels of today, true to the traditions of a thousand years ago, are as spiritual as their mighty ancestors.[11]'.

Tipperary won the day by 5-5 to 2-0.

Approaching the game with a positive attitude was always emphasised by Semple. Negative thoughts were not to be tolerated and were to be cleared from

---

[10] Interview by Paddy Doherty, Ardnacrusha, Thurles, with Jack Murphy, Iona Ave, Thurles (29 June 1981).
[11] *Nenagh News*, 26 Apr. 1913.

Thurles Sarsfields– Tipperary Senior Hurling Champions 1939

Back row (l.-r.): William Leahy, Paddy Brolan, Jim Maher, Michael Callanan. Third row (l.-r.): Dan Mackey, Ger Cornally, Tom Mason, Tommy Lanigan, Mick Murphy, John Maher, John Lanigan, Willie Bowe. Second row (l.-r.): Eddie Gleeson, Tim Nyhan, Gerry Doyle, Jim Lanigan Captain, Danny Doyle, Paddy Bowe, Paddy O'Gorman. Front row (l.-r.): Seamus Bowe, Tommy Doyle, Paddy Maher (W), Tommy Semple, John Delaunty, Jimmy 'Pip' O'Connell.

the mind, as they were destructive to ambition and success. 'Never brook defeat,' was a saying he regularly used on the training field or in the dressing room before a game.[12] **Semple's "never brook defeat" attitude and statement was recalled by Johnny Ryan, when Mick Mackey scored a goal in the first minutes of the 1937 Munster Final. "I will always remember the speech the 'Old Blues' captain gave that day in the dressing room. It sent the blood racing through our veins. We remembered what he had said when the green flag went up after Mick Mackey's goal. We knew there must not be a repetition of 1936."[13] Tipperary prevailed in that great Munster final, and went on to All-Ireland victory.**

Tom Semple was a great believer in the team ethic. To get the best out of his players he constantly emphasised the value of team-work and working together as a unit rather that individual effort. Many commentators on Semple's era stress that it was the excellent, highly developed quality of their team-work that made the Thurles team such a match-winning unit. Before a game the hurlers had it drummed into them by Semple, that individual glory was but secondary to the benefit of the team as a whole. 'And this reliance on team-work was something that was to be carried on by their successors, who became the finest club combination in the land... And even when Sarsfields struck lean days, the blue jersey with that strange mystique that seems to surround it, still commanded the greatest respect in the local championships'.[14]

In March 1930, Thurles railway workers threatened to withdraw support from certain town traders who did not support the railway service. The workers were: Front row seated (l.-r.): J. O'Gorman, M. Hyland (chairman), Jack Murphy (secretary), J. Mooney. Front row standing (l.-r.): C. Blythe, T. Temple, Jer Cornally, J. Kane. P. Donoghue, P. Doherty, Willie Bowe, W. Cantwell, Tom Semple, J. Kennedy, W. Quinn, J. McGrath, S. Whittaker, M. Ryan. Second row (l.-r.): John Kennedy, W. Delaney, J. Dunphy, R. Dargen, James Donoghue, J. Scally, P. O'Connor. Back row (l.-r.): T. Walsh, T. Leahy, M. Carroll, A. O'Connor, R. Carroll, P. Ferriter and T. Shortt.

---

[12] Liam Ó Donnchú's recollection of conversations with John Lanigan, Árd Mhuire, Thurles.
[13] Raymond Smith, *Clash of the Ash* (Dublin, 1972), p. 243.
[14] Ibid, *Decades of Glory* (Dublin, 1966), pp 62-4.

CHAPTER 23

Tom Semple's Second Marriage

WINIFRED CREAGH was born in Grogan near Rathdowney, Queen's County (County Laois). She was the second youngest of four daughters and two sons. She attended the St John of God Sisters Convent School in Rathdowney and after finishing her schooling, she worked as a teacher's assistant with the nuns in what was then the infants programme.

In the early 1920s she sailed from Queenstown (Cobh), County Cork, to join cousins in New York city and worked there for twelve years. She returned to Ireland to visit her parents every four or five years and on one of those visits, in 1934, when she was travelling from Ballybrophy station to Kingsbridge station (Hueston), Dublin, she met my father on the Cork-Dublin train, where he was the guard. He had lost his wife a few years before. They struck up a conversation and he began visiting her at her parents' home in Grogan. At times, she would also come up to Thurles and stay with her sister, Mrs. Kit Loughnane. My father would have known our Auntie Kit's husband, Jimmy Loughnane, a bootmaker/cobbler since he was very active in the I.R.A. during the War of Independence. As noted elsewhere, Jimmy Loughnane's younger brother, Willie, was shot as an act of reprisal in his parents' home in Thurles.

Winifred Creagh with her father John, at Grogan, Co. Laois.

My mother certainly understood and knew the role of my father in the War of Independence. She remembered the Black and Tans coming to her home in Grogan late one night, when the whole family was asleep. The 'Tans' pounded on their door with the butts of their rifles and when it was opened immediately marched in and grabbed her two brothers, Jack and Jim Creagh and dragged them out of the house. The family thought their end was imminent. In fact, some of the I.R.A. members had cut down a tree a few hundred yards from their home and shoved it across the roadway to block the military lorries carrying the 'Tans'. The 'Tans' forced the two Creagh boys to cut through the downed tree and remove it from the roadway so that the trucks could pass and then they were allowed to return to their home.

Winifred Creagh with her friend, Madge Dineen-Sheridan, a native of Skibereen, Co. Cork. Both met on the voyage to the U.S.A. (Photograph taken in New York)

My mother's other brother-in-law, Dan Daly, was married to her oldest sister, Mary. He was a native of Rathdowney and a staunch and loyal supporter of the G.A.A. He would have been thoroughly familiar with my father's role as the captain of the 'Blues' and as a referee and administrator. I remember my Uncle Dan cycled from Rathdowney to Thurles on the Munster final Sundays in the 1940s, for the game at Thurles Sportsfield. He would park his bicycle in our back yard and while he had a meal before he walked up to the game, would regale us with his stories of our father's stewarding and the crowd control at the previous finals.

My mother often told me that my father wanted to keep their courtship extremely low key, and in fact he never told any of his friends in Thurles that he was courting my mother. They were married in the parish church in Grogan in 1934. She described how they then travelled on the train from Ballybrophy to Dublin for a short honeymoon. To avoid his many friends in Kingsbridge station (Hueston), who got word of the wedding and wanted to meet and congratulate their railway colleague and his wife, my father moved to the back of the train and when it arrived in Kingsbridge, they got out on the opposite platform to avoid their well-wishes.

They celebrated their wedding by having dinner in my father's favourite restaurant in Dublin, The Red Bank. My mother also told me that she remembers them visiting Galligan's on Henry Street, where my father bought his clothes and had his suits and even his railway uniforms tailored.

The Red Bank, 19/20 D'Olier Street, Dublin.

In the hallway in our home at 3 Fianna Road, Thurles, there is a large photo of the gathering on the steps of the Cathedral of the Assumption, Thurles, in 1934, on the 50th anniversary of the founding of the G.A.A. That gathering occurred soon after my mother and father were married. My mother often pointed to my father standing in the front row of that photo, and on one occasion she recounted how my father led the gathering after the Mass from the cathedral through Liberty Square to Hayes's Hotel. My mother was one of the many onlookers that crowded both sides of the street as the procession came forward. When my father saw my mother, he immediately took off his raincoat and walked across from the head of the procession and handed it to her so that he could walk in the sunshine and lead the dignitaries and delegates to the G.A.A. Congress. They processed through the Square where they circled the Croke Memorial and ended in Hayes's Hotel. I always thought that my father's action, stepping from the head of the parade to hand my mother his overcoat, was his way of introducing his new wife to Thurles and to all his friends in the G.A.A.

My mother took over a household of five sons, Tommy, John, Michael, Paddy and Joseph (Jobey). Tommy married and moved to his own accommodation soon after she arrived. Michael moved to Cardiff and Paddy moved to Bristol to find work in the later 1930s. Jobey trained as an electrician in Thurles and lived in Fianna Road, until he moved to the Liverpool area in the early 1940s, a number of years after his father's death. John worked on the railway with C.I.E., until he moved to live with his brother Paddy and work on the railway in Bristol in 1956.

My mother's first son, James (Jim) was born on 3 October 1935; the only daughter in our family, Anne, was born on 22 March 1937 and Martin was born on 19 November 1940. Anne and Martin were named after Tom Semple's parents.

My mother described how my father always had an 'open door' to his friends from the town and particularly from the Sarsfields, who visited on a regular

Winifred Semple with her three children, (l.-r.) Anne, Martin and Jim.

basis. She described how it was common when my father and his friends would have a drink in Delahunty's pub off the top of Fianna Road, they would then come to our house to visit and very often engage in the discussions and strategies for the Sarsfields and the Tipperary team. Even after my father's death, a number of those friends continued to visit, the one that I can remember the best was Jack Lanigan, the father of Jim and John Lanigan, whom my father trained for the Sarsfields and the county teams. Jim Lanigan captained the 1937 Tipperary All-Ireland champions.

Less than five years after they were married, my father suffered his first stroke and was significantly incapacitated from that point on. My mother ensured that he could continue to meet with his friends at our home, and in what was obviously a very difficult situation for him, continue to be involved to the extent that he could with the Sarsfields, the county teams and their trainers, and the Sportsfield. She took care of him at home through his final illness, until he suffered his last stroke and died on 11 April 1943.

She often described to me and my brother and sister, how my father would control the crowds in the stadium that eventually would be named for him, especially on the Munster final days; how he had all of his stewards organised and in place to ensure the crowd was well behaved and would not encroach on the playing field from the sideline seats. She said that he did that just by a wave of his stick. I recall her telling me that Archbishop Morris once spoke with her of his recall of how Tom had this great ability and talent as a leader, which was shown particularly when he acted as the chief steward at the major games in Thurles Sportsfield and how he could stop a crowd or even redirect it with a wave of his ash plant. My mother was quick to tell him that Tom always had a blackthorn walking stick that he used to direct and control the crowds and lead his stewards. That blackthorn walking stick had a place of honour in our home as long as I could remember.

My mother's devotion to my father's memory was quite complete. Because of her own broad experience and travels, having lived in the U.S. for twelve years, she fully recognised the great talent and skills that he had, especially as a leader and administrator in the G.A.A. She often commented and perhaps with a bit of nostalgia, that his heart and soul were always with the G.A.A., the Sarsfield and Tipperary teams, and Thurles Sportsfield. She wanted to ensure that his role with those organisations would not be forgotten, and it was with that in mind that she presented the Thomas Semple Perpetual Cup to the Sarsfields in December 1976, to honour his memory. She would be especially pleased that the Sarsfields have organised an international festival during which clubs from U.S., Britain, European continent and Ireland compete for the cup that she presented.

It was a great but extremely pleasant surprise to her when the Thurles Sportsfield, which her husband was instrumental in founding and particularly developing as the premier venue for Munster hurling, was named Semple Stadium in 1971. When it was announced that the All-Ireland hurling final would be held in Semple Stadium on the centenary year of the founding of the G.A.A., she believed that my father's commitment to the development of

Martin and Fr. Jim with their mother Winifred. Photograph taken in 1961 shortly after Fr. Jim's ordination.

the stadium was fully vindicated. She remembered that he was particularly disappointed in 1934 when the All-Ireland was not played in Thurles, as he and his colleagues had fully expected it would be. Unfortunately, my mother died in 1981 and did not see that great assembly and celebration in Semple Stadium in 1984.[1]

TOM AND WINIFRED'S FAMILY

Tom and Winifred had three children, James (Jim), Anne and Martin. Jim, who attended Thurles C.B.S. and St Patrick's College, Thurles,

Martin and Fr. Jim celebrate the Silver Jubilee of Fr. Jim's ordination, June 1986.

was ordained in the Cathedral of the Assumption on 11 June 1961 and then served for fifty-three years as a priest in the diocese of Salt Lake City, Utah. He served as the pastor of many parishes, assistant director of Catholic Charities and director of the Bishop's Fund. Father Jim returned almost every year to visit with his mother in Thurles until her death and then later with his sister, Anne.

On the morning of the centenary All-Ireland hurling final in Thurles, 2 September 1984, Fr. Jim celebrated Mass in the cathedral. During the ceremony, Fr. James Feehan, Thurles, introduced him and other members of the Semple family who were present. As the Semple family left the cathedral that morning, Thurles Silver Band, led by Joe Ryan, a Fianna Road neighbour, were playing in the cathedral yard and Cardinal Tomás Ó Fiaich was arriving with Archbishop Thomas Morris, who introduced the cardinal to Fr. Jim.

On Sunday, 12 June 2011, at the Church of St. James the Worker, Salt Lake City, Fr. Jim celebrated his Golden Jubilee in the priesthood. Among those celebrating with Fr. Jim was his fellow priest in Salt Lake City, Fr. Paddy Carley, a native of Iona Avenue, Thurles and a former Sarsfields hurler. On Friday, 12 August 2011 at 12 noon, Fr. Semple celebrated Mass in the Cathedral of the Assumption, Thurles, to mark the great occasion, with family and friends in the

---

[1] Recollections of Martin Semple – Tom and Winifred's youngest son.

town of his birth. Father Jim died on 7 February 2014, and his remains were returned to Thurles and after Mass in the cathedral he was buried in St Patrick's cemetery.

Anne is the only daughter in the Semple family. She was named after Tom Semple's mother and after attending the Presentation Convent School in Thurles, like her grandmother, she became a registered nurse (R.G.N.) from Mercer's Hospital,

Fr James Semple preaching at his outdoor Golden Jubilee Mass at St Joseph the Worker parish in West Jordan, Utah in 2011.

Dublin. She served as a nursing sister in the Irish Army Nursing Corps at Collins Barracks, Cork, and she is a Foundation Fellow of the Royal College of Nursing

Tom and Winifred Semple's family – Martin, Fr James and Anne, at their father's grave at St Mary's, Thurles, in August 2011.

of Ireland (F.F.R.C.N.I.). Thereafter she worked at and became the Director of Services in the St John of God Carmona Services which provide educational, training and residential programmes for children and adults with intellectual disabilities in County Dublin southeast areas. She is married to Sean Gunning and lives in Stillorgan, County Dublin, and in the Semple home in Fianna Road, Thurles. Anne continues to be an avid fan and supporter of Thurles Sarsfields and the Tipperary hurling teams.

Martin and Jo Ann Semple, Denver, Colarado at Tom Semple's memorial in St Mary's.

The Semples' youngest son, Martin, was named after Tom Semple's father. He attended the Christian Brothers School and St Patrick's College in Thurles. In his student days, he was actively involved with the Thurles N.A.C.A. club, St Joseph's Athletic Club and served as its secretary. He participated in and organised numerous track and field sports programmes at Thurles Sportsfield. He followed his brother Jim to the United States, did graduate studies in law at a number of U.S. universities and set up his law practice in Denver, Colorado, where he lives with his wife, Jo Ann, and continues to work at his law firm. Martin keeps current on Thurles, Tipperary and Semple Stadium activities through the *Tipperary Star*, which he has read every week since he left Thurles. He and Jo Ann are regular visitors to Thurles and his home on Fianna Road.

SOIL TO CASEMENT PARK

Jim Semple, at the age of 17 in 1953, made his own piece of G.A.A. history. That was the year that the G.A.A. venue in Belfast, known as Casement Park, was opened. To coincide with the opening, a silver urn containing soil from Thurles Sportsfield, which had been dug by Tipperary captain Tommy Doyle,

In June 1953, a casket of soil was carried in relay from Thurles Sportsfield to Casement Park, Belfast. Photograph shows (l.-r.): Mickey Byrne, Pa Joe O'Brien, Phil Purcell (Tipperary G.A.A. Secretary), and Tommy Doyle.

At Hayes's Hotel, Very Rev. R. Power Adm. Thurles, presented the casket of soil to Jimmy Semple, Fianna Road, the first runner in the relay. Others in the photograph are: Very Rev. Philip Canon Fogarty P.P., Templemore, Cormack Boomer, Corrigan A.C., Belfast, Joe Campbell (Thurles Sportsfield) and Tommy Doyle.

was carried to Belfast by a relay of runners. The soil would be spread on the new pitch, providing a symbolic link between it and the birthplace of the G.A.A. Very Rev. R. Power, Adm., Thurles, blessed the soil and presented the urn to the first runner leaving Hayes's Hotel, Thurles. The relay of runners was organised by the N.A.C.A. Local athlete, Jim Semple, Fianna Road, son of Tom Semple, carried the urn on the first leg of the journey, as far as Drish bridge. Running beside Jim was Cormac Boomer, Corrigan A.C. Belfast, who was one of twenty-seven Northern Ireland athletes that had come to Thurles to provide an escort for the bearers. At Drish bridge, Jim handed the urn to forty-four year old Tom Ryan, St Joseph's A.C. Thurles, a former long-distance runner.[2] The relay continued to Croke Park, where soil was added to the urn from the spot on the pitch where Mick Hogan was killed, on Bloody Sunday 1920. The relay continued through the night, arriving at Casement Park, Belfast, the following afternoon.

An old Thurles streetscape, looking from the River Suir up Thomond Road on to Fianna Road and Croke Street. Tom Semple's residence was at 3 Fianna Road.

---

[2] *Tipperary Star*, 20 June 1953.

CHAPTER 24

The Final Whistle – 1943

TOM SEMPLE died on 11 April 1943, on the eve of his sixty-fourth birthday, at his home, 3 Fianna Road, Thurles. For some years prior to his passing, Tom was in delicate health; still the end came unexpectedly early on Sunday morning. He passed to his reward with all the consolations of the Catholic Church, to which he was devotedly attached.

The *Tipperary Star* reported the death as follows:- 'By the death of Thomas Semple, there passes from the scene of mortal life a Tipperary man whose name was known, wherever Tipperary men made a home here or beyond the seas. To many thousands of Irishmen besides, the name of Semple was synonymous with Tipperary hurling prowess around thirty years ago. Active on the field and for many years in the hurling counsels of Tipperary, Tom Semple was a dominant and esteemed figure, just as in a quieter way, he was an earnest and faithful worker for his country's freedom in her time of trial.

Tom Semple

'To a generation of Tipperary men, now in middle age, Tom Semple was the idol of boyhood years. Though many of them were not to know him in the flesh, for years after they were familiar with his hurling exploits from the stories told by their fathers or elder brothers. Those were not the days of special trains and motor cars and the details of great contests had to be learnt from the newspapers – and the few who were fortunate enough to be comparatively near the venues. The times have changed rapidly and the G.A.A. has now a

Tom Semple's funeral cortege rounds the top of Liberty Square.

patronage that would seem incredible in those bygone years yet there was a homeric touch about those contests that does not seem to be there now. The stature of the men was different then and one had only to know Tom Semple to realise that fact.

'It was perhaps in his ability to control and manage a team that he stood so much apart. Good hurlers may be plentiful, but the great captains are few... He did his utmost to ensure, before the game, that all that was possible to be done was done. To the Semple watchfulness on and off the field Tipperary Gaeldom owes many victories. Most of his time, energy and resourcefulness had been devoted to the promotion of Gaelic games and the revival of the Gaelic tradition. Nothing else appealed to him with such forcefulness. From his boyhood, his delight was to be with the Gaels, whether on or off the playing field.'[1]

Numerous messages of sympathy were received, among them the president of the G.A.A., Pádraig McNamee and general secretary, Pádraig Ó Caoimh. Dan Breen T.D.'s message included the following, 'A great Tipperary man gone, please accept deepest sympathy'.

On Monday, following his death, his coffin, draped with the Tricolour and the colours of Thurles Sarsfields, was borne to the Cathedral of the Assumption,

---

[1] *Tipperary Star*, 17 Apr. 1943.

by members of the 'Old Blues' and Sarsfields Club. The attendance included Very Rev. J.J. Meagher P.P. Anacarty, Chairman of Tipperary County Board and Johnny Leahy, secretary.

On the following day, Requiem Office and High Mass were offered, the officiating priests being: Very Rev. T.J. O'Connor Adm., Rev. Philip Fogarty C.C., Rev. T. Mulvihill C.C. and Rev. R. Power C.C. The funeral to St Mary's cemetery, Thurles, was of exceptionally large proportions and representative of all sections. Outside the cathedral, members of the Thurles 'Old Blues' formed a guard of honour as members of Sarsfields club carried the coffin all the way to the graveside. Seán McDermott Pipers' Band, Thurles played appropriate music. The 'Old Blues' present were: Jack Mockler, Paddy Brolan, Martin O'Brien, Joe McLoughney, Jack Mooney, Hugh Shelly, Jim 'Hawk' O'Brien, Paddy Burke and secretary of that era, J.M. Kennedy. At the graveside a firing party representing the Old I.R.A. fired three volleys and 'The Last Post' was sounded.

At a special meeting of Thurles Sarsfields Club, moving tributes were paid to the late Tom Semple, who for many years as player, trainer, chairman and recently club president, had guided the club with distinction and success.

Tom's son, Martin, recalled, 'Fr. Jim told me regarding our father's funeral in 1943, The Sarsfields carried Tom Semple's coffin from Fianna Road to the cathedral. The coffin was draped in the Sarsfields colours. As the cortege passed Mixie O'Connell's premises on Liberty Square, Mixie came out and placed the Tricolour on the coffin'.[2] This was seen as recognition by Mixie, who was involved himself in the War of Independence, for another who had played his part.

Mixie O'Connell

Following Tom Semple's death, the *Tipperary Star* included this reference to Tom's part in the national struggle:- 'From his native Drombane, he came to Thurles as a young man and entered the service of the Great Southern Railways. In course of time, he was appointed passenger guard on the main Cork-Dublin line and was well known to thousands of rail travellers. In the position which he held, he was a valuable service to the I.R.A. in the years of the fight for freedom. He took numerous risks but took them willingly and with all the knowledge of the consequences. He was steadfastly Gaelic, too, in the sterner field of national endeavour.'[3]

[2] Martin Semple in conversation with Liam Ó Donnchú (21 Feb. 2014).
[3] *Tipperary Star*, 17 Apr. 1943.

In a letter to the *Tipperary Star* newspaper, following Tom Semple's death in 1943, Jimmy Leahy, who was commandant of the Second Tipperary Brigade I.R.A. wrote:-

> 'Tall is his form, his heart is warm,
> His spirit is light as any fairy,
> His wrath is fearful as the storm
> That sweeps the hills of Tipperary.'

'One would think that Thomas Davis, who wrote these lines, knew Tom Semple. Big in stature, big in heart, big in everything that goes to make a man, a Gael among Gaels, a great general on the playing fields and a great judge of team material. Such was Tom.'

Another poet wrote:-

'Our land shall call but not in vain, For fighting lines of hurling men.'

Jimmy Leahy.
(Photo courtesy Seamus Leahy)

'When our land did call, though Tom was past the hurling stage, he answered and through those trying years he had the very dangerous task as courier between G.H.Q. and the fighting men in the south.

'Tonight, perhaps he is in goodly Gaelic company, the old guard of the 'Blues' talking of battles won and lost – Jer Hayes, Gaffer Kenna, The Keff Kirwan, Tom Kerwick, Denny Dwyer, pardon me for omitting the complete roll.

'He is gone, but let us hope and trust his spirit will be with us to help the young Gaels to place our county in the peerless position, he led it to forty years ago.

'God be with you Tom Semple and may the green sward of Tipperary rest lightly on you.'[4]

At the Tipperary G.A.A. Convention of the following year, Very Rev. J.J Meagher, chairman, paid the following tribute to Tom Semple:- 'Since our last

---

[4] *Tipperary Star*, 24 Apr. 1943.

meeting we had many deaths, but none more deserving of remembrance than that of the prince of Gaels, the late Tom Semple. Tom, for a generation, was one of our greatest Gaels. We remember well his massive frame, his clean and polished hurling, his rugged eloquence and his sound judgment. Perhaps he excelled as captain and trainer of our inter-county teams. He was very proud of having led our hurlers to Brussels, and played on the historic battlefield of Fontenoy. For his upright life and example, together with his paternal interest in the boys, he was like a missionary in his native town. He was a credit to his religion, and a bright ornament to the game he loved. Go ndéana Dia trócaire ar a anam.'[5]

St Mary's, Thurles.

---

[5] *Tipperary Star*, 12 Feb. 1944.

WINIFRED SEMPLE R.I.P.

After his death, Tom Semple's widow, Winifred, raised their three young children at their home in Fianna Road, where she continued to live until her death on 10 March 1981, after a short hospitalisation. After her children left home, she was actively involved in many community groups in Thurles and was especially active in the Legion of Mary and the Apostolic Society up to her final years. She always took good interest in the G.A.A. in general and Semple Stadium in particular. She was dedicated to Tom's memory and his G.A.A. legacy and in December 1976, Winifred presented the Tom

Winifred Semple (Photo taken 1970).

Semple Perpetual Cup to Thurles Sarsfields. The patron of the G.A.A., Most Rev. Thomas Morris, archbishop of Cashel and Emly, presided at the concelebrated Requiem Mass in the Cathedral of the Assumption, Thurles, and the principal celebrant was her son, Rev. James Semple, Boston College, Massachusetts and Salt Lake City, Utah, U.S.A. The Very Rev. Augustine O'Donnell, President, St Patrick's College, Thurles, delivered the eulogy. Members of the Thurles Sarsfields Club, many of them former players trained by Tom Semple, carried her coffin at the cathedral and at its arrival at St Patrick's cemetery in Thurles, for burial where Right Rev. Dean Christopher Lee officiated at her graveside.

Winifred Semple at the opening of Thurles Sarsfields Social Centre, 30 October 1977.
From left to right: Fr. James Feehan, Patron; Liam Ó Donnchú, Secretary; Con Murphy, G.A.A. President;
Winifred Semple; Tommy Butler, Club President; Paddy Doyle, Club Chairman.

CHAPTER 25

Thurles Sportsfield to Semple Stadium

FOLLOWING the death of Tom Semple, Rev. Philip Fogarty C.C., Thurles, was elected chairman of Thurles Sportsfield committee. No major development took place at the venue until the mid 1960s, when work began on transforming the field into a modern stadium. This involved the erection of Ardán Uí Chuinneáin, Archbishop Kinane[1] Stand. It replaced the old galvanized stand and open stand and cost in excess of £100,000. This stand, which accommodated 16,000 patrons, was completed in 1967 and opened on 9 June 1968. The contractors were Messrs Malachy Bourke Ltd., Galway.

Ardán Uí Chuinneáin, Dr Kinane Stand was opened in June 1968.

---

[1] Archbishop Jeremiah Kinane (1884-1959) was archbishop of Cashel and Emly and G.A.A. patron from 1946 until his death in 1959.

At Thurles Sarsfields annual convention on Sunday, 21 January 1968, club chairman, Fr. James Feehan C.C., suggested that the memory of Tom Semple should be suitably commemorated by the naming of this new stand in Thurles Sportsfield in his honour. While this suggestion was unanimously approved, it developed no further at the time but was not forgotten.

Fr. James Feehan C.C., Chairman of Thurles Sarsfields

Three years later at Sarsfields convention in 1971, chairman Rev. James Feehan C.C. suggested that the trophy for the Tipperary senior hurling championship should be replaced by a cup to be named the Semple Cup and that he himself would be the first subscriber towards such a trophy. As the discussion progressed among the fifty delegates present, it was decided that, subject to the approval of the Semple family, to submit a motion to County Convention asking that Thurles Gaelic Sportsfield be named in memory of the late Tom Semple.[2]

At the county convention, which convened at Scoil Ailbhe, Thurles on 31 January 1971 the following motion was proposed by Fr. James Feehan C.C., Thurles Sarsfields chairman:-

'That Thurles Sportsfield be named Semple Park to perpetuate the memory of the late Tom Semple.'

In proposing the motion he said that the idea of it was to honour a man who was a legend in his lifetime. 'At the opening of the century Tom Semple was the only Thurles man on the Two-Mile-Borris team that won the All-Ireland in 1900 and by 1906 he had moulded the 'Blues' to smash Cork's six years unbroken reign in Munster. It was recorded that the late Paddy Leahy described Tom Semple as the greatest captain of them all'.

Fr. Feehan outlined at length the career as a player and official of the late Tom Semple mentioning the part he played in bringing the Croke Memorial to Thurles and said that Rev. Dr Michael O'Dwyer, Dalgan Park, a team-mate of Tom Semple's said that it was to Sarsfield's everlasting shame that they had done nothing to perpetuate the memory of Tom Semple. His Grace, Most Rev. Dr Thomas Morris, archbishop of Cashel and Emly, and Very Rev. Canon

---

[2] *Tipperary Star*, 9 Jan. 1971.

Fogarty had given their blessing to the motion. He concluded by saying that there could be no better symbol to our youth than that the name of Tom Semple be over the Sportsfield gate.[3]

The motion was seconded by Boherlahan/Dualla delegate, Philly O'Dwyer N.T. Gaile, who added that it was high time Thurles Sportsfield was given a name. He also suggested that the title Semple Stadium would sound more attractive than Semple Park. This was agreed and the motion was carried unanimously.

John Lanigan, Thurles Sarsfields, related how Tom Semple was instrumental in bringing the first big Munster championship game to Thurles in 1926 and added, 'Since then hundreds of thousands of people had come to the town for games and hundreds of

Philip O'Dwyer, Boherlahan/Dualla.

thousands of pounds had been spent in it by them.'

1984 – G.A.A. CENTENARY HURLING FINAL

In the late 1970s, as the centenary of the foundation of the G.A.A. was approaching, the idea of staging the All-Ireland hurling final of 1984 at Semple Stadium was slowly gaining momentum. This had been a shattered dream for Tom Semple and Tipperary G.A.A, in the golden jubilee year of 1934. The first major step towards preparing Semple Stadium for such a historic event was the erection of a new covered stand, Ardán Ó Riain,[4] on the northern side of the ground, with a capacity of 11,000. This was completed in June 1980.

G.A.A. Centenary Crest 1984.

Completed also was the newly-terraced Town End, accommodating 15,000. The 'Town End' was renamed to the memory of Maurice Davin, Carrick on Suir – first president of the G.A.A. Duggan Bros., Templemore were the building contractors and Horgan & Lynch the architects.

[3] *Tipperary Star*, 6 Feb. 1971.
[4] Note:- Ardán Ó Riain is named in memory of Canon M.K. Ryan, who was instrumental in the purchase of the grounds that became known as Semple Stadium. For more information see Appendix 1.

Planning the G.A.A. Centenary Celebrations 1984 (l.-r.): John Lanigan, Treasurer; Fr. Pierce Duggan, Chairman and Tomás Ó Baróid, Tipperary G.A.A. Secretary.

At the Tipperary convention, held at Nenagh on 25 January 1981, an Upperchurch/Drombane motion calling for the amendment of the appropriate rule in the official guide, to allow the 1984 All-Ireland hurling final to be played at Semple Stadium, Thurles, was unanimously adopted. The motion was proposed by Rev. Pierce Duggan C.C., chairman of Semple Stadium Centenary and Development Committee. At Easter, this motion was passed with an overwhelming majority at the G.A.A. Congress in Killarney.

Following the passing of the motion minds became more focused on the magnitude of the project to be undertaken. As in 1934, the ability of Thurles and Semple Stadium to accommodate the event was questioned in the press.

Stamps issued in 1984 for G.A.A. Centenary

In 1983, after months of controversy and doubt, G.A.A. President, Paddy Buggy, gave the green light to the completion of the development at Semple Stadium. The president was

Blessing and official opening of Semple Stadium by His Grace Most Rev. Dr. Thomas Morris, 31 May 1984. Included are Brendan Vaughan, Chairman Munster Council; Rev. Pierce Duggan, Chairman Semple Stadium Development Committee; Liam Ó Maoilmhichil, Árd Stiurthóir, G.A.A.

addressing the Tipperary county convention at Clonmel on 30 January. Six major sub-committees were set up to co-ordinate the planning of facilities and events of centenary year:- Accommodation – Martin O'Connor, All-Ireland Festival – Michael Maher/Tomás Ó Baróid, Press and Communication – Liam Ó Donnchú, Museum – William Corbett, Stewarding – Matt Hassett, Traffic and Transport – Michael Lowry.

The completed Semple Stadium was officially opened on 31 May 1984. The Killinan End was terraced and the side-line capacity was now three thousand. The stadium could now accommodate 65,000 spectators.

For a week before the All-Ireland, Thurles was en fête and on Sunday, 2 September the town was the focus of Gaeldom. From early morning it was grey and overcast, but the rain held off and the absence of sunshine was made up by the hordes of supporters from all quarters that thronged the town-centre hours before the game. As the time ticked away, the town was pulsating with life as the pre-match tension built up to a crescendo. From overhead the drone of helicopters was heard as they ferried Uachtarán na hÉireann President Patrick Hillery and An Taoiseach Garrett Fitzgerald to Semple Stadium, who along with Cardinal Tomás Ó Fiaich were welcomed by G.A.A. President Paddy Buggy. The attendance of leaders of church and state marked this historic occasion with special significance.

All the hours of planning and meticulous preparation proved worthwhile as the historic event was a huge success. As to the games, the minor match between Limerick and Kilkenny ended in a draw, 1-14 to 3-8. With less than a minute remaining, Kilkenny scored a goal to put them one point ahead. The final seconds were hectic, with Limerick having barely time to equalise. But equalise they did and went on to win the replay, at the same venue, by 2-5 to 2-4, in another classic game. Paddy Downey, in the *Irish Times*, summed up the general feeling when he wrote, 'It is probably true to say that there never has been a better minor All-Ireland final'. The senior final between Cork and Offaly turned out to be an anti-climax largely because Cork were so dominant. The first-half saw 'The Rebels' slow to settle, leading by just two points at the break. But they found their form after the resumption and coasted to victory. Captained by John Fenton, they won by 3-16 to 1-12. The legendary broadcaster of Gaelic games, Mícheál Ó hEithir, was present and commented, 'This was a stirring occasion, superbly and efficiently organised despite the

G.A.A. Centenary All-Ireland Hurling Final at Semple Stadium 2 September 1984
(Photograph courtesy: The Irish Times. Photographer: Dermot O'Shea)

Celebrating the G.A.A. Centenary, 2 September 1984.
Semple group at 3 Fianna Road, Thurles (l.-r.): T.J. Semple, Mrs. Josephine Semple, Fr. Jim Semple,
Máirín Semple Thomas, Ann Semple Gunning, and Martin Semple.

doubting Thomases, who had predicted chaos. It was a great day to be in Semple Stadium'.[5] John O'Grady, *Cúlbáire*, writing in the *Tipperary Star* stated, 'Climactic Day ... the eyes of Ireland and further afield were on Thurles – and Thurles looked mighty good in all respects, from viewpoints aerial or earthbound. The great, controversial project succeeded...'[6]

The pitch at Semple Stadium was in pristine condition for all the major matches played there during centenary year. Its accolade as the finest hurling pitch in the G.A.A. was upheld. The work and dedication of the grounds staff of Jim Hickey, Tommy Max and Bobby Mockler was lavishly praised. There was praise too for the organisers of the centenary celebrations led by Fr. Pierce Duggan – Chairman, Tom O'Hara – Secretary, John Lanigan – Treasurer, County Chairman and Secretary Mick Frawley and Tomás Ó Baróid and the countless volunteer workers. They had undertaken a task and had not been found wanting. For the record, the attendance of 59,814 was over seven times the

[5] Michael O'Hehir, *My Life and Times* (Dublin, 1996), p. 122.
[6] *Tipperary Star*, 8 Sept. 1984.

normal Thurles population and all enjoyed a historic and memorable occasion.

Pádraig Ó Fainín (Pat Fanning), former G.A.A. president, summed up the occasion succinctly:- 'But such was the sense of occasion, such the atmosphere, such the sense of history prevailing the scene and the fervour of the crowd that the hurling did not matter. It was the occasion that counted. Here was the living G.A.A., the evidence that the spirit of Croke and Cusack and Davin prevailed, and the certainty that in 1984 the people were proud of what they are, and determined to profess and preserve it. In the streets of Thurles one felt the Irishness of it all. One believed that one shared in and was part of a significant national occasion. Dare I say it now: All-Ireland 1984 could not have celebrated the centenary more properly,

Munster Final programme cover 1984. Tipperary hurlers Tom Semple, Tony Wall and Jimmy Doyle with Cork hurlers Christy Ring and Gerald McCarthy. Archbishop Thomas Croke is seen in the background.

more suitably, than in the place where it all began back in 1884. On Sunday last and in the days preceding the great event, Thurles and Tipperary stood vindicated. Semple Stadium was the place, the only place in all Ireland in which to stage our hurling All-Ireland of 1984'.

It was more than an All-Ireland final, it was a celebration. It was a memorable occasion to witness and to savour. Long after other and better games are forgotten, this one will be remembered. Tom Semple's dream had become reality.

Plaque and mural at Semple Stadium.

CHAPTER 26

Remembering Semple in Thurles

1948 – MONUMENT TO TOM SEMPLE

EARLY IN 1944 a committee was formed for the purpose of raising funds for the erection of an appropriate monument to the memory of Tom Semple. The officers of the committee were:- chairman – Fr. Philip Fogarty C.C., Thurles, vice-chairmen – Johnny Leahy and Phil Purcell, secretary – T.J. Egan, Slievenamon Road, Thurles and treasurers – James Maher, William Leahy, both of Thurles Sarsfields.[1] The fund was very well supported, with Thurles Sarsfields among the most generous con-

Celtic cross at Tom Semple's grave in St Mary's cemetery, Thurles.
(Photograph courtesy George Willoughby)

tributors contributing the sum of twenty pounds. Although it was planned to complete the fund-raising at the end of the 1944, subscriptions still poured in

---

[1] *Tipperary Star*, 29 Apr. 1944.

from far and wide, well into the following year.[2] Fund-raising continued through 1946 and in June 1947 the Semple Memorial committee placed an order with Messrs T. & W. Burnell, sculptors, Mitchel Street, Thurles, for a Celtic Cross, which was erected over the grave, in St Mary's churchyard.[3]

T. & W. BURNELL,
SCULPTORS,
Headstones, Crosses and Kerbs erected anywhere. Renovations and Lettercutting. Moderate charges. Estimates and Designs free on application.
Mitchel Street, Thurles.

The inscription on the memorial reads:-

Gaedhil Thiobrad Árann
agus roinnt charad
taobh amuigh den chonndae
a thóg an leacht so
i ndil chuimhne
Thomáis S. Seimpeil
Captaoin Foirne Thurles Blues
D'éag 11-4-1943
Aois 64 bliadhna
SUAIMHNEAS SÍORRAIDHE D'Á ANAM.[4]

1976 – THE TOM SEMPLE PERPETUAL CUP

In December 1976, Mrs Winifred Semple, widow of the late Tom Semple, presented 'The Tom Semple Perpetual Cup' to Thurles Sarsfields Club. The club decided that a senior hurling tournament for the cup would be a most appropriate way of honouring the memory of Tom Semple. To add status to the tournament it was hoped that the top hurling clubs in the country would be invited to participate. This proved more difficult than expected in an already overloaded championship calendar. By the mid 1980s the tournament had been successfully contested on only two occasions with James Stephens of Kilkenny, in 1980, and Tipperary's Moycarkey/Borris being successful. The latter defeated Thurles Sarsfields in the 1986 final and Tom Semple's grandson, T.J., presented the cup and trophies to the winners. Mrs Josephine Semple also attended the final at Semple Stadium.

In 1997 Thurles Sarsfields hosted an Under-21 hurling tournament for the 'Tom Semple Perpetual Cup'. The final was played in mid-September at Semple

---

[2] *Tipperary Star*, 10 Feb. 1945.
[3] Ibid, 28 June 1947.
[4] *Note:-* The inscription translates as follows – Tipperary Gaels and some friends from outside the county erected this headstone in memory of Thomas J. Semple, Captain of the Thurles Blues, who died on 11-4-1943, aged 64. May he rest in peace.

Mrs. Winifred Semple presented 'The Tom Semple Perpetual Cup' to Thurles Sarsfields Club in December 1976. Back row (l.-r.): Thomas Callanan, Jimmy Doyle, Michael Dundon, Paddy Doyle (Chairman), Tommy Butler (President), Winifred Semple, John Lanigan, Paddy Kenny. Front row (l.-r.): Tommy Barrett, Mícheál McElgunn, Donal O'Gorman (Secretary), Jack Carew.

Stadium, between Thurles Sarsfields and Na Piarsaigh, Cork. In a tough bruising battle, Sarsfields were lucky to come through, winning by 2-14 to 2-12.

During the following years the cup seemed destined to remain in the trophy cabinet at Thurles Sarsfields Social Centre. However, in recent years it has seen a great revival, being now the trophy presented to the winners of the premier competition of Thurles Sarsfields International Hurling Festival. This annual tournament, which has been running since 2011, was the brainchild of John Enright, a former chairman of Thurles Sarsfields, who with Michael Dundon and Liam Ó Donnchú developed the idea of promoting the game of hurling internationally and by doing so to generate tourism in the hurling heartland of mid-Tipperary.

The Semple family have been very supportive and closely associated with the tournament. Tom Semple's youngest son, Martin, presented the trophy in 2014, while Tom's only daughter, Anne, did the honours on each of previous years.

THURLES SARSFIELDS INTERNATIONAL HURLING TOURNAMENT

Division 1 – The Tom Semple Perpetual Cup

Roll of Honour

2011 – Kilburn Gaels, London

2012 – Kilburn Gaels, London

2013 – Causeway, Co Kerry

2014 – Coolderry, Co. Offaly

Tom Semple's son, Martin, presenting 'The Tom Semple Perpetual Cup' to the Coolderry captain, Brian Kelly, in July 2014.

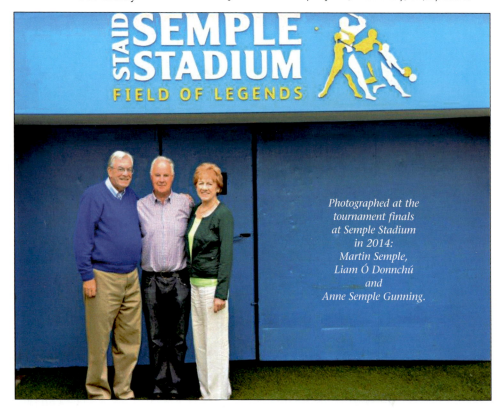

Photographed at the tournament finals at Semple Stadium in 2014: Martin Semple, Liam Ó Donnchú and Anne Semple Gunning.

SEMPLE VILLAS

Semple Villas (Bailtíní Semple), a housing development erected by Thurles Urban Council, was named in honour of Tom Semple. These houses are situated at Bohernanave beside Semple Stadium and were constructed in the early 1980s. On his many journeys to Thurles Sportsfield as a player and G.A.A. administrator, Tom Semple would have walked past where these houses now bear his name.

Semple Villas, Bohernanave, Thurles.

1984 – TIPPERARY G.A.A. CONVENTION – SEMPLE REMEMBERED

On 5 February 1984, the patron of the G.A.A., Most Rev. Dr Thomas Morris, celebrated Mass in the Cathedral of the Assumption, Thurles, prior to the start of Tipperary G.A.A. Convention at Hayes's Hotel. After Mass, representatives of every club in Tipperary assembled with their club banners and marched behind the Thurles Silver Band to St Mary's cemetery, Thurles. Here a wreath was laid on the grave of Tom Semple by Michael Frawley, Tipperary G.A.A. chairman. Prayers were recited by Right Rev. Dean Christopher Lee, a former chairman of Thurles Sarsfields Club and the club's banner was carried by Mickey Byrne and Tommy Doyle.

Tipperary G.A.A. Chairman, Michael Frawley, lays a wreath on the grave of Tom Semple, prior to the Tipperary G.A.A. Convention, February 1984. In the background are: Fr. James Feehan, Michael Lowry and Tommy Doyle, who is holding the Sarsfields banner.

Commemorating the 50th anniversary of the death of Tom Semple in 1993
From left to right: Mickey Byrne, Mícheál McElgunn, Mrs. Bridget Wort, Johnny Wort, Seán Fogarty,
Peter Fogarty, Dick Maher, Matty Connolly, Anne, Thomas and T.J. Semple, Mrs. Josephine Semple,
Fr. Pat O'Gorman, Gerard Corbett, Seán Maher, Conor O'Dwyer, Liam Ó Donnchú, Archbishop Dermot
Clifford, Willie Corbett, Pat O'Shea, Enda Walsh, Denis Maher.

1993 – 50th ANNIVERSARY OF TOM SEMPLE'S DEATH

The fiftieth anniversary of the death of Tom Semple was commemorated on Sunday, 11 April. The ceremonies commenced with an anniversary Mass at St Joseph's and St Brigid's Church, Bohernanave, concelebrated by the patron of the G.A.A., Archbishop Dermot Clifford and Rev. Pat O'Gorman, Thurles Sarsfields patron. The ceremonies were organised by Thurles Sarsfields and members of the Semple family present included T.J. Semple, grandson, seven year-old Thomas Semple, great-grandson and Mrs Josephine Semple, daughter-in-law. After Mass, a wreath was laid at Tom's grave in St Mary's and the archbishop led the gathering in prayer. Liam Ó Donnchú, chairman of Thurles Sarsfields, in a graveside oration paid appropriate tribute to Tom Semple. Later that afternoon, at Semple Stadium, the semi-finals of the Tom Semple Memorial Cup tournament were cancelled due to inclement weather. Loughmore/Castleiney was due to play Tullaroan, as were Thurles Sarsfields and Graigue/Ballycallan.

2000 – PLAQUE AT ST MARY'S

The memory of Tom Semple was honoured with the erection of a stone plaque at the entrance of St Mary's Church of Ireland in Thurles, on 27 July 2000. In the presence of a large gathering, the plaque was unveiled by Tom Semple's daughter, Mrs Anne Gunning. The plaque was sponsored by Thurles Sarsfields GAA Club and erected in association with Dúrias Éile Eliogarty Memorial Committee.[5]

---

[5] Dúrlas Éile Eliogarty Memorial Committee was co-founded by Pat Walsh and John Wort in 1999. It aims to increase awareness of the immense contribution local people have made to historical events at home and abroad.

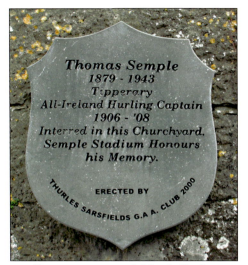
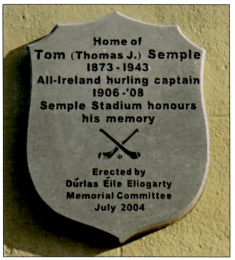

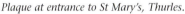

Plaque at entrance to St Mary's, Thurles.   *Plaque at 3 Fianna Road, Thurles.*

A wreath was laid at Semple's grave by Thurles Sarsfields Club president, Mickey Byrne. A decade of the Rosary in the Irish language was recited by Rev. Eugene Everard, Adm., Thurles and patron of Thurles Sarsfields. As the rain threatened to spoil the ceremony, the attendance moved into St Mary's Church where Liam Ó Donnchú, vice-president of Thurles Sarsfields Club, outlined Tom Semple's career and his contribution to Thurles, to Tipperary and to the G.A.A. This quiet dignified ceremony concluded with a social evening in Sarsfields clubhouse. Incidentally, the plaque was the work of local Thurles monumental sculptor, James Slattery, Fianna Road, the street on which Tom Semple resided.

2004 – PLAQUE AT FIANNA ROAD

A plaque indicating the home of Tom Semple at 3 Fianna Road, Thurles, was erected by Dúrlas Éile Eliogarty Memorial Committee in 2004.

2004 – MEMORIAL AT ST MARY'S

The patron of the G.A.A, Archbishop Dermot Clifford, on a glorious Easter Sunday morning, 11 April 2004, unveiled a memorial, sculpted by James Slattery, to the memory of Tom Semple. The year marked the 125th anniversary of Semple's birth in 1879.

The memorial was erected by the local Dúrlas Éile Eliogarty Memorial Committee with support from Thurles Sarsfields G.A.A. Club, who were represented by chairman Tom Barry, Thurles town manager, and vice-president Liam Ó Donnchú. Several hundred people were present, including Semple's son and daughter, Martin Semple, Denver, Colorado and Anne Semple Gunning,

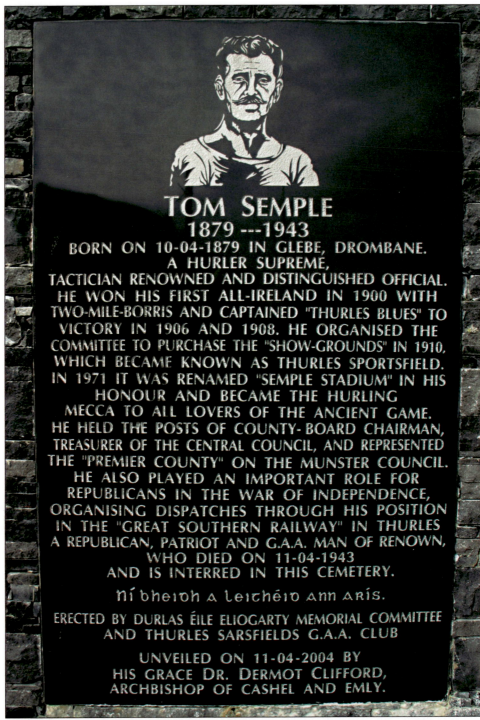

This memorial to Tom Semple at St Mary's, Thurles, was erected by Dúrlas Éile Eliogarty Committee 2004 and unveiled by Archbishop Dermot Clifford, on Easter Sunday, 11 April 2004.

Photographed at the unveiling of the memorial (l.-r.): Sean Gunning, Anne Semple Gunning, Josephine Kennedy Semple, Martin Semple, T.J. Semple, Máirín Semple Thomas, Anne Twomey Semple, Michael Smith, T.D., Minister for Defence, Most Rev. Dr Dermot Clifford, Archibishop of Cashel and Emly, Thomas Semple, Ken Thomas, Tom Thomas, Monica Thomas. In front (l.-r.): Odhran, Calum and Andrew Thomas.

Dublin accompanied by her husband, Seán. Other relatives present included Semple's grandson, T.J. Semple and his wife, Anne and son, Thomas; Mrs Josephine Semple, daughter-in-law of Tom Semple; Máirín Semple Thomas, grand-daughter of Semple and her husband, Thomas.

There was a parade to the graveyard led by Sean Treacy Pipe Band, Moycarkey/Borris, who later played the National Anthem and Faith of our Fathers. A guard of honour drawn from the Third Field Artillery Regiment of the F.C.A. under the command of Sergeant Tommy Mockler was inspected by the Archbishop and Defence Minister, Michael Smith. Sergeant Jim Hynes, drummer and Sergeant R. Kelleher, trumpeter of the band of the Southern Command, Cork were also on duty.

Martin Semple, on behalf of the Semple family, thanked all and particularly those of the Memorial Committee for the great honour given to his father. He said, "My father was very involved with the erection of the memorial to Dr Croke in Liberty Square. Canon Fogarty, chronicler of the Tipperary G.A.A. story, who had ministered to my father in his last days, described Tom Semple in his book as symbolic of Matt the Thresher, a born leader of men on and off the field. As well as leading the Thurles 'Blues' Tom Semple played his part in Cogadh na Saoirse (War of Independence) and what most people do not know is that he was a captain in the first Irish army founded in the Free State. He never wanted to stay in that army very long and he came back to Thurles because first, last and always he was a member of the Thurles community. He wanted to stay here. My mother told me that on many occasions he was asked by the railway company, G.S. & W.R., to take jobs in various parts of the country and he always refused, because he wanted to live all his days in Thurles. And he gave his life to the town of Dúrlas Éile Uí Fhógartaigh. The great stadium that he and the men of his generation founded was a symbol of the G.A.A. throughout the country. He also recognised how important this town was in the life of the G.A.A. and how important the G.A.A. is to the life of Ireland. And for that reason we are really proud that this memorial in the Garden of Remembrance will be unveiled to him today. It's just within steps of his last resting place", said Mr. Semple.

Archbishop Dermot Clifford recalled when the Black and Tans surrounded the gathering at Liberty Square, when the foundation stone for the Croke memorial was being laid. 'Archbishop Harty did the blessing and Tom Semple stood at his right hand. Archbishop Harty said that the people of Thurles would guard the Croke Memorial as they would their own lives. We will guard this memorial to Semple and hold it in great honour. It is a privilege for me to be here to bless it and to unveil it', said Dr Clifford.

Defence Minister, Michael Smith, said: 'Easter Sunday, a day of great celebration for the Christian world that marks renewal, hope and salvation. We are here to celebrate a man who made such a lasting impact. To few people is given the capacity to do things in their lives which do not die with them.'

Addressing Martin Semple, Mr. Smith said, 'He was admired as a player and as a sportsperson, but his hurling feats were not the only strength he had. He was a key figure in making the I.R.A. more effective in the fight for freedom. His life spread itself wide with great generosity, great love for our national game and for our national identity.'[6]

---

[6] *Tipperary Star*, 17 Apr. 2004.

CHAPTER 27

What others said about Tom Semple

RAYMOND SMITH

RAYMOND SMITH, who started his career in journalism with the *Tipperary Star,* has written extensively on Gaelic Games for the *Sunday Independent.* Raymond grew up on Thomond Road, fifty yards from Tom Semple's residence at 3 Fianna Road and as a youngster he would have known and seen Tom Semple in his neighbourhood. He had a passionate love for the game of hurling and several of his books are on that subject. This piece relates to 'The Thurles Blues':-

'Paddy Leahy expressed the opinion to me one night in Thurles that the Old Thurles Blues were the most perfect machine that ever graced a hurling field and that Tom Semple was the greatest captain of them all. I take Paddy's word for it. He should know as he played against the Old Blues as a stripling young hurler with Boherlahan. Tom Semple was born to lead. A towering figure of a man, he immediately commanded respect and the wonderful effect of his example and enthusiasm, inspired the players around him with the burning desire for victory. He led the Blues selection

Journalist, Raymond Smith at Tom Semple's grave in 1984.

295

to all-Ireland successes in 1906 and 1908 and when he died in 1943 the Premier County mourned one whose name symbolised all that was great in Tipperary hurling. His shadow still looms in the background, it always seems to me, when Sarsfields or Tipperary are engaged in titanic struggle.

'After his retirement he became a noted administrator. His voice was always listened to with respect in the council chambers. More than anyone else he built up the reputation which Thurles gained for excellent stewarding on the days of big matches. Semple, of the broad shoulders with his hat at a rakish angle, was like a general in command on these occasions.

'It was the excellent, highly developed quality of their team-work that made the Thurles team such a match-winning unit. And this reliance on team-work was something that was to be carried on by their successors, Thurles Sarsfields, who became the finest club combination in the land. Indeed no club has remained as true to their proud past. And even when Sarsfields struck lean days, the blue jersey with that strange mystique that seems to surround it, still commanded the greatest respect in the local championships.'[1]

PADDY MEHIGAN – 'CARBERY'

Paddy Mehigan[2] was on the Cork team that lost by a disputed goal to Tipperary, captained by Tom Semple, in the 1908 Munster hurling final at Fermoy. Having hurled against Semple, he was in an ideal position to observe Tom in action. As the years went by, Mehigan got to know Semple personally and was very familiar with Tom's activities as an administrator and with the development of Thurles Sportsfield. He has left us several references to Semple. Using the pen-name 'Carbery', Mehigan wrote:-

Paddy Mehigan – 'Carbery'.

'Tom Semple was a tall athletic man, six feet and one inch in height, with a great stride and sweep of arm. In a prolific Tipperary period, Tom Semple usually played mid-wing on a seventeen aside team. He was a smooth stylish hitter, with great ball control. His drives on the sod or in the air were of

---

[1] Raymond Smith, *Decades of Glory* (Dublin, 1966), pp 62-4; *The Hurling Immortals* (Dublin, 1969), p. 111.

[2] Patrick D. Mehigan (1884-1965) was a sportsperson and journalist. Born in Ardfield, County Cork, he played hurling with Robert Emmets G.A.A. and with the London senior inter-county team in the early 1900s. Mehigan later served as the leading Gaelic games journalist from the 1920s until the 1960s. He was correspondent for the *Cork Examiner* under the pseudonym 'Carbery'. During his era he produced several issues of *Carbery's Annual*. Mehigan also wrote for the *Irish Times* under the byline Pato.

tremendous length and perfect in direction. He was a handsome deer-like man. He always 'played the ball' but when the battle was hottest, he could mix it with the best. Semple was a great leader of men and it was under him that the famous Thurles Sarsfields reached their peak. He was a charming companion. In clubroom or council chamber Tom Semple showed rare judgment and far-seeing wisdom. His love of hurling and hurlers was profound. For long, he was the idol of Tipperary and played a noble part in the 'troubled times'. I often visited his grave at Thurles. Tom and his blackthorn were all-commanding on the crowded and excited side-lines in many a Munster final at the Thurles Gaelic Field'.[3] When the Anglo-Irish War was hot, Semple played a noble part. He was in the intimate confidence of the national leaders and was entrusted with missions of highest importance. He was faithful to the end, highly esteemed in the railway circles of his employment.[4]

'Few men playing the game in Ireland today have achieved the fame that the Thurles captain – Tom Semple – has known. As an organiser and as a player he deserves a high place in any story of the progress of hurling during the infancy of the twentieth century. Tom is a conspicuous man, there is no chance of mistaking another player for Semple … In build, Semple is one of the tall, sinewy type, more of a thoroughbred than a hunter, if I may express myself. He is well over six feet in his 'vamps', and, like most Tipperary men, square cut and as hard as nails. Considering his great height, he is light all over him, particularly at the waist and limbs. A grand ball player, he is a most dangerous wing scorer. On the ground he has a fine 'slog' off left or right and always sends the ball where his centre can't help scoring. But his favourite stroke is a lift, catch with left, turn to deceive an opponent and shoot low and long. It is as quick and spectacular a movement as one could wish to see and countless scores have come off those efforts. He doesn't throw up the ball when he handles it – it simply drops to his swinging stick. When a rival is too close for him to catch, he trusts to the drop-puck … and a most deceptive ball it is to save. He doesn't love close work and generally makes room for himself by dribbling before he strikes. It generally pays a team to set a man specially to watch Semple for his backs feed him invariably.'[5]

MEHIGAN ON SEMPLE'S STYLE

'Having played against him (for Cork) in several Munster championships, I had ample opportunity of studying his style. He was universally regarded as the greatest winger and roving commissioner of his era. He landed points out of number from frees and from play. A born leader, he could rally a team with one shake of his hurley high above the field. Mighty was his physique, he relied

---

[3] Patrick D. Mehigan, *Carbery's Annual*, p. 86.
[4] Ibid, 'Carbery', 'Five Great Hurling Captains' in *Carbery's Annual*, 1943-'44, pp 19-25.
[5] Ibid, *Cork Examiner*, Dec. 1908.

on clean open hurling and polished hitting. When entering the councils of the G.A.A. his sound judgment, his sportsmanship and firmness as a referee did much to put hurling on the map as a fine spectacular sport.'[6]

MEHIGAN – THE BEST MEN OF MY TIME

In the Christmas number of *'The Gaelic Sportsman'* in the mid fifties, P.D. Mehigan picked his best hurling team of the previous fifty years. He was a shrewd observer of the game and had seen over fifty All-Ireland hurling finals. He selected Tom Semple at left half-forward with following comment:- 'On the left wing I can find no peer for the great Tom Semple of Thurles, County Tipperary. A deer of a man and a glorious striker of the ball, he captained great teams'.

Mehigan's best hurling fifteen were:- John 'Skinny' O'Meara, Tipperary; Dan Coughlan, Cork; Seán Óg O'Hanley, Limerick; Mick Derivan, Galway; Pat Stakelum, Tipperary; James Kelleher, Cork; Dick Grace, Kilkenny; Lory Meagher, Kilkenny; Jim Hurley, Cork; Eugene Coughlan, Cork; Mick Mackey, Limerick; Tom Semple, Tipperary; Mattie Power, Kilkenny; Martin Kennedy, Tipperary; Christy Ring, Cork.

FR. DOLLARD – 'SLIEVENAMON'

Rev. James Bernard Dollard (1872-1946) was born at Ballytarsney, Mooncoin, County Kilkenny. He was ordained to the priesthood in 1896 and served his ministry in Canada. At least four volumes of his poetry were published in Canada. Under the pen-name 'Slievenamon', he published several articles, including the following, which was reprinted in 1960:-

'They dream of hurling in Tipperary. Life down there consists of looking forward to the next game. The pride of a family tradition in hurling, counts

Fr James Dollard.

for far more than royal blood. Their tales are of the heroic men of the hurling field – Mickey Maher of Tubberadora, the human tornado who won a pocketful of All-Ireland medals by his reckless daring; the giant Tom Semple who towered over his rivals and shot points from eighty yards; the 'iron man' Paddy Maher 'Best'; the peerless hawk-eyed goalman, Jack O'Mara; the lovable Johnny Leahy; the sweet-striking Phil Cahill, who cut in points off the ground from seventy yards out on the touchline.'[7]

[6] P.D. Mehigan, 'Carbery', 'Five Great Hurling Captains' in *Carbery's Annual*, 1943/44, p. 23.
[7] 'Slievenamon', Rev. James B. Dollard, Official Programme,All-Ireland Hurling Final, 4 Sept. 1960, p. 13.

CANON PHILIP FOGARTY

Canon Philip Fogarty was one of Tipperary's longest serving administrators, being chairman of the Mid Board from 1929 to 1948 and Tipperary County Board chairman from 1948 until 1970. He knew Tom Semple personally and was well aware of his achievements and of his status among the Gaels of Tipperary and further afield. In his book, *Tipperary's G.A.A. Story*, he wrote:-

Canon Philip Fogarty.

'Tom Semple, a Tipperary man whose name was known far and near as a giant in a day of giants. To thousands, the name of Semple was synonymous with Tipperary prowess. Captain of the Sarsfields (better known at the time as the 'Blues'), he steered that famous team to many successes and won with their selection the All-Irelands of 1906 and 1908. Literally he towered high on the field and his fine athletic figure caught the eye, but it was as a captain he excelled. He dominated his team; his discipline was rigid but never disputed. He was an outstanding personality, a champion among champions.'[8]

EGAN CLANCY

Egan Clancy, Grange, Limerick, was a noted member of the famous Castleconnell selection and was captain of Fedamore and Limerick All-Ireland teams, 1913-'15. As sports editor of the *Irish Echo*, New York, he wrote:-

"There is one name that looms large at the mere mention of Thurles, that 'smiling Tipperary town' and that is the celebrated Tom Semple, for years 'skipper' of the Sarsfield hurling club, better known as the 'Thurles Blues'. Tom was one of the greatest players that ever struck a free puck, as he rarely ever failed to register even at formidable ranges. He had a sweet graceful style that was a treat to watch and no matter how strenuous the contest he never became ruffled, always acquitting himself in creditable fashion. This towering prototype of 'Oisín' that has been eulogised in the 'Hurler' by 'Slievenamon', was a thorough typification of the Gael."[9]

PADDY BROLAN

Paddy Brolan was a team-mate of Tom Semple on the Thurles and Tipperary teams and used hurl beside him on the field. He recalled:-

---

[8] Philip Fogarty, *Tipperary's G.A.A. Story* (Thurles, 1960), p. 372.
[9] *Tipperary Star*, 4 May 1929.

'And if Tom Semple got a ball nearly ninety yards out, you could mark down a score as sure as if it were only a free in the goal area. He was surely a great hurler and leader of men. And he would drive a ball over the bar from sixty yards out, off the ground, if he got half a chance. If he saw you stopping a ball he would shout, 'Go home, if you won't pull'.'

PRAISE FROM CORK

Keen as the rivalry was between Cork and Tipperary, an admirable mutual admiration also existed between them. This good feeling was expressed well in the *Cork Weekly Examiner* from the southern city:-

'By winning the senior and junior championships of the hurling district of Tipperary, the Thurles club has given a great proof of vitality, despite many adverse conditions, which to a less vigorous club would mean disaster and extinction. The two notable wins will give satisfaction to many of our Cork hurlers, who to a large extent are familiar, since the Brussels tour, with the genial sports of the Thurles club. As most of our hurlers know, the Thurles club stands for all that is decent in the association and its members play the game as it should be played. The rough tactics of bygone days are not those of the Thurles team, which like all the principal clubs, place greater reliance on speed and science than on the antiquated bustling methods which in the past prevented the free development of the game on proper lines.'

The *Cork Evening Echo* was not to be outdone. It commented:-

'For more years than we care to recall, we have been familiar with the name of Thurles in the Gaelic area. Not alone that in the Cathedral Town the G.A.A. was conceived and fostered, or that from within its walls the ever to be lamented Gaelic Archbishop, Dr Croke, sent forth his famous letter, which became and still remains the creed of the Gael, but that there were there, ever since the inception of the G.A.A. hardy camán wielders able to make their name and fame ring all over the land. Thurles hurlers have a reputation for playing a decent manly game and its representatives are highly respected for their integrity and ability.'[10]

JIM CROKE

Jim Croke, who lived near where Teach an Chúinne, Parnell Street, Thurles, is now, said to me, about seventy years ago that, 'It was easy for those forwards to be good, there was always two marking Semple.'[11]

---

[10] *Tipperary Star*, 29 July 1911.
[11] Interview with Larry Ryan, Kilmacud/Crokes, Dublin and formerly Thurles (6 Mar. 2014).

BR JOSEPH PERKINS

In 1993, Br Joseph Perkins, a native of Drombane, Thurles, wrote:- My longest memory and only recollection of Tom Semple was seeing him, hat on head, walking down Friar Street, Thurles. 'There's Tom Semple', someone said to me, 'the great captain'. Being only a nipper myself, I kept looking at this giant of a man.[12]

Br Joseph Perkins

IRISH INDEPENDENT JUBILEE SUPPLEMENT 1934

In 1934, the Golden Jubilee of the foundation of the G.A.A. was celebrated in fine style in Thurles. It was a time of recalling the great days of the association and the national newspapers published lavish supplements to mark the occasion. Writing on Tipperary's contribution to the association, the *Irish Independent* correspondent included the following reference to the Thurles Blues:-

'The Thurles Blues led by their captain Tom Semple replaced the old 'reliables' in 1906. With the team must be associated the name of Canon M.K. Ryan. Inborn beauty and brainy field-craft were the chief characteristics of Semple's hurlers, whose reign, though short, supplies us with a memory and a wonderful history, which still lingers. They brought Tipperary from the valley of shadows, dispersed the mist and won two more national titles in a great epoch of hurling.'[13]

CARMEL McLOUGHNEY

Regarding Tom Semple, Carmel McLoughney, daughter of Joe McLoughney recalled:- 'Daddy always spoke well of him, he was a very good captain and always encouraged them on the field. They had great respect for him and maybe were a little bit afraid of him. But it was all to the good as he would drive them on and get the best out of them. He always spoke well of Tom Semple.'[14]

JACK MURPHY

Jack Murphy, Iona Avenue, Thurles, long time member of North Tipperary County Council, who knew Tom Semple well since he worked with him at Thurles railway station recalled, 'Tom was a fine man, six feet four or five, a man in a million. He had a beautiful head of wavy hair; you'd never be tired looking at him in his young days. He was a big man, sixteen stone and well able to carry it, a great captain. Whatever Tom said, there was no more about it, that

---

[12] *Tipperary Star*, Tales of the Gaels, 10 Apr. 1993.

[13] *Irish Independent*, G.A.A. Golden Jubilee Number, Easter 1934, p. 87.

[14] Interview by Paddy Doherty, Ardnacrusha, Thurles, with Joe McLoughney's daughter, Carmel (12 Aug. 1980).

Jack Murphy

was it. There was no questioning his authority. He was in charge in the Sportsfield at the big matches, the chief marshal. He used wear a big white pullover on those days. In Thurles that time, the match would be hurled in every house, in every pub, on every street-corner until the next match. As a young-lad in 1909 I saw Tom hurl with the Blues against Dungourney in Tipperary town. Every man, woman and child from Thurles were there. There wasn't a soul left in the place. I remember the poem:-

We marched to the field and were placed in our line,
By our captain Tom Semple, an athlete so fine.
The whistle was blown and the ball was thrown in,
But Dungourney were certain they surely could win.

Tom was a great man that day. He played at mid-field. At that time when a goalman would be striking out a ball, Tom would name his man that was to take that ball – He'd say 'Mooney that's your ball' or 'Shelly that's your ball' and so on.

Oh! The Gaffer Kenna was a sweet hurler. He was from up around Mitchel Street, I think. He loved a few drinks after the game. That was o.k. with Tom, but there was no drinking between matches, it was out completely. If a fella was seen drinking, he was off the team. When the team was called, he wasn't on it. No one questioned it. That was the discipline they had. Oh! The Thurles 'Blues' were a great team, fine men, not one of them under five feet ten'.[15]

PHILLY O'DWYER

Philly O'Dwyer, Gaile, recalled these memories:- 'In those days being captain meant a lot more that being captain at the present time. A captain now doesn't do much more that lead his team in the parade, call the toss and all that, but in Semple's time the captain played a big part in picking the team and he placed his team before the match and he gave the pep-talk. He also made changes during the game. Years ago I heard this story about Tom Semple. Thurles were playing an important match and he was undecided between two players as to

Philly O'Dwyer

[15] Interview by Paddy Doherty, Ardnacrusha, Thurles, with Jack Murphy, Iona Ave, Thurles (29 June 1981).

which he'd play and which he'd leave off. What he did was, he called out the team, lined up the seventeen and left himself out and immediately they were all running to him and calling, 'I'll stay off', 'I'll stay off'. I thought 'twas a great act of diplomacy. I heard he used lead the 'Blues' in long walks from the Square in Thurles out around the country roads and back into the town again. There were no special trainers or coaches that time, the captain had to do it all. He was a wonderful man and the 'Blues' were a wonderful combination, a real machine. I remember hearing about a great game played in Cashel. It was the first time Boherlahan beat the 'Blues'. Boherlahan won by a point and to those who saw it, it was the greatest hurling match ever played. Arthur O'Donnell was the star for Boherlahan and Tom Kerwick was the champion of the 'Blues'.'[16]

CHRISTY FOGARTY

Christy Fogarty, Bohernanave, recalls being at the 1926 Munster final games in Thurles Sportsfield:- 'Tom Semple was brilliant organiser. When I was growing up, Tom was finished hurling but was rated locally as a good but not exceptional player. Organising was his great skill. I remember coming home on the train from the All-Ireland final in '37. That was played in Killarney and Tom and the team were on the train. They were all mad for a drink and Tom knew where to stop the train. We all got out and crossed a field to a pub. I can't remember exactly where it was. None of us were in any hurry home.'[17]

EAMONN MANSFIELD

'Tom Semple always stood four-square for the games of the Gael and who, by his personal prowess and skill on the field, and his tact had done much to raise at the same time the standard of manly sport and the banner of the county in the athletic arena. It was men like Semple who, on the field and in the council, enabled the G.A.A. to outlive the opposition and the sneers of some of the very people who now obtrude with anxious condescension a patronage it can barely tolerate. To Dr Croke, Maurice Davin, Michael Cusack and such men Ireland owed much. The national spirit was

Eamonn Mansfield

resurrected by the G.A.A. To it the Gaelic League and all that it denotes in spirit, in literature, in nationality, owed its existence. Such men as Tom Semple were unconscious torch-bearers of the fire, the custodians of the latent patriotic

---

[16] Interview by Paddy Doherty, Ardnacrusha, Thurles, with Philly O'Dwyer, Gaile, Thurles (1 June 1981).

[17] Interview with Christy Fogarty, Bohernanave, Thurles (27 July 2000).

spirit, the links in national continuity. I had the pleasure of seeing his first game and his last. He was ever a true sport, loyal to his comrades, fair to his opponents. To him, more than any other man, Thurles owed that fine monument, that striking tribute to the late Rev. Dr Croke, whose historic letter was as a trumpet call to the dying spirit of a disheartened Ireland.'[18]

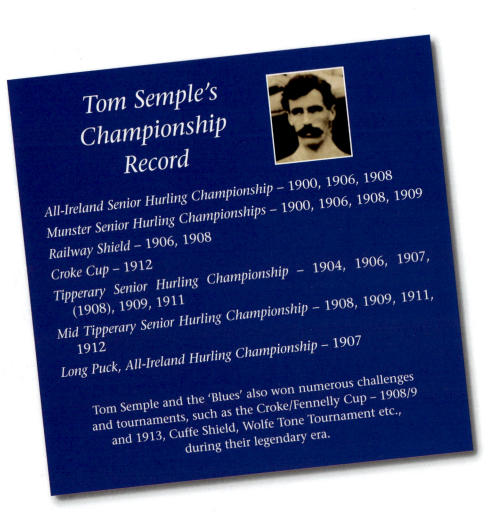

Tom Semple's Championship Record

All-Ireland Senior Hurling Championship – 1900, 1906, 1908
Munster Senior Hurling Championships – 1900, 1906, 1908, 1909
Railway Shield – 1906, 1908
Croke Cup – 1912
Tipperary Senior Hurling Championship – 1904, 1906, 1907, (1908), 1909, 1911
Mid Tipperary Senior Hurling Championship – 1908, 1909, 1911, 1912
Long Puck, All-Ireland Hurling Championship – 1907

Tom Semple and the 'Blues' also won numerous challenges and tournaments, such as the Croke/Fennelly Cup – 1908/9 and 1913, Cuffe Shield, Wolfe Tone Tournament etc., during their legendary era.

---

[18] *Tipperary Star*, 6 Dec. 1930. Eamonn Mansfield (1878-1954), Cullen, County Tipperary. He was president of the Irish National Teachers' Organisation (INTO) in 1910-11 and a member of the first Seanad Éireann in 1922.

APPENDIX I

Meet 'The Blues' – Pen Pictures of the Hurlers

These biographical accounts are of the hurlers that played under the captaincy of Tom Semple, either with Thurles or Tipperary. They appear in alphabetical order by surname. Club officers are also included.

TOM ALLEN

TOM WAS a farmer's son from Ballydavid, Littleton,[1] born 1881. He came to prominence as a skillful hurler in the final years of the nineteenth century, playing with the local Two-Mile-Borris team. Tom won Tipperary county championships in 1900 with Two-Mile-Borris, 1904 with Thurles, 1905 with Two-Mile-Borris and 1906 with Thurles. All-Ireland success came his way in 1900, when Two-Mile-Borris had the county selection and in 1906 with the Thurles selection. He

Tom Allen

also won a Railway Shield in 1906 with Munster, Two-Mile-Borris selection. In the 1907 Munster championship, Tom was on the Thurles selection that lost to Cork in the Munster final, Cork (Dungourney) 1-6, Tipperary (Thurles) 1-4.

Photograph taken at Galboola cemetery in 2002 (l.-r.): Pat Kearney, Tom Harold, Mairéad Kearney, Dan Kearney, Fr. Paudie Moloughney, Tommy Maher, Harry Ryan and Michael Power.

Tom died on 20 June 1952 aged seventy-one and is buried in Galboola cemetery, Littleton. A headstone in his honour was erected in October 2002 by Dan Kearney, Rahinch, and unveiled by Fr. Paudie Moloughney, Laharden, Littleton.[2]

RODY BERKERY

Rody Berkery

THE BERKERY family came originally from the townland of Cooleen in the parish of Templederry. Rody Berkery was born in 1877[3] and as a young man both he and his brother Jack lived at Leugh Beg and were employed as agricultural labourers on the Trant estate at Dovea, outside Thurles.

Described as a dark-haired, moustached, well-built man of above average height, he possessed a fine athletic figure and was very interested in all sports especially hurling.

Rody first played with Thurles in the championship of 1898 and won Tipperary county championships in 1904 and 1906. Rody was a substitute on the Tipperary team, Thurles selection, in 1906 that won the All-Ireland.

Berkery gravestone, Loughmore cemetery.

Rody's brother, Jack, played with Thurles in 1901 and 1902. Another brother Andy emigrated to New York, where he played with the Tipperary team there. Andy was on the team of Irish/American hurlers that toured Ireland in 1911 and played a game at Thurles Sportsfield against a Tipperary selection.

Rody married Johanna (Hannie) Meagher of Killahara, about the year 1908. She was a cousin of Rev. John Meagher, Ashfield, Littleton, who was Tipperary G.A.A. chairman from 1927 to 1948.[4] In the census of 1911, Rody and Hannie are living at Leugh Beg and Rody's occupation is described as a farmer. They had a family of two sons – Denis and Philip and three daughters – Anastasia (Statia), Mary (May) and Margaret (Peg). Rody's eldest son, Denis, like his father, is remembered as a fine hurler, and played with Thurles, until he emigrated to Australia. Sadly, he died at a young age due to a work-related accident.[5]

Rody always held the view that unless hurling was strong and vigorous in Moycarkey and Two-Mile-Borris that county hurling would not be at its best. Though Thurles and Moycarkey were keen rivals, this was a great tribute from a member of one club to the other.[6]

Rody's cousin, John Berkery, was grand-father of Donie O'Connell, Killenaule, who won All-Ireland medals with Tipperary in 1989 and 1991.

Donie O'Connell

Rody, who farmed at Leugh, died, following a brief illness, at St Anne's nursing home, Thurles, on 1 October 1952. His wife, Johanna, died on 18 June 1917.[7] Both are buried in Loughmore cemetery.

JIMMY BOURKE

JIMMY BOURKE was a native of Rathcunikeen, Two-Mile-Borris. He was born on 30 December 1884. He first came to prominence as a hurler in 1905, hurling with Two-Mile-Borris and winning the year's county title. Jimmy won a Railway Shield medal in 1906 with the Two-Mile-Borris selection. He was on the Thurles team that won the 1906 county final and the Thurles selection that won both 1906 and 1908 All-Irelands. As a hurler, he was not as tall as most midfield players but is remembered for his powerful stroke on the ball. It was said that by the

Jimmy Bourke

sound of the crack of the ash on the leather, it was possible to know that Jimmy Bourke had struck the ball. Those who remember him in his heyday class him as one of the hardest, toughest and most devastating tacklers of a time when fibre and sinew needed to be stronger and sterner than the present day demands. Jimmy took over the captaincy of Two-Mile-Borris in 1911, when Ned Hayes retired, and he led them to two consecutive victories in the 'Otway Cuffe Shield' tournament.

Jimmy Bourke and Mary Delaney (Rahinch) on their wedding day, 16 February 1927.

Jimmy, who was a successful farmer at Rathcunikeen, died in April 1950. Six members of the 'Blues' All-Ireland team of 1906, wearing mourning armlets, carried his coffin[8] to his place of rest in Two-Mile Borris.[9]

PADDY BOURKE

Paddy Bourke

PADDY BURKE was from Kylecrue in the parish of Borris/Ileigh, where the parishes of Borris/Ileigh, Inch and Upperchurch meet. He was son of John and Bridget Bourke and was born in 1880.[10] Paddy was one of a family of fifteen and the Bourkes were well known because they owned a water mill to which people came from near and far to have corn dried and ground. The mill was a great source of income for the large family and is still set in motion occasionally by Paddy's nephews John, Joe and James Bourke.

Two of Paddy's uncles, Captain Charles Bourke and James Bourke were involved prominently in the Fenian Rising in 1867. During the action, Captain Bourke marched his men to Barnane (Devil's Bit), where many were arrested by the military from Templemore barracks but most fled for their lives. Soon afterwards the British authorities offered £50 for his arrest,[11] but Charles escaped to France and from there to the city of Troy in New York state. His brother, James, was arrested at Gortahoola, Drombane and charged with being a member of the armed party that burned Roskeen barracks and he was lodged in Thurles Jail. He was later released in a very weak condition and died at the early age of twenty years.

Paddy was a splendid hurler, who in his younger days played with Borris/Ileigh and also with Inch,[12] but it was while playing with Thurles 'Blues' that Paddy really blossomed as a hurler.

Former days at Bourke's, Kylecrue

Paddy won three Tipperary senior hurling championships, three Munster championships and All-Ireland medals in 1906 and 1908. However, he was on the losing side in the 1909 All-Ireland final. Paddy also won medals in these competitions: Railway Shield, Croke/Fennelly Cup and Wolfe Tone Tournament. He was on the 1910 Tipperary team that went to Brussels for the Pan Celtic Congress and played hurling matches at historic venues, such as Fontenoy.

Paddy possessed many sterling qualities of head and heart and had a quiet and unassuming manner and was regarded as a most lovable character by all his G.A.A. friends and associates.

Paddy's brothers, Jim and Charles, were regulars on the Borris/Ileigh hurling and football teams until around 1919. Charles, played on a few occasions with Tipperary, while Charles's son, Dermot, and grand-son, Cathal, hurled with Ballinahinch. Paddy, who was unmarried, died on 24 June 1945 and is buried in St Brigid's cemetery, Borris/Ileigh.[13] His grand-nephew, Seamus Bourke, is a current senior hurler with Borris/Ileigh.

WILLIAM BOWE, Club Treasurer

WILLIAM (Willie) Bowe was born in 1882 and lived at Main Street, Thurles, now Liberty Square, in a property leased from Eliza Stapleton. According to the 1911 census, he was married to Nan and they had one daughter, Mary M.[13a] Willie was employed as a stoker with the Great Southern and Western Railway, a company which also employed Tom Semple. The Bowes had a bar and grocery business, which was run by Nan. They also supplemented their income by keeping lodgers and boarders in the house. Some of these were employees of the railway company.

William Bowe

In 1909, Willie succeeded Phil Molony as treasurer of Thurles Sarsfields Club, a post he held for that year. This was one of the busiest years ever for the 'Blues', as they played thirteen championship games for club and county, including three All-Ireland finals, a record in itself.

Phil Bowe

Willie's sons – Billy, Seamus and Paddy –

Sarah McKevitt

were great supporters of Thurles Sarsfields. Paddy won Tipperary senior hurling championship medals with the club in 1935, 1936, 1938 and 1939.

The link with Thurles Sarsfields continues to the present as Seamus's grand-daughters, Sarah and Jane Ann McKevitt, are prominent players on the club's camogie and ladies football teams.[13b]

Willie died in 1943, aged sixty-one, and is buried at St. Patrick's cemetery, Thurles.

PADDY BROLAN

PADDY BROLAN was born in 1881 and during his life he lived in Ballyduag, and later Mitchel Street (Opposite Well Lane, the Quarry) and at 10 Bohernanave, Thurles. His schooldays were spent at Rahealty National School and later at Thurles C.B.S.

Paddy's usual playing position on the hurling team was at wing-forward and he was a regular on Tipperary teams from 1906 until 1913. In that time he won four Tipperary senior hurling championships, four Munster titles – 1906, 1908, 1909, 1913 and All-Ireland medals in 1906 and 1908.

Paddy Brolan

A typical Brolan attack from the 1906 final was described thus:- 'From the puck out Brolan is away, picking up possession just inside the half-way line and coming along the left wing at terrific pace, he eludes opponent after opponent passing no less than eight Dublin players and finishes up with a truly brilliant piece of play by shooting a marvelous point'.

Paddy also won medals in these competitions:- Railway Shield, Ottway Cuffe, Croke Cup, Croke/Fennelly Cup and Wolfe Tone Tournament. He was on the 1910 Tipperary team that went to Brussels for the Pan Celtic Congress. Paddy was also on the Tipperary selection in 1909 and 1913 that was beaten in the All-Ireland final. One of Paddy's greatest performances was against Leinster in a Railway Shield match, when he scored ten points.

Talking with John D. Hickey of the Irish Independent, Paddy Brolan said that the best hurler of his time was Tom Kerwick of Thurles, particularly for his display against Cork in the 1909 Munster final. Brolan remarked, 'That game was the best game I ever saw. I would have Kerwick in preference to any man in Ireland'.[14]

Paddy Brolan

Paddy's son, Frank, recalling his father said, 'My father was a lightly built man of about 5 ft. 9 ins. in height. In the early years he worked for a farmer in Brownstown and on match days he was up very early, milking twenty cows and running or cycling to the railway station to catch the train to the match. After the match it was always a dash back for the milking. From 1944 to 1956, he was caretaker at Thurles Sportsfield. He was very particular about the field. It was hard to satisfy him and even when the grass was cut I would have to pluck any long tráineens (long grasses) that escaped the mower. My sister Kathleen often helped to line the field. My father got to know some of the great hurlers of the time. Jim Barry of Cork used say that anyone who could not hurl in Thurles should not bother handling a stick. He remembered the embankments at the sportsfield being built with cinders from Thurles sugar factory. They had to pay something for them, so one penny per ton was agreed'[15]. Paddy cared for 'the field' with loving hands and even worked to a late hour there on the night preceding his death.

As caretaker at Thurles Sportsfield, Paddy was in an ideal position to assess the evolution of the game of hurling. He commented,' Players nowadays do not hold their place on the field as we did. If they did, the game would be much more spectacular. In my day, you beat your man or he beat you. There was no cover up that you were helping out somewhere else. Your place was your place and it was your business to be there. In my time, I often saw the ball travel the length of the field half a dozen times in the air and no one marveled at the spectacle, just accepted it as part of the game'.

Paddy Brolan trained the Tipperary 1937 senior hurling team to All-Ireland success. Recalling his tactics he commented, 'you wouldn't see any of them stopping the ball; I just wouldn't have it, if I was going to train them'. First-time hurling was the order of the day. 'Don't stop a rolling ball, keep it moving no matter where you are playing and whether it is on the ground or in the air', he would comment.

Regarding Brolan, the sports editor of the *Irish Echo* in New York, Egan

Clancy, wrote, 'Paddy 'Daddy' Brolan was a very snappy stylish hurler and so earned the sobriquet through his artful handling of the 'camán'. He was an adept at combination and needed a whole lot of watching as his sense of direction was almost uncanny. 'Daddy' was in the front rank of Ireland's best centre wing men'.[16]

Paddy's son, also Paddy, recalls his father as a very easy going, placid man who, after his day's work, loved gardening, a good game of draughts and on Sundays a long walk of maybe ten miles in the country. He mentioned that the war years were very tough for his father. Working with a laundry, and as there was no petrol to be had, they reverted to the horse and cart and Paddy had to go to Templemore and Roscrea to collect and deliver items. As regards the hurling, he often heard that his father could be short-tempered and that first time pulling, getting rid of the ball and never mind trying to lift it was what he believed in.[17]

Paddy Brolan was married to Julia Bradley, a native of Athy, County Kildare.[18] He had a family of nine children and was the laundry van driver at the Presentation Convent, Thurles. He died on 21 July 1956, aged seventy-five years, on the eve of the Munster final. He is buried in Shyan cemetery, Thurles. Paddy played an active role in the War of Independence and three volleys were fired over his grave by members of the Thurles A and B companies of the Old I.R.A., following prayers recited by Rev. Jack McElgunn, who was home on holidays from his missionary work in Nigeria.[19]

JACK CAHILL

Jack Cahill

JOHN (JACK) CAHILL, Leugh Beg, Thurles, was born in 1883, son of John and Ellen Cahill.[20] His school-days were spent at Leugh National School and showed promise as a hurler from those days.

His name first appears with Thurles in the senior hurling championship of 1905. Jack was described as being of powerful build, broad-shouldered and about 5ft. 11ins. in height. He usually played at centre-forward on the team. Jack won two Tipperary county championships with Thurles 'Blues', in 1906 and 1907. He won one All-Ireland medal as a substitute in 1906. He retired from hurling about 1910. At the 1911 Mid final in Rossmore, Jack was a spectator but Sarsfields were short a player, as Tom Semple failed to arrive. Jack Cahill was pressed into service and, though out of practice, got through the game with considerable credit, beating Borris-Ileigh.

The 1907 county hurling final was played in Cashel on 17 February 1908. Jack Cahill was selected on the team but missed his lift to the match. Luckily, he met Mickey Bowe in Thurles, who gave him a loan of his bicycle. Jack cycled to Cashel and was in time to line-out with the 'Blues' and they duly won the county final. Described as one of the most reliable men on the team, he stood firm through thick and thin, in victory or defeat and smiled all the while.[21]

Jack Cahill spent his adult life farming on the family farm at Leugh and always had a great interest in the fortunes of Thurles

Jim Cahill

Sarsfields. Jack married Catherine Cantwell of Lisaticy, Moyne in January 1925 and their family consisted of four sons – John, Anthony, Jim, Michael and three daughters –Anne, Aileen and Margaret.[22]

Their eldest son, John died when only nine years of age. The other three of Jack's sons – Mick, Jim and Anthony, all played hurling. Mick won an All-Ireland junior medal with Tipperary in 1953 and several championships with Thurles Sarsfields. Jim was a star hurler with Leugh/Rahealty in the Rural Schools competition in 1945, while Anthony won a Mid Tipperary junior championship with Drom/Inch in 1951.[23] Jack's grandsons have lined out with Drom/Inch and J.K. Brackens in recent years. Jack's great-grand-son, Michael O'Dwyer, Kilrush, Thurles, plays with Thurles Sarsfields at present, having won Under 21 county hurling finals in 2012 and 2013.

Jack's son, Jim, was a committee member of Thurles Sarsfields for several years and held the position of vice-president at the time of his death in 2000.

Jack Cahill, who had been in failing health for some time, died on 11 September 1953 and is buried in Ballycahill cemetery. His coffin was draped in the Sarsfields colours and was carried by club members.

Michael O'Dwyer

ANDY CALLANAN

ANDREW (Andy) Callanan, Ardbawn, Thurles was born in 1891. He was the third son of John and Ellen Callanan.[24] He was a member of a widely-known and well-respected Gaelic family, where hurling lore was the topic of the day. His uncle Con Callanan was on the Thurles team that won the first ever Tipperary championship in 1887 and he was also on the Tipperary team, Thurles selection, playing in all the games up to the All-Ireland final.

Andy hurled with Thurles Sarsfields and won Mid Tipperary senior championship titles in 1909, 1911 and 1915. His usual position on the playing field was in the half-

Andrew and Ellen Callanan.

forward line. He also won Tipperary county championships in 1909 and 1911. He was on the Tipperary team, Thurles selection that contested the 1911 Munster hurling championship. In the semi-final they defeated Cork at Dungarvan, on 23 July, with the final score:- Tipperary (Thurles) 5-2, Cork (Blackrock) 0-3. The Munster final took place at the Cork Athletic Grounds on 19 November against Limerick. Tipperary was captained by Hughie Shelly and led 2-1 to 0-2 at half-time. An unexpected score, completely against the run of play, set the whole Limerick camp on fire and they went on to finish winners by 5-3 to 4-3. Andy was on the Tipperary junior hurling team that won the Munster championship in 1910 and 1911. At this time, the junior championship was confined to the province.

However, for Andy Callanan, an injury received while playing championship hurling in Mid Tipperary prematurely ended his hurling career.[25] Andy always reckoned that Hughie Shelly was the best hurler he ever saw in action.

Andy married Ellen (Nellie) Maher, Lower Killinan. She was the eldest daughter of Denis and Johanna Maher. Denis was Tipperary's first senior hurling captain and Nellie was sister of John Maher,[26] Tipperary's All-Ireland winning captain in 1945. Andy and Nellie reared twelve sons and four daughters – Ellen, Josie, Maura and Margaret. All their sons hurled at various times with Thurles Sarsfields:-John, Denis, Con, Andrew, Jim, Michael, Dick, Paddy, Gus, Thomas, Andrew and Eamon. Andy's son Dick won five senior Tipperary championships with Thurles Sarsfields 1961-'65. Dick was also chairman of Dúrlas Óg G.A.A. Club from 1997-'99. Andy's son Michael (Mick) hurled with Faughs, Dublin, while another son, Jim, hurled for years in New South Wales, Australia.

Andy Callanan

Andy's younger brother John Joe (1894-1970) was a noted hurler with Sarsfields and Tipperary. He captained Tipperary to All-Ireland success in 1930-Triple Crown Year. While a student in Dublin (1919-'25), John Joe hurled with Faughs winning a Dublin county hurling championship with them in 1920. Also in 1920, he was on the Dublin senior hurling team which won the All-Ireland. On Bloody Sunday, 21 November 1920, he and Bob Mockler, Horse and Jockey, were umpires at the fateful Tipperary/Dublin football match in Croke Park. While in Dublin, John Joe was active in the War of

John Joe Callanan

Independence as a courier for Michael Collins. On his return to Thurles, in the mid twenties, he resumed his hurling with his colleagues of old and was a vital cog in the break-through of 1929, when Thurles Sarsfields won the county championship after a lapse of eighteen years. When his playing days were over John Joe was a successful county senior hurling selector in the forties and fifties. He was also Tipperary's representative on Central Council from 1928 till 1930 and chairman of Thurles Sarsfields in 1946 and 1947. In 1940, John Joe refereed the All-Ireland hurling final between Limerick and Kilkenny.

On the days of major games at Thurles Sportsfield, Andy would be seen stewarding the sideline. He loved such occasions as it afforded him the opportunity to meet old hurling colleagues of yesteryear.

Andy Callanan, who farmed the family farm at Ardbawn, died on 1 May 1971.[27] His wife, Nellie, died on 2 March 1982 and both are buried at Killinan cemetery, Thurles.

ANTHONY CAREW

ANTHONY BERNARD CAREW was the youngest son of Patrick and Catherine Carew (née English). He was born in Rossmore about the year 1889, where his parents had a farm, shop and public house.

Anthony Carew

As a young lad he walked on a darning needle, which went through his foot. Later, at the age of sixteen years, he got a severe pain in his knee. There was no relief for it and the doctors decided to open the knee in order to discover the cause. They found the darning needle had made its way up to his knee and removed it to his great relief.[28]

Having come to Thurles, Antony joined the local hurling club, where his talent was quickly recognised. Carew was an outstanding hurler and a great scorer of goals as the records of the 'Blues' reveal. In time, Anthony won two Tipperary senior hurling championships, 1909, 1911 and two Munster championships in 1908 and 1909. He was on the 1908 All-Ireland winning team and also won medals in these competitions:- Ottway Cuffe, Croke/Fennelly Cup and Wolfe Tone Tournament. He was on the 1910 Tipperary team that went to Brussels for the Pan Celtic Congress.

This verse, praising Carew was penned by an Irish exile, Edmund Murphy, Washington:-

> *Of Tipperary's camán wielders,*
> *No forward of their hosts,*
> *Could so crush opposing fielders,*
> *Could so humble all their boasts;*
> *Or send the sliotar spinning,*
> *His blows upon it ringing,*
> *While hats the crowds were flinging,*
> *As he shot it through the posts.*[29]

In the 1911 census, Patrick Carew is a spirit merchant and resident at Main Street, Thurles, while his son, twenty-one year old, Anthony, resides with him.

Anthony's occupation is described as commission agent.[30] He was employed at this time by the Singer sewing machine company.

The 1911 Mid senior hurling final, between Thurles Sarsfields and Borris/Ileigh, was played in Carew's field, Rossmore, on 2 July of that year. Getting the match to Rossmore was a coup for Anthony. There is a theory that there was a bit of canvassing behind the scenes and that Anthony Carew, who was Thurles club secretary at the time, was behind the motion to get the match to Rossmore, where his father, Patrick had a farm and public house. The farm had a field suitable for hurling and the pub would come in handy for a crowd at a match.

On the night of 20 January 1930, a fire destroyed Anthony Carew's licensed premises on lower Liberty Square (Suirside). Anthony, at this time, lived alone on the premises and the Carew's held the public-house under lease dated 28 February 1905. The house and drapery store next door, the property of Catherine Flynn was also damaged. The famous Croke/Fennelly cup, which Sarsfields won outright, was mislaid for some time and discovered again in the rafters of Carew's house following the fire. Anthony believed the fire was started maliciously and took an action against Thurles Urban Council for £800 damages. However, he lost the case and left Thurles shortly afterwards.

Carew was a skilled G.A.A. administrator, as Thurles Sarsfields secretary in 1912 and as Tipperary county secretary from 1913 to 1922. He was present in Croke Park on the grimmest and most violent day in the War of Independence, Sunday, 21 November 1920, a day that became known as 'Bloody Sunday'. An inter-county football challenge game had been arranged between Tipperary and Dublin and Anthony was present in his role as Tipperary county secretary.

Anthony Carew married Mary (Molly) Boyle, daughter of Michael and Ellen Boyle, Cassestown, Thurles. Mary worked as a shop assistant at McGraths on Main Street, Thurles.[31] They had one daughter, Catherine (Kathleen), who married Thomas O'Mahony of Moyaliffe. They had four children:- Seán, Anthony (Tony), Maura and Frank and lived at Durrow, County Laois. Molly died on 16 November 1914, aged twenty-five years. She is buried in St Mary's churchyard, Thurles.

Anthony later married Bridget Green. They moved to Southampton in the south of England and Anthony was employed as a hotel barman. Anthony Carew died at the local borough hospital on 3 January 1943, aged fifty-three years. His grave, in Hollybrook cemetery, Southhampton, was 'discovered' some years ago by his grandson, Seán O'Mahony.[32]

TIM CONDON

TIM CONDON, son of Michael and Johanna Condon, was born in 1876. He was a native of Ballinure and started his hurling career with neighbouring Horse and Jockey. He quickly established himself as a skilled hurler. Tubberadora included him on their winning All-Ireland selection in 1896 and 1898. In 1899, Tim captained Horse and Jockey to Tipperary and All-Ireland success.

Tim was on the Thurles team in the 1906 county final against Lahorna De Wets. He also was on the winning Munster final team of that year. However, he played no part in the All-Ireland final other than being listed among the substitutes. In 1906 he also won a Railway Shield medal with Munster, Two-Mile Borris selection. Tim was also a respected referee, taking control of major club games.

Tim Condon

In his early working life Tim was a noted stonemason and slater but as the years passed it was as a builder and contractor that he is best remembered. In 1904, Tim was among those who built the handball alley at Horse and Jockey.

He was a most unassuming and gentle character. No matter who sought his aid, it was freely given. The big occasion never phased him, he was the same lining out for a Munster final as he would with a group of schoolboys pegging an old 'thread ball' at a crossroads on a summer's evening. He treated victory and defeat just the same.

Tim's brother, Mikey, was a fine athlete, winning numerous prizes at sports meetings at local and national level. He excelled in the high jump but also had successes in the long jump and hurdle events, competing at events in Dublin, Cork and Limerick. Mikey's son, Michael, won a minor hurling All-Ireland with Tipperary in 1933. On the path to that final, Michael scored the winning goal against Cork in the Munster final and notched four against Kilkenny in the semi-final. Another son, Niall was also an accomplished high jumper, winning Tipperary high jump titles in 1944, 1952 and 1953.[33] Niall also hurled with Thurles Sarsfields and won a Munster senior championship medal with

Billy Quinn   *Niall Quinn*   *Niall Condon*

Tipperary in the 'Foot and Mouth' year of 1941. Niall's sister, Mary, married Billy Quinn, Rahealty, who played with Tipperary minors in four successive years, 1950-1953, captaining the team to victory in 1953. Billy played senior with Tipperary in the mid fifties and was also a star with Faughs, winning several Dublin titles. Their son, Niall Quinn, grand-nephew of Tim Condon, won a Leinster minor hurling championship with Dublin in 1983 and was on the losing side to Galway in that year's All-Ireland minor hurling final. Niall progressed to becoming a renowned soccer player with Arsenal, Manchester City and Sunderland. In an international career, 1986-2002, he gained ninety-two caps and scored twenty-one goals for the Republic of Ireland.

In 1908, Tim Condon was chairman of Mid Tipperary G.A.A. Board and continued in this position for three years. He died on 21 May 1918, aged 42 and is buried in Ballinure cemetery. At a meeting of the old Horse and Jockey Hurling Club, following his death, the following resolution was passed:-

'That we, the members of the old Horse and Jockey Hurling Club, beg to tender to Mr. Michael Condon and family our sincere regret in the great loss they have sustained in the death of a worthy son and brother. And our grief is no less poignant to lose a worthy colleague and genial companion.'

Those present at the meeting were:- P.W. Hogan, Richard and James O'Keeffe, William and John Gleeson, Dan Mullins and Paddy Maher (Best).

TOM DWAN

TOM was born in 1889 at Lisnagonoge, Beakstown, a townland in Holycross/Ballycahill that borders the parish of Thurles. His schooldays were at Thurles C.B.S. and he spent all his adult life farming at Beakstown. Tom was the best known of a great hurling family, which included his brothers

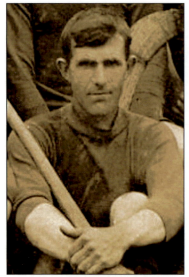

Tom Dwan

Stephen Dwan

Patrick, Willie, Stephen and Rody. Tom's career as a hurler is mentioned as far back as 1906, when he was a member of the Holycross team beaten by Thurles Sarsfields. In 1908 Tom played with Holycross in the early rounds of the championship and in the same year lined out with Thurles in the county semi-final against Lahorna De Wets.[34] In 1909, Tom was goalkeeper for Thurles 'Blues' in that year's county final. Tom's height was 5ft. 11 ins. and he weighed about twelve stone. He is remembered as an above average goalkeeper, taking over from James 'Hawk' O'Brien, when he retired, but he also played at half-back. Between 1910 and 1915 Tom was a member of the Tipperary junior hurling team, winning an All-Ireland in 1913, a year that Tom also helped Tipperary win the Croke Cup. In 1915 Tom captained Tipperary to another junior All-Ireland victory. From then until 1923 Tom was a member of the county's senior side, winning Munster and All-Ireland medals in 1916 as goalkeeper, with the Boherlahan selection.

Tom's usual position on the field was at right corner-back, but his versatility was shown by playing in goal at All-Ireland level. He was a close marking defender, who wasted no time in lifting the ball, but cleared first-time to safety. The ballad-maker in 1916 had this to say about Tom:-

I'd say my memory was gone
Said the Sean Bhean Bhocht.
Not to mention Tom Dwan
Said the Sean Bhean Bhocht.
He was placed between the sticks
Where he played some crafty tricks
And had Kilkenny in a fix
Said the Sean Bhean Bhocht.

Tom won the Munster championship in 1922 and retired following the All-Ireland defeat of that year. His brother Willie (1895-1977) was a fine hurler and played with both Thurles and Tipperary, winning a Munster senior championship medal in 1922.

Stephen Dwan (1896-1976) also hurled senior championship with Thurles. He won a junior hurling All-Ireland with Tipperary in 1924. Stephen also played an active role in the War of Independence. He later emigrated to Australia and died in Sydney.

Rody Dwan played a prominent role in the War of Independence in the Thurles region. He was employed at J.K. Moloney's, Liberty Square, Thurles,

Rody Dwan

and also acquired a farm at Glenbane, Holycross. He died, aged eighty-four years, on 1 October 1982 and is buried in St Patrick's cemetery, Thurles. He was predeceased by his wife Bridget, who died in April 1948.

Tom Dwan's nephew, Rody Curran, Fianna Road, Thurles, won three Tipperary senior hurling championships with Sarsfields in the 1930s. Rody's grandson, Paul Curran, Mullinahone, won a senior hurling All-Ireland with Tipperary in 2010, playing at full-back, and captained the team in 2012.

Tom Dwan, who was married with two children, was chairman of Thurles Co-Op Creamery for over thirty years. Tom died in May 1980 and is buried in St Patrick's cemetery, Thurles. He was the last survivor of the victorious 1916 Tipperary hurling team.

Paul Curran

TIM (THADY) DWYER

TIMOTHY (THADY) DWYER was son of Thomas and Johanna Dwyer, the Commons, Thurles. He was born about the year 1888 and grew up on the family farm on the Holycross Road, Thurles. Thady was an ardent hurler and one of the most skilful of 'the Blues'. He won Mid titles in 1908, 1909, 1911 and 1912. He also won county titles in 1909 and 1911. In 1909 Thady was on the Tipperary team that won the Munster final but were defeated by Kilkenny in the All-Ireland final. In September of that year, Thady was on the Tipperary team, Thurles selection that won the inaugural Croke/Fennelly Cup tournament at Fethard.

Tim Dwyer

Thady was a member of the 1910 Tipperary team that travelled to Brussels for the Pan Celtic Congress. He was also on the Tipperary junior hurling team that won the Munster championship in 1910 and 1911.

Thady, described as 'a veritable prince of sportsmen,'[35] was an enthusiastic coursing follower and the mainstay of the Thurles Coursing Club for many years. Such was his interest in the sport that the local annual coursing meeting was held on his lands at the Commons. He was also one of the founders of Thurles greyhound racing track and a director since its inception. Tim, who was unmarried, was a lifetime supporter of hurling and a regular at the games at all levels. He died in tragic circumstances in a fire at his home on Wednesday, 27 December 1961. Tim Dwyer is buried in Ballytarsna cemetery.

Philip O'Dwyer. Thurles Sarsfields Junior A Hurling captain,   *T.J. O'Dwyer*
Mid Tipperary Champions 2014

The O'Dwyer links with Sarsfields have continued down through the years to the present day. Thady's grand-nephew, the late "Black" Johnny Dwyer, Mathew Avenue, Thurles, played for the club and was a stalwart follower until his untimely death in a car accident in 1994. Currently, two other grand nephews, Johnny's cousins, T.J. and Philip (Philly) O'Dwyer, who reside at the family home on Holycross Road, and who are sons of Michael O'Dwyer, nephew of Thady, are playing members of the club. Two great-grand-nephews, Brian and Peadar Graydon, Monadereen, Thurles, also played with the club before moving away from town.

PAT AND JOHN FITZGERALD

EVEN THOUGH they shared the same surname and address Pat and John were not related. Pat was son of John and Ellen Fitzgerald, Poyntstown, Glengoole (New Birmingham) and was born in 1879 while John, also of

Poyntstown, was born two years later. Around 1907, both were showing their mettle as great skillful wielders of the camán. Pat with a height of six feet two inches, had a fine athletic figure, noted for his fitness and stamina and usually played in a defensive role. The success of the Fitzgeralds encouraged other locals and Glengoole entered a team in the south Tipperary championship in 1908. This was the first such championship, the south Tipperary Board having been formed the previous year. Led by their captain Pat Fitzgerald, they defeated Clonmel, Racecourse (Cashel) and in the final completely outclassed Killenaule, both Fitzgeralds playing leading roles. That same year, Pat's talents were recognised by the Thurles selectors, who included him on their team that defeated north champions, Lahorna de Wets, in the county semi-final. The 1908 county final between Thurles and Glengoole was played in Cormack's field, Glengoole and Thurles overconfidently expected to retain their title. Tom Semple did not take the Glengoole challenge seriously and only brought a make-shift team. 'It was the saddest day Tom Semple saw in his hurling career', according to Pat.[36] They fielded a much weaker team than in the semi-final, but to the delight of the locals, Thurles were beaten by 4-2 to 2-6. The result was much disputed with Thurles focusing on the fact that Pat Fitzgerald had played with two clubs in the same championship, even though one of the clubs was Thurles. The Glengoole line-out for the final clearly showed that there was scant regard for parish boundaries in those far off days.[37] The controversy dragged on until 1910 when Tipperary G.A.A. convention decided to drop the 1908 hurling championship and declared it null and void.

Pat Fitzgerald

John Fitzgerald

Both Fitzgeralds were on the Thurles selection that won the 1908 All-Ireland final, beating Dublin in the replay, 3-15 to 1-5. This game was the only game in the championship in which they played.

They were also on the Tipperary team – Thurles selection for the 1909

Pat and Patsy Fitzgerald.

championship, winning the Munster title and playing in all the games including the All-Ireland final, losing to Kilkenny, 4-6 to 0-12.

Both John and Pat were also on the 1910 Tipperary team that went to Brussels for the Pan Celtic Congress. Both also hurled on the Two-Mile-Borris selection that won the 1910 Cuffe Shield tournament, beating Wexford (Castlebridge) in the final. Toomevara also selected Pat on the Tipperary team that won the Croke Cup final in 1913, played on 1 June at Dungarvan.

Travelling to matches in those days was not easy, Pat recalled, 'Pakie Holland would come out from Littleton with his pony and side-car and take John and myself to Thurles where we would meet up with the rest of the team. We would get a meal in Jim Maher's and then off with us to the train. We would bring about 2/6 with us going to an All-Ireland. That is as much as we would spend during the day'.[38]

John Fitzgerald was unmarried and died in 1925. Mourning his passing, his former captain, Tom Semple said, 'No man could claim first with John Fitz as a hurler; he was the flower of our flock, known and noted throughout the length and breadth of the country.'[39] John is buried in Boulick cemetery.

Pat married Catherine (née Croke) and their family consisted of two sons and three daughters.

Pat's son, Patsy, Poynstown, Glengoole, was a hero of Irish athletics. In a glittering career that spanned almost two decades, Patsy won an incredible thirty-four All-Ireland medals and numerous county and provincial honours over

Patsy Fitzgerald

324

cross-country and track circuits. One of the races that he fondly recalls was at Fontenoy, Belgium, where his father had hurled in 1910.[40] Patsy and his brother Tom hurled with Glengoole in the 1950s. Their victory in the 1956 Mid No. 2 junior championship is well remembered, when Patsy was 'Man of the Match' with his winning goal. For many years, the local G.A.A. club had use of one of Fitzgerald's fields as a training pitch.

Pat died on 26 June 1970, aged eighty-nine. His wife Catherine died on 2 April 1984. Both are buried in Glengoole Cemetery. He was the second last survivor of the old Thurles 'Blues', Fr. Michael O'Dwyer being the last.

JOE FITZPATRICK

JOE FITZPATRICK, Pouldine, was born in 1886, son of Daniel and Elizabeth Fitzpatrick. He attended Pouldine school and came to the fore as a hurler with Two-Mile-Borris, with whom he won the Mid Tipperary senior hurling championship in 1910. Joe was on the Tipperary team, captained by Hugh Shelly that beat Cork in the 1911 Munster championship semi-final with the score:- Tipperary (Thurles) 5-2, Cork (Blackrock) 0-3. In the Munster final against Limerick, Joe played in the half-back line but they lost by 5-3 to 4-3. In later years Joe played mostly in the forward line, being described as 'a fierce and vicious forward'.[41] In 1913, Joe was on the Tipperary team, Toomevara selection that lost to Kilkenny. However, he won an All-Ireland medal in 1916, with the Boherlahan selection

Joe Fitzpatrick

and a Munster medal the following year. As a wing forward Joe was rated the best in the game in a long playing career which stretched from 1910 until 1926. His classic displays against Kilkenny's Dick Grace were the stuff of legend. He won further Munster championships in 1922 and 1924. In 1926 Joe emigrated to the U.S.A. and while there he played with the Tipperary team for four or five years. Joe was among the welcoming party that greeted the touring Tipperary team in 1931. He returned to Ireland in June 1939, six months before his death.[42] Joseph Fitzpatrick died unexpectedly, following a brief illness, in December 1939 and was buried in Galboola cemetery.

JERRY FOGARTY

JERRY (JEREMIAH) FOGARTY, a native of Ballydavid, Littleton, was born on 4 July 1892.[43] He was son of John and Margaret Fogarty (née Mullaney), who

Jerry Fogarty

were married in Moycarkey church on 2 February 1886. In his early twenties, Jerry worked as a shop-assistant at Ryan's, Main Street,[44] Thurles for some years and hurled with Thurles Sarsfields. He was a regular on the club and county teams between 1909 and 1912.[45] He won Tipperary senior championships with Thurles Sarsfields in 1909 and 1911. Jerry played on the Thurles selection in the 1911 Munster final losing heavily to Cork's Blackrock selection by 5-2 to 0-3. Jerry played on the Tipperary junior hurling team that won the Munster championship in 1910.

About the year 1913, Jerry emigrated to the U.S.A. Prior to his departure, his Thurles club mates presented him with a gold medal. For the

Sadhbh Leahy

Philip Leahy

Patrick Leahy

remainder of his working life Jerry was in the employ of the Wabash Railroad Company. He was also the business agent for his local of the railway clerks' union. Jerry married Catherine Lavin and they had one son, John, born 1929.

Jerry Fogarty died in Missouri Baptist Hospital, St Louis, Missouri, on Thursday, 24 September 1953. Rev. Edward T. O'Meara, St Louis, a nephew of the deceased, celebrated his Requiem Mass. He was buried at Calvary cemetery, St Louis.

Many descendants and cousins of Jerry Fogarty are staunch supporters of Moycarkey/Borris G.A.A., particularly Leahys – Ballydavid, Mahers – Galboola. Cousins also are very involved in Thurles Sarsfields – former player and present treasurer Philip Leahy and current players Patrick and Sadhbh Leahy.

JACK GLEESON

Jack Gleeson

JACK GLEESON was a member of a great sporting family from Dromboe, Horse and Jockey. He was a top-class miler and half-miler as well as being a renowned hurler. Jack won three All-Irelands:- 1899 with Horse and Jockey, 1900 with Two-Mile-Borris and 1906 with Thurles. He also won a Railway Shield in 1906, Two-Mile-Borris selection and the Cuffe Shield in 1910. In his day Jack was regarded as one of the best full-forwards in the game. He exemplified the 'Tipperary dash' to a degree not in evidence in the modern game. A friend commented, 'Jack knew not the meaning of the word danger. In he went and the ball went with him'. On one occasion the Tipperary goalie asked Jack where he would drop the ball. 'At my feet,' was the reply and sure enough, when the request was complied with, ball, man and all ended in the back of the net. Jack won the following Tipperary county championships:- 1901 Ballytarsna, 1904 Thurles, 1905 Two Mile Borris, and 1906 Thurles. In 1908, Jack played in his usual forward position in the All-Ireland final against Dublin, which ended in a draw, 2-5 to 1-8. Due to some unexplained dispute, the players from Horse and Jockey (Bill Harris, Joe O'Keeffe, Jack Gleeson and Bob Mockler) did not line out in the replay, which Tipperary won by 3-15 to 1-5.

In 1901, Jack won a mile race at Shepherd's Bush, London at the August bank holiday sports. That same weekend, he also lined out at the same venue with the Tipperary hurlers which defeated a London selection by 3-15 to 1-3.

Jack was a good handballer and was renowned for his strength on the local tug-of-war team. This great sportsman died on 20 January 1957, aged seventy-eight years and is buried in Moycarkey cemetery.

MICHAEL GLEESON

MICHAEL GLEESON was born in the Pike (now Kickham Street), Thurles in 1886, son of Patrick and Hanora Gleeson. He was educated in the local national school and by his mid-teens his occupation was described as a railway painter. His father was working as a railway ganger in 1901. Later that decade the family moved residence to New Street (now Parnell Street).[46] Michael, in his twenties was working as a builder and contractor and proprietor of the Gaelic Stores on the street.

Michael 'Mickey' Gleeson

Mickey, as he was affectionately known, first played with Thurles Sarsfields in the county senior championship of 1905 and he went on to win three county championship medals with the club. He won one All-Ireland medal as a substitute in 1906. He played in the 1907 Munster championship, which lost the Munster final to Cork. Playing days over, Mickey continued his involvement in Sarsfields club as their representative on mid and county board.

His son Eddie Gleeson, Sean Treacy Avenue, Thurles, was an All-Ireland winner in 1945, scoring two goals in the final against Kilkenny. Mickey's grandson, Michael (Glossy) won a senior county championship with Sarsfields in 1974 and was on the Tipperary senior hurling panel in 1975, 1976 and 1977. He was a county selector in various grades including senior in 2011 and 2012. His sons Eamon, Michael and Cian all hurled with Thurles Sarsfields, with Michael winning four county senior hurling titles.

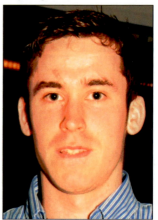

Michael Gleeson

Another of Mickey's sons, Billy, was on the Tipperary minor team that won the Munster championship but lost the All-Ireland final in 1945. He emigrated to England in 1945 and spent the remainder of his life there.

Michael Gleeson died, aged forty-five, unexpectedly at St Vincent's Hospital, Dublin, in November 1932. At the weekly meeting of the Sarsfields Club, James Maher proposed and Patrick Brolan seconded, 'That this committee extends to the relatives of the late Michael Gleeson sincere regret and deepest sympathy in their sad bereavement'. The meeting then adjourned[47].

Mid Board chairman, Rev. Philip Fogarty said, 'Tonight we mourn the passing of an ardent supporter of our native pastimes. We will not soon forget the enthusiasm with which he worked to have his native town the 'one bright spot' in hurling circles.

Remembering Mickey Gleeson, Tom Semple, his former team-captain said, 'One of our old team is gone. He took a great interest in the games to the end and the G.A.A. has suffered a great loss'. Michael Gleeson was buried in St Mary's cemetery, Thurles.

TIM GLEESON

TIM GLEESON was born at Cloonyross, Clogher in the parish of Clonoulty/ Rossmore in 1881. A skilful hurler, though of light build, Tim always kept himself in the peak of physical condition. Regular training included many sessions up and down Cody's hill beside his home and it was customary for him to walk to and from matches in Thurles. The result was an extraordinary consistency of high-class performance. Renowned for his determination, he literally put his heart into every game, which was typical of his general character.

Tim Gleeson

Tim, who always made his own hurleys, lined out with Drombane in the championship of 1905. He was with Thurles the following year, winning the county final against Lahorna De Wets. He was on the Thurles selection that won Munster and All-Ireland medals in 1906 and 1908 and a Munster title in 1909. To all these victories he contributed in large measure by his crisp, clean, powerful defensive hurling, from his favourite left half-back position. He sorely regretted losing the 1909 final, as he felt Tipperary were good enough to win it. In 1906 and 1908 Tim Gleeson also won Railway Shield medals with Munster.

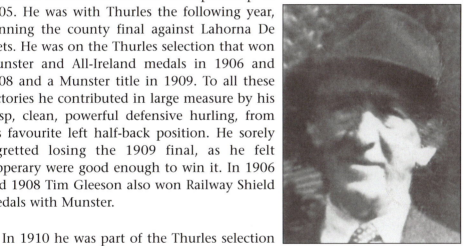

Tim Gleeson – 1930s.

In 1910 he was part of the Thurles selection that represented Tipperary at the Celtic Congress in Belgium. Tim captained the Tipperary team that lost the Munster semi-final to Cork at Limerick in 1910 but won the Cuffe Shield medal that year. When the power base of Tipperary hurling swung towards Toomevara, Tim was also part of their selection that lost the All-Ireland final of 1913 but he won a coveted Croke Memorial medal that year, beating Kilkenny at Dungarvan on 1 June. Following this victory the Toomevara anthem – 'Hurrah for Toomevara' was penned and includes the line:-

Give one cheer for Timmy Gleeson – that hero tried and true...[48]

Like his father, also named Tim, he was a National Teacher by profession, having trained at De Le Salle College, Waterford. He succeeded his father in the principalship of Cloneyharp N.S. Tim also taught at Turraheen and Ballagh and was principal of Clonoulty N.S., when he retired in 1946.

One of the hurlers that Tim admired most was Jamsie Kelleher, who captained Dungourney, the great Cork team of his era. Their tussles with the Thurles 'Blues' were epic. Mickey Byrne, the legendary Sarsfields corner-back, was also a favourite of Tim's, both revelling in a no-nonsense approach to hurling.

A keen observer of the game, who saw him in action recalled, 'Then there was Tim Gleeson, the school-master hurler from Drombane, whose ground drives were some of the most spectacular things which I ever witnessed on a hurling field. Tim found no difficulty in cutting the ball off the ground – often the full height of the playing pitch and frequently scoring points, in this manner from his own half-back position'.[49]

On the administration side of the G.A.A., Tim was treasurer of Tipperary County Board from 1910 to1915. At the Tipperary convention in January 1916, Tim Gleeson was elected county chairman, a position he held for that historic year. He was also chairman of Mid Tipperary Board in 1925 and 1926 and served many years as the Mid Tipperary's representative on the county board. Tim refereed the Mid senior hurling final, between Thurles Sarsfields and Borris/Ileigh, which was played in Carew's field, Rossmore, on 2 July 1911. He was also in charge of the 1910 county hurling final between Toomevara and Racecourse. Tim was a member of the Rossmore team beaten by Thurles in the 1911 semi-final. He retired from hurling after the 1913 championship.

Tim, who was renowned for his good-humour, loved a visit from his old hurling comrades to his home at Cloonyross. Jack Mockler was a regular as was Wedger Meagher, the famous captain of Toomevara 'Greyhounds'.[50]

Tim, who was in failing health for some time, was aged seventy-eight when he died in February 1960. He is buried in Kilvalure cemetery, Drombane.

Tim's grandson, Mícheál Treacy married Patricia McElgunn, daughter of former Thurles Sarsfields backman, Mícheál 'Rocky' McElgunn. Their son, Cian, hurls with Thurles Sarsfields at present.

Cian Treacy (Captain), Thurles Sarsfields Mid Intermediate champions 2014.

JOHN HACKETT

JOHN HACKETT was a native of Grawn, Two-Mile-Borris and was born in 1876. He was one of four brothers, all of whom had very close association with the local Two-Mile-Borris teams in the early years of the last century. John was on the 'Borris team that won the Tipperary championship in 1900 and along with his brother Ned were substitutes on the Tipperary team, Two-Mile-Borris selection, that won the All-Ireland that year.

Shortly after 1900, Ned moved to Dublin and continued his hurling with clubs in the city. He was later proprietor of the Belvedere Hotel, Gardiner Row, a landmark for G.A.A. supporters near Croke Park. Ned died in 1951.

John Hackett

In 1909 John (Johnny) was on the Tipperary team, Thurles selection, captained by Tom Semple, which lost the 1909 All-Ireland final to Kilkenny by 4-6 to 0-12. In 1911, he was a member of the winning Tipperary team that captured the Cuffe Shield. This was a Two-Mile-Borris selection captained by Jimmy Bourke, Rathcunikeen. John had a lifelong interest in the G.A.A. and particularly the Moycarkey/Borris club, a tradition he handed on to subsequent generations of the Hackett family. John's son, Tom, played with Rahealty. Another son, Pat, played with Moycarkey/Borris and was captain and full-back on the Tipperary junior hurling team in 1947.[51]

John Hackett's grandsons, John and Liam, are very involved with the Moycarkey/Borris club. Liam is the current chairman and John has been club secretary and treasurer. They were both members of the club team that won senior county titles in 1982 and 1984 and a Munster title against Patrickswell in 1982. John captained the intermediate team that won the 1985 county title against Killenaule. Liam played at midfield in that final.

John Hackett   *Liam Hackett*

John Hackett died on 24 December 1962, aged eighty-six years and is buried in Two-Mile-Borris cemetery.

BILL HARRIS

William (Bill) Harris's headstone in the old cemetery, Moycarkey.

BILL HARRIS, son of John and Mary Harris (née Croke), was born in the townland of Lurgoe, Killenaule in 1883,[52] but when he was one year old, the family moved residence to Liskeveen, Littleton. His schooldays were spent at Moycarkey N.S., Pouldine, and later, as a teenager, he became part of the local workforce as a general labourer. In his adult life Bill is remembered as having operated a threshing steam-engine, which provided a useful service for the local farming community.

There was a strong hurling tradition in the family, his father, John Harris (Addish), was a hurler of note with Moycarkey in the late 1880s.[53] In 1906, Bill Harris made his first appearance for Moycarkey in the championship, beaten by Thurles, 3-13 to 2-3, following a replay. In the first round of the 1908 Munster hurling championship, Tipperary (Thurles) met Waterford at Fermoy, on 27 September. It was a facile victory for Tipperary on a score of 7-16 to 0-5 and it was Bill's first game representing Tipperary. In the Munster semi-final against Cork, also at Fermoy, Bill scored the winning goal for Tipperary in their 2-11 to 3-7 victory. Following a Munster final victory over Kerry, Bill played in his usual forward position in the All-Ireland final against Dublin, which ended in a draw, 2-5 to 1-8. Due to some unexplained dispute, the players from Horse and Jockey (Bill Harris, Joe O'Keeffe, Jack Gleeson and Bob Mockler) did not line out in the replay, which Tipperary won by 3-15 to 1-5.

In 1914, Bill Harris was on the Tipperary, Two-Mile-Borris selection that retained the Cuffe Shield, under Jimmy Bourke's captaincy, defeating Limerick in the final. Bill continued to hurl with parish clubs until 1917.

Bill married Margaret Ryan, Curraheen, Horse and Jockey and they lived at Kylenoe. They had a family of five children,[54] one of whom, Jack, a nonagenarian is residing at Ballinure. Margaret Ryan's uncle, Jimmy Ryan 'Remedy' was a member of the Horse and Jockey team, which won the 1899 All-Ireland hurling final.

Bill Harris died aged fifty-six on 13 February 1939. He had been ill for some time and his death was not unexpected.[55] His wife, Margaret, died on 14 August 1958. Both are buried in the old cemetery at Moycarkey.

JER HAYES

JEREMIAH (JER) HAYES, a native of Leugh, Thurles, was born on 17 May 1877. His school-days were spent at the local Leugh N.S. and he showed prowess as a hurler from an early age. Jer was described as a man of large build, possessing great natural strength. He was vice-captain on the 'Blues' during their most successful era.

Jer Hayes

Jer's name first appears on a Thurles team in 1898. He went on to win Tipperary championships in 1904, 1906 and 1907, his usual position on the hurling team being at full-back.[56] In 1906, he was vice-captain of the Tipperary, Thurles selection, that won Munster and All-Ireland titles. He was also holder of a Railway Shield medal with Munster. Jer played in the 1907 Munster final, losing to Cork.

Jer was a skilful hurley-maker and supplied hurleys for the 'Blues' team. After retiring from the game he continued to serve the club as vice-chairman and committee member.

Jer was a progressive farmer and had a number of threshing engines. The family suffered a huge loss in July 1913, when an accidental fire broke out in the haggard attached to the house in Leugh. Jer was at the fair in Thurles and the mills of his two threshing machines, a hay-barn and outhouse etc. were destroyed. In the days following the accident, Jer's neighbours, team-mates and friends came together in Leugh school and a committee was formed to collect subscriptions to indemnify Jer for his loss.

Jer and his wife Nora, née Callanan, Leugh bridge, had a family of ten children, six sons and four daughters. His son Dan was on the first team from Thurles C.B.S. to win the Dr Harty Cup, in 1933.

Jer died, aged forty-six, on 6 September 1923. He is buried in Moyaliffe cemetery, Drombane.[57] His death, at a relatively young age, was hastened by an old hurling injury.

TOM KENNA

TOM KENNA was born in Church Lane (St Mary's Avenue) Thurles in 1884. He was son of William and Ellen Kenna and his early education was at the Presentation Convent School nearby. In 1891, Thomas was enrolled at

Tom Kenna

A tombstone crafted by William Kena in the old cemetery at Moycarkey.

Sculptures by Tom Kenna.

Moycarkey N.S., Pouldine, where he finished his education. His address is recorded as Turtulla, on the outskirts of Thurles, where his grand-father, Patrick Kenna, resided.

Popularly known as 'Gaffer', he is listed as playing with Thurles 'Blues' in the 1905 Tipperary county championship and was a regular on the team until 1909. Kenna was a great believer in the importance of training and would be seen regularly perfecting his hurling skills in Butler's 'glen' field beside his house in Turtulla.[58] A skill that used to enthuse and amaze the locals was Tom's innate ability of keeping the ball pucked in the air and meeting it, time after time, as it fell. He won Tipperary championships in 1906 and 1907 and was on the Tipperary team, Thurles selection, that won Munster and All-Ireland winning titles in 1906 and 1908. In the 1907 Munster championship, Tom was on the Thurles selection that lost to Cork in the Munster final, Cork (Dungourney) 1-6, Tipperary (Thurles) 1-4. 'Gaffer' also won a Railway Shield medal in 1908.

Tom Kenna, like his father, William, was a stonemason and sculptor by trade and examples of their craftsmanship can still be seen in the Moycarkey area, particularly in local cemeteries.

JAMES M. KENNEDY, Club Secretary

JAMES M. KENNEDY was born in 1882. According to the census of 1901, James (Jimmy) then eighteen years of age, was living over a shop at New Street (now Parnell Street), Thurles, with his uncles, John and James Moloney, both postmen in the town.[59]

Jimmy was then employed as a mail messenger but was dismissed from the service because of his republican sympathies and activities. He was an active member of the Irish Republican Brotherhood and since 1909 gave years of service to the cause of Sinn Féin. As Thurles 'centre' for the I.R.B., Jimmy enrolled members

James Kennedy and Johanna Fogarty on their wedding day.

in the organisation and administered the 'oath'. In a statement to the Bureau of Military History, Jimmy Leahy, Tubberadora, who was later commandant of the Second Tipperary Brigade I.R.A., stated, 'In January or February 1916, I was sworn into the I.R.B. by Jimmy Kennedy, the town clerk in Thurles, and the local I.R.B. centre. It was he who was responsible for the reorganisation of the Irish Volunteers in the town in 1915. I was still in Thurles when the rising occurred in Dublin in Easter 1916. Jimmy Kennedy was in direct contact with the leaders of the rising. A dispatch was received by him on Easter Sunday, or on the previous day, from Dublin. I am not aware or the contents of this dispatch... He called a meeting of the Thurles I.R.B. circle at which he told us about the rising in Dublin and also made arrangements for the transfer of five or six rifles from Thurles to Annfield, and, as far as I can remember, a couple of automatic pistols. At any rate, I think this meeting took place on Easter Monday and on the following Wednesday the guns were removed … In the summer of 1916, the I.R.B. 'centre', Jimmy Kennedy, summoned the circle and announced his intention to revive the Volunteer movement.[60]

Éamon Ó Duibhir, Ballagh, Gooldscross, who later became Tipperary county 'centre', Irish Republican Brotherhood and assistant brigade quartermaster, 3rd Tipperary Brigade I.R.A., stated:- 'One day when I was in Thurles and James Kennedy, who was later the very efficient town clerk of Thurles, brought me in amongst the machinery in the *Tipperary Star* office. There he administered the I.R.B. oath to me'.[61]

Another statement to the Bureau by Frank McGrath formerly commandant Tipperary No. 1, North Tipperary Brigade states, 'Whilst I am not positive, I am almost certain that it was some time in that year 1915 that I was sworn into the Irish Republican Brotherhood by James Kennedy of Thurles. At that time, too, I was in close contact with the Volunteer leaders in Dublin including Thomas

J. Clarke and Michael O'Hanrahan but principally with The O'Rahilly and Cathal Brugha...'.[62]

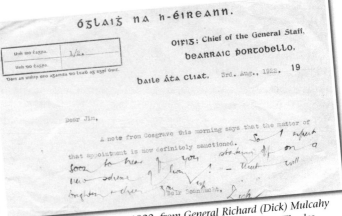

Letter, dated 3 August 1922, from General Richard (Dick) Mulcahy to Jimmy Kennedy confirming his appointment with Thurles Urban District Council.

In the pre-1916 Rebellion days, Jimmy was a frequent visitor to Tom Clarke's shop on Parnell Street, Dublin and was a close confidant of Seán Mac Diarmada. Both Clarke and Mac Diarmada were signatories of the 1916 Proclamation of the Irish Republic.

Jimmy recalled the Irish Volunteer manoeuvres in Thurles at Easter 1916. The Volunteers had assembled on the Square near where the Croke memorial now stands and marched down past Hayes's Hotel. They were met with verbal abuse and the contents of many chamber pots from the local residents, particularly those from the lanes off the Square, while a bemused band of R.I.C. watched them from the other side of the road. The parade ended their manoeuvres.[63] Jimmy was also a friend of Pierce McCan, Ballyowen House, Dualla and campaigned successfully for his election as a member of parliament for the East Tipperary constituency in 1918. When hostilities developed in the Anglo-Irish War (War of Independence, 1919-'21), James was one targeted by the British forces and consequently he went 'on the run' for several periods of time.

Jimmy Kennedy was an active participant in the movement to revive the Irish language, an ideal he shared with Richard (Dick) Mulcahy to whom he taught Irish in the early years of the century, at Gaelic League – Conradh na Gaeilge classes in Thurles.[64]

Following the Anglo Irish Treaty, signed in December 1921, James took the anti-Treaty side during the Civil War and was imprisoned for a period at Templemore barracks, which was then occupied by the National Army. Despite the bitterness of the war, James never lost his friendship with General Richard (Dick) Mulcahy, commander in chief of the pro-Treaty forces, who supported Jimmy's appointment as town clerk. In later years, Mulcahy often called to the Kennedy home on Parnell Street, Thurles, and is remembered for his generosity at Christmas and Easter by Jim and Pat Crone, who were resident with Jimmy in the 1950s and early 60s.

James Kennedy was secretary of Thurles Sarsfields G.A.A. Club from 1906 to 1911, a period when the club led Tipperary to two All-Ireland successes. He is remembered for his loyalty, efficiency and organisational acumen. While secretary he designed a new crest for the club which included a shamrock in blue and white and bearing the phrase – Thro' the Thatch.

According to journalist and author Raymond Smith, 'The game of hurling was everything to James Kennedy and I admired greatly his detachment from inter-club and inter-county rivalries. This true spirit of sportsmanship was to me the greatest legacy of the Tom Semple era'.[65]

Local knowledge and local history were two of Jimmy Kennedy's attributes and delights. He left a rich legacy of source material relevant to Thurles and was a lifetime collector of Thurles lore. Apart from his many contributions to the *Tipperary Star*, Kennedy published *A Chronology of Thurles* (Thurles, 1939) and *Historic and Important dates in the Civic Life of Thurles* (Thurles, 1941).[66]

For close on fifty years Jimmy worked in the service of Thurles Urban Council, firstly as a rate collector[67] and then twenty-five years spent as town clerk. He was an outstanding Thurles man, who worked tirelessly for its betterment. He presided over the transformation of the town's physical appearance and economic life. His foresight in the area of development gave the town a head-start over similar towns. He played a major role in securing the sugar factory as well as providing up-to-date water and sewage amenities. Much of the progress, in housing particularly, made in Thurles in the quarter century prior to his death had been due to his foresight and energy.

James married Johanna Fogarty, Brittas, Thurles. At the time of his death, 29 June 1964, James, had one brother and three sisters living in Australia. He was almost eighty-three years of age. He was predeceased by his wife Johanna, who died in May 1949. Both are buried in St Patrick's cemetery, Thurles.[68] Incidentally Jimmy was town clerk when this cemetery was opened, on 11 May 1928, a fact recorded on a plaque in the cemetery.

Páraic Crone, Furze, who hurls at present with Thurles Sarsfields is a great grand-nephew of Jimmy Kennedy. Páraic won Dr Harty and All-Ireland Colleges medals with Thurles C.B.S. in 2009, Munster Club S.H. with Sarsfields in 2012 and an All-Ireland intermediate

Páraic Crone

hurling medal with U.C.D. in 2013/14. His sister, Sinéad, also plays camogie with Thurles Sarsfields.

Remembering Jimmy Kennedy, town clerk E.F. Murphy paid this tribute, 'He laid the foundation of everything we have today. He was a great Thurles man and a great Tipperary man, but I think he would like, above all, to be regarded as a great Irishman, and that he truly was'.[69]

TOM KERWICK

Tom Kerwick

TOM KERWICK, son of Pierce and Catherine (Kate) Kerwick, was born in 1886. He was enrolled as a pupil in Leugh N.S. but later transferred to Moycarkey N.S., Pouldine, when the family moved residence to Maxfort in the parish of Moycarkey/Borris. Following the death of his father, the family moved to Thurles and lived at Nicholas Street (now Cúchulainn Road). Tom was a carpenter and joiner by trade.[70]

Tom won four Tipperary senior hurling championships, three Munster titles – 1906, 1908, 1909 and All-Ireland medals in 1906 and 1908. He also won medals in these competitions:- Railway Shield, Ottway Cuffe, Croke Cup, Croke/Fennelly Cup and Wolfe Tone tournament. He was on the 1910 Tipperary team that went to Brussels for the Pan Celtic Congress. Tom was also on the Tipperary selection in 1909 that was beaten in the All-Ireland final.

Team-mate Paddy Brolan recalls, 'In the 1909 Munster final in Tipperary town against Cork, the hurling that Tom Kerwick did that day had to be seen to be believed. Every ball he hit, and I can tell you he hit many, he drove seventy to eighty yards, whether he hit it off the ground or in the air.' Jack Murphy recalled, 'Tom Kerwick was a great full-back for a light bit of a lad – not a big man by any means'.[71]

Regarding Kerwick, the sports editor of the *Irish Echo* in New York, Egan Clancy, wrote, 'Tom Kerwick with the surprising delivery was undoubtedly a rattler of the back division. The ball used to leave his hurley with bullet-like velocity and woe to the human target it came in contact with. Tom, although inclined to be the serious type, was nevertheless well able to tell a yarn and crack a joke with any of the 'boys in blue'.[72]

Tom Kerwick was an ardent worker in the cause of the Gael; his love and life's service he gave to the promotion of native pastimes. Few were on a par with him as a handball and football player, but it was as a hurler with the 'Old Blues' selection that his fame was highest.[73]

Tom Kerwick died unexpectedly on 9 February 1929, at Hillside, Westport, County Mayo. Aged forty-two, he had been resident in Westport for about ten years, where he was employed as a manual instructor under the Department of Technical Instruction. But it was as a Gael that Tom Kerwick figured with remarkable prominence. P.D. Mehigan, 'Carbery' had written of him that, 'He was the one man that possessed all the attributes of the perfect hurler, viz., science, speed, stamina and strength'.[74] He was indeed one of the finest exponents of hurling, during his era. Tom Kerwick, who is buried in Killinan cemetery, also served as chairman of Tipperary County Board from 1909 to 1914.

Recalling Kerwick, John Joe Hayes, Moycarkey, stated, 'In the days of the Thurles 'Blues', he proved himself the most perfect exponent of the hurling code in Ireland'.

PADDY MAHER-BEST

PADDY MAHER (Best) was born in 1878 at Ballybeg, in the parish of Moycarkey/Borris. He was an extraordinary athlete excelling at middle and long distance events. A man of boundless energy and stamina, with an iron constitution and could run and did run to many a venue many miles distant and afterwards compete, before running home later. As a hurler he first came to fame with Two-Mile-Borris and was on their selection that won the 1900 All-Ireland.

He won his second All-Ireland as part of the Thurles selection in 1906. In that year Paddy also won a Railway Shield medal representing Munster, Two-Mile-Borris selection. One of his finest displays was against Leinster in the shield semi-final at

Paddy Maher-Best

Deerpark, Carrick-on-Suir, when Paddy came on as a substitute and scored 2-5 in fifteen minutes to earn a draw for Munster.

Group taken at the unveiling of the memorial in 1979. Back row (l.-r.):- John Phelan, Paddy Moloney, Harry Ryan, T.K. Dwyer, Jim Burke, Joe Ryan, Bill Moloney, Liam Hennessy, Eamonn Barry, Jimmy Tobin, Seán Barry, Harry Melbourne, Billy Shanahan, Liam Ryan. Front row (l.-r.):- Bill O'Keeffe, Johnny Ryan, John Mullins, John Joe Hayes, Tommy Gleeson, Paddy Ryan (S), Thomas O'Keeffe, Tommy Fogarty.

He had a fine athletic build and his usual position was at centre-field, where his high fielding of the hurling-ball was renowned. In total Paddy won four Tipperary hurling county championships:- 1900, 1904, 1905 and 1906.

In 1907 Paddy won an All-Ireland junior cross-country title with Tipperary and was second in the Irish one mile championship, with a time of 4 mins. 29¼ secs. Later that year at the Thurles sports, he outran McNamara of Tulla, then Irish champion, also defeating the legendary Tipperary runner, Tim Crowe, Bishopswood, Dundrum.

Paddy also had a great interest in ploughing and was a regular winner at ploughing matches all over Tipperary.

Tales of his feats of strength and endurance are legion. One such tale tells of how he was due to travel by train with the 'Blues' to the 1908 All-Ireland final at Athy. As they left Thurles, Paddy was nowhere to be found. Their consternation turned to amazement as they arrived in Athy to find that Paddy 'Best' had cycled the whole journey and was in the process of finishing a hearty dinner. His comment was, 'What kept ye?'[75]

Paddy died on 9 June 1954, aged seventy-six, and was buried in the old cemetery in Moycarkey. In January 1979, a memorial was unveiled over his grave, by a sub-committee of the Moycarkey/Borris G.A.A. Club.

PAT 'WEDGER' MEAGHER

Pat 'Wedger' Meagher

PAT 'WEDGER' MEAGHER was born at Coole Lane,[76] Toomevara in 1890 and attended Clash National School. He is remembered as a great captain, a fine hurler, a tenacious and utterly capable corner-back. He was nicknamed 'Wedger' after a County Waterford family noted for breeding race horses.

'Wedger' made his first appearance for Tipperary on the Thurles selection against Kilkenny (Tullaroan selection) at Dungarvan on 28 July 1912, losing by 3-3 to 2-1.

'Wedger' was a natural leader, both on and off the field, leading the Toomevara 'Greyhounds' to county honours in 1910, 1912, 1913, 1914 and 1919. In 1913 the Toomevara selection was unlucky not to capture the All-Ireland title, losing to Kilkenny by 2-4 to 1-2. Earlier that year, victory in the Croke Cup final over Kilkenny, then All-Ireland champions, earned for 'Wedger' and his team a status, never to be forgotten, in hurling lore. The victory gave birth to the ballad – 'Hurrah for Toomevara':-

'Then hurrah for Toomevara, may your banner never fall!
You beat Galway and Queen's County, you're the boys can play the ball!
But I never will forget the day Kilkenny's pride went down
Before the skill of Wedger's men in sweet Dungarvan town.[77]

During the War of Independence, 'Wedger' played an active role as did many of the Toomevara 'Greyhounds', being participant in numerous guerrilla actions, endured a hunger-strike and was imprisoned on a number of occasions.[78]

On the administration side of the G.A.A. 'Wedger' was an efficient North Tipperary secretary from 1914 to 1920 and county secretary from 1920 to 1927, the year he emigrated to the U.S.A. For twenty-nine years he was Gaelic sports editor of the *Irish Echo*, where his column 'With the Gaels' made him a household name among the Irish emigrants.

Pat 'Wedger' Meagher died on 20 February 1959 and was buried in St Charles cemetery, Farringdale, Long Island, New York.

BOB MOCKLER

Bob Mockler

ROBERT (BOB) MOCKLER was born in 1886.[79] He was the eldest son of Thomas and Bridget Mockler, Curaheen, Horse and Jockey. His father was a boot-maker by trade. When his school-days were over at Moycarkey N.S., Pouldine, Robert worked for local farmers. From an early age he showed great promise as a hurler with the local Horse and Jockey team. Mockler first came to prominence on the inter-county scene as a member of the Tipperary senior hurling team, Thurles selection, in 1908. He made his first appearance, at midfield, in that year's All-Ireland decider as Tipperary faced Dublin. A 2-5 to 1-8 draw was the result on that occasion. Tipperary won the replay, however, Bob Mockler played no part in the replay and his absence is unexplained. In 1909, Bob lined out again with the Thurles selection, winning the Munster final, but losing the All-Ireland to Kilkenny. He was also a member of the Tipperary team, Toomevara selection that lost the 1913 All-Ireland final, again to Kilkenny. In 1914, Bob moved to Dublin and got work as a van-driver with a Dublin bakery. He joined the Faughs club in 1914, winning six Dublin county championship medals with them, including back-to-back championship medals in 1914 and 1915. He gave great service to Faughs, wearing their jersey for over twenty-five years. With Dublin he won three All-Irelands: 1917, 1920 and 1924. In 1920 he captained the Dublin team to victory. Bob was also holder of five Leinster senior championship medals. He played in a total of eight All-Ireland finals, three with Tipperary and five with Dublin. On Bloody Sunday, 21 November 1920, Bob Mockler and John Joe Callanan were umpires at the fateful Tipperary/Dublin football match in Croke Park.

Remembered as a vigorous and towering centre-field player, capable of taking scores from behind his own centre-field line and that in days when the sliotar was much heavier and much less water-resistant than now.[80] One of his last visits to Tipperary was to support Moycarkey/Borris in the 1962 county hurling final at Thurles Sportsfield.

Bob was also a prominent handballer, referee and administrator and regarded as one of the best hurlers Tipperary ever produced. Bob Mockler died in 1966.[81]

JACK MOCKLER

Jack Mockler

JOHN (JACK) MOCKLER was born in 1885 at Brittas Road, Thurles. He was the eldest son of Thomas and Hanora Mockler.[82] He grew into a powerful man and to a height of 5ft 10ins. Jack was a man of tremendous physical endurance, he always seemed to be impervious to the weather, no matter how cold. He certainly made many younger men wonder at his strength and hardiness. He also enjoyed weight-lifting, a sport that came naturally to him.

In his professional life, Jack was a pharmacist and had the confidence and respect of a large clientele who frequented his premises on Liberty Square, Thurles.

As a hurler, Jack was a great believer that hurling was a team game, where the individual was useless without the team working together. He was a regular on Tipperary team from 1906 until 1912 and in that time Jack won four Tipperary senior hurling championships, three Munster titles, All-Ireland medals in 1906 and 1908. He also won medals in these competitions:- Railway Shield, Ottway Cuffe, Croke Cup, Croke/Fennelly Cup and Wolfe Tone

Margaret and Jack Mockler.

Tournament. He was on the 1910 Tipperary team that went to Brussels for the Pan Celtic Congress. Jack's regular position was at centre-field, often beside team-captain Tom Semple. Hughie Shelly and Paddy Brolan were speedy forwards running beside them. Jack rated Jim Kelleher, Dungourney, Cork, as the best backman he ever saw and that Dick Grace was the best Kilkenny man of his time.[83]

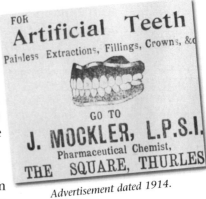

Advertisement dated 1914.

Jack was part of the Tipperary back-room team in 1945 and the team, that went on to win the All-Ireland, was often selected in a room at the back of his chemist's shop. As a great judge of hurling, his opinion was always valued and it was Jack that recommended the young Mick Murphy, to replace the injured Johnny Ryan for the All-Ireland final of that year. Right through his life, Jack, loved 'first-time' hurling. He was of the opinion that the Wexford team of the fifties was the nearest he saw to his own 'Blues' era.

Jack married Margaret Russell, Ballyduag, as he said himself, 'I walked from Grange up the sleepers to Loughmore to marry Margaret'.[84] Apart from hurling, Jack was known far and wide as a sportsman with dog and gun or fishing for pike on the local rivers. He died, aged seventy-three, at 'Flora Villa', Thurles on 13 July 1957. His wife, Margaret, died on 25 May 1973 and both are buried in St Patrick's cemetery, Thurles.

THOMAS MOCKLER

THOMAS 'TOSS' MOCKLER, Brittas Road, Thurles, who was born in 1891,[85] was a younger brother of Jack Mockler. During his lifetime Toss was one of the keenest sportsmen in Tipperary. In particular he was a splendid athlete excelling as both hurler and footballer. Toss, whose pharmacy was on Patrick Street, Templemore, had the then unique distinction of playing both senior hurling and football for Tipperary on the same day. He won Mid and county hurling championships with Thurles Sarsfields in 1909 and 1911 and a Mid championship in 1912. He was also on the Thurles Mitchels team that won the Mid Tipperary senior football championship in 1909, the inaugural year of the competition. As a hurler, he was perhaps unlucky in that when he came to his prime, the best years of Thurles 'Blues' had just passed. However he won a Croke Cup with Tipperary in 1912.

Toss was on the Tipperary junior hurling team that won the Munster championship in 1910 and '11. At this time, the junior championship was confined to the province.

Thomas married Mary (Mai) Ryan, daughter of Hugh Ryan, West Gate, Thurles and they resided over the pharmacy on Patrick Street, Templemore. They had two sons Vincent and Hugh, four daughters Elizabeth, Eileen, Mary, Delia.[86]

He gave great service as a chemist in Templemore for almost forty years, where his advice and skill was eagerly sought by customers from a wide area.

As a horse breeder, Toss enjoyed much success at the Dublin spring and horse

Toss and Mai Mockler.

The Vets Scour Specific.

The safe, speedy and certain Cure for White Scour in Calves.

Every Packet Guaranteed. Price, 3s. 6d.

To be had from the Manufacturers:

MOCKLER'S, The Chemists,

THURLES and Templemore.

Advertisement dated 1916.

shows. He was an ardent rider to hounds but it was perhaps as a greyhound breeder and coursing man that he is principally remembered.

Thomas 'Toss' Mockler was in his mid-sixties when he died on 7 February 1957. His wife Mai predeceased him on 11 February 1951 and both are buried in Templemore cemetery.

PHIL MOLONY, Club Treasurer

PHILIP (PHIL) MOLONY was born in Rossestown (Lewagh Beg), Thurles in 1885,[87] son of James and Mary (née Maher). He was one of a family of nine children that grew up on the family farm. At this time Phil's uncle, Con, was owner of a drapery business at 15/16 Liberty Square, Thurles and also owned a farm and racecourse at Killinan, on the outskirts of the town. In 1911, Philip, now twenty-six years of age, was learning the drapery trade from his uncle and residing on his premises.[88] The drapery shop was situated where Liberty Square meets Slievenamon Road and was known as the 'Corner House'. At that time, the name Cornelius Molony was over the door.[89]

About the year 1916, Phil acquired the premises and business on Liberty Square from his uncle Con, and Phil's brother, Pierce, became owner of Killinan in 1921.

Phil was treasurer of the Thurles Sarsfields G.A.A. Club from 1906 to 1908. This was the period in which the club led Tipperary to two All-Ireland hurling successes.

Phil married Josephine (Josie) Benson, a native of Drombane, and they both lived over their business premises, which

Phil Molony

continued as a drapery. They had a family of eleven:- Christine, Margaret, Maura, Philip, Jack, Josephine, Lou, James, Marie, Ann (Nance) and Mary.[90]

Wonderful Value
in
All-Spring Fashions

We have now in stock our full selections of Ladies' Coats and Costumes, Frocks, Hats, Gloves, Bags, etc., etc.

Irish Tweed Coats from ...... £4-4-0.

Very smart semi-fitting Coats, all shades, from .... £5-18-9.

Sty-lex hand-tailored models in Coats and Costumes. See our very smart selection in everything that is new.

NYLONS for Spring. All good brands in stock: Bear Brand from 3/11; fully-fashioned from 7/11; Non-run in several brands, 12/11; very fine Bear Brand, F.F., 8/11.

SPECIAL SALE IN HANDBAGS
Shoulder Bags from .... 7/11.
Very smart Handbags, all shades, from .... 9/11.
See our selection.

Men's Sports Coats and Sports Pants in a large selection. We stock DUBTEX Pants.

INSPECTION INVITED.   SEE WINDOWS.   TERMS: CASH.

MOLONYS
THURLES
The Corner House,

An old advertisement for Molony's Corner House.

Both Phil's sons, Philip and Jack, were excellent rugby players. Jack, better known as Jacko, played at lock for Ireland in the Five Nations competition against Scotland in February 1950.

Recalling bygone days in Thurles, an article in the *Tipperary Star* newspaper stated, 'Phil Molony's, the 'Switzers' of Thurles. Like the designer clothes of the present times, if you bought anything from Phil Molony's you'd nearly display the receipt on the outside'.[91]

Phil was a keen golfer and an honorary member of Thurles Golf Club, of which he was one of the founders.[92]

Phil Molony's grand-nephew, Fr Pierce Duggan, Two-Mile-Borris, was chairman of Tipperary G.A.A. Centenary and Development Committee, which was responsible for the redevelopment of Semple Stadium, Thurles, in preparation for the G.A.A. centenary celebrations, including the staging of the All-Ireland hurling finals at Semple Stadium, in September 1984.

Phil Molony, who had been in failing health for some time, died at his residence on Slievenamon Road, Thurles, on 20 November 1962. He was seventy-eight years of age. His wife Josephine died on 1 June of the following year. Both are buried in St Patrick's cemetery, Thurles.

Fr Pierce Duggan

JACK MOONEY

JACK WAS born in Clonmel on 3 March 1883 and christened John Farrell. Following the death of his father, his mother remarried a man named Mooney, so Jack also took the surname Mooney. When he moved to Thurles, he lived at Limekiln Lane and later at Mitchel Street. He married Annie Coady, Fennor Hill, Gortnahoe and they had a family of eight children.

In his youth Jack was a very useful boxer and was a founder member of Thurles Boxing Club[93] but it was hurling with Thurles 'Blues' that he gained sporting fame. His name first appears on the Thurles team lists for the 1906 Tipperary county championship and remains there every year until 1914. In

Jack Mooney

that time Jack won five Tipperary senior hurling championships and three Munster championships. He was a substitute on the 1906 All-Ireland winning team and played at centrefield in the 1908 victory. Jack also won medals in these competitions:- Railway Shield, Ottway Cuffe, Croke Cup, Croke/Fennelly Cup and Wolfe Tone Tournament. He was on the 1910 Tipperary team that went to Brussels for the Pan Celtic Congress.

Jack Murphy, Iona Avenue, Thurles, recalled talking to Jack about his training and he said, 'At the time he was hurling with the Old 'Blues', he was driving a horse-drawn oil-car for O'Meara's. To improve his fitness he used to tie the reins to the side of the car and run after the horse and car all the way to Ballingarry'.[94]

It was said that Jack's stocky build was capable of withstanding almost any shock. Despite his great strength and boxing skill, he always played the game fairly and never, even in the heat of battle, lost the good humour and joviality for which he was noted.[95] Jack was always the mainstay of the team when hope seemed darkest, he never bowed to defeat but valiantly fought to the last ditch for the honour, glory and the prestige of the Thurles 'Blues'.[96]

Jack later worked as a turf accountant (bookie) on Liberty Square and was well known and popular at horse- racing and coursing fixtures. His son Jimmy, Fianna Road, won minor hurling All-Irelands in 1933 and 1934 and was also on the Tipperary junior hurling team in 1938.

Jack, who lived at Mitchel Street, Thurles, died at a nursing home in Waterford, on 1 December 1950 and is buried in St Patrick's cemetery, Thurles.

NED McGRATH

NED (EDDIE) McGRATH was born in 1888 at New Street (now Parnell Street), Thurles. Having finished school locally he served his time to the carpentry trade.[97] Ned showed promise on the hurling field from a young age and was on the Thurles club teams from 1907 to 1917. In the early years he played with the junior team, Thurles Emmets and was remembered as an impressive full-forward.

In 1908 Ned, now aged twenty, emigrated to the U.S.A., possibly to relations in Tacoma or Spokane, Washington.[98] At a meeting of Thurles G.A.A. before he left, Tom Semple proposed and it was agreed that he be presented with a gold watch suitably inscribed and costing less than one pound.[99] The presentation was made by Denis O'Keeffe, club chairman, at a function in the Confraternity Hall. While making the presentation O'Keeffe stated that over forty-three club members had emigrated in the previous three years. On the following Saturday, most of Ned's team-mates were at Thurles railway station to bid him farewell, safe journey and every success.[100]

By 1910 Ned was back in Thurles and hurling with the 'Blues'. He won a Munster junior hurling championship with Tipperary in 1910 and 1911. In 1913 he won his only All-Ireland, when Tipperary won the All-Ireland junior hurling title. This victory gave Tipperary the distinction of being the first county to win an All-Ireland junior title.

From 1912 to 1914 he was on the senior team, Thurles Sarsfields, and he contested the championships in these years. In 1912 Ned hurled with the Tipperary team, Thurles selection that won the Croke Cup under the captaincy of Tom Semple.

In later years Ned was employed as a carpenter and caretaker at the Ursuline Convent, Thurles. He is remembered as a quiet unassuming man who enjoyed fishing, shooting and a stroll in the countryside. He died in the early 1960s.

JOSEPH McLOUGHNEY

JOSEPH McLOUGHNEY was born at Coldfields in the parish of Moycarkey/Borris on 10 June 1887, the youngest of a family of nine children. His school-days were spent at Two-Mile-Borris N.S. and later at Tonagha N.S. As a teenager in 1905, Joe secured a position as draper's assistant at Denis O'Keeffe's drapery, West Gate, Thurles and later at Con Molony's drapery store on Main Street, Thurles. This business was later run by Phil Molony, a former Thurles Sarsfields treasurer.

Joseph McLoughney

Joe McLoughney's early hurling was with Two-Mile-Borris but he is best remembered as a stalwart of the Thurles 'Blues'. He joined the Thurles club in 1905. Joe was about 5ft. 9 ins. in height, of slim build and noted for his speed. His usual position on the playing field was at wing-forward. His brothers played with 'Borris and never spared him when they crossed camáns.

Joe won four Tipperary county championships with Thurles 'Blues', two All-Ireland medals, one as a substitute in 1906 and as a team member in the

1908 decider. However, Joe was on the losing team in the 1909 All-Ireland final against Kilkenny. Joe also won medals in these competitions:- Railway Shield, Croke/Fennelly Cup and Wolfe Tone Tournament. He was on the 1910 Tipperary team that went to Brussels for the Pan Celtic Congress.

In Easter 1916, Joe was anxious to join in the rebellion in Dublin, and had organised leave from work to travel, but news of the surrender in Dublin ended his plans.

In August 1917, Joe opened a ladies and gents drapery shop at 23 Liberty Square, Thurles, having purchased the premises, Hibernian Hotel, from Henry Barry for the sum of £700. Barry had originally purchased the hotel for £400. The premises was formally McGlades and Ryans.

Joe joined Sinn Féin in 1917 and was on the local committee with James M. Kennedy (later town clerk), D.H. Ryan and Pat Hunt. He was arrested in 1918, as were many local Gaels, among them J.M. Kennedy and Michael Eustace. Following his release, his republican activities intensified with the outbreak of the War of Independence in January 1919. Joe was involved with next door neighbour Mixie O'Connell, 24 Liberty Square, Bridget Fitzpatrick, Ballynonty (later married Colonel Jerry Ryan) and Mai Moloney, Lackelly, Emly, in sending the historic telegrams regarding the arrested Seán Hogan, on 13 May 1919. This led to the famous Knocklong rescue.[101]

When Inspector Hunt R.I.C. was shot on 23 January 1919 after Thurles races, Joe had to hide for a time. On 20 January 1920, when Luke Finnegan was shot, the R.I.C. went on the rampage, shooting up the town. A shop assistant at Joe McLoughney's shop, J. Corbett, escaped when two bullets came through the fourth floor bedroom. Joe was accosted in his room when going to bed, by the military, but they did not find anything on him, but his shop windows were smashed and a lot of goods went missing.

Later that year, on Monday 1 November, Joe's front door and windows were smashed and goods from the shop were looted. This happened following the capture of Littleton barracks. As it was now too dangerous for his staff to stay over the premises, they were moved to safer accommodation. Joe was again targeted on 10 March 1921, when Larry Hickey and Willie Loughnane were shot by the R.I.C. They tried to gain access to Joe's by the back door, in the lane behind his shop, but failed, not before leaving several bullet holes in the kitchen door. Joe had escaped, over the flat roof, then over Burrough's, Ryan/Walsh's and Butlers down the lane into gardens behind the National Bank, now Lár na Páirce museum. This was a route he used to escape on several occasions. He was always 'on the run' during the years of the 'troubles'. When

Joe McLoughney and his son Eamonn outside his premises in 1932.

Joe was 'on the run' his former team-mate, Martin O'Brien, would manage the shop in his absence.

During the Civil War, Joe took the Republican side but, like so many others, spoke very little about the period. Even though his friend and neighbour, Michael 'Mixie' O'Connell, took the other side, they remained great friends and Mixie would 'tip him off' about when to 'disappear' for a few days.[102] Some years later, Joe was presented with his War of Independence 1919-1921 active service medal.

In 1921 Joe was elected to Thurles Urban Council, a position he held until 1939. He was always very conscious of the importance of employment for the local economy and was very proud of the part he played in securing the sugar factory for Thurles in 1934.

Joe married Nora Purcell, Kyle, the Commons, Ballingarry. She had served three years apprenticed to the drapery business at William J. Moloney's (later J.K. Moloney's), which carried an annual fee of £16. In 1918 Nora took up a position in Joe's drapery. Nora's brothers Dick and Tom were active in the War of Independence, while her sister, Bridie, was in Cumann na mBan. Joe and Nora arranged to marry in June 1923. The wedding was to take place in Ballingarry but as Joe was still 'on the run', they were married by Fr. M.K. Ryan in the cathedral, Thurles at 6.30 a.m., then took the early train to Dublin and sailed from the North Wall to Liverpool for their honeymoon. Joe and Nora had six children, four of whom lived to adulthood.

Joe McLoughney was Sarsfields club secretary for a period in 1917. Club loyalty was vital to Joe, who continued to line-out with Sarsfields in both hurling and football until 1922. He was also treasurer of Tipperary County Board from 1923 until 1932. When the Tipperary hurling team toured the U.S.A. in 1926, Joe did not travel, as his first child (Carmel) was due in July of that year.

One of Joe's great pastimes was in breeding greyhounds at which he had his successes, breeding some good ones such as 'Mark Off' father of 'Dash off Dick' which won the Irish Cup and the Puppy Derby in Clonmel. He was a member of the Irish Coursing Board from 1924 and when Thurles greyhound racing track was opened on 14 March 1950, Joe was very involved with the project from the beginning.

Playing days over, Joe kept up his friendship with the hurlers of his era. G.A.A. correspondent, P.D. Mehigan, 'Carbery', was a special friend, who always called to the house after big games in Thurles Sportsfield and sometimes stayed in McLoughneys. Mehigan had hurled with Cork against Thurles Blues in the 1908 Munster final. Dan Breen was also a regular and welcome visitor, until he became infirm.

Joe's son, Jim, played Dr Harty Cup hurling with Thurles C.B.S. in the early 1950s. Jim's son Rory McLoughney, with the Powerball product, was Thurles Sarsfields main sponsor in 2010, 2011 and 2012.

Joe's daughter, Nora Troy, 'Darby Villa', Kickham Street, Thurles, has been

Paddy and Nora Troy

involved in the promotion of Scór, the G.A.A,'s Irish cultural competition, at local and county levels for many years, while her late husband Paddy was treasurer of Thurles Sarsfields sub-committee responsible for the construction of their Social Centre in the 1970s.

Joseph McLoughney died on 30 January 1962 and is buried in St Patrick's cemetery, Thurles.

JIM 'HAWK' O'BRIEN

Jim 'Hawk' O'Brien

JAMES O'BRIEN was born in 1876 at the Pike, Thurles and later lived at Pony's Lane, Rossestown. As a young man he moved to Dublin with his sister Mary. While in Dublin, he was employed by Dublin Corporation and was gaining a name for himself as a hurler. When this became known to the Thurles club, they requested that he return to Thurles and play with the 'Blues'. This he agreed to do on the condition that he got a similar job in Thurles. So James worked for years with the urban council in Thurles.

In his day he was the idol of Tipperary hurling enthusiasts and known all over Ireland by the sobriquet of 'The Hawk'. A champion goalkeeper, famed for his amazing quick eye, the speed of his reaction and his ability to deal with the flying 'tan'[103]. Nature did not cut him out as a goalkeeper, for his was a fragile frame, yet what was denied him in physique was recompensed in agility and hurling craft.[104] He could pick balls out of the air and liked to indulge in a little fancy stick-work.[105] It was with Thurles 'Blues' that he made his name and earned the well-deserved fame as the champion of his era between the sticks and in his day there were four of them, including point-posts.

James 'Hawk' O'Brien with his son, Jimmy.

In a brilliant hurling career the 'Hawk' won four Tipperary senior hurling championships, three Munster titles, All-Ireland medals in 1906 and 1908. He also won medals in these competitions:- Railway Shield, Ottway Cuffe, Croke Cup,

Croke/Fennelly Cup and Wolfe Tone Tournament. In July 1915, Thurles G.A.A. Club organised a testimonial to James on the occasion of his 'forthcoming marriage'.[106] Subscriptions were collected and a presentation made as a token of the esteem in which he was held. He had five sons: Timmy, Paddy, Eddie, James and Michael and two daughters Bridget and Margaret.

NEW CINEMA, THURLES.

ON TUESDAY NIGHT,

March 29th

THAT SUPER PICTURE:

'SPORTING LIFE'

WILL BE SCREENED IN AID OF THE " HAWK " O'BRIEN TESTIMONIAL.

The promoters of the Testimonial to this famous old Thurles Goalie expect a " Full House " on the occasion. Admission—2s. ; 1s. 6d., and 1s.

'Hawk' was a great friend of Tom Semple and would regularly call into Semple's home on Fianna Road, particularly on Saturdays, when the family would drop him in, while they were shopping in town.[107] His daughter, Margaret,

Advertising 'Hawk' O'Brien testimonial in 1915.

usually accompanied him. Jack Mockler was also a close friend.

James had been in delicate health for some years prior to his death on 3 February 1951, at the age of seventy-five. He is buried in the old graveyard in Moyne.[108]

MARTIN O'BRIEN

MARTIN O'BRIEN was born in 1886, son of James and Bridget O'Brien, Patsy's Cross, Drombane, Thurles. He was one of a family of twelve, eight boys and four girls. In 1906 Martin moved residence from Drombane to Thurles. He was a butcher by trade and his premises were on the New Road (now Parnell Street).

Martin was one of the greatest hurling defenders of his day and was considered among the best right full-backs Tipperary ever produced. Consistency was one of the hallmarks of his greatness and he was never known to leave club or county down. He was a fearless determined

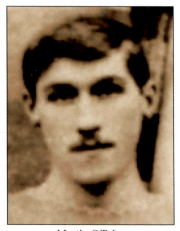

Martin O'Brien

tackler, who pulled fast and free and never resorted to unsporting tactics to beat an opponent. The best forwards in Cork and Kilkenny were pitted against him, but all to no avail.

Martin won five Tipperary senior hurling championships, three Munster titles and All-Ireland medals in 1906 and 1908. He also won medals in these competitions:- Railway Shield, Ottway Cuffe, Croke Cup, Croke/Fennelly Cup and Wolfe Tone Tournament. He was on the 1910 Tipperary team that went to Brussels for the Pan Celtic Congress. He hurled his last match for Thurles Sarsfields, losing to Boherlahan at Coolcroo in 1917.

Martin's younger brother, Tom (1893-1966), played with Faughs, Dublin, winning Dublin senior hurling league and championship in 1914 and 1915. Tom was on the Dublin team that won the 1917 All-Ireland, beating Tipperary. Having played, in his usual corner-back position in the early championship matches, he was a substitute in the final and received a medal. Tom went off the hurling scene during the War of Independence and Civil War but later played with Faughs into his forties.

Martin O'Brien was a well-known owner and breeder of greyhounds and he achieved great success not alone in Ireland but also in Britain. He bred and owned the famous bitch 'Beaded

Martin with his daughters, Biddy on left and Nonie, c1936.

Biddy' that achieved success at Shelbourne Park, Dublin and White City, London in 1927. The ballad-maker, Cathal MacGarvey, Cahir, wrote:-

> *'In the green vales of famed Tipperary*
> *Neath the shadow of sweet Slievenamon*
> *Of late there was littered a puppy*
> *The best ever eyes looked upon*
> *By Martin O'Brien of old Thurles*
> *This marvelous puppy was bred*
> *And there's no better judge of the 'long tails'*
> *In Ireland than Martin, 'tis said'.*
>
> *Chorus*
> *Then here's to her-grand 'Beaded Biddy.'*
> *As gentle and fleet as the fawn*
> *From the green glens of gallant Tipperary*
> *Smiled down on by sweet Slievenamon'...*[109]

In September 1922 Martin married Mary (Molly) Mockler of Brittas, Thurles, at the Cathedral of the Assumption in the town. Molly was a sister of Jack Mockler who was also on the Thurles Blues team. Martin and Molly O'Brien had two daughters – Bridget (Biddy) and Nora (Nonie). Bridget (Biddy) married Tommy Dwyer. He was nephew of Tim (Thady) Dwyer, the Commons, Thurles, who also hurled with the 'Blues'. Their son John, 'Black' Johnny (1953-1994), played for Thurles C.B.S. and Sarsfields in late sixties and seventies. Biddy's grandson's (i.e. Martin O'Brien's great grand-children) Peadar and Brian Graydon, Monadreen, Thurles, both played for Sarsfields up to recently.

Peadar Graydon   *Brian Graydon*

In 1942, there was a revival of interest in camogie, with the formation of a new club in Thurles, named in memory of Piaras Mac Canna (Pierce McCann).[110] Martin O'Brien's daughter, Nonie, was one of the foremost of the Thurles camogie players. At that time, there was a great emphasis on the use of the Irish language and members of the club were exhorted to foster its spread. There were very close links between the camogie club and the local branch of the Gaelic League (Conradh na Gaeilge). Nonie, who played in the full-back line, was the team's vice-captain in 1942 and 1943. Thurles were county finalists in 1943 and Nonie was on the Mid Tipperary selection and the county team in subsequent years, until she emigrated to London in 1946. Nonie maintained a lifelong interest in hurling especially Tipperary hurling and accompanied her father, Martin, to many big matches down through the years. In September 1960, Nonie, married Larry Hickey, who was reared at 25 Liberty Square, Thurles. Larry hurled for Thurles C.B.S., Sarsfields and Tipperary at minor level. He won a Frewen Cup medal, Munster Colleges Junior Football, with the school in 1937, Dean Ryan in '39 and was on the Harty winning teams of 1938 and 1939. He also represented Munster at inter-provincial colleges level. Larry played for Tipperary minors in 1939 but they were beaten in the first round by Limerick. He worked with the Sugar Company in Carlow from 1951 until

Larry Hickey

1960 and then at Thurles sugar factory until he retired in 1981. Nonie died on 23 April 2006, aged 79[111] and Larry died on 14 January 2008 aged 86.

Larry Hickey was named after his father, Laurence, who was originally from Derricknew in the parish of Killenaule. In 1916, Laurence purchased 25 Liberty Square, Thurles, which at that time was a public-house and grocery shop combined. He married Catherine, née Maher, and continued to run the business until he was shot in his home by the R.I.C., on 10 March 1921.[112] His wife, Catherine, was pregnant at the time of the killing and gave birth to her son, Larry, seven months later on 2 October 1921. Laurence, aged forty years, was buried in the churchyard in Killenaule.

Martin O'Brien, who resided at Brittas Road, died on Christmas Eve 1958 in St Anne's nursing home, Thurles. He was aged seventy-three and is buried at St Patrick's cemetery.[113]

MICHAEL O'DWYER

MICHAEL O'DWYER was born at Skeard, Holycross, on 27 September 1887. He was educated at Holycross N.S., Thurles C.B.S. and at St Patrick's College, Thurles and at Maynooth, where he was ordained in 1912.

His postgraduate studies at the Dunboyne Establishment, Maynooth, earned him an M.A. and D.D. in 1915, after which he spent five years as professor of theology at St Patrick's College, Thurles.[114] He was a welcome and valued addition to the then infant Maynooth Mission to China (St Columban's Society), which he joined in 1920. He was their superior general from 1924 until 1947. He was then retained as Director in Ireland and Counsellor until 1962.

Fr Michael O'Dwyer. Photograph was taken around the time of his ordination.

In his youth Michael was a noted hurler. His cousin was the famous Tubberadora goalkeeper, Ned Maher, who had won four All-Irelands, three with the Tubberadora selection in 1895, 1896, 1898 and one with Two-Mile-Borris in 1900.

In his clerical student days, Michael often played tournament games with Glengoole such as one at the Feis in Tullaroan against Sim Walton's Tullaroan team. Another student cleric, Jerry Kinane of Upperchurch, also lined out on the same team. He later became Archbishop Jeremiah Kinane of Cashel and Emly. Both were regular visitors to Glengoole in their student days.[115] In 1908, Michael played with Holycross in the early rounds of the county championship.[116] Later that year, his prowess as a hurler was recognised by the Thurles selection and Michael was in their plans as they prepared for the All-Ireland final with Dublin. Because of restrictions placed on clerical students at

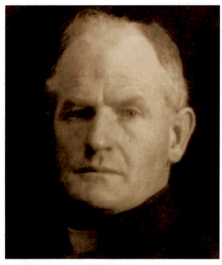

Fr Michael O'Dwyer

this time Michael was not allowed leave of absence to participate in the final. The game ended in a draw and for the replay, at Athy, Michael was available as special permission was sought from Archbishop Fennelly, through the good offices of Canon M.K. Ryan.[117] Commenting on the replay, Canon Philip Fogarty wrote, 'In a much lauded team, one player stood out: he was Mick Dwyer of Holycross, then a student in Maynooth and later one of the directors of the Maynooth Mission to China. The Rev. Michael, together with the Fitzgeralds of Glengoole, were brought on the team to deputise for the Horse and Jockey hurlers, who were absent.'[118]

In the 1909 Munster championship, Mick was one of the stalwarts of the Thurles victory over Dungourney, Cork and was in the back-line when they overcame Galway by four points in the All-Ireland semi-final. Sadly, Michael had returned to his studies at Maynooth before the All-Ireland final and was not available to line out. His loss was very significant, the backline was weakened and the team lost to Kilkenny by 4-6 to 0-12.

Michael was on the 1910 Tipperary team that went to Brussels for the Pan Celtic Congress.

Regarding O'Dwyer, the sports editor of the *Irish Echo* in New York, Egan Clancy, wrote, 'The formidable defence and crafty generalship of the mighty Mick Dwyer, as he came out of fierce tussles on the goal-mouth with possession and saving the situation with a long powerful drive, will long be spoken of on the Maynooth campus, where he is now a Doctor of Divinity, and by many a cross-roads of his native county'.[119]

Bill Hennessy of the great Dungourney team from Cork, in a conversation with John D. Hickey of the *Irish Independent*, rated Mick Dwyer the best Tipperary hurler he had ever seen.

In February 1920, Dr Michael O'Dwyer was chairman of Thurles Gaelic League-Conradh na Gaeilge. Thurles Urban Council gave the Gaelic League committee the task of suggesting alterations to the street names in Thurles. Some of the old street names were seen as meaningless and in some cases distasteful. The league's suggestions were adopted and an Irish language version of each name was provided by the committee and given priority.

Dr Michael was always a keen angler, an excellent horseman in his younger days; he was a scholar and an apostolic leader, who remained a straight-talking man's man, esteemed and beloved by all. Friendly, square-jawed, with a steady blue-eyed gaze, he was also a clear-headed theologian who never lost the common touch and whose counsel was widely sought. Bishop Quinlan, Borris/Ileigh, the veteran missionary of China and Korea had been a student under Dr O'Dwyer in Thurles.[120]

Dr Michael's grand-nephew is Michael Cahill, Leugh, Thurles, who won a senior hurling All-Ireland with Tipperary and an All-Star award in 2010 and is holder of four Tipperary senior hurling medals with Thurles Sarsfields.

Dr Michael O'Dwyer died on 13 February 1975 and is buried at Dalgan Park, Navan, County Meath, as are his two nephews Fr. Michael and Fr. Paddy O'Dwyer. He was the final living member of the famous Thurles 'Blues'.

DENIS O'KEEFFE, Club Chairman

DENIS O'KEEFFE was chairman of the Thurles club from 1906 to 1908, when the 'Blues' were at their peak. Denis, who was born in 1871,[121] was a member of the far-famed O'Keeffe family of the Horse and Jockey. His schooldays were spent at Moycarkey N.S., Pouldine. Coming from a family steeped in hurling lore, it was not surprising that Denis joined the Thurles club, when he moved residence to West Gate, Thurles, where he had a drapery shop. In 1894, he was treasurer of the club and in his younger days was a noted hurler and referee. An ardent Gael, he was prominent in all the Irish-Ireland movements. Denis was national trustee of the G.A.A. in 1901 and also chairman of Tipperary G.A.A. County Board in 1905 and 1906. In 1901

Denis O'Keeffe

and 1902, Denis was Tipperary's representative on the Munster G.A.A. Council.

Regarding Thurles Sportsfield, an entry in the diary of Jim Maher, Parnell Street, Thurles, reads, '5 April 1910. Had small meeting in small room of Confraternity Hall, composed of Fr. M.K. Ryan, Denis O'Keeffe, Denis McCarthy and myself. Decided on calling a meeting of the people of the town to discuss advisability of purchasing grounds for the benefit of the people of the town'.[122] This led to the purchase of the grounds from the Thurles Show Committee, in June of that year. Denis O'Keeffe was also a member of the first committee to manage the venue and he contributed generously to the purchase and development of the sportsfield, now known as Semple Stadium.

In 1971, Denis O'Keeffe's daughter, Lil, wrote to the *Tipperary Star* stating:-' They (i.e. Jim Maher and Denis O'Keeffe) supplied all equipment – railings, stands etc., jerseys, hurling sticks, balls, medals, cups etc., and even paid expenses for the players when they played 'away' matches. All this and more out of their own pockets.' She also bemoaned the lack of recognition given, by the G.A.A. to both Denis O'Keeffe and Jim Maher, Parnell Street.[123]

Denis's brothers Jim, Joe and Dick were winners of a total of seven All-Ireland senior hurling medals. Jim won in 1898 with Tubberadora, 1899 with Horse & Jockey and 1900 with Two-Mile-Borris. Joe played with 'The Jockey in 1899 and with Thurles in 1906. Dick won with Tubberadora in 1898 and with the Horse & Jockey in 1899.

Denis married Bridget O'Grady in 1897. They had six daughters:-Ellen Patricia, Mary, Kathleen, Anastatia, Judith and Bridget. The family resided over the shop at West Gate, Thurles. Denis contracted influenza in the severe epidemic of 1918 and died in November of that year. He is buried in the old cemetery at Moycarkey.

Jack O'Keeffe

Denis's cousin, Jack O'Keeffe, Fianna Road, was caretaker at Thurles Sportsfield/Semple Stadium in the late 1960s and early 1970s.

ELIAS 'BUD' O'KEEFFE

ELIAS O'KEEFFE was born in Chapel Lane, Templetuohy in 1886 and named after his grandfather. He was son of John and Elizabeth O'Keeffe (née Wright).[124] John O'Keeffe was a native of Larkin's Lane, Borris-Ileigh and a tailor by trade, a craft that he handed on to his son, Elias. Elias, affectionately known as 'Bud', showed athletic promise from a young age, being particularly keen on hurling and football. His usual playing position was full-forward, where he was noted for his dash and determination. In 1907, when he was twenty-one years of age, he was selected on the Tipperary team, Thurles selection, for the Munster final against Dungourney, Cork. This low-scoring game was played at

Elias 'Bud' O'Keeffe

Dungarvan with the Tipperary side playing second fiddle throughout. Bud played in his familiar forward position but on the day they were unable to overtake the Leesiders. Cork (Dungourney) 1-6, Tipperary (Thurles) 1-4, was the final score.

Bud was on the Munster team, Thurles selection, which won the 1908 Railway Shield beating Leinster, 8-9 to 1-8 at Thurles Sportsfield. More success followed in 1910 when Bud was a member of the Tipperary junior hurling team that won the Munster championship, beating Clare 5-1 to 2-0 in the final at Limerick. With the local Templetuohy senior football team, Bud was on the team that defeated Thurles in the 1911 Mid final, 3-0 to 2-1. He captained Templetuohy, the following year. In 1913, Toomevara selected Bud on their county selection. They went on to win the Croke Cup, a success immortalised in song by Newport songwriter, Michael Bourke:-

'And our hero Wedger Meagher, he is the lad can fly:
Not forgetting Murphy and O'Keeffe, the Templetuohy boy'.

However, the Toomevara selection, remembered as the 'Greyhounds', lost the 1913 All-Ireland final to Kilkenny by 2-4 to 1-2. Also in 1913, Bud was elected vice-chairman of the Tipperary G.A.A. Board. In the following year, he won a mid and county senior football title with Templetuohy/Castleiney. During his playing days and for years after his retirement from competitive sport, Bud was a popular referee.

Elias played a prominent role in the national movement, and is remembered as a man of high integrity and was utterly trustworthy.[125] In April 1919 Elias was one of five arrested for holding a collection in aid of the Gaelic League (Conradh na Gaeilge) on St Patrick's Day. They were all members of the Gaelic League and were brought into custody in Templemore as they had not received an official permit for the collection, from the Royal Irish Constabulary. Having refused bail, they were held on remand in Limerick jail, until their trial in Templemore on 7 May 1919.[126] All five were found guilty as charged of unlawful assembly, but were deemed to have spent sufficient time in jail and were discharged. During the War of Independence, Bud also became a member of 'B'

Company (Templetuohy Company) 2nd Battalion, 2nd Mid Tipperary Brigade of the Irish Republican Army.[127]

Bud's love for coursing was equal to his passion for hurling and football. He spent most winters attending coursing meetings.[128] Over the years he bred and trained many successful greyhounds, one of the best being 'Suirside Hero' in 1957.

Cyril Bourke and Eoin O'Flaherty, Clonmel, grand-nephews of 'Bud' O'Keeffe, holding the O'Keeffe Cup.

On 21 December 1924, Bud married Nora Tobin at Dunkerrin church. They had no children. Throughout his working life Bud was known far and wide as an outstanding tailor and ran a very successful business. Elias 'Bud' O'Keeffe died on 2 April 1958 and is buried in Templeree cemetery, Castleiney. The Mid Tipperary minor football cup is named in his memory and was presented to the Mid Tipperary G.A.A. Board by the Moyne/Templetuohy Club in 1963.

JOE O'KEEFFE

JOE O'KEEFFE, Horse and Jockey, was born in 1878 and won his first All-Ireland with Horse and Jockey in 1899. Joe was on the Thurles team in the 1906 county final against Lahorna De Wets. He also was on the winning Munster final and All-Ireland team of that year. He also won a Railway Shield medal with Munster in 1906.

In 1908, following the Munster final victory over Kerry, Joe played in the All-Ireland final against Dublin, which ended in a draw, 2-5 to 1-8. Due to some unexplained dispute, the players from Horse and Jockey (Bill Harris, Joe O'Keeffe, Jack Gleeson and Bob Mockler) did not line out in the replay, which Tipperary won by 3-15 to 1-5.

Joe O'Keeffe

Joe won the following Tipperary county championships:- 1899 Horse and Jockey and 1906 Thurles.

Joe farmed at Rathmanna and later at Gaile. He died in 1967 aged 89 years.

FRANK O'MEARA

FRANK O'MEARA was a native of the parish of Holycross/Ballycahill and was born about the year 1885. In 1908 Frank and his brother Ned lined out for Holycross in the championship, losing to Cashel.[129] In 1909 Frank was on the Tipperary team, captained by Tom Semple, which won the Munster final but were defeated by Kilkenny in the All-Ireland final.

Frank, who lived at Killeenyarda, was married and employed by the county council.[130]

PIERCE PURCELL

PIERCE PURCELL, a native of Bawnmore, Johnstown, County Kilkenny, was born in 1891, son of William and Hanora Purcell. He went to school at Crosspatrick, where hurling was the only game played. Pierce had two elder brothers, John and William Purcell, playing for Crosspatrick at the time and young Pierce was at every match.

At twelve years of age he went to St Kieran's College, Kilkenny and having completed his education Pierce was apprenticed to the drapery business of J.K. Moloney at Thurles. He spent every spare hour practicing at Thurles sports-ground where he came across many hurlers of All-Ireland fame and as a hurler he developed into a brilliant wing forward. He captained Thurles Emmets in 1909.

Pierce Purcell

Pierce got a place on Sarsfields senior side when eighteen years of age but rosy prospects were offered to young Purcell by friends in America and his restless ambition urged him thither. He played many star matches with Tipperary N.Y. team during his comparatively short time in the U.S.A. Pierce figured prominently with the All-American team who toured Ireland in 1911.

In the summer of 1911, Pierce had an urgent call from home, to come and help on the family farm. This he did and though he had arrangements made to return to America, Pierce found himself back in business in Thurles where he had full opportunity of perfecting his hurling technique. Pierce played several senior matches with the 'Blues' but he was still eligible to play junior inter-county and he was on the Tipperary junior team that won the Munster and All-Ireland Junior championships in 1913.

Pierce left Thurles for a drapery post at Killenaule and from there to the Monster House, Kilkenny. He won two county senior championships, with Johnstown and then transferred to Tullaroan. With Kilkenny, he played in the Leinster semi- final in 1915 that lost to Laois, 4-1 to 2-6.

Next we find Pierce moving to Waterford but he finished the County Kilkenny championships with Tullaroan before transferring to Young Irelands, Waterford, winning two county championships and playing in all Waterford's inter-county games until 1921.

Pierce played a role in the War of Independence and was arrested in June 1921, and banished to Spike Island prison. A daring successful escape gave Pierce a taste of freedom but more warfare followed for Pierce. He took the Republican side after the Treaty and near the end found himself at Newbridge (Droichead Nua) internment camp – the old British barracks, handed over after the Treaty.

Following his release, Pierce now took up a post in Dublin. But he could not be kept from the hurling. Small persuasion tempted him to play his last match with the Drapers team. After that last game, Pierce Purcell, at thirty-two, hung up his boots, ending a remarkable career, having played inter-county hurling for Kilkenny, Tipperary and Waterford.[131]

PADDY RIORDAN

THE RIORDANS of Rosmult in the parish of Upperchurch/Drombane were a renowned sporting family. Few families can match their achievements with all three sons, John (Jack), Patrick (Paddy) and James (Jim) winning senior county medals. Their father, John, hailed from Ballincollig, Cork, and was a member of the R.I.C., stationed at Roskeen barracks.[132] Paddy and Jim completed a unique feat in winning All-Ireland medals in different codes on the same day, 13 March 1896 (1895 championship), Paddy hurling with Tubberadora and Jim with the footballers of Arravale Rovers. However there is one single achievement that ensures the Riordan name in the record-books, that being Paddy's phenomenal scoring feat in the 1895 All-Ireland, when he scored Tipperary's (Tubberadora) entire total of 6-8, in their defeat of Kilkenny.

Paddy was on the Drombane team that won the 1894 county hurling final beating Thurles by 2-2 to nil. On Whit Monday 1896 Paddy Riordan was part of the 'Gaelic Invasion' of England, where Munster beat Leinster, by 5-7 to 2-8, at Stamford Bridge, London. In 1906 Paddy lined out with Thurles in the county final against Lahorna De Wets and also played on their selection in the Munster and All-Ireland final. In 1906 Paddy Riordan also won a Railway Shield medal with Munster, Two-Mile-Borris selection.

Paddy Riordan

Team-mate Paddy Brolan recalling the 1906 All-Ireland final said, 'Paddy Riordan hit the crossbar on one occasion and it was such a terrific shot that the ball rebounded sixty yards out the field. After that the Dublin goalie would not stay in goal when Paddy would be on the ball and let me tell you he was a wise man. Paddy, take it from me, was the greatest forward ever, he used to play full'.

In late November 1907, the officers of the Thurles club became aware that Paddy, one of their hurling stars, was about to emigrate to the U.S.A. A subscription list was opened to pay for a gold chain and medal, which was presented to Paddy on the Saturday prior to his departure.[133] He landed in New York at noon on 1 December, just in time to be rushed over to help Tipperary beat King's County (Offaly) in the New York hurling final at Celtic Park, before an attendance of 20,000. Reardon's hurling was described as 'simply grand'. Captain of the Tipperary team in New York was a Thurles man – William (Bill) Ryan. Paddy was back in Thurles in 1911 when a team of exiles returned and played some exhibition matches against Tipperary in Thurles and Cashel.

Paddy usually played at full-forward and was described at the time as 'the perfect machine in the art of scoring'.[134] Regarding Riordan, the sports editor of the *Irish Echo* in New York, Egan Clancy, wrote, 'Paddy Riordan, the fiery flash from Drombane, was a wizard on the front division. He could double a ball almost from any angle between the uprights and like Kilkenny's Sim Walton, was the terror of the backs and goalmen'.[135]

Paddy died in Long Island, New York, on 19 February 1941 aged 69 years and is buried in St John's cemetery there.

MICHAEL RYAN (MACK)

Michael Ryan (Mack)

MICHAEL RYAN, locally known as Mike Mack was born in Thurles, in 1887. He played with Thurles Blues and won Mid Tipperary championships in 1908, 1909 and Tipperary county championships in 1906 and 1907. He was also on the Tipperary team, Thurles selection that won the first Croke-Fennelly Tournament at Fethard in 1909.

Hovever, he emigrated to America in September 1909 and before his departure he was presented with an Omega pocket-watch, which had been purchased from J. Rudd, jewellers, Thurles.

Michael returned to Thurles and married Judy O'Gorman, Pudding Lane and later of the Derheen. Judy was the eldest of seventeen children.[136]

Mike and Judy emigrated to the U.S.A. and lived in New Jersey. Some years later, they returned and set up home at 2 Bohernanave. They had two children, Michael and Margaret. Michael (Mickey) was a great supporter of Thurles Fennelly's and hurled with them in his youth. Margaret recalls the hustle and bustle of Bohernanave on big match days at Thurles Sportsfield, now Semple Stadium. On such days, her mother was on the catering staff of Jim Lambe's Glenmorgan House, Parnell Street. The Ryan home in Bohernanave looked onto the Sportsfield and to supplement their income Mike allowed supporters to park their bicycles, at sixpence each, on his premises.[137]

Mike died on 24 April 1959 and is buried in St Patrick's cemetery, Thurles. Judy, who reached the ripe old age of one hundred died in December 2003.

Front and rear view of the watch presented to Michael Ryan (Mack) in 1909. The watch is on display in Lár na Páirce, the museum of Gaelic Games in Thurles.

CANON M.K. RYAN

MICHAEL KENNEDY RYAN (Lacken) was born at Knockfune, Newport on 29 September 1868, into a family steeped in the Gaelic and national traditions of the country. He studied for the priesthood at St Patrick's College, Thurles and at Maynooth, where he was ordained on 25 June 1893. Following a temporary mission in Westminster diocese, he was appointed professor at St Patrick's, Thurles in 1901. In 1906 he was appointed to the Thurles parish. While in Thurles he was very involved in the community. As chairman of Thurles G.A.A. Club, from 1916 until 1924, he was their trusted guiding light. He regarded the cultivation of the games as the sheet anchor and salvation of young men.[138]

Canon M.K. Ryan.

While in Thurles, he started a Brass and Reed band in the town, which survived until the instruments were smashed by the Black and Tans.[139] Canon M.K. Ryan had been among the deputation of local Thurles Gaels that negotiated the purchase of Thurles Sportsfield from the Thurles Agricultural Show Committee, in 1910.

On his appointment as parish priest of Latin and Cullen, in December 1924, Canon M.K. Ryan resigned the chairmanship of Tipperary G.A.A. Board and he was succeeded by Captain Johnny Leahy, Boherlahan. The canon had been seven years in the position, difficult years of trial and turmoil for Ireland. In a letter to Tipperary's annual convention he expressed regret at having, unavoidably, to sever his connection with the board. He continued, 'I will follow your every moment in the field, with close and anxious attention. Be Gaels in the council room! Be Gaels in the field, proud of the traditions that you have inherited and upholders of them, at their best. Keep at the game! Keep Knocknagow alive!'[140] Many

ERECTED BY THE PARISHIONERS
TO THE MEMORY OF THE
VERY REV. M.K. CANON RYAN
WHO MINISTERED FOR EIGHTEEN
YEARS IN THE PARISH OF THURLES
AND DIED P.P. OF LATTIN ON
APRIL 3RD 1925 AGED 57 YEARS

HE WAS A LEARNED, PIOUS
AND ZEALOUS PRIEST·

R · I · P ·

Canon M.K. Ryan is remembered at the Cathedral of the Assumption, Thurles.

glowing tributes were paid to him at the convention.

Three months later, Canon Ryan suffered a paralytic seizure and died without gaining consciousness, on 3 April 1925. Archbishop Harty, in paying tribute to Ryan said, "He was a great man and a great priest … He spent nearly half of this life in Thurles. He had a big heart and he loved the people of Thurles, recognising in them a good people and the people of Thurles loved him in return, as a priest, a true and big-hearted Irishman and great Tipperary man'.[141]

At a specially convened meeting of Thurles G.A.A. members, it was proposed by Tom Semple and seconded by James Butler that, 'We tender to the archbishop, clergy and relatives of the late Canon M.K. Ryan, who was hon. president of our club and through whose able counsel the youth of this town and parish stood by the G.A.A. in trying times and under trying circumstances, our sincere sympathy.'

When a new stand was erected at Semple Stadium in 1980, it was named Ardán Ó Riain, as an enduring monument to Canon M.K .Ryan. He was interred in the grounds of Latin church.

HUGH SHELLY

HUGH SHELLY, Parnell Street, Thurles, was born in 1883. Always perfectly trained, he was one of the best forwards in the game. Hugh Shelly was on the county selection during the 1906 championship and was a regular member of the starting team until his retirement after the 1923 championship. He was winner of three All-Ireland medals, 1906, 1908 with Thurles Sarsfields selection and in 1916 with the Boherlahan selection. He won six Munster medals 1906, 1908, 1909, 1913, 1916, 1917 and six Tipperary senior championship medals 1904, 1906, 1907, 1909, 1911, 1922. Hughie also won medals in these competitions:- Railway Shield, Ottway Cuffe, Croke Cup, Croke/Fennelly Cup and Wolfe Tone Tournament. Hugh captained the Tipperary team that lost the Munster final to Limerick at Cork in 1911.

Hugh Shelly

Hugh Shelly and Margaret Maher on their wedding day.

In 1913 when Toomevara were representing Tipperary, Hugh was part of the famous Croke Cup and Thomond Feis Shield victories. He is commemorated in the third verse of the Toome anthem, "Hurrah for Toomevara" –

> *"God bless you, Meara and McGrath, Raleigh and Hackett too,*
> *Like wise brave Bobby Mockler, you were always loyal and true;*
> *There's Kelly and Gilmartin – they never miss a ball,*
> *And the Thurles boy, Hugh Shelly, would hole a four foot wall."*[142]

Following the 1916 All-Ireland final, 'Carbery' wrote, 'Perhaps the most interesting personality in the combination is little Hugh Shelly of Thurles, whose three goals in the last half-hour turned the tables in Tipperary's favour. Shelly is a small, though neatly made man, meek and modest to a fault. Meet him at a coursing match, before a hurling game or in his own home in Thurles, he is always the same gentle individual. He strikes one as the last type of man in the world to lead a daring charge on an opposing citadel amidst a sweeping forest of hurleys, at a critical stage of a great game. Yet again and again Shelly has proved himself absolutely fearless. Then his fine pace serves him immensely in racing for a ball. He strikes with equal freedom off either hand and rarely mistakes the net's whereabouts…'[143]

In March 1917, the Gaels of Tipperary, under the chairmanship of Rev. M.K.

Ryan, decided to make a presentation to Hugh Shelly on the occasion of his marriage. Subscriptions from all corners of Tipperary and beyond were many and generous.

Regarding Shelly, the sports editor of the *Irish Echo* in New York, Egan Clancy, wrote, 'Hughie Shelly the hero of many a hectic encounter, was a dashing wing-forward. My, what speed that boy had! His hurley was like a

céad míle fáilte at the Thurles House for Gaels.

HUGHIE SHELLY, PARNELL ST

STOCKS THE BEST IN WINES & SPIRITS & GROCERIES.

PERSONAL ATTENTION.

Advertisement for Hughie Shelly's public house in 1930.

magnet. No matter how fast he travelled, he could pick the ball and send it singing for the objective. Hughie was one of the most popular players that ever wore the Sarsfield sweater and we have every reason to know that he richly deserved the esteem of his team-mates and fellow citizens'.[144]

An evening in Thurles in 1915 was described by G.A.A. journalist 'Portobello':- 'Myself and Austin Stack[145] of Tralee walked up to the Sportsfield in Thurles. The gate was locked but a fierce game was in progress in Bohernanave. Outposts on the watch for R.I.C. did not signal hostile forces as we went straight on. An old battered kettle on the one side with a rock on the other were doing duty as goalposts at the near end, a coat and a cap lower down marked the distant scoring area. Surrounded by half dozen 'back' men, the forward succeeded in driving the ball through and proud of the success let forth a shrill yell of delight. On no other occasion would the scorer show such marked pleasure. Winning by a narrow margin in one of the great championship games he would, no doubt, feel pleased, but there would be no demonstration. With the 'kids' it was different. It was a blushing Shelly that came forth to greet Stack... After a long chat on Gaelic matters we separated. Stack remarked, as we passed on, that it was great to find such an expert hurler of so great a record, playing on the roads with schoolboys showing by the fact a rare old *grá* (love) for the game.[146]

Hughie was an exceptional hurler, possessing speed in abundance, combined with hurling skill, grit and an eye for a score. Hughie was also noted as a sprinter, winning numerous prizes at sports meetings nationwide.[147] He continued participating in sport until 1931. Hugh also loved breeding and training greyhounds, which he did successfully.

It was said of Hugh that:- 'No one has played more matches for Tipperary or talked less about what he did, than Hugh Shelly'.[148]

> *There is gentle Hughie Shelly,*
> *Says the Sean Bhean Bhocht.*
> *Of his deeds, sure I could tell ye,*
> *Says the Sean Bhean Bhocht.*
> *He's little, but he's wise,*
> *He's a terror for his size,*
> *And he does not advertise,*
> *Says the Sean Bhean Bhocht.*

Hugh Shelly, who was a successful publican on Parnell Street, married Margaret Maher, Borrisoleigh, and had a family of five children. Hugh's only sister, Bridget, married Michael (Mixie) O'Connell, 24 Liberty Square, in 1917. Hugh Shelly died on 3 May 1957, aged seventy-three and is buried in St Patrick's cemetery, Thurles.[149]

WILLIAM SMEE

William (Bill, Willie) Smee was the youngest son of John and Bridget Smee. He was born about the year 1888 and grew up on the family farm at Brittas, Thurles. Willie was an accomplished hurler with the 'Blues' and under the captaincy of Tom Semple he won Mid Tipperary titles with in 1909, 1911 and 1912 and Tipperary county titles in 1909 and 1911. Willie was on the Tipperary junior hurling team that won the Munster championship in 1911.

Stephen and Willie Smee.

Willie's hurling career was cut short as he worked as a radio operator aboard ship, a position that took him to the four corners of the globe and far from the hurling-fields of Tipperary. When news spread of the fateful sinking of the Titanic on 15 April 1912, Willie was on board a ship sailing from Australia.[150] Willie emigrated to Canada and later settled in Detroit, U.S.A., gaining employment at the Ford Motor Company.

In 1927, Thurles Urban Council planned to lay a new road linking Friar

The old Smee residence at the limekiln, Garryvicleheen.   *The limekiln.*

Street with Castle Avenue and Parnell Street. The lands through which the new road, Mathew Avenue, would run was owned by Willie Smee, an inheritance from his mother. Willie was happy to sell the lands to the council, as he wrote in a letter home, 'I am glad to see the town going ahead'.

Willie married Margaret Gleeson, a native of Moyaliffe, Drombane, Thurles and they raised a family of eight children. Willie died, aged ninety-seven in 1985.

Willie's older brother, Steven, lived at the Lime Kiln, Garryvicleheen, Thurles. Smee's owned and worked the lime-kiln, which supplied lime to the local farming community for the improvement of their lands. Lime was also in big demand for the making of white-wash which, at the time, was painted on houses and farm buildings.

Willie's cousin, Jimmy Smee, was born in Cahirciveen, County Kerry, on 8 July 1910. As a teenager, he spent some years living in Thurles with the Smee family of the Lime Kiln. Jimmy was a good footballer but it was in Thurles that he learned the art of hurling, playing with the local club and Thurles C.B.S. Jimmy emigrated to New York in the late 1920s and he continued to play hurling and football in the 'Big Apple'. He won a record twenty-four New York championships in both hurling and football, dividing his talents between Kerry and Tipperary.[151] In 1932, he represented New York against Ireland in the Tailteann Games played

This stone marks the location of Stephen Smee's Cornstore, in which, according to legend, a subscription dinner was given to Daniel O'Connell during the Repeal Movement. The old Pallottine College, known as 'Jerusalem' stood here from April 1911 to July 1984.

at Croke Park. He continued to play into the early 1950s. Jimmy was a very welcoming and generous host to many G.A.A. players that visited New York during his era. Jimmy married Betty Flaherty, a native of Crotta, County Kerry and they lived in the Bronx. They had two sons, Timmy and Jimmy.

Liam Dwan and Jimmy Smee.

Jimmy Smee died on 22 June 1996, aged eighty-five years.

Early in the twentieth century, the Smee family owned property at the corner of Pike Street (Kickham Street) and College Lane (Eliogarty Road). Buildings on the property included an old corn-store and three two-storey, slate-roofed stone buildings. This property was sold by Eliza Smee, relict of Stephen Smee, to the Pallottine Fathers in 1908.[152]

Their grandson, Steven (Stevie) Smee, Bohernanave, is also Willie's cousin. Stevie hurled with Thurles Kickhams, winning a county junior chamoionship in 1962 and won a Tipperary senior hurling championship with Thurles Sarsfields in 1965. The lands now known as Dr Morris Park were owned by Stevie and were sold to Tipperary G.A.A. Board in 1994 and officially opened on 16 July 1998.

WILLIAM WADE

William (Billy) Wade was born at Drish, Thurles, about the year 1879. His father was a herdsman on the nearby Langley estate[153] and Billy was the eldest in the family.[154] He attended Tonagha National School. His father died in Billy's youth and the family then moved residence to Quarry Street (Mitchel Street), Thurles.

Billy hurled with Thurles 'Blues' in the early years of the twentieth century, under the captaincy of Tom Semple. Indeed, Billy knew Tom Semple very well as they were schoolmates at Thurles C.B.S. However, his

William Wade.

hurling career was cut short as he emigrated to South Africa. There he secured employment in the mining centre of the Transvaal.

Billy died at the young age of forty-three, on 10 October 1922, at Transvaal Phthisis Hospital. The dreaded, Phthisis (miners) disease, a chronic disease of the lungs, from which Billy died, claimed many lives at the time. Billy was a keen sportsman and a first-class big game shot, having hunted all over Africa. He was survived by his widow and three children.

---

[1] N.A.I., Census of Ireland 1901.

[2] *Tipperary Star*, 26 Oct. 2002.

[3] N.A.I., Census of Ireland 1901, 1911.

[4] Interview with Mrs. Statia Ryan, Templemore (Rody's Daughter) (15 June 2001).

[5] Interview with Paddy Berkery, Mullaunbreac, Thurles (12 June 2014).

[6] *Tipperary Star*, 25 Oct. 1952.

[7] Interview with Tom Ryan, Rody's grandson (19 Aug. 2014).

[8] Raymond Smith, *The Centenary Co-Operative Creamery Society 1889-1989* (Dublin, 1989), p. 105.

[9] *Tipperary Star*, 10 Apr. 1950.

[10] N.A.I., Census of Ireland 1901.

[11] *Irish Times*, 8 May 1867, p.3.

[12] Philip Fogarty, *Tipperary's G.A.A. Story* (Thurles, 1960), p. 373.

[13] Interview with Dermot Bourke (Paddy's nephew), Munnagh, Newport (25 May 2014).

[13a] NAI, Census of Ireland 1911.

[13b] Interview with Mary McKevitt, née Bowe, Willie's grand-daughter (30 Mar. 2015).

[14] *Irish Independent*, 17 Dec. 1952.

[15] Interview with Frank Brolan (Paddy's son) (8 Aug. 2001).

[16] *Tipperary Star*, 4 May 1929.

[17] Interview by Paddy Doherty, Ardnacrusha, Thurles, with Paddy Brolan's son, Paddy (12 Aug. 1981).

[18] Interview with Kathleen Quinn (Paddy Brolan's daughter) (1 May 2014).

[19] *Tipperary Star*, 28 July 1956.

[20] N.A.I., Census of Ireland 1901.

[21] Philip Fogarty, *Tipperary's G.A.A. Story* (Thurles, 1960), p. 378.

[22] *Tipperary Star*, 19 September 1953.

[23] Interview with Mick Cahill (Jack's son) (13 May 2001).

[24] N.A.I, Census of Ireland 1901, '11.

[25] Interview with Andy's son, Denis Callanan, Boheravoroon, Thurles (21 June 2014).

[26] Note:- John Maher's son, Michael, is the current chairman of Thurles Sarsfields club.

[27] *Tipperary Star*, 8 May 1971.

[28] Seamus J. King, *Clonoulty-Rossmore 13th Vintage Rally* Booklet, pp 13-15.

[29] *Tipperary Star*, 6 Jan. 1917.

[30] N.A.I., Census of Ireland 1911.

[31] Ibid.

[32] Seamus J. King, *Mid Senior Hurling Final 1911* in Clonoulty/Rossmore Vintage Club programme 2013, pp 13-15.

[33] Joe Tobin, "Athletes from 'The Jockey' and Pouldine" in Liam Ó Donnchú (ed.), *Pouldine School – Inné agus Inniu* (2009), p. 58.

[34] Bob Stakelum, Gaelic Games in Holycross/Ballycahill 1884-1990 (Holycross, 1991), p. 15.

[35] *Tipperary Star*, 30 Dec. 1961.

[36] Raymond Smith, *Decades of Glory* (Dublin, 1966), p. 70.

[37] John Guiton (ed.), *The History of Gortnahoe/Glengoole G.A.A. 100 Years* (Thurles, 1984), p. 10.

[38] Raymond Smith, *Decades of Glory* (Dublin, 1966), p. 71.

[39] Philip Fogarty, *Tipperary's G.A.A. Story* (Thurles, 1960), p. 254.

[40] Interview with Patsy Fitzgerald, Pat's son, Poyntstown (28 May 2014).

[41] *Moycarkey Borris G.A.A. Story* (Thurles, 1984), p. 11.

[42] *Tipperary Star*, 16 Dec. 1939.

[43] Division of Health of Missouri, Standard Certificate of Death, (Filed 15 Oct. 1953).

[44] N.A.I., Census of Ireland 1911.

[45] *Tipperary Star*, 12 Oct. 1953.

[46] N.A.I, Census of Ireland 1901 and 1911.

[47] *Tipperary Star*, 19 Nov. 1932.

[48] 'Hurray for Toomevara' was written by Michael Bourke, a native of Newport.

[49] Dan J. Stapleton, 'Hurling Reminiscences', in Séamus Ó Ceallaigh (ed.) *Gaelic Athletic Memories*, (Limerick, 1945), pp 137- 41.

[50] Liam Ó Donnchú, Interview with Josephine (Jo Jo) Treacy, daughter of Tim Gleeson (28 Jan. 2014).

[51] Information supplied by John Hackett, Grawn, Two-Mile-Borris (31 Dec. 2014).

[52] N.A.I., Census of Ireland 1901.

[53] Philip Fogarty, *Tipperary's G.A.A. Story* (Thurles, 1960), p. 47.

[54] Interview with Bill's grandson, Liam Harris, Grallagh, Horse and Jockey, Thurles (29 April 2014).

[55] *Tipperary Star*, 18 Feb. 1939.

[56] *Nenagh News*, 15 Sept. 1923, p. 2.

[57] Interview with Fr. Conor Hayes, Jer's grandson (15 June 2001).

[58] Interview with Joe Tobin, Turtulla (22 Feb. 2014).

[59] N.A.I., Census of Ireland 1901.

[60] Irish Bureau of Military History, 1913-21, Document No. W.S. 1454. Statement by James Leahy, Nenagh, County Tipperary.

[61] Irish Bureau of Military History, 1913-21. Éamon Ó Duibhir, Ballagh, Gooldscross. Document No. W.S. 1403.

[62] Irish Bureau of Military History, 1913-21, Document No. W.S. 1558. Statement by Frank McGrath, Nenagh, County Tipperary.

[63] Interview with Jim Crone, Grange, Brittas, Thurles (24 Aug. 2014).

[64] W. Corbett and W. Nolan (eds), *Thurles-The Cathedral Town* (Thurles, 1989), pp 24-5.

[65] Raymond Smith, *Decades of Glory* (Dublin, 1966), p. 72.

[66] J.M. Kennedy, *A Chronology of Thurles*, first published in 1939, was updated in 1978 by Donal O'Gorman, Laurence Long and Michael Dundon.

[67] N.A.I., Census of Ireland 1911.

[68] Interview with Pat Crone, Furze and his brother Jim, Grange, Brittas, Thurles, both grand-nephews of J.M. Kennedy (24 Aug. 2014).

[69] *Tipperary Star*, 4, 11 July 1964.

[70] N.A.I., Census of Ireland 1911.

[71] Interview by Paddy Doherty, Ardnacrusha, Thurles, with Jack Murphy, Iona Ave, Thurles (29 June 1981).

[72] *Tipperary Star*, 4 May 1929.

[73] Philip Fogarty, *Tipperary's G.A.A. Story* (Thurles, 1960), p. 286.

[74] *Tipperary Star*, 16 Feb. 1929.

[75] Raymond Smith, *Decades of Glory* (Dublin, 1966), p. 65.

[76] *The Green and Gold Years, Toomevara G.A.A, 1885-1895* (Toomevara, 1985), p. 167.

[77] *Hurrah for Toomevara*, composed by Michael Bourke, Newport.

[78] Seamus J. King, *A History of the G.A.A. in the North Tipperary Division* (Nenagh, 2001), pp 585-6.

[79] N.A.I,, Census of Ireland 1901.

[80] Seamus Leahy, 'A Sensational Final – The 1917 All-Ireland' in *Tipperary G.A.A. Yearbook 2014*, p. 27.

[81] Marcus de Búrca, *One Hundred Years of Faughs Hurling* (Dublin, 1985), p. 69; Liam Ó Donnchú (ed.), Horse and Jockey Centenary 1899-1999, p. 19.

[82] N.A.I., Census of Ireland 1911.

[83] Raymond Smith, *Decades of Glory* (Dublin, 1966), p. 65.

[84] Interview with Frank Mockler (Jack's son) (1 May 2014).

[85] N.A.I., Census of Ireland 1901.

[86] Interview with Dan Ryan, Dublin Road, Thurles (18 Feb. 2015).

[87] N.A.I., Census of Ireland 1901.

[88] Ibid, 1911.

[89] *Note:-* Executive Menswear now occupies these premises.

[90] Interview with Pierce Duggan, The Castle, Two-Mile-Borris, Thurles (grand-nephew of Phil Molony) (2 May 2014).

[91] Dan Leahy, 'Do you remember Thurles?' in *Tipperary Star* (6 Apr. 2001).

[92] *Tipperary Star*, 24 Nov. 1952.

[93] Interview with Jack's grandson, Eddie Mooney, Thurles (15 May 2001).

[94] Interview by Paddy Doherty, Ardnacrusha, Thurles, with Jack Murphy, Iona Ave, Thurles (29 June 1981).

[95] Philip Fogarty, *Tipperary's G.A.A. Story* (Thurles, 1960), p. 376.

[96] *Tipperary Star*, 4 May 1929.

[97] N.A.I., Census of Ireland 1901 & 1911.

[98] Interview with Billy Taylor, Abbey Road, Thurles (10 Jan. 2015).

[99] Minutes, Thurles G.A.A. Club, 21 Oct. 1908.

[100] *Nationalist*, 28 Oct. 1908.

[101] Interview with Nora Troy, née McLoughney, (Joe's daughter) (16 Apr. 2002).

[102] Interview by Paddy Doherty, Ardnacrusha, Thurles, with Joe McLoughney's daughter, Carmel (12 Aug. 1980).

[103] Common name for a sliotar or hurling ball in Thurles.

[104] Philip Fogarty, *Tipperary's G.A.A. Story* (Thurles, 1960), p. 377.

[105] *Irish Independent,* 16 Feb. 1951.

[106] *Tipperary Star*, 7 Aug. 1915.

[107] Recollections of Martin Semple, (4 Dec. 2013).

[108] Interview with Margaret Ryan née O'Brien (Daughter) (10 Feb. 2001).

[109] *Tipperary Star*, 20 Aug. 1927.

[110] Pierce McCan, Ballyowen House, Dualla, Cashel, was a founder member of Sinn Féin in 1905. He joined the Gaelic League in 1909 and was a member of the Irish Volunteers from 1914 onwards. In May 1918, he was arrested and detained in Gloucester Jail. While incarcerated, he was elected as a Sinn Féin MP for the East Tipperary constituency at the 1918 general election. McCan never sat in Dáil Éireann, having died in prison in 1919.

[111] Interview with John Hickey (Martin O'Brien's grandson) (25 June 2014).

[112] For further information see:- Seán Hogan, *The Black and Tans in North Tipperary* (Nenagh, 2013), pp 331-4. Irish Bureau of Military History. James Leahy WS 1454, p. 68.

[113] *Tipperary Star*, 3 Jan. 1959.

[114] Martin O'Dwyer, *A Biographical Dictionary of Tipperary* (Cashel, 1999), p. 308.

[115] John Guiton (ed.), *The History of Gortnahoe/Glengoole G.A.A. 100 Years* (Thurles, 1984), p. 9.

[116] Bob Stakelum, *Gaelic Games in Holycross/Ballycahill 1884-1990* (Holycross, 1991), p. 15.

[117] *Tipperary Star*, 22 Feb. 1975.

[118] Philip Fogarty, *Tipperary's G.A.A. Story* (Thurles, 1960), pp 142-3.

[119] *Tipperary Star,* 4 May 1929.

[120] *Tipperary Star*, 22 Feb. 1975.

[121] N.A.I., Census of Ireland 1911.

[122] Diary of James Maher, loaned by his son Mícheál, Castlemeadows, (15 June 2008).

[123] Letter, dated 18 Apr. 1971, written by Lil Skehan, née O'Keeffe, to the editor *Tipperary Star*.

[124] N.A.I., Census of Ireland 1901.

[125] *Tipperary Star*, 12 April 1958.

[126] W. J. Hayes (ed), *Moyne-Templetuohy, A Life of its Own* (Thurles, 2001), Vol. 2 pp 427-8, Vol. 3 pp 152,3,4,7, 184, 396.

[127] Margaret Cormack, *Moyne/Templetuohy Newsletter 2009*, p. 83.

[128] Ibid, p. 66.

[129] Bob Stakelum, *Gaelic Games in Holycross-Ballycahill* (Thurles, 1991), p. 15.

[130] Interview with Tomás Ó Baróid, Thurles (12 Dec. 2014).

[131] P. D. Mehigan, *Carbery's Annual 1950/51.*

[132] Tim Quinlan, 'The Riordans of Rosmult' in *Upperchurch/Drombane Historical Journal 2012*, p. 76.

[133] Thurles Sarsfields Club Minutes 1907.

[134] John G. Maher & Philip F. Ryan, *Boherlahan/Dualla, A Century of Gaelic Games* (1987), p. 31.

[135] *Tipperary Star*, 4 May 1929.

[136] *Tipperary Star*, 3 Jan. 2004.

[137] Liam Ó Donnchú, interview with Margaret Ryan (7 Nov. 2013).

[138] John Lanigan, Very Rev M. K. Ryan in match programme, *Official Opening of Semple Stadium*, (ed.) Liam Ó Donnchú, 31 May 1984.

[139] Walter G. Skehan, *Cashel and Emly Heritage* (Thurles, 1993), p. 17.

[140] Philip Fogarty, *Tipperary's G.A.A. Story* (Thurles, 1960), p. 253.

[141] Michael Collins, Denis Floyd, *By the Mulcaire Banks*, (Nenagh, 1986), pp 65-9.

[142] *Hurrah for Toomevara*, composed by Michael Bourke, Newport.

[143] P.D. Mehigan, 'Carbery's' Column in *Weekly Examiner*, 3 Feb. 1917.

[144] *Tipperary Star*, 4 May 1929.

[145] Note:- Austin Stack (1879-1929) was elected an M.P. in 1918. He opposed the Anglo-Irish Treaty of 1921, and took part in the subsequent Civil War. He was captured in 1923 and went on hunger strike for forty-one days before being released in July 1924. He was elected to the Dáil in subsequent elections but Stack's health never recovered after his hunger strike and he died on 27 April 1929.

[146] *Tipperary Star*, 3 Mar. 1917.

[147] Ibid, 11 May 1957.

[148] 'Portobello', *Tipperary Star*, 3 March 1917.

[149] Interview with Bridie Shelly (daughter) and Michael Bowe (grandson) (14 May 2001).

[150] Interview with Willie's niece, Bridget (Bridie) Kennedy (née Smee), Abbey Road, Thurles. 6, 15 Aug. 2014.

[151] *Irish Echo*, 10-16 July 1996.

[152] Donal McCarthy S.C.A., The Irish Pallottines, in W. Corbett & W. Nolan, (eds) *Thurles – The Cathedral Town* (Dublin, 1989), pp 253-4.

[153] Interview with Seamus McGrath, Kickham Street, Thurles (grand nephew) (18 Sept. 2014).

[154] N.A.I., Census of Ireland 1901, '11.

The Foundation of the Gaelic Athletic Association: A Local Perspective

*By J.M. Tobin**

HE INAUGURAL meeting of the GAA, on Saturday, 1 November 1884,[1] at Lizzie J. Hayes's Commercial Hotel on Main Street, Thurles,[2] has been the subject of much debate among historians of Irish sport. Apart from the date and venue, they have agreed on little else.[3] The motivation of those who responded to Michael Cusack's and Maurice Davin's letter of invitation has attracted divergent interpretations.[4] Likewise, the number present has been recorded as between seven and thirteen.[5]

The Thurles gathering was the culmination of a lengthy campaign by the Clare-born Cusack for the 'reform' of Irish athletics[6] and, from the end of 1882, a belated interest in the revival of hurling.[7] A schoolteacher by profession,[8] Cusack had been associated with athletics since his youth.[9] Moreover, he had been a member of the Dublin Amateur Athletic Club, the Irish Champion Athletic Club, the City and Suburban Harriers, the Cross-Country Association of Ireland, and the Dublin Athletic Club.[10] In April 1881 he had begun to publicly articulate his opinions on track and field issues when he contributed the first in a series of articles to the *Irish Sportsman*.[11] Having failed to win support for his cause in Dublin, Cusack turned his attention to the provinces. By the summer of 1884 he had established contact with a number of groups, including one in Cork,[12] and with a party of radical land agitators at Loughrea, County Galway.[13] He was also satisfied that north Kerry was on his side through the efforts of the Fenian William Moore Stack.[14] More importantly, he had been

---

* Joe Tobin, Turtulla, Thurles, is a post-primary teacher at Thurles C.B.S. A local historian, whose main area of research is the history of sport, particularly athletics, on which he has written extensively. At present he is compiling a publication to mark the bicentennial of the Christian Brothers in Thurles.

in communication with Maurice Davin, the former international athlete from Carrick-on-Suir.[15] Davin, a moderate proponent of self-regulation, had been a member of the Irish National Athletic Committee in 1877 when an unsuccessful attempt was made to establish a governing body for Irish athletics.[16] Despite his contact with Davin, Cork was Cusack's preferred location for the establishment of the new sports organisation. As late as October 1884 he was arguing for the formation of a society for the preservation and cultivation of national pastimes based in Cork, because most 'of the champion athletes of Ireland come from Munster'.[17] Yet he could not have garnered much support in that city following his boorish behaviour at the previous year's Cork Amateur Athletic Club sports.[18] In the ensuing press controversy, Cusack launched a bitter attack on J.F. O'Crowley, secretary of the promoting club.[19] O'Crowley, in turn, accused Cusack of visiting the southern city to promote his 'Gaelic mission'.[20] Recalling those years, Patrick Davin observed that 'Michael Cusack's influence, as far as athletics were concerned, was practically nil outside Dublin, and even there he was anything but popular.'[21]

Having decided that the time was opportune to launch the new organisation, Cusack commenced a carefully orchestrated campaign through the columns of *United Ireland*. In an article entitled 'A Word about Irish Athletics' on 11 October 1884 he wrote of 'the tyranny of imported and enforced customs and manners' and of a 'foreign and iniquitous … system' that had to be eradicated. 'Swarms of pot-hunting mashers … formed harrier clubs'. The modernising and progressive AAA had, in his estimation, driven the Irish people from their traditional playing fields.[22] Davin's response was published by the same paper on 18 October. The Carrick man found no fault with Cusack's detested harrier clubs and considered the AAA rules to be 'very good in their way'. Nevertheless, he went on to point out that the English handbooks neglected to legislate for weight-throwing, and jumping events popular in Ireland. He also regretted that these disciplines were often omitted from the programmes of leading fixtures.[23] The following week Cusack announced that a meeting would be held at Thurles on 1 November, the purpose of which would be the development of Irish games and to discourage the growth of English sports in which Irishmen 'can be easily beaten'. Typically unapologetic, he singled out foot-racing as such a sport.[24] On 27 October, two days after the announcement of a proposed gathering, Cusack issued a circular letter from his Civil Service Academy at 4 Gardiner's Place, Dublin.[25] The document, which was endorsed by both he and Maurice Davin, invited participation in the following terms:

> Dear Sir –You are earnestly requested to attend a meeting which will be held at Thurles on the 1st November to take steps for the formation of a Gaelic association for the preservation and cultivation of our national pastimes and

for providing rational amusements for the Irish people during their leisure hours. The movement which it is proposed to inaugurate has been approved of by Mr Michael Davitt, Mr Justin M'Carthy, MP, Mr William O'Brien, MP, Mr T. Harrington, MP, and other eminent men who are interested in the social elevation of the race. The place of meeting will be determined on at the Commercial Hotel, Thurles, at 2 o'clock on the day of the meeting.

Maurice Davin, Carrick-on-Suir.

Michael Cusack, Dublin, hon. sec. pro tem.[26]

Cusack must have been greatly disappointed when he entered the hotel for the two o'clock appointment. Not only did the modest-sized structure prove large enough for those who arrived, the group was accommodated, apparently, in the hotel's billiard room.[27]

WHO WAS PRESENT?

In his account of the occasion, as published by *United Ireland* and *The Irishman*, Cusack wrote:

> At a well-attended meeting, which was held in Miss Hayes's Commercial Hotel, Thurles, last Saturday, a Gaelic association for the preservation and cultivation of national pastimes was formed. The meeting was called by a circular signed by Mr Maurice Davin, Carrick-on-Suir, and Mr Michael Cusack, Dublin. In addition to the gentlemen who called the meeting, there were also present – Mr J.W. Power, Leinster Leader, Mr P.J. O'Ryan, [sic] solicitor, Callan and Thurles, Mr J. M'Kay, Cork, Mr Bracken, Templemore, Mr St George M'Carthy, Templemore, etc. etc.[28]

A generation later, T.F. O'Sullivan maintained that 'notwithstanding the fact that Mr Cusack placed a few etceteras after the names of those attending' only the seven listed above were present.[29] However, a subsequent assertion by Séamus Ó Riain that O'Sullivan had done considerable research in the files of national and provincial papers in the preparation of his history, proved to be untenable.[30] Marcus de Búrca argued that 'by adding the cryptic and infuriating phrase "etc, etc" to his authoritative list of seven,' Cusack 'gave a false impression that more than that number had attended.'[31] De Búrca also made the inaccurate claim that newspapers hostile to Cusack named twelve people as having attended, whereas supportive organs purportedly gave the figure as seven.[32] As to why Cusack's rivals would boost his cause by inflating the attendance at Thurles, he offered no explanation.

The Thurles-based *Tipperary Leader* was certainly not opposed to the Clare man's aspirations. A contemporary advertisement described the journal as advocating 'everything calculated to improve the condition of the people, and to work out the objects of the National League'.[33] Advance publicity was provided by the paper for Cusack's project in its issue of 31 October.[34] The following week's edition covered the transactions of the inaugural event in considerable detail:

Revival of Irish National Pastimes Meeting in Thurles

On Saturday last a meeting was held in Miss Hayes's Commercial Hotel, for the purpose of establishing an association to promote, foster, and cultivate the national pastimes of the country, which, it is to be regretted, are rapidly falling into disuse, and are being succeeded by sports more enervating, less manly, and pre-eminently English. Even where the old sports still obtain, and where annual sports are held, the meetings are conducted under English rules, to the great disadvantage of competitors. The movement, so auspiciously set on foot in Thurles on Saturday, has been inaugurated by Mr Michael Cusack, of 4, Gardiner-street, Dublin, and, since his project has seen the light in the columns of United Ireland, he has been ably seconded in his efforts by that well-known champion athlete, Mr Maurice Davin, of Carrick-on-Suir. ... Amongst those present at the meeting were – Messrs Michael Cusack, M. Davin, J. Wyse Power (Naas and Kildare Club), J.R. Bracken [sic], Templemore, John M'Kay (Cork Athletic Club), Joseph Ryan, solr, Callan, St George M'Carthy, DI, RIC, Templemore, W. Foley, Carrick-on-Suir, E. Dwyer, Charles Culhane, Wm Delahunty, M. Cantwell, Thurles, and John Butler, Ballyhudda.[35]

The *Tipperary Advocate* published a list containing twelve of the above names. However, Charles Culhane was described as 'D.C. Culhane'[36] which was probably a conflation of 'E. Dwyer' and 'Charles Culhane' as reported by the *Tipperary Leader*. Briefer reports in the *Nenagh Guardian* and the *Clonmel Chronicle*, both of unionist outlook, merely provided the names of the officers: Davin, Cusack, Wyse Power, and McKay.[37]

There is compelling evidence for the veracity of the *Tipperary Leader's* report of the foundation meeting. Thurles in 1884 was a small and intimate community; the recent census had returned its population at 4,850 people.[38] The town's newspaper, with a limited circulation, depended on local news for its very survival. Readers were reminded that 'every miscellaneous item of local news' was attended to by 'correspondents in every parish' and that news was 'also taken verbally at the office from the general public'.[39] If anything newsworthy occurred in Thurles the *Leader* was sure to have the details, and in this instance it had almost an entire week, and a number of sources from whom to verify the facts.

Two of the founders, Charles Culhane (1858-1926)[40] and Michael Cantwell (1865-1932),[41] were known to the editor of the *Leader*, Patrick Gorman, through their involvement in the Thurles Young Men's Society.[42] Gorman had attended the launch of that society in 1883 and promised that 'their meetings ... would be fully and faithfully reported' in his paper. He also offered 'magazines and newspapers for their use.'[43] Indeed, some weeks later he gave them permission to conduct all future business on the newspaper's premises.[44] The Culhane family, in particular, had strong associations with the local news industry. The *Tipperary Leader*'s immediate precursor, a publication entitled *Tipperary*, had been printed at their store on Pudding Lane (later Hall Street) in the early 1880s.[45]

If Gorman did not know John Butler (1839-1912)[46] of Ballyhudda personally, he certainly knew him professionally. Butler was a regular, and at times provocative, contributor to many Tipperary publications, including the *Leader*. The Moycarkey man's correspondence invariably included his townland address.[47] This tempts one to speculate that perhaps he had an influence on the local paper's account of the proceedings at Hayes's Hotel, as his was the only name ascribed to a precise location.

William Delahunty (1852-1930)[48] would have been known to the editor on a personal basis. As recently as 25 September both men had attended a meeting, in the *Leader* office, to organise funds for William O'Brien MP.[49] Delahunty was the owner of a licensed grocery, livery, dining, and accommodation business at Cathedral Street.[50] A member of a Ballingarry family,[51] he had been involved in the commercial life of the town for a considerable time.[52]

'E. Dwyer' (recorded by the *Freeman's Journal* as Dwyer)[53] was almost certainly a misprint for T.K. Dwyer (1848-1926)[54] of Littleton, the one mile champion of Ireland in 1878.[55] No suitable candidate bearing the former name can be traced from contemporary sources. According to tradition, Dwyer was among those who assembled in Lizzie Hayes's hotel. However, when a family member shared this information in the 1930s with Fr Philip Fogarty, the future author of *Tipperary's GAA Story*, his contribution was dismissed as spurious.[56]

Even though Séamus Ó Riain and Marcus de Búrca supported T.F. O'Sullivan's contention that only seven were present at the meeting of 1 November, the results of ongoing research[57] led both men to concede that others were present in the hotel that afternoon.

De Búrca suggested that a 'handful ... stayed out of the billiards-room' because 'they would not join a group that included a police officer'.[58] It is highly unlikely that T.K. Dwyer, who had served a jail sentence for boycotting during the Land War,[59] and Charles Culhane, afterwards incarcerated in Wormwood Scrubs for Sinn Féin activities,[60] would be intimidated by the presence of a policeman. Moreover, the officer in question, Thomas St George

MacCarthy, was not noted for his devotion to duty.[61] William Delahunty, on the other hand, would have been quite at ease in the company of a police officer as his family's public house was a rendezvous for both the police and the military.[62] In a subsequent publication de Búrca tentatively put the attendance at thirteen, but, apparently unconvinced, he immediately suggested that 'possibly only seven were present'. As if to underscore his unease with the former figure, he then twice in quick succession alluded to 'the seven accepted founders'.[63]

Ó Riain's claim that although 'the other named six' came 'to meet Davin ... to express their support for the movement ... they did not take part in the meeting in the billiard room',[64] is implausible. It is simply not credible that one of that six, William Foley of Carrick-on-Suir, who was in all probability Davin's former rowing colleague,[65] would have travelled to Thurles to wish his friend well in the lobby of a hotel when he could have done so more conveniently in their home town. Equally implausible is that the gregarious and somewhat egotistical John Butler would have missed the opportunity to join such interesting company in their proposed venture.

It would appear that both Ó Riain and de Búrca were compromised by their admiration for T.F. O'Sullivan, who had been a distinguished member of the GAA and also its first historian.[66] Ó Riain, a conservative, former president of the association,[67] and de Búrca, its latter-day apologist, were reluctant to challenge what had become official dogma. In contrast, William Dooley, in his well-researched history of Irish athletics, took a different view of matters at Hayes's Hotel and recorded the thirteen surnames as above, without qualification.[68]

Various attempts have been made to link a number of others to the inaugural event. The principal figures in this group include Henry Joseph Meagher of Tullaroan, County Kilkenny, Frank R. Maloney of Nenagh, and the Clonoulty native Hugh Ryan.[69] The assertion that Meagher had 'attended the founding meetings' [sic], accompanied by his neighbours Ned Tehan[70] and Jack Hoyne, can be safely discounted.[71] Apart from the lack of any supporting evidence, it should be noted that Tehan and Hoyne, who won senior All-Ireland hurling medals with Kilkenny in the championship of 1905,[72] were born c.1874 and c.1883 respectively.[73]

Both W.F. Mandle's[74] and Marcus de Búrca's[75] contention that Frank R. Maloney was in attendance has been ably refuted in Nancy Murphy's biographical essay on the alleged founder.[76]

The case for Hugh Ryan, a Thurles shopkeeper,[77] is again unsubstantiated. He is reputed to have been at the second meeting of the organisation in Cork and was 'therefore a delegate from the foundation meeting'.[78] This line of reasoning fails to explain why many others in attendance on that second occasion did not require delegate status to gain entry to the Victoria Hotel venue.[79] A recent historian of Thurles Sarsfields GAA Club has attempted to endorse this argument[80] by invoking the *Cork Examiner's* inaccurate report of the first meeting which referred to 'Mr O'Ryan (Thurles)' and 'Mr Ryan, solr, Callan.' The unreliable nature of the *Examiner's* version is emphasised by the omission of Thomas St George MacCarthy's[81] name from its list of seven.[82] Hugh Ryan's family name was never recorded with a prefix in local newspapers, official documents, or indeed by himself.[83] On the other hand, Joseph O'Ryan's surname was usually reported at that time with a prefix.[84] John McKay, who supplied the *Examiner's* account, was clearly unaware that O'Ryan had a practice in both Callan and Thurles. In fact, only a fortnight previously O'Ryan had presented a case at the Thurles quarter sessions.[85] There can be little doubt that 'Mr O'Ryan (Thurles)' and 'Mr Ryan, solr, Callan' were merely confused references to one Joseph O'Ryan, solicitor of Callan and Thurles.

We leave the final word on the subject to Cusack who, on reflection when the details were still clear in his memory, declared that the association had been founded – 'by about a dozen Irishmen'.[86]

WHY WERE THEY THERE?

Having established beyond reasonable doubt that thirteen men, among them three Thurles residents, and two from Moycarkey-Borris, were present at the formation of the GAA, we now attempt to uncover possible explanations for their attendance.

Cultural Nationalism – The Irish Language

A significant number of those who gathered in Hayes's Hotel had a strong interest in the revival of the Irish language. Cusack's letter to Davin of 26 August had been written on the headed notepaper of the Gaelic Union,[87] of which the former was an enthusiastic supporter and treasurer.[88] The similarity between the titles of the Gaelic Union for the Preservation and Cultivation of the Irish Language,[89] and that of the Gaelic Association for the Preservation and Cultivation of National Pastimes[90] is obvious. Again it was no coincidence that the patron of the Gaelic Union Archbishop Croke[91] would go on to play a vital role in the development of the GAA. A series of Irish lessons for beginners found among Maurice Davin's papers attest to the Carrick man's interest in the language. Such lessons were prepared by members of the Society for the Preservation of the Irish Language (SPIL) and published in several national newspapers.[92] Davin also subscribed to the *Gaelic Journal*.[93] John Wyse Power, an

Irish language enthusiast from County Waterford, had been a member of SPIL, and following the establishment of the Gaelic Union, assisted John Fleming in editing the aforementioned *Gaelic Journal*.[94]

At a time when there was no public interest in the Irish language issue in mid-Tipperary, John Butler's was a lone, if not slightly eccentric, voice crying in the wilderness. As early as 1869 he had written to Canon Ulick Bourke of St Jarlath's College, Tuam, and to the Reverend John Taylor Coffey, rector of Magorban, enquiring about the etymology of 'Ballyhudda'.[95] In 1879 he referred to the Irish language as 'the only landmark left to distinguish our race from our cruel calumniators and oppressors'.[96] The following year finds him enquiring as to the correct pronunciation of the phrases 'Céad míle fáilte' and 'Fág a ballagh'.[97] The formation of the Gaelic League in 1893[98] appears to have renewed his enthusiasm for the cause. Writing to *The Nationalist* he noted:

> I perceive that there are a few of the sons of our dear old country determined on doing something towards the resuscitation of our fast-dying language; but the efforts of a few are unavailing for the accomplishment of such a grand design. How can we sustain any object if a little inconvenience and sacrifice are avoided? This is not the way the Welsh people act under similar circumstances. Surely, indolence and sluggishness should not be cast to us as a good reason why we have not cultivated our native tongue. ... Then, let us be up and doing, and prepare ourselves to preserve the language of our sires-the only "landmark" left to distinguish our race. Let us follow the example of several clergymen and laymen in gallant Tipperary and elsewhere ... Nothing short of a combined effort on the part of our people can effect a successful result.[99]

Athletics

A passion for athletics was obviously a crucial determinant for many of those who founded the Gaelic Athletic Association. Maurice Davin, the newly-elected president, had won ten Irish titles for weight throwing between 1875 and 1879.[100] Davin then came out of retirement to win the hammer-throw and shot-put disciplines at the English AAA championship of 1881.[101] Michael Cusack too was a former shot-putter of note and won an Irish title in 1881 with a respectable performance.[102] John McKay also had an interest in athletics and attended the Thurles meeting as a member of the 'Cork Athletic Club'.[103]

Joseph O'Ryan had been a member of the defunct Carrick-on-Suir Amateur Athletic Cricket and Football Club. At the inception of that club in 1879, Maurice Davin was appointed perpetual chairman and O'Ryan one of the joint treasurers.[104] The latter acted as call steward for the inaugural club sports in November 1879,[105] a position he filled at a number of fixtures over the following two years.[106] He was also in attendance when the City and County Dublin Harriers travelled to meet the Carrick-on-Suir Harriers for a cross-country challenge at Knocknaconnery in the winter of 1881.[107] It would appear that O'Ryan's interest in athletics was enduring, and as late as 1898 he acted as assistant secretary to the Thurles sports committee.[108] He was subsequently appointed to a subcommittee charged with the selection of prizes, along with M. Callanan, Hugh Ryan, D.H. Ryan, J.L. Johnston, and Thomas Ryan.[109] Again, he was actively involved on the day of the meeting in the dual capacity of lap steward, and call steward.[110]

Whereas O'Ryan's sporting interests tended to be in the sphere of administration, his fellow Carrick man William Foley had enjoyed a successful competitive career. For it would appear that, in addition to his rowing exploits, Foley had been a useful sprinter in the early years of the previous decade.[111]

The majority of the local founders were athletics enthusiasts. T.K. Dwyer of Ballyvinane, Littleton, had been a middle-distance runner of considerable talent. A consistent performer on the local Tipperary circuit,[112] he raced to a sensational victory at Trinity College in 1877.[113] Dwyer went on to win the Irish one mile championship in 1878 with a performance of 4 minutes and 39¼ seconds.[114] In fact, his winning time had been the best recorded since 1873, when A.C. Courtney ran a fraction quicker to take the inaugural title.[115] That the Moycarkey man was also an able administrator is attested by his efficient handling of an athletics meeting at Littleton in 1877, where he acted as secretary.[116]

Although an infrequent competitor, Charlie Culhane had been a capable sprinter. His name is listed on the programme for the 100 yards race at the Littleton meeting, but it is not known if he contested the preliminary rounds.[117] Culhane had a very rewarding outing at Thurles in July 1878 when he won both the 100 yards open event and the 220 yards race for the 'Thurles Champion Cup'.[118] He reclaimed that trophy in September 1880 when he beat the holder J.L. Worrell of the National Bank.[119] The following month he travelled to Carrick-on-Suir where he finished second in the 100 yards open event.[120] Culhane's taste for athletics endured into middle age. He is described as one of the 'judges of running' at the Thurles sports in 1906,[121] and in 1913 subscribed to a testimonial for Tim Crowe,[122] the champion long-distance runner from Bishopswood, Dundrum.[123]

It would appear that John Butler had a brief association with the sport in his youth. He was almost certainly the 'John Butler' who won a foot-race, organised by his friend and neighbour Charles Langley,[124] at Coolkennedy in 1866.[125] Again it was he, we presume, who eleven years later was recorded, by his cousin and secretary T.K. Dwyer,[126] as an entrant in the two miles walk at the athletics sports in Littleton.[127]

William Delahunty, a neighbour of Joseph O'Ryan in Thurles,[128] shared the latter's penchant for administration. Delahunty performed the duty of steward at the Littleton event in 1877,[129] and was along with O'Ryan a member of the organising committee for the Thurles sports of 1898.[130]

Fenianism

In 1934 Thomas Markham, in a contribution to the *Irish Press* entitled 'It was Kindled from the Fenian Fire', attempted to trace the GAA's origins back to the teachings of old Fenians such as John O'Mahony. Some years after the Young Ireland debacle of 1848, O'Mahony is reputed to have organised a hurling match at Carrick-on-Suir, in order to arouse in the participants a spirit of independence.[131] Markham had been a senior British civil servant in Dublin Castle and his access to files on the period in question lends credibility to his evidence.[132] He went on to claim that:

> Having in mind the keynote of O'Mahony's teaching – "self-restraint, self-discipline, self-sacrifice" – leading members of the IRB [Irish Republican Brotherhood] held a council meeting in 1883, and decided thereat to initiate an athletic movement which would attract the young manhood of Ireland. Later in the same year, a sub-group, consisting of P.N. Fitzgerald, Pat Hoctor, John Menton, and Jim Boland, ... considered ... that prominent anti-constitutionalists should not, in the initial stages at all events, openly appear to dominate an organisation whose ostensible object would be to bring the games of the Gael under executive control. Hence the Fenian quartet, who met at Blackrock to decide the matter, looked around for a capable organiser. Their choice fell on Michael Cusack.[133]

Some of these details are possibly inaccurate,[134] and the latter claim is almost certainly an exaggeration as Cusack was a man of strong and independent mind. Yet both parties could work together to achieve a common goal. It was, after all, the age of the New Departure,[135] when disparate elements of Irish nationalism came together in an alliance of convenience. That Cusack was willing to co-operate with proponents of physical force nationalism is attested by his meeting with the IRB activists P.W. Nally in the spring of 1879,[136] and P.N. Fitzgerald in December 1886.[137] At the former encounter he and Nally discussed the feasibility of founding a national athletics association. Moreover, in 1899 Cusack would claim that nobody had done more than Nally to persuade him to found a body like the GAA.[138] Indeed, though they were advocates of parliamentary methods in their middle years, it is quite likely that both Cusack[139] and Davin[140] had joined the Fenians in their youth.

Whereas the two main founders might have had a brief association with radicalism, J.K. Bracken and John Wyse Power were long-term advocates of the separatist creed. Wyse Power, the recently-appointed editor of the *Leinster Leader*, had been dismissed from his post in Dublin Castle because of his membership of the Young Ireland Society which the authorities regarded as a front for the IRB.[141] At the time of the foundation meeting he is described as an associate of 'the extreme section of Irish nationalists'.[142] He would go on to take part, along with P.N. Fitzgerald, John Menton, and J.K. Bracken, in the IRB-inspired Parnell Leadership Committee.[143] However, a police report from the early 1890s suggests that though he still espoused the separatist philosophy, his enthusiasm was beginning to wane.[144]

The IRB member Joseph Kevin Bracken,[145] a business manager in the family firm of monumental sculptors and builders[146] at Templemore, was one of two rebel siblings. His brother, William, who had been imprisoned because of his involvement in the Fenian movement and released only on condition he left the country, settled in Bradford, Yorkshire.[147] A priest in Templemore denounced J.K. Bracken for his subversive activities declaring that he was 'worse than a Protestant, or even an atheist' and that 'he was leading the Roman Catholic youth of the country astray'.[148] As late as 1896 the police described him as still 'a warm advocate of physical force' and as a man who despised parliamentary methods as a solution to Irish grievances.[149] By this time also, Bracken had changed allegiance to the Irish National Alliance.[150]

It would appear that Joseph O'Ryan was a moderate nationalist. Yet it is significant perhaps, that both he and Patrick Davin had served their apprenticeships in Dublin with the Menton law firm. As alluded to above, John Menton, a member of that family, attended the IRB meeting at Blackrock in 1883 when it was decided to establish a nationalist athletics association.[151]

A similar pattern of political activism can be discerned among the local founding fathers. While no definite proof exists, there is a strong possibility that T.K. Dwyer had taken the Fenian oath.[152] It will be recalled that he had endured a term of imprisonment for intimidation during the land campaign. An extract from his notebook and diary (evidently recorded by his wife) indicates an unconventional lifestyle for a tenant farmer. Under a heading entitled 'Days he did not work', which coincided with a period of intense land agitation at local and national level, are the following entries:

> 25 August 1880 on the bed.
> 27, 28 [August] went away and we don't know.
> 8 September half-day sleeping in garden.
> 10 September half-day on bed went away p.m.

11 [September] on the bed.

27 December Thurles races went away.

Easter Saturday [1881] went to meeting in Thurles.

6 May away to Cashel.

8 May went to England and remained away to 12 May.

30 May Cashel races.

22 June half [-day] went to see the barrister.

27 July half [-day] went to see emergency men.

11 August half [-day] went from hoeing turnips to writing letters.

22, 23 [August] dressed himself up and went away.[153]

Dwyer's role in the funeral of the Fenian leader Charles Kickham, which arrived in Thurles on 27 August 1882, provides some additional clues as to his political sympathies. As a member of a select group he was involved in the reception of the remains, and on the following day made the twenty-mile journey to Mullinahone for the interment.[154] The identities of those on the funeral committee were not disclosed by the local press, and it was not until 1945 that their names were published by James Kennedy, a former 'centre' of the IRB in Thurles.[155] Dwyer's son, James, who took an active part in the War of Independence, served his apprenticeship with Cannock & Co. of Limerick where a tradition of IRB membership existed among the staff.[156] One such activist was the Rossmore-born D.H. Ryan, a founder of the Limerick Commercials Football Club and a driving force behind the fledgling GAA in that city.[157] On returning to his native Tipperary, Ryan was closely associated with the GAA club in Thurles,[158] and the IRB, of which he was the local centre.[159]

Although it must be conceded that the details of his early life are quite sketchy, we are on surer ground when we investigate the political career of Dwyer's fellow athlete Charlie Culhane. At a time when clubs and societies were often formed or infiltrated for IRB purposes, he was one of the leading lights in the establishment of the Thurles Young Men's Society in 1883.[160] When Culhane proposed 'certain names to form a committee (with power to add to their numbers)' he was outmanoeuvred by Fr Cantwell and his supporters who insisted that the committee should be elected by ballot.[161] Within a few years the society's affairs were being orchestrated by a cadre of advanced nationalists, most notably the secretary[162] and IRB suspect James Butler.[163] Culhane, on the other hand, who was a member of a prosperous merchant family,[164] seems to have avoided police attention. Oral tradition records that in later years his business trips to the United States were used as opportunities to collect funds for the nationalist cause.[165] A former employee recalled that he often set out for these, and other, journeys dressed in his work clothes as a ploy to deceive the authorities.[166] Two statements issued by a New York bank, found among his papers, raise some intriguing possibilities. The first document, dated 1 June 1925, shows a credit balance of $77,694.40, while a statement for a 'special' account, dated 2 November 1925, reveals a balance in credit of $15,384.66.[167]

Following the launch of the GAA, Culhane seems to have disappeared into the anonymity of small-town life. He emerged again in 1892 when he was returned as a member of the Thurles branch of the Irish National Federation,[168] an anti-Parnellite organisation which had been founded the previous year.[169] Towards the end of 1892 he made a generous contribution to a collection organised by the INF in support of evicted tenants.[170] Culhane threw himself wholeheartedly into the movement to erect 'in Thurles a suitable memorial to celebrate the memory of the martyred heroes of 1798'.[171] When the original committee fell into abeyance a new energetic group appointed him as chairman, and the IRB man D.H. Ryan as secretary.[172] At least three of the others involved, Andrew Callanan, Hugh Ryan, and Denis McCarthy, were also members of the brotherhood.[173] At a meeting under the auspices of the United Irish League in May 1900 'to take up the work where they left off at the time of the split', Culhane proposed that a branch of the organisation be established in the town. The resolution, which was passed unanimously, was seconded by Andrew Callanan of the IRB.[174] Speaking at a gathering of that group some time later, Culhane, betraying a little of his political philosophy, averred, 'if you have some energetic men in a parish it makes very little difference whether you have the priests or not'.[175] He would express similar sentiments at a town council meeting in 1906 when he dismissed as 'rubbish' a motion of commendation for a local policeman. He then proceeded to disparage the proposer for allowing the council to be used as a 'cat's paw'.[176] Despite his advancing years, Culhane continued to be involved in a number of nationalist organisations, particularly Sinn Féin and the Irish Volunteers. Among his companions in the Thurles unit of the Volunteers were IRB members Michael Eustace, James Kennedy, and James Leahy of Tubberadora.[177] Towards the end of the decade when Eustace and others were accused of illegal drilling, Culhane, by then a prominent Sinn Féin official, was injured in a baton charge near the courthouse.[178] That he was also an advocate of cultural nationalism is attested by his presence at the railway station in February 1915 when 'Thurles gave a royal welcome to Dr Douglas Hyde' of the Gaelic League.[179] The outbreak of hostilities in 1919 saw him come under increased police scrutiny. A party of police and military raided his house in Friar Street and his business premises in Hall Street, but 'nothing of any consequence was found'.[180] He was less fortunate the following year when:

> some glass in the house of Mr Charles Culhane, president of the local Sinn Féin club, was broken. Very extensive damage was done to this house on the night of 20-21 January; and the owner, who has since been sent to Wormwood Scrubs prison, though over sixty years of age, had a narrow escape with his life.[181]

While in prison Culhane participated in the general hunger strike 'with all the perseverance and spirit of self-sacrifice which animated his younger compatriots of the prison cell'. He was released shortly after the truce but never deviated from his political convictions.[182] Culhane was chairman of Thurles UDC when the terms of the Anglo-Irish Treaty were discussed. A republican to the last, rather than accept a motion for approval he vacated the chair. In his absence the vote for acceptance was unanimous.[183]

Michael Cantwell's first overt political act occurred in December 1882 when Charles Dawson MP, lord mayor of Dublin, paid a visit to the local Christian Brothers schools. Cantwell, a senior pupil, was chosen to read the customary address of welcome.[184] Evidently a youth of conviction, he was treasurer of the town's Juvenile Temperance Society, as a member of which he made a donation to the Parnell National Tribute collection.[185] A talented musician and singer,[186] he was, like his fellow CBS alumnus Charlie Culhane,[187] a member of the Thurles Young Men's Society.[188] Perhaps it was in the convivial surroundings of the latter that he was first inveigled into the shadowy world of radical politics. Then again it is possible that such a transformation occurred when he moved to Dublin, where he would eventually settle permanently. While in that city he spent various periods as a medical student, clerk in the National League office, journalist, commercial traveller, advertising canvasser, and employee of the insurance firm – MacDonagh and Boland.[189] In January 1896 the police noted that Cantwell, who 'was a most active IRB organiser' in Thurles, had left for Dublin to take up the 'position of traveller for Messrs Mitchell and Co. wine merchants, Belfast, vacated by suspect P.J. Hoctor.'[190] A file compiled at the start of the following year provides some further insight into his activities:

> Although this man's name does not appear on the B list his movements have been reported on during previous visits to Thurles. ... I beg to report that the above named suspect arrived here by the 9 p.m. train on 23rd inst. ... during his stay here, he kept indoors during the day time, but was most active at night and kept very late hours. He was to be seen each night in the company of [the IRB organiser][191] James Ryan (Scales) L.C. Doyle, John Walsh, Thomas Ryan and John Murphy. Cantwell told a friend here that John E. Redmond's visit to America was for the purpose of consulting the leading IRB men as to the amount of support he (J.E. Redmond) and his friends in Ireland would receive from the advanced society men in America.[192]

The young Michael Cantwell grew up in a staunchly nationalist environment. When Archbishop Croke returned in triumph from Rome in May 1883 'at Miss Cantwell's house in the main street a banner bearing the word "welcome" was suspended.'[193] 'Miss' Cantwell was in fact Mrs Bridget Cantwell, a shopkeeper and the proprietor of a high-class confectionary operation.[194] Indeed, this popular business would survive under her daughter

Margaret's name until the middle of the following century.[195] Remembered as 'a tough customer', Mrs Cantwell 'cursed' a daughter who married a member of the RIC and hoped that she would 'never give birth to a live child'.[196] The enterprising Cantwell women supplemented their income by taking in boarders. One such resident was Joseph MacDonagh, a customs official,[197] whose brother, Thomas, was an occasional visitor at weekends.[198] Following the latter's execution for his role in the 1916 Rising, Joseph MacDonagh entrusted Margaret Cantwell, his former landlady, to deliver a letter of condolence to his sister-in-law Muriel Gifford.[199] The friendship between Margaret Cantwell and the MacDonagh family was enduring. When the Thurles-born[200] Mary MacDonagh married Frank Lemass in 1937 her father's 'true friend',[201] Miss Cantwell, was an honoured guest at the ceremony.[202] Her brother, Michael, had died in greatly reduced circumstances some years earlier.[203] He was laid to rest, without display, near his former conspirator, and GAA founder Charlie Culhane.[204] Also nearby lie the remains of Lady Elizabeth Thurles, a progenitor of the British royal family;[205] totems of a political and cultural system they once so bitterly opposed.

Whether the GAA was founded as a direct result of an IRB plot is largely irrelevant. Nevertheless, evidence from both national and local sources indicates that the influence of the secret oath-bound organisation was considerable. The utilisation of sport for political purposes was not new. Separatists from previous eras, such as James Hope, Thomas Francis Meagher, John O'Mahony, and Charles Kickham, had recognised the value of sport as a vehicle for promoting the cause of national self-determination.[206] It was a phenomenon that was not confined to Ireland. Two decades before the emergence of the GAA, patriotic Czechs had formed gymnastic societies to help restore their native culture and to confront the threat of Germanisation.[207]

REFERENCES

This article was first published in the *Tipperary Historical Journal* of 2014.

[1] *Tipperary Leader*, 7 Nov. 1884, p. 3 (henceforth *TL*).
[2] George Henry Bassett, *The Book of County Tipperary: A Manual and Directory for Manufacturers, Merchants, Traders, Professional Men, Land-Owners, Farmers, Tourists, Anglers and Sportsmen Generally* (Dublin, 1889), pp 370, 379 (henceforth Bassett, *Book of Tipperary*).
[3] However, a recent essay carelessly locates the foundation meeting in Dublin, and refers to the existence of GAA clubs in the United States from the 1850s, see Paul Darby, 'Gaelic Games and the Irish Diaspora in the United States', in Mike Cronin, William Murphy and Paul Rouse (eds), *The Gaelic Athletic Association 1884-2009* (Dublin, 2009), p. 205.
[4] Pádraig Puirséal, *The GAA in its Time* (Dublin, 1982), p. 35 (henceforth Puirséal *GAA*); Séamus Ó Riain, *Maurice Davin (1847-1927): First President of the GAA* (Dublin, 1994), p. 53 (henceforth Ó Riain, *Davin*); W.F. Mandle, *The Gaelic Athletic Association & Irish Nationalist Politics 1884-1924* (London, 1987), pp 9-10 (henceforth Mandle, *GAA*).
[5] T.F. O'Sullivan, *Story of the GAA* (Dublin, 1916), p. 8 (henceforth O'Sullivan, *Story of GAA*); William Dooley, *Champions of the Athletic Arena* (Dublin, 1946), p. 10 (henceforth Dooley, *Champions*).

[6] Marcus de Búrca, *Michael Cusack and the GAA* (Dublin, 1989), p. 77 (henceforth de Búrca, *Cusack*).

[7] Ibid. p. 71.

[8] Liam P. Ó Caithnia, *Micheál Cíosóg* (Dublin, 1982), pp 21-54 (henceforth Ó Caithnia, *Cíosóg*).

[9] de Búrca, *Cusack*, pp 16, 25.

[10] Ibid, pp 45-55.

[11] *Irish Sportsman*, 9 Apr. 1881, p. 5, 2 July 1881, p. 5, 1 Oct. 1881, p. 11, 10 June 1882, p. 5 (henceforth *IS*).

[12] GAA Museum, *The Gaelic Athletic Association through History and Documents 1870-1920* (Dublin, 2008), Document 1 Letter Michael Cusack to Maurice Davin suggesting the first meeting of the GAA – 26th August 1884 (henceforth GAA Museum, *Documents*); Ó Riain, *Davin*, p. 51.

[13] de Búrca, *Cusack*, pp 88-90.

[14] GAA Museum, *Documents*.

[15] Ibid.

[16] *IS*, 3 Nov. 1877, p. 10, 1 Dec. 1877, p. 11, 15 Dec. 1877, p. 9.

[17] *The Shamrock*, 11 Oct. 1884, p. 30; Marcus de Búrca, *The GAA: A History* (Dublin, 1999), p. 12, misquotes Cusack (henceforth de Búrca, *GAA*).

[18] *Cork Examiner*, 24 May 1883, p. 2 (henceforth *CE*); *Freeman's Journal*, 24 May 1883, p. 7 (henceforth *FJ*); *Irish Times*, 24 May 1883, p. 7 (henceforth *IT*); *IS*, 2 June 1883, p. 5, 9 June 1883 p. 5; de Búrca, *Cusack*, p. 78, appears to be inaccurate.

[19] *IS*, 26 May 1883, p. 5, 2 June 1883, p. 5, 9 June 1883, p. 5, 16 June 1883, p. 5, 23 June 1883, p. 6.

[20] *IS*, 16 June 1883, p. 5.

[21] Pat Davin, *Recollections of a Veteran Irish Athlete: The Memoirs of Pat Davin, World's All-Round Athletic Champion* (Dublin, 1938), p. 43.

[22] *United Ireland*, 11 Oct. 1884, p. 5 (henceforth *UI*); *The Irishman*, 11 Oct. 1884, p. 233 (henceforth *TI*).

[23] *UI*, 18 Oct. 1884, p. 2.

[24] *UI*, 25 Oct. 1884, p. 2.

[25] Seán McNamara, *Man from Carron* (Ennis, 2005), pp 37-8; Ó Caithnia, *Cíosóg*, p. 54.

[26] O'Sullivan, *Story of GAA*, p. 6; *CE*, 3 Nov. 1884, p. 4; Puirséal, *GAA*, pp 39-40.

[27] *TL*, 7 Nov. 1884, p. 3; Mandle, *GAA*, p. 6; O'Sullivan, *Story of GAA*, p. 7, misquotes Cusack.

[28] *UI*, 8 Nov. 1884, p. 6; *TI*, 8 Nov. 1884, p. 295.

[29] O'Sullivan, *Story of GAA*, p. 8.

[30] Ó Riain, *Davin*, p. 58.

[31] de Búrca, *Cusack*, p. 103.

[32] Ibid.

[33] *TL*, 15 Feb. 1884, p. 2.

[34] *TL*, 31 Oct. 1884, p. 3.

[35] *TL*, 7 Nov. 1884, p. 3.

[36] *Tipperary Advocate*, 8 Nov. 1884, p. 1

[37] *Clonmel Chronicle*, 5 Nov. 1884, p. 2 (henceforth *CC*); *Nenagh Guardian*, 8 Nov. 1884, p. 4 (henceforth *NG*).

[38] Bassett, *Book of Tipperary*, p. 369.

[39] *TL*, 15 Feb. 1884, p. 2.

[40] Thurles RC parish, baptismal register 1858 (henceforth *BR*); *Tipperary Star*, 9 Jan. 1926, p. 5 (henceforth *TS*); *NG*, 9 Jan. 1926, p. 5.

[41] Thurles RC parish, BR 1865; *TS*, 31 Dec. 1932, p. 6.

[42] *TL*, 7 Nov. 1884, p. 2.

[43] *TL*, 10 Oct. 1883, p. 3.

[44] *TL*, 31 Oct. 1883, p. 2.

[45] Notebook of Daniel Maher, Thurles, County Tipperary, p. 101 (MS in private keeping); Joseph C. Hayes, 'Guide to Tipperary Newspapers (1770-1989)' in *Tipperary Historical Journal*, ii (1989), p. 11 (henceforth *THJ*); Liam Ó Donnchú, 'The Genesis and Early Development of the Gaelic Athletic Association in a Thurles Context' (MA thesis, UCC, 1999), p. 84, is inaccurate (henceforth Ó Donnchú, 'Genesis of GAA in Thurles').

[46] Moycarkey RC parish, BR 1839; *TS*, 30 Nov. 1912, p. 5.

[47] *Tipperary Free Press*, 26 Feb. 1867, p. 3 (henceforth *TFP*); *Cashel Gazette*, 9 Oct. 1880, p. 5, 24 Sept. 1881, p. 2, 1 Oct. 1881, p. 3 (henceforth *CG*); *TL*, 4 Oct. 1882, p. 2, 11 Oct. 1882, p. 3; *NG*,

14 Sept. 1881, p. 3, 21 Sept. 1881, p. 2, 8 Oct. 1881, p. 4, 6 Sept. 1882, p. 2, 17 Dec. 1884, p. 2; *CC*, 12 May 1880, p. 3, 20 Oct. 1880, p. 2, 17 Mar. 1883, p. 2, 24 Mar. 1883, p. 3, 28 Aug. 1886, p. 2; *The Nationalist*, 13 Sept. 1890, p. 4, 19 Aug. 1891, p. 4, 12 Sept. 1894, p. 4, 13 July 1895, p. 4, 28 Aug. 1895, p. 3, 18 Sept. 1895, p. 3 (henceforth *TN*); *Cashel Sentinel*, 30 Apr. 1892, p. 4 (henceforth *CS*).

[48] Ballingarry RC parish, BR 1852; *TS*, 18 Jan. 1930, p. 6.

[49] *TL*, 26 Sept. 1884, p. 3.

[50] Bassett, *Book of Tipperary,* pp 377, 379, 381, 387.

[51] *TS*, 22 June 1912, p. 5.

[52] *TN*, 16 Mar. 1892, p. 4.

[53] *FJ*, 3 Nov. 1884, p. 7.

[54] Moycarkey RC parish, BR 1848; Ballycahill graveyard, Dwyer headstone; Interview with T.K. Dwyer of Turtulla, Thurles, County Tipperary (15 Aug. 1985).

[55] 'Carbery', *Fifty Years of Irish Athletics* (Dublin, 1943), p. 49 (henceforth Carbery, *Irish Athletics*).

[56] Interview with T.K. Dwyer (11 Mar. 1997).

[57] T.K. Dwyer, 'Who Was There?' in Liam Ó Donnchú (ed.), *Cluichí Ceannais Iomána na Mumhan: Clár Oifigiúil* (Thurles, 1979), p. 8; T.K. Dwyer and Jimmy Fogarty (eds), *Moycarkey-Borris GAA Story* (Thurles, 1984), pp 10-11 (henceforth Dwyer & Fogarty, *Moycarkey-Borris GAA*); Nancy Murphy, 'Frank R. Maloney: Nenagh's GAA Pioneer' in *THJ*, x (1997), pp 74-6 (henceforth Murphy, 'F.R. Maloney').

[58] de Búrca, *Cusack*, pp 104-5.

[59] *CC*, 2 Feb. 1881, p. 1.

[60] *TS*, 9 Jan. 1926, p. 5.

[61] Marcus de Búrca, 'The Curious Career of Sub-Inspector Thomas St George McCarthy' in *THJ*, i (1988), pp 202-3.

[62] *NG*, 2 Nov. 1872, p. 4; Ó Donnchú, 'Genesis of GAA in Thurles', pp 86-7.

[63] de Búrca, *GAA*, pp 13-14.

[64] Ó Riain, *Davin*, p. 58.

[65] *CC*, 23 Aug. 1865, p. 2, 8 Sept. 1866, p. 2, 14 Aug. 1867, p. 2, 5 Aug. 1868, p. 2.

[66] Richard McElligott, *Forging a Kingdom: The GAA in Kerry 1884-1934* (Cork, 2013), pp 123-4, 126; Brendan Fullam, *The Throw-In: The GAA and the Men who Made It* (Dublin, 2004), p. 6; Mandle, *GAA*, p. 156.

[67] See William Nolan, 'Séamus Ó Riain: An Appreciation' in *THJ*, xx (2007), pp 187-8.

[68] Dooley, *Champions*, p. 10.

[69] *TS*, 8 Mar. 1919, p. 4; *TN*, 8 Mar. 1919, p. 7.

[70] Spelling as in 1901 and 1911 census.

[71] Brendan Fullam, *Giants of the Ash* (Dublin, 1991), pp 165-6.

[72] Ibid; Tom Ryall, *Kilkenny: The GAA Story 1884-1984* (Kilkenny, 1984), pp 23-6; Raymond Smith, *A Century of Gaelic Games: A Comprehensive Record of Results and Teams (1887-1987)* (Dublin, 1987), p. 196.

[73] National Archives Ireland, Census 1901, New England, Ballybeagh, County Kilkenny (henceforth NAI).

[74] Mandle, *GAA*, p. 7.

[75] Marcus de Búrca, *The Story of the GAA to 1990* (Dublin, 1991), p. 22.

[76] Murphy, 'F.R. Maloney', pp 74-6.

[77] Interview with Daniel Ryan of Thurles, County Tipperary (15 Aug. 2013); Bassett, *Book of Tipperary*, p. 379.

[78] Interview with Daniel Ryan (25 Apr. 2004).

[79] *CE*, 29 Dec. 1884, p. 2.

[80] Ó Donnchú, 'Genesis of GAA in Thurles', p. 52.

[81] NAI, Census 1911, Newport, Newport East, County Mayo; *TS*, 20 Mar. 1943, p. 3; Denis G. Marnane, 'Remembering to Remember (1862-2012) Thomas St George MacCarthy and the Abbey School Tipperary' in *THJ*, xxv (2012), p. 109.

[82] *CE*, 3 Nov. 1884, p. 4.

[83] *TN*, 15 June 1892, p. 4, 15 Oct. 1892, p. 3, 15 Mar. 1893, p. 4, 30 May 1894, p. 1, 8 Mar. 1919, p. 7; NAI, Crime Branch Special, 13114/S (henceforth CBS); NAI, Census 1911, Main Street,

Thurles, County Tipperary.

[84] *CC*, 22 Nov. 1879, p. 4, 31 Mar. 1880, p. 3, 7 July 1880, p. 3, 20 Oct. 1880, p. 2, 2 Mar. 1881, p. 3, 27 Apr. 1881, p. 3.

[85] *CC*, 18 Oct. 1884, p. 2; Bassett, *Book of Tipperary*, p. 381.

[86] *UI*, 15 Nov. 1884, p. 2.

[87] GAA Museum, *Documents*.

[88] *Gaelic Journal*, i, No. 10 (Aug. 1883), p. 333 (henceforth *GJ*).

[89] Ibid.

[90] *CE*, 3 Nov. 1884, p. 4.

[91] *GJ*, i, No. 1 (Nov. 1882), p. 32.

[92] Ó Riain, *Davin*, pp 41-2.

[93] *GJ*, i, No. 10 (Aug. 1883), p. 336.

[94] Marie O'Neill, *From Parnell to De Valera: A Biography of Jennie Wyse Power 1858-1941* (Dublin, 1991), pp 29, 52-3 (henceforth O'Neill, *Wyse Power*).

[95] *CS*, 30 Apr. 1892, p. 4.

[96] *CG*, 7 June 1879, p. 3.

[97] *CC*, 12 May 1880, p. 3.

[98] F.S.L. Lyons, *Ireland since the Famine* (London, 1971), p. 222.

[99] *TN*, 12 Sept. 1894. p. 4.

[100] Carbery, *Irish Athletics*, p. 50; Ó Riain, *Davin*, p. 38, is inaccurate.

[101] Peter Lovesey, *The Official Centenary History of the Amateur Athletic Association* (Enfield, 1980), pp 187-8.

[102] Tony O'Donoghue, *Irish Championship Athletics 1873-1914: GAA and IAAA Championships Ireland v Scotland Cross-Country Championships* (Dublin, 2005), p. 24 (henceforth O'Donoghue, *Irish Championship Athletics*).

[103] *CE*, 3 Nov. 1884, p. 4.

[104] Minute Book of Carrick-on-Suir Amateur Athletic Cricket and Football Club, p. 4 (MS in private keeping).

[105] *CC*, 22 Nov. 1879, p. 4.

[106] *CC*, 31 Mar. 1880, p. 3, 7 July 1880, p. 3, 20 Oct. 1880, p. 2, 27 Apr. 1881, p. 3.

[107] *TFP*, 25 Feb. 1881, p. 2; *CC*, 2 Mar. 1881, p. 3.

[108] *TN*, 20 Aug. 1898, p. 3.

[109] *TN*, 27 Aug. 1898, p. 3.

[110] *TN*, 17 Sept. 1898, p. 3.

[111] *CC*, 7 Aug. 1872, p. 2, 16 Apr. 1873, p. 3, 25 June 1873, p. 2, 24 Sept. 1873, p. 2.

[112] *IS*, 29 Mar. 1879, p. 7; Dwyer & Fogarty, *Moycarkey-Borris GAA*, pp 302-3.

[113] *IT*, 16 June 1877, p. 3; *IS*, 29 Mar. 1879, p. 7.

[114] *IS*, 29 Mar. 1879, p. 7.

[115] O'Donoghue, *Irish Championship Athletics*, pp 11-21.

[116] Dwyer & Fogarty, *Moycarkey-Borris GAA*, p. 11.

[117] *Littleton Athletic Sports* (Thurles, 1877), p. 3 (henceforth *Littleton Sports*).

[118] *NG*, 17 July 1878, p. 2; *TFP*, 19 July 1878, p. 1; *CC*, 20 July 1878, p. 3. This impressive silver trophy, which survives in private keeping, is inscribed 'Champion Cup | Thurles | For 220 Yards Flat | 1878'.

[119] *CC*, 25 Sept. 1880, p. 2.

[120] *CC*, 20 Oct. 1880, p. 2.

[121] *TN*, 14 July, 1906, p. 4.

[122] *TS*, 22 Mar. 1913, p. 2.

[123] J.M. Tobin, 'National Athletics Champions 1885-1922 GAA Rules' in *Tipperary GAA Yearbook* (2003), pp 77, 79.

[124] *CC*, 28 Aug. 1886, p. 2.

[125] *CC*, 11 Aug. 1866, p. 3.

[126] Dwyer & Fogarty, *Moycarkey-Borris GAA*, p. 11.

[127] *Littleton Sports*, p. 3.

[128] Alf MacLochlainn, 'From Tipperary to Joseph's Prairie: The Story of Joe Ryan, the Seventh Man in Hayes's Hotel' in *THJ*, xv (2002), p. 164 (henceforth MacLochlainn, 'Joe Ryan').

[129] *Littleton Sports*, p. 1.
[130] *CC*, 17 Sept. 1898, p. 3.
[131] *Irish Press,* 14 Apr. 1934, p. 56 (henceforth *IP*).
[132] William O'Brien and Desmond Ryan, (eds), *Devoy's Post Bag 1871-1928* (2 vols, Dublin, 1953), ii, 545-6; Tim Pat Coogan, *Michael Collins: A Biography* (London, 1990), p. 81.
[133] *IP*, 14 Apr. 1934, p. 56.
[134] See David Fitzpatrick, *Harry Boland's Irish Revolution* (Cork, 2003), p. 19.
[135] Conor Cruise O'Brien, *Parnell and his Party 1880-90* (London, 1974), pp 5-6.
[136] de Búrca, *Cusack*, p. 48.
[137] Ibid. pp 148-9.
[138] Ibid. p. 50.
[139] Ibid. p. 93; Richard Ellmann, *James Joyce* (Oxford, 1983), pp 61, 459.
[140] *TN*, 30 Jan. 1927, p. 3; de Búrca, *Cusack*, p. 93; Ó Riain, *Davin*, p. 17.
[141] O'Neill, *Wyse Power*, pp 29-30.
[142] NAI, CBS 11207/S; Mandle, *GAA*, p. 7.
[143] *IT,* 11 Dec. 1890, p. 5; Marcus Bourke, *John O'Leary: A Study in Irish Separatism* (Athens, 1967), p. 204.
[144] NAI, CBS 11207/S.
[145] NAI, CBS 12844/S; CBS District Inspectors Crime Special 521/184/S (henceforth DICS).
[146] Nancy Murphy, 'Joseph K. Bracken: GAA Founder, Fenian and Politician' in William Nolan and Thomas G. McGrath (eds), *Tipperary History and Society: Interdisciplinary Essays on the History of an Irish County* (Dublin, 1985), p. 379; Bassett, *Book of Tipperary*, pp 353-4.
[147] Charles Edward Lysaght, *Brendan Bracken* (London, 1980), pp 21-2.
[148] NAI, CBS 126/S; Lysaght, op. cit. p. 22, misquotes this report.
[149] Lysaght, op. cit. p. 22.
[150] NAI, CBS 11628/S; CBS 12844/S.
[151] MacLochlainn, 'Joe Ryan', p. 164.
[152] Interview with T.K. Dwyer (25 Apr. 1980).
[153] Diary of Timothy K. Dwyer, Littleton, County Tipperary, p. 99 (MS in private keeping).
[154] Interview with T.K. Dwyer (25 Apr. 1980); J.M. Kennedy, *A Chronology of Thurles* (Thurles, 1945), pp 38-9.
[155] Kennedy, op. cit. p. 49; Pádraig Ó Haicéad, *Keep their Names ever Green* (Nenagh, 2003), p. 442 (henceforth Ó Haicéad, *Keep their Names*).
[156] Interview with T.K. Dwyer (20 Apr. 1995).
[157] *TS*, 16 Oct. 1937, p. 2; Séamus Ó Ceallaigh and Seán Murphy, *One Hundred Years of Glory: A History of Limerick GAA 1884-1984* (Limerick, 1987), p. 32; *TS*, 27 Apr. 1929, p. 3.
[158] NAI, CBS 2786/S; Fogarty, *Tipperary GAA*, p. 55.
[159] NAI, CBS 12929/S; CBS DICS 521/11222/S; CBS DICS 521/12026/S; CBS DICS 521/12144/S.
[160] *TL*, 6 Oct. 1883, p. 2
[161] *TL*, 10 Oct. 1883, p .3
[162] Bassett, *Book of Tipperary*, p. 375.
[163] NAI, CBS 1360/S; CBS 2786/S.
[164] Isaac Slater, *Royal National Commercial Directory of Ireland: Including, in Addition to the Trades Lists, Alphabetical Directories of Dublin, Belfast, Cork and Limerick* (Manchester, 1856), p. 357; Thurles Christian Brothers School, register 1865 (MS in private keeping), (henceforth Thurles CBS, register); *NG*, 25 June 1892, p. 4; *TN*, 3 Aug. 1898, p. 4; NAI, Census 1901, Main Street, Thurles, County Tipperary; *Nenagh News*, 13 June 1903, p. 3; *TS*, 9 Jan. 1926, p. 5.
[165] Interviews with William Gaynor of Thurles, County Tipperary (25 Apr. 1994), William Maher of Thurles, County Tipperary (9 Nov. 1997).
[166] Interview with Mary Davern of Thurles, County Tipperary (25 Apr. 1984). Culhane was a feather and hide dealer, see note 164 above.
[167] The National Park Bank of New York, statements 1 July 1924 - 2 Nov. 1925.
[168] *TN*, 29 June 1892, p. 3.
[169] *TN*, 11 Mar. 1891, p. 2.
[170] *TN*, 23 Nov. 1892, p. 2.
[171] *TN*, 18 Feb. 1899, p. 4.

[172] *TN*, 24 Dec. 1898, p. 3, 18 Feb. 1899, p. 4.

[173] NAI, CBS 13114/S; CBS DICS 521/184/S; CBS 2786/S; CBS DICS 521/12144/S; CBS DICS 521/6395/S; CBS DICS 521/12026/S; CBS DICS 521/13664/S.

[174] *TN*, 23 May 1900, p. 4.

[175] *NG*, 8 Aug. 1900, p. 4.

[176] *Midland Counties Advertiser*, 18 Oct. 1906, p. 4.

[177] *TS*, 26 Sept. 1914, p. 4, 16 Feb. 1918, p. 3, 25 July 1953, pp 4-5; Ó Haicéad, *Keep their Names*, p. 442.

[178] *NG*, 16 Mar. 1918, p. 3.

[179] *TN*, 10 Feb. 1915, p. 6; *TS*, 13 Feb. 1915, p. 3.

[180] *TN*, 13 Sept. 1919, p. 6.

[181] *TS*, 6 Mar. 1920, p. 4.

[182] *TS*, 9 Jan. 1926, p. 5.

[183] *TS*, 7 Jan. 1922, p. 3.

[184] *TL*, 9 Dec. 1882, p. 3.

[185] *TL*, 21Apr. 1883, p. 2.

[186] *TL*, 3 Feb. 1883, p. 2.

[187] Thurles CBS, register 1865. William Delahunty was also a past pupil, see Thurles CBS register 1861.

[188] *TL*, 7 Nov. 1884, p. 2.

[189] Interview with Mary Lemass of Dublin (20 May 1999); NAI, CBS Précis 31 Jan. 1896; *TS*, 31 Dec. 1932, p. 6; NAI, Census 1901, Killarney Parade, Inns Quay, Dublin; Census 1911, Grenville Street, Rotunda, Dublin; See *TS*, 7 Jan. 1922, p. 3.

[190] NAI, CBS Précis 31 Jan. 1896.

[191] Ibid.

[192] NAI, CBS 12958/S

[193] *TL*, 26 May 1883, p. 3.

[194] Bassett, *Book of Tipperary*, p. 377; NAI, Census 1901, Main Street, Thurles, County Tipperary.

[195] Interview with Mary Tobin of Turtulla, Thurles, County Tipperary (1 Sept. 2012); *TS*, 11 Jan. 1947, p. 1.

[196] Interview with Joan Weymes of Dublin (19 May 1999).

[197] *TN*, 20. Aug. 1913, p. 3; *CC*, 1 Sept. 1917, p. 5.

[198] Interview with Mary Lemass.

[199] Roche Williams, *In and Out of School: In the Home of the MacDonaghs* (Nenagh, 1999), p. 75.

[200] Interview with Mary Lemass.

[201] Williams, op. cit. p. 75.

[202] *TS*, 28 Aug. 1937, p. 4

[203] Interviews with Joan Weymes and Mary Lemass.

[204] *TS*, 31 Dec. 1932, p. 6, 9 Jan. 1926, p. 5.

[205] James Condon, 'Elizabeth, Lady Thurles: Her Ancestry and her Role in the Rebellion of 1641' in William Corbett and William Nolan (eds), *Thurles the Cathedral Town: Essays in Honour of Archbishop Thomas Morris* (Dublin, 1989), pp 42, 44.

[206] Séamus Ó Ceallaigh, *Story of the GAA: A History and Book of Reference for Gaels* (Limerick, 1977), pp 13-14; *IT*, 1 Sept. 1984, p. 33.

[207] Allen Guttmann, *Sports: The First Five Millennia* (Amherst, 2004), pp 280-1; Joseph M. Bradley, *Sport, Culture, Politics and Scottish Society: Irish Immigrants and the Gaelic Athletic Association* (Edinburgh, 1998), p. 14.

APPENDIX III

Tom Semple –
The Legend and the Legacy

By SEAMUS LEAHY*

I WAS thirteen and that was more years ago than I care to remember when I put a leading question to an old hurler who had won his first senior All-Ireland in 1916 and who was involved with Tipperary teams up to the mid 1960s. It was a question I was in the habit of asking of heroes of past times – "What was the best team you ever saw?"

He looked deeply into his cup of tea for a longish while before he answered but when he did there was an emphatic quality in his voice. "It was the old 'Blues'," he answered, 'Semple's crowd'.

Over the years that followed, my curiosity was to lead me to ask many more questions of men who had won their hurling spurs in the early years of the century; and the more I asked the more I became aware of the admiration which 'Semple's crowd' had commanded among those who saw them in their heyday. The Tubberadora men and the Moycarkey men who had preceded the

Tom Semple

---

* Seamus Leahy, Clonmel, is a noted writer and historian and a member of the famous Leahy family from Tubberadora. Seamus, now in retirement, taught at Rockwell College, Cashel, for many years. He has written extensively on many subjects, particularly the game of hurling. During the Anglo-Irish war, his father, Jimmy Leahy, was commandant of the Second Tipperary Brigade I.R.A. Jimmy Leahy and his brother Mick were well known to Tom Semple, all having hurled together with Thurles.

'Blues' and with whom the young Tom Semple had played in the twilight of their careers had recognised 'Semple's crowd' as the peers of those who had brought to the county five All-Irelands between 1895 and 1900. The Boherlahan men who were the successors of the 'Blues' as the county's next All-Ireland honours winners looked on the 'Blues' with something approaching awe. This was a feeling shared by all those who had seen Semple's men in their prime.

Something of that same awe took hold of my youthful self, though all my experience of them was through the reminiscences of their contemporaries. I contributed to the reverential whisper which passed through the crowd in Thurles about 1944 when the aged 'Hawk' O'Brien, the legendary goalkeeper of the 'Blues', wearing dark glass and stick in hand made his way along the sideline. I stared so intently at Paddy Brolan the old wing forward in Liberty Square that he called me over and asked me my name. I stood in the doorway of Hugh Shelley's pub in Parnell Street on the day of a Cork-Limerick Munster final until I espied the old centre-forward serving thirsty Corkmen, many of whom, I fancied, must surely have been aware of his exploits forty years before. And I travelled from Nenagh with my father to attend the funeral of Jack Mooney the old 'Blues' centrefield stalwart.

I remember vividly on the evening of a game in Nenagh when Mike Condon, a Nenaghman who had been a follower of hurling since the early 1890s, came to our house to show to Johnny Leahy, the old Boherlahan captain, a magnificent mounted photograph of the old Tubberadora team which had played against the famous Lahorna De Wets in a tournament in 1904 which Mike claimed was Tubberadora's last game. And seated among the veterans of Tubberadora, who were reinforced by a strong representation from Horse and Jockey, was a youthful Tom Semple. His inclusion in the team obviously marked him in the eyes of the winners of a bag of All-Irelands as a coming man.

'Will you just look at the wild eye of Semple!' exclaimed the Boherlahan man and for a few minutes the two men who had seen so much of G.A.A. history were lost in the past as they spoke nostalgically of the man who had done so much to bring pride into the lives of all lovers of hurling and particularly to the hearts of Tipperary men. Undoubtedly, Tom Semple, with the physical attributes and the leadership qualities of a Greek hero, had those qualities that continue to fascinate and captivate those who saw them in their prime long after they have departed the mortal scene.

In the early years of the 20th century when Cork men who had hurled against Tipperary were uniquely fitted to judge the qualities of Tipperarymen,

P.D. Mehigan, played for Cork. He was later to become the father figure of all G.A.A. scribes; under the pseudonym 'Carbery' he was the sports correspondent for a lifetime of the *Cork Examiner*; for many years he was the Gaelic games correspondent of the *Irish Times*; he was the weekly contributor of the famous "Carbery calling from Ireland's Hills and Glens" column in the New York *Irish Echo*; and he was the author and compiler of the much-loved *Carbery's Annual*.

When *Carbery's Annual* appeared during the Christmas season of 1943 it contained what must have been the most authoritative and most heartfelt portrait of the 'Blues' captain from the pen of one who had confronted him on the field and admired him as a spectator and a friend –

> 'I had heard much of Tom Semple's prowess with ashen blade before I first laid eyes on him in action – in the home final of the 1900 championship, played at Terenure Gaelic Park against Ardrahan, Galway. Two-Mile-Borris represented Tipperary that year and they called on the choicest hurlers of Mid-Tipp. I think Tom Semple was the only man called on from Thurles town. I took particular notice of him that rich September day – a glorious antelope of a man.

> 'Tom Semple stood six feet two inches in hurling togs, long limbs beautifully turned; whippy body, good hips and shoulders, powerful arms and the head of an Adonis, fresh complexion, glowing with health; straight Grecian features, crowned with a mass of close brown curls. He had an immense stride, his swing of ash was long and graceful. He was a stylist if ever there was one, yet he had typical Tipperary fire and spirit in the close clashes then a feature. He hit balls half a field's length from his post on the left wing and helped materially to build Tipp's score – 5-7 to 0-1.

> 'A month later I saw him at Jones' Road (Croke Park) against a mighty London-Irish side that beat Cork the following year. The 1900 final was memorable. Tipp had won four titles in five years and were reckoned impregnable; yet Sean Oge Hanley of Kilfinane fame led them brilliantly and Tipp were a point down, ten minutes to go. They got two crashing goals and won a sensational game....that was the day Tom Semple hit the railway wall from the left wing 100 yards away – a flying catch and mighty sweep of long arms.

> 'Tom Semple captained the Thurles Sarsfields (Blues) through the 1906 and 1908 championships, retaining his wonderful pace and brilliance right up to 1912. Having played against him (for Cork) in several Munster championships I had ample opportunity of studying his

style. He was universally regarded as the greatest winger and roving commissioner of his time. He landed points out of number from frees and from play. A born leader, he could rally a team with one shake of his hurley high above the field. Mighty as was his physique, he relied on clean open hurling and polished hitting. When entering the councils of the G.A.A., his sound judgment, his sportsmanship and firmness as a referee did much to put hurling on the map as a fine spectacular sport.

'For decades he was Tipperary's mighty man in every sense – as organiser, as representative, as friend. His word was law...When the Anglo-Irish War was hot, Semple played a noble part. He was in the intimate confidence of the national leaders and was entrusted with missions of the highest importance...'

That his leadership qualities remained with him long after his playing days had ended was demonstrated at the two replays of the Munster final drawn game between Cork and Tipperary which were played in Thurles in the summer of 1926. It was a time when G.A.A. fields were not equipped to deal with huge crowds and the first drawn game played in Cork had ended after fifteen minutes when the field was invaded and, the stewards being unable to deal with a crowd of twenty-six thousand spectators, the match was abandoned. It was replayed in Thurles a fortnight later and this time there was a special emphasis on stewarding and the organising and directing of this was entrusted to the old 'Blues' captain. For the first and second replay there was no hitch, no encroachments on the field and there was wide comment and praise for Semple's part in the success of the two events, each of which had hosted an estimated thirty thousand spectators.

My own mother, having passed her century in years, still recalled with the greatest enthusiasm the scene in Thurles as Tom Semple strode along the sideline seventy years before, stick in hand, military-style, directing stewards who rushed to obey his commands. Not having seen him hurling, she recalled at the age of 103 how she realised then that the control over men which he had exercised on the hurling field was an innate gift which he still enjoyed. He pointed his stick to an area of the field and stewards rushed to do his bidding. He radiated authority. Whether as an athlete or otherwise he was a natural leader of men.

In an age when captains are appointed by team managers and take instruction from backup teams, it is difficult for us to understand the degree of authority wielded by a team captain in the early days of the G.A.A. A captain was party to the organising of every detail of a team's preparation for a game (if not the sole organiser), the selection of a team and the travel arrangements; he spoke on behalf of the team at all times and in every situation. Above all he was the leader on the field, the one who was expected to lend inspiration to the team by voice and by performance.

Before the advent of the 'Blues', the outstanding example of the Tipperary captain had been Mikey Maher who still shares with Kilkenny's Drug Walsh and Cork's Christy Ring the record of having captained three All-Ireland winning teams. It was an achievement which narrowly eluded Tom Semple when the Tipperary men went down to Kilkenny on a cold wintry day in Cork in December 1909, when in boggy conditions they failed to display the fiery spirit which they had displayed through the previous summer months.

But the tradition of Tipperary being noted for an inspiring and assertive captaincy had been renewed in Tom Semple. The mere phrase 'Semple's crowd' conveyed the general attitude towards the 'Blues'. The captain was representative of the team and its followers. The idea of the Thurles men taking the field without the leadership of the tall warrior was unthinkable.

There was another important facet of the Semple years. All of the eight All-Irelands won for Tipperary up to the time of his retirement had been won by selections from a small group of Mid Tipperary clubs. This would continue to be a feature of successful Tipperary teams until 1951 when Jimmy Finn, having captained the Borrisoleigh team that had won its way in the previous year out of the north Tipperary division to a county championship victory, went on to captain the All-Ireland winning team of that year.

And a by-product of this predominance of Mid-Tipperary clubs would be to copper-fasten the unique place which Thurles had enjoyed in G.A.A. affairs since the founding of the association there three years before a Thurles team won the first All-Ireland in 1887.

When his playing days were ended Semple, like his predecessor Mikey Maher, did much to establish the tradition of outstanding players continuing to play a leading role in the affairs of the association in their counties. For many years he acted as mentor to Tipperary teams and to represent Tipperary at inter-county meetings. For many years after his retirement he appeared among mentors of county teams and many photographs of Tipperary teams taken during those years of his active retirement show that majestic form towering over many of the players. And when the county's senior, junior and minor teams which had captured all the All-Ireland honours in 1930 were assembled for a famous unique photograph, the old 'Blues' captain not being able to attend for the taking of the photograph, a photo of him in his prime was inserted with that of the three teams.

Father Dollard, the Kilkenny poet-priest home on holiday from missionary activity, captivated by the hurling of the period and the striking qualities of contemporary captaincy, penned 'The Hurler' a poetic gem which he dedicated to the three great captains of the time – Drug Walsh of Kilkenny, Jim Kelleher of Cork and Tom Semple –

The Hurler

"Upon his native sward the hurler stands
To play the ancient pastime of the Gael,
And all the heroes famed of Inisfail
Are typified in him – I see the bands
Of the Craobh Ruadh applauding with their hands,
The Fianna shouting over Cliú-Máil,
Oisín and Finn with eager faces pale,
Caoilte and Goll are there from fairy lands.

And fierce Cuchulain comes, his Godlike face,
With yearning wild to grip in hand once more
The lithe camán and drive the hurtling ball,
In Walsh's, Kelleher's and Semple's grace.
He sees again his glorious youth of yore
And mourns his dead compeers and Ferdia's fall."

– *Fr James Dollard*

APPENDIX IV

Ballads, Books and James Joyce on The 'Blues'

Thurles Abú[1]

Nearer the 'final' is coming, beware boys!
The great day's at hand when you take to the field,
And battle once more for the laurels of fame boys,
Determined that never shall gallant Tipps yield.

Chorus:
Forward to victory then, on for the Leinster men,
Let Erin see what the 'Blues' can do;
Practise at dawn and noon, train hard and train soon,
On! On! The battle cry is Thurles Abú.

What is your fear boys whilst Semple is with you?
That gallant old captain who leads in the fray,
Why should you doubt when you think of the past boys?
The one word 'Dungourney' ought all trouble allay.

Send in your best boys, your fleetest, your bravest,
The fight will be fierce; you must use your best shot.
Pick out the keen-eyed, the sure stroke, the swift man,
Another All-Ireland then you'll notch to those got.

– Templemorensis

---

[1] Note: The final referred to is the 1909 All-Ireland final. The poem refers back to the victory over Cork's Dungourney in the Munster final, which many considered was Tom Semple's finest hour as Tipperary captain. See Chapter 10 for more details.

Tom Semple

It was in 1943
Tom Semple passed away
Well-known to all Tipperary men
And throughout the G.A.A.

The stadium that bears his name,
On many a day he trod
And played the game that brought
    him fame
On that emerald sacred sod.

Not only did he train his men
To act honourably and win,
But built up teams with character
Through splendid discipline.

As captain of the Thurles Blues
We think of Semple's name;
In 1906 and '08
He won All-Ireland fame.

And then in 1930
When Tipperary won renown
It was Semple trained the teams
    that won
The famous Triple Crown.

As he travelled on the train each
    day
He risked his life and name;
Through troubled days he bravely
    played
The patriotic game.

He spent his days in Gaelic ways
As many a Gael can tell;
He led the way in the G.A.A.
And served his country well.

Drombane oft speak of him with
    pride;
They keep his memory green;
But 'tis in St Mary's cemetery
His lonely grave is seen.

Now fifty years have passed away;
Yet, no plaque or script adorn
The Gaelic home where he had
    dwelt
Or the place where he was born.

'Though his deeds are past, his
    name will last,
As long as thousands come
To see the game, in that field of
    fame –
Renowned Semple Stadium.

– Joseph Perkins[2]

The Old Sport

I love to see two rival teams
Upon a 'sporting ground',
Beneath the mellow Autumn beams
With eager crowds around,
Prepared with might and main to
vie,
Until the game is won-
For I could make the leather fly
When I was 'twenty-one'.

I love to see our young athletes,
With clean and healthy frames,
Display their strength in manly
feats,
Their nerve and skill in games,
And not like drones to sit or lie
Supinely in the sun –
For I could make the leather fly
When I was 'twenty-one'.

Your fathers, boys, had lots of snap
Which some call nerve or vim;
Your ginger you must keep on tap
To be the peers of them.
Then fame and honour were the
prize
The victors sought and won-
For sports were never worldly wise
When I was 'twenty-one'.

I know young fellows always hate
To hear an old man brag,
But those you now deem 'up-to-
date'
Will soon begin to lag.
O! once I could with Semple vie
Or emulate Bob Quane-

For I could make the leather fly,
When I was twenty-one.

Then, hurrah for him who makes a
goal,
And him who scores a point,
And may their limbs be always
whole
And never out of joint.
I see them play with many a sigh
For happy days long gone-
When I could make the leather fly
And I was 'twenty-one'.

Then each should in some game
engage,
If games with them agree,
Or else he'll croke when half my
age
And I am sixty-three.
Enough-I see it in your eye,
You're sceptical, my son-
That I could make the leather fly
When I was 'twenty-one'.

– *J.J. Finnan (Myles)*

Magnificent Tipperary 1906

Cheer after cheer broke forth from the thousands strong
Greeting our hurlers in 'Ye Faire Citie'
Loudly in praise rose the voice of the great throng,
Crying 'Magnificent Tipperary'.
On then brave Knocknagow, show them your prowess now,
Let not your spirit or courage vary.
Thurles and Borris men; fleet Tubberadora men,
Work for Magnificent Tipperary.

Swift as the deer that roams the great mountains
Keen as the eagle guarding his eyrie.
Strong as the force of the wild rushing fountains
Such are the men of bold Tipperary.
On then brave Knocknagow; win back your laurels now,
Be not in strength or skill ever chary.
Toil now with all your might; strive in the noble fight,
Work for 'Magnificent Tipperary'.

The battle's half over the capital's leading
But Kickham's men are not cold and weary.
They will triumph yet-danger unheeding
And win the day for old Tipperary.
Play up brave Knocknagow, show your opponents how
To play a game cool, deft and airy.
Prove now that you are men, ready to win again,
All-Ireland honours for Tipperary.

Then onward they rushed with a wild fierce hurrah
Yet quite graceful and light as a fairy.
And loud cheers rent the air as out from the fray came
The victorious men of Tipperary.
Hurrrah! Brave Knocknagow; you've kept the Thresher's vow,
And cwowned yourself by a grand victory.
Ireland is proud of you, grand sons of Róisín Dubh,
And of Magnificent Tipperary.

– Risteard M. O'Hanrahan

Tipperary v Dublin 1908

Two stauncher teams never did *camáns* wield
Than in Athy for highest honours met –
Dublin's athletes marched proudly on the field,
Tipp's matchless sons composed the other set.
What tales their deeds of valour can forget?
Or ever saw them on the battleground
Against the greater odds to fume or fret,
Although of difficulties oft beset?
But press the foe to meet the ball's dull bound,
Nor yield one inch before they heard the whistle sound.

From far and near the anxious Gaels had come
To see those teams already known to fame,
Nor lacked their martial sounds of fife and drum,
Although such things might then appear quite tame
Compared with the excitement of the game
Which brought into the field eight thousand souls
To see the Capital make good its claim-
While still the human tide through benches rolls
The ball's thrown in and rushed down to the Dublin's goals.

But Grace was there and promptly sent it back
To Kelleher whose blow had changed its course,
And won first blood, and staved off the attack;
So the Metrops are yelling themselves hoarse,
While Leonard from the side a goal did force,
And with unerring aim he shot it through;
But to long pucks the Tipps had now recourse,
Then back to Leinster's posts the leather flew,
And twice the flag went up, for Semple's aim was true.

Tipperary's puck-out was closely watched;
Fast work was done and Dublin's uprights raided-
Burke, Shelly, Kenna, Fitz, some plot have hatched,
And in full force the east preserves invaded,
And points banged in while Leinster's smile had faded,
Quinn's blow caused now a lull in the assault-
A splendid stroke and few that could have made it,
Which ended in a point through no one's fault;
The pace had grown so hot both sides were glad to halt.

The second-half had opened like the past-
Strong hopes of victory each side had swayed;
They've struck a gait which surely cannot last,
So fast and furious the game they played,
So grand is the impression they have made
That the vast crowd looks on with baited breath
While Grace against the south directs a raid,
And Dublin's fans shout 'victory or death!'
While Tipps with grim resolve strive for their native heath.

Forth comes Will Leonard cheered by Dublin's hosts,
Imparting to the Faughs both hope and pride,
As dashing with their swift and powerful stride
They shot the ball down through the other side.
Intense and more intense excitement grows,
And on the ball they land with all their power,
For this great contest now drawn to a close-
Should Leinster prove the master of the hour?
Swift pucks both Fitz and Shelly quickly land,
And Dublin's backs before their goalposts cower;
For Semple now was using head and hand,
And Carew's fresh attack was deemed superbly grand.

The nervous tension still was at its height
Though the Metros could scarcely hope to win,
Yet shouts arose of 'Dublin to the fight',
As Tipps the onslaught led through thick and thin;
Till Carew's smashing drive a goal shot in,
Then Leinster's chance seemed hopelessly to slip,
While Semple flagged amid the deafening din,
Then swelled the roar 'Hurrah for gallant Tipp,
The Premier county's sons have won the championship!'

– *Edmund Murphy*

The Voice of the People (Songs and History of Ireland). Song 18 in the McCall Collection, National Library of Ireland. Note: Reference in the sixth stanza to Faughs should correctly be Kickhams.

Semple Stadium

Gaeldom revels at this revelation –
Edifice to a great figure, on and off the field.
What memories Semple Stadium evokes?
Its sod, its atmosphere on Munster Final Day.
The actors that have trod its stage seem infinite.
Some great performers come to mind.
Dinny Barry Murphy scoring from his own line.
Stakelum on the ground or in the air,
Finn the halfback supreme.
Phil Cahill scoring in full flight.
Ring without question the most successful player.
Mackey, the colossal thundering goalwards.
Jimmy Doyle the greatest hurler-
He was the flawless version of the Celtic art.
September sees the climax of Centenary year.
From the four corners, they'll come to Semple Stadium.
The kith and kin of all the Gael
To see the ancient Celt exhibit
His treasure of a hundred – a thousand years.

– Gerard Ryan, Inch.

Tipperary Boys Again

(Air: A Nation Once Again)

When Semple to Kilkenny came
In the year nineteen-o-seven
Of gallant Tipp to uphold the fame
With five men and eleven.
'McCormack brave' said giant Tom
'You'll need those mighty men
To battle with the swift and strong
Tipperary Boys Again'.

'You'll need those mighty men
'You'll need those mighty men,
To battle with the swift and strong
Tipperary Boys Again'.

The Thurles boys marched out quite calm
With the lads from 'Borris' 'knacky',
And two stout veterans from Drombane
Backed up by brave old 'Jockey'
Tipperary ne'er before had known
Such stalwart hurling men
Go forth at dawn – with sweet *camán*
Tipperary Boys Again.

Such stalwart hurling men
Such stalwart hurling men
Go forth at dawn – with sweet *camán*
Tipperary Boys Again.

The coin is spun, *camáns* are crossed,
Hurray! The Tipps are slashing-
The bounding leather as it's tossed
By Barna's fierce ash crashing;
The play was right magnificent-
Tho' poured the drenching rain;
Still on they went, with one intent-
Tipperary Boys Again.

Tho' poured the drenching rain;
Tho' poured the drenching rain;
Still on they went, with one intent-
Tipperary Boys Again.

The whistle shrill rings out full-time
Tipperary is victorious;
'Riordan, Gleeson, 'Hawkeyed' Brien
Bear on the flag before us'.
The honours of All-Ireland
We have not sought in vain,
Oh splendid team, sweet seventeen,
Tipperary Boys Again.

We have not sought in vain,
We have not sought in vain,
Oh splendid team, sweet seventeen,
Tipperary Boys Again.

– Dan English, Rossmore.

Hurrah for Gallant Thurles

Hurrah for the gallant Thurles team
That Munster failed to beat;
There lurks in their frank and fearless mein
And in their dark eyes fiery gleam
A pride that scorns defeat.

When Holycross for honours tried-
A stalwart aggregation,
Their hopes were quickly dashed aside
Though Horse and Jockey with you tied
You beat them in rotation.

In each encounter since you've shown
You're masters of the field,
First Limerick's defeat was known,
Then Clare's picked team was overthrown,
And Cork was forced to yield.

Excitement ne'er was more intense
Since Cork had picked its best;
Besides the gathering was immense
For a championship was in suspense;
With giants to contest.

Tipperary! Scarce the shout arose
Before you smashed the ball,
And dealt it out such telling blows
That though you met their stubborn foes,
Proud Cork was doomed to fall.

'Borris great triumphs gained in vain,
Discretion's what they lacked;
Or else upon Kilmallock's plain
To clinch their victory they'd remain,
Nor leave themselves sidetracked.

Such follies Thurles will avoid,
No chance they'll let slip;
Semple, whose wisdom will they guide,
The Gleesons and Mahers at his side
Will win the championship.

– Edmund Murphy in the 'Boston Pilot'

Oh, to be in Thurles!

Oh, to be in Thurles, when the final there is played,
A sight to cheer the hearts of all who wield the ashen blade,
A hosting of the Gaelic clans from districts far and wide,
When age and youth and beauty fair foregather side by side.

Oh, to be in Thurles as the rivals take the sward,
To weigh their form and pick the team to win the grand award,
Then while the Babel voices call each favoured one by name
And lusty clansmen stridently their county's worth proclaim.

Oh, to be in Thurles at the throw in of the ball
When tense first seconds speechless hold the multitude enthral
And then to hear reverberate one grand tumultuous roar,
In cadence mixed of joy and gloom to greet the opening score.

Oh, to be in Thurles and to note the pluck and dash,
The scientific striking of those heroes of the ash.
The eager forwards sweeping down, spectacular and fine
'Till the *cúlbáire*, with doughty drive relieves his harassed line.

Oh, to be in Thurles and to watch some veteran back
Opposing craft to youthful speed beat off each fierce attack.
And when some boy till then unknown reveals his hurling skill
To hear the Gaelic host, as one, applaud with right goodwill.

Oh, to be in Thurles as opposing fortunes sway
And in the closing minutes tense, a point divides the play,
Then souls in transport rise above humdrum, mundane affairs,
And hurling takes pre-eminence o'er tariffs, markets, fairs.

Oh, to be in Thurles at the Munster final game,
Regardless of the teams engaged, the thrills are much the same,
But surely the Olympian gods would ask no finer fare,
Than this sporting epic battle of old rivals Cork and Clare.

– Joseph Senan Considine – Munster Final 1932

The Hurler

Upon his native sward the hurler stands
To play the ancient pastime of the Gael
And all the heroes famed of Inisfáil
Are typified in him – I see the bands
Of the Craobh Rua applauding with their hands,
The Fianna shouting over Cliú Máil
Oisín and Finn with eager faces pale
Caoilte and Goll are there from fairylands.

And fierce Cú Chulainn comes, his godlike face
With yearning wild to grip in hand once more
The lithe camán and drive the hurtling ball
In Walsh's, Kelleher's and Semple's grace.
He sees again his glorious youth of fore,
And mournes his dead compeers and Ferdia's fall.

– Rev. J.B. Dollard *(Slievenamon)*

Tipperary's Treble Crown – 1930

It's not a crown of diamonds
Nor yet a crown of gold,
But a Treble Crown of laurels
That speaks of fame untold.

– *Ms Brigid Hayes, Cashel*

Munster Final 1909

At Tipperary Town August 29th 1909 – Tipperary v Cork

Of contests Tipp was oft the scene
Where Arra flows the hills between,
But never had Tipperary seen
Excitement run so high,
And when the Corkmen took their
stand
Against the champions of Ireland,
The Munster Championship to
land –
Conclusions for to try.

Then high enthusiasm ran-
Each hurler swung his gay camán;
There was not on the field a man
Stood listless at the call;
So prompt were they to take their
place,
To watch the ball each other face
For they were leaders in the race-
Now one of them must fall.

Then for the sphere the rebels go,
But Gleeson checked them down
below,
And Shelly hit a frightful blow
For one who looked so mild.
Then Kelleher for Cork did score,
And he and Ronayne scored once
more,
While Fleming made the green flag
soar,
And Cork roared themselves wild.

Not yet Cork's winning gait grows
slack-
'Tis Walsh now leads the attack;
But gallant Thurles beat them back-
The play was very hot.
The Tipps were not to be denied,
In every blow was local pride,

Cork's forwards Semple threw aside,
While Mockler made the shot.

A point and goal at once they score
Tipp's sympathisers cheer and roar;
Throughout the half, which now is
o'er,
They played against the wind,
But favoured with the wind and
weather,
Although opposed not caring
whether,
Unsparingly they welt the leather
And Cork's uprights they find.

The furious shots Tipp's forwards
gave,
And many a goal did Fitzy save,
For never yet worked backs so brave
As he and 'Hawk' O'Brien.
Though Cork had victory almost
earned,
A bitter lesson yet they learned-
Tipp's speed and strength the tables
turned,
They win for the third time.

Tipp's gallant captain worked things
through,
James Bourke was there and Brolan
too,
And to crush Cork in rushed Carew
And piled up score on score.
And keener now excitement grew-
To end it all the whistle blew
Mid shouts of 'Tipps! Long life to
you!
You're champions o'er and o'er'.

– *Edmund Murphy, Washington D.C.,*
Sept. 14th 1919.

The Poetry Reading at Semple Stadium

The first poetry reading
I ever attended
was at Semple Stadium
in the early days
of my love affair
with Tipperary.

Everyone else thought
it was a hurling match
but I knew it was a reading,
when I heard the poet
rhapsodise the names
of G.A.A. clubs
through the charged aura
of a hurling stadium
from his bunker
beneath the New Stand.

Isolated on his podium
by ticket sellers

counting out their takings,
the Ezra Pound of Thurles
shocked me with the excitement
of the spoken word.

As he read out the names
Carrick Davins, Lorrha,
Boherlahan-Dualla,
Moycarkey, Roscrea,
Kilruane MacDonagh
And Borris-Ileigh,
The fans cheered their players
And their clubs.

And I cheered the poet
for giving me back
my love of language.

– *Arthur Broomfield*

IN MONAVALLA

Such was the fame of Tom Semple that the author Joseph
Brady mentions him in his novel on Irish country
life *In Monavalla*:-

> 'After dinner Paddy Coady of Coolagh and Bill
> Devine of Stoneyfort arrived with melodeon and
> fiddle. The advent of the Kilkenny men sparked
> off a discussion on the respective merits of the
> Tipperary and Kilkenny hurlers and footballers.
> The debate developed into something like a game
> of chess in which there were no pawns, for all the
> figures were knights. Dan Meagher was check-
> mated by 'Dara' Donovan, Tim Walton by Paddy
> Leahy, Dan Grace by Tom Semple...'[3]

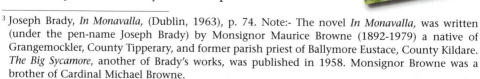

---

[3] Joseph Brady, *In Monavalla*, (Dublin, 1963), p. 74. Note:- The novel *In Monavalla*, was written
(under the pen-name Joseph Brady) by Monsignor Maurice Browne (1892-1979) a native of
Grangemockler, County Tipperary, and former parish priest of Ballymore Eustace, County Kildare.
The Big Sycamore, another of Brady's works, was published in 1958. Monsignor Browne was a
brother of Cardinal Michael Browne.

JAMES JOYCE'S *'FEARLESS THURLES'*

In James Joyce's *A Portrait of the Artist as a Young Man* something has happened to one of Stephen Dedalus's student friends, Davin. Joyce weaves a picture of the G.A.A. and particularly the game of hurling from Tom Semple's time. While the book was not published until 1916, Joyce's first draft was in 1906, which well establishes that the 'Fearless Thurles' is an obvious reference to the Thurles 'Blues.' The central passage of the relevant section reads as follows:-

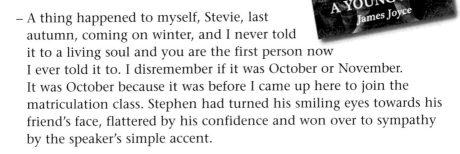

– A thing happened to myself, Stevie, last
   autumn, coming on winter, and I never told
   it to a living soul and you are the first person now
   I ever told it to. I disremember if it was October or November.
   It was October because it was before I came up here to join the
   matriculation class. Stephen had turned his smiling eyes towards his
   friend's face, flattered by his confidence and won over to sympathy
   by the speaker's simple accent.

– I was away all that day from my own place over in Buttevant.

– I don't know if you know where that is – at a hurling match
   between the Croke's Own Boys and the Fearless Thurles and by God,
   Stevie, that was the hard fight. My first cousin, Fonsy Davin, was
   stripped to his buff that day minding cool for the Limericks but he
   was up with the forwards half the time and shouting like mad. I
   never will forget that day. One of the Crokes made a woeful wipe
   at him one time with his camán and I declare to God he was within
   an aim's ace of getting it at the side of his temple. Oh, honest to
   God, if the crook of it caught him that time he was done for.[4]

---

[4] James Joyce, *A Portrait of the Artist as a Young Man* (1916; Corrected Edition. 1967), Chap. 5, p. 184.